Readings in Public Choice Economics

Readings in Public Choice Economics

Jac C. Heckelman, Editor

THE UNIVERSITY OF MICHIGAN PRESS
Ann Arbor

302.13
R287

Copyright © by the University of Michigan 2004
All rights reserved
Published in the United States of America by
The University of Michigan Press
Manufactured in the United States of America
○∞ Printed on acid-free paper
2007   2006   2005   2004   4   3   2   1

A CIP catalog record for this book is available from the British Library.

Library of Congress Cataloging-in-Publication Data

Readings in public choice economics / Jac C. Heckelman, editor.
    p.   cm.
Includes bibliographical references.
ISBN 0-472-03021-3 (pbk. : alk. paper)
1. Social choice.   2. Welfare economics.   I. Heckelman, Jac C.

HB846.8.R43   2004
302'.13—dc22   2004058015

Contents

Acknowledgments

The desire to create this reader has been supported by many individual instructors and scholars. Of particular note, Larry Kenny was kind enough to send me a copy of his course syllabus and provided suggestions on my original proposed topics coverage. P. J. Hill reviewed the introductory essays, offered detailed feedback through multiple correspondence, and proposed some alternative readings, most of which have been incorporated into the present selection or in the additional readings sections. This volume is much stronger than its original form due to his specific comments and suggestions, for which I am grateful.

Readings appear with permission of the publishers and, where required, the authors as well. Every effort has been made to obtain all necessary permissions. Support has been provided by a grant from the Research and Publication Fund, Wake Forest University.

Preface

The lack of a standard undergraduate public choice textbook has forced many public choice instructors to create a "readings" course that is developed around a core set of academic articles and book chapters. Since most academic articles are written in such a way that only other scholars can understand, it is a tedious and time-consuming process to find articles that speak to the state of knowledge undergraduate economics majors have attained. The purpose of this volume is to provide instructors with a ready-made set of papers from which to build a course around. The volume is intended to supplement, rather than replace, traditional lectures and hopefully generate a basis for good classroom discussion.

The particular readings included in this volume represent my assessment of the most interesting and accessible readings that have appeared on various instructors' syllabi. Students in my public choice courses have been required to base their own papers on articles not found on my regular course listing of assigned readings. Their searches have helped me to better gauge a reasonable level of technical proficiency for them. Some of the papers included here were first brought to my attention through this process.

The papers that follow in this volume represent a mix of overview (or survey) readings and extensions in both theoretical and empirical dimensions. Papers are presented in their entirety. Inclusion therefore requires the information to be comprehensible for a typical student having only a background in undergraduate intermediate theory courses and a preliminary knowledge of basic statistical analysis. Theory pieces contain a minimal amount of notation and are well explained. Empirical studies make use of only standard regression techniques, but instructors may wish to familiarize their students with rudimentary regression analysis to get the most out of some of these readings. Even here, students should find they can read around the technical details and still absorb the material. Thus, the focus of the empirical readings is on what and how they test, rather than on statistical details.

Thus, while the papers represent a diverse view of topics and methodologies, the more technical nature of public choice has been specifically avoided. Just as the study of economics has undergone a mathematics revolution, so too has public choice. Cutting-edge theory often employs game-theoretic modeling techniques, and much of social choice utilizes vector analysis and number set theory. Empirical studies have become more econometrically advanced as well. These improvements are to be lauded and are important for generating new insights not otherwise obtainable. Their exclusion here is not meant to de-emphasize their importance but rather to ensure the volume is comprehensible to the typical student in an undergraduate public choice course.

Each section contains two or three papers on a related topic, so instructors are able to pick and choose those that most closely represent their particular interests. The survey pieces in particular will help students obtain a broad overview of the topic, and instructors may wish to highlight individual sections and provide additional details in class. As an aid, each section contains a brief descriptive introduction to the general theme and explains its importance and evolution. Questions are presented for each of the readings for students to assess their degree of comprehension. Suggested additional readings are presented at the end of each section, including slightly more technically advanced ones that are listed separately.

PART I

Overview

The field of public choice applies neoclassical economic analysis to areas of political interest. There are two broad categories within public choice: institutional political economy, which from a positive view considers the role of institutional design in government structures, and social choice theory, which is typically more concerned with normative issues in how different voting rules will affect incentives and outcomes.

One way to view the evolution of institutional political economy is from a reaction against the traditional welfare economics of the 1950s and 1960s, where perceived market failures, such as monopoly power and externalities in production and consumption, led economic policy to prescribe government intervention in the marketplace to correct these failures. Since Adam Smith's notion of an "invisible hand" leading private economic agents (motivated purely by self-interest in profits and utility) to engage in activities that also happened to maximize social welfare would only hold under the purely blackboard conditions of perfect competition and the absence of externalities, any true society was thought to be far from this ideal. The underlying assumption behind intervention was that government was in a position to determine what was best for society and was eager to carry out this task.

Some economists eventually questioned these assumptions. It had already been established that a firm is not truly an entity in itself but rather it is composed of managers and workers, whose self-interest may not coincide with the interests of the owner. The analogy is expected to hold for government as well, in which the politicians (managers) and bureaucrats (workers) may have self-interests that do not coincide with the interests of the taxpayers (owners). In this case, government intervention may not have the desired effects.

By modeling politicians, bureaucrats, and voters as rational, self-interested economic agents, instead of as purely altruistic sacrificers, the expected consequences of government intervention became dire. Government was now seen to be self-serving and self-promoting. The "visible hand" of government intervention could no longer be ensured of promoting social welfare. The study of institutional political economy is concerned with how the current institutional environment skews incentives and how to develop institutions to limit the potential harmful consequences.

On the other hand, social choice theory focuses primarily upon the incentives facing voters under alternative voting arrangements. In order for government officials to properly make decisions, if they were so inclined to promote social interests, they would need to know what their citizens' preferences are. This is the role of elections, and this analogy holds true for any social group trying to reach decisions. If the entire group cannot agree, how should consensus be determined? The implications of various vote rules are considered both in terms of individual voting incentives and aggregation to group decisions.

Social choice analysis has revealed that the decision reached by a group may not be considered "fair" by certain members of the group and the group decision can be a very skewed representation of what its members actually want. One aspect of social choice theory is thus designed to determine how well a given voting rule will lead to outcomes that best represent the desires of the group members. Furthermore, group members as voters may not reveal their true preferences if they determine that voting differently will better their chances for a more favorable outcome. This type of "strategic voting" may further skew the revealed preferences of the group members. Voting rules are considered for their impact on voting incentives or their ability to generate "sincere voting" from group members.

The Public Choice Revolution

James Gwartney & Richard E. Wagner

Review Questions

1. How does self-interest in the political process affect policy outcomes? Who are the relevant actors in the political policy process and what are their motivations?
2. What is the relationship between rent seeking and economic stagnation?
3. Why do special interests often win out over the general interest?
4. How do elections affect the timing and incentives for economic policy?
5. What is the incentive structure bureaucrats face?
6. How can the inefficiencies of the political process be lessened?

In the 1950s and 1960s, economists with rare exception treated government as a corrective device available to right the economic wrongs of this world. While *hypothetical* competitive markets allocated resources efficiently, the real world was characterized as being replete with market failure. Externalities, public goods, lack of competition, and imperfect information all were thought to plague market economies. Economists typically saw their function as one of developing "solutions," which in turn would be faithfully adopted by democratic governments to promote the general welfare.

Gwartney, James, and Richard E. Wagner. "The Public Choice Revolution." *Intercollegiate Review*, spring 1988, 17–25.

Despite this near consensus within the academy, thoughtful students of that era were troubled by the chasm that separated the classroom view of government from simple observations of the real world. It did not take a genius to determine that real world governments not only failed generally to adopt the optimal solutions of economists, but often intervened in ways that promoted economic inefficiency, thereby clashing sharply with the economists' prescriptions for good government. For example, while most economists opposed tariffs, particularly those protecting concentrated industries such as steel and automobiles, the political process nonetheless led to trade restrictions in these areas. Similarly, while most economists opposed agricultural price supports, minimum wage legislation, rent controls, and various government-imposed barriers restraining market competition, such policies seemed to be a natural outgrowth of the political process. Observing the policies of the real world, many students of economics during the 1950s and 1960s found themselves asking: "If government is a device for correcting market failure, why do governments often adopt policies that are obviously wasteful and inefficient?"

The public choice revolution provided the answer. Government is *not* a corrective device. It is *not* a pinch hitter we can count on to supply a base hit whenever we fear the market might strike out. Government is not a person, it has no mind or conscience. It is simply a set of processes by which people relate to one another. Governmental decisions and policies are simply the outcomes of the interactions of the people who relate to one another through a particular political system or constitutional order. If we want to know if and when government can be expected to yield preferable outcomes compared to the market, we must systematically analyze how the political process works. This is precisely what public choice theory does. Public choice analysis is to government what traditional economic analysis is to markets.

Public Choice and the Political Process

During the last 25 years, public choice scholars have made great strides in expanding our knowledge of how democratic political processes work. Public choice, which has now developed to the point where one of its founders, James M. Buchanan of George Mason University, was awarded in 1986 the Nobel Prize in Economics, is often described as representing the application of economic reasoning to politics.[1] Just as economic reasoning holds that people are predominantly self-interested creatures, so public choice holds that political processes are likewise dominated by self-interest. This is not to deny the existence of benevolence, but only to note that benevolence provides an inadequate basis for social organization. Self-interest is pervasive in the organization of human affairs and it would be futile and foolish to think otherwise. As Adam Smith noted: "It is not from the benevolence of the butcher, the brewer, or the baker that we expect our dinner, but from their regard to their own interest. We address ourselves not to their humanity but to their self-love, and never talk to them of our own necessities but of their advantages."[2]

Just as economics studies the interactions among self-interested creatures within market processes, so public choice does the same thing within political processes. The voter who selects among political alternatives is the same person who selects among market alternatives. If Jones is influenced by the expected personal benefits and costs when he makes choices in the department store, it makes sense that he will also be influenced by personal interests when he makes choices in the voting booth. Similarly, the men and women working in government as politicians and bureaucrats are pretty much the same as their counterparts in the private sector. If pursuit of such rewards as personal wealth, power, and prestige motivates people in the marketplace, there is every reason to believe that these same elements will motivate them in the political arena.[3] A pivotal implication of public choice scholarship is that political outcomes will depend importantly on how political institutions and constitutional rules influence the incentives people face and not just on who in particular is elected or appointed to political office.

The key players in the democratic political process are citizen-voters, politicians, and bureaucrats. While politicians may be motivated by a broad range of factors, their ability to achieve both private and public objectives is dependent upon one thing—winning elections. Understandably, politicians will seek to promote an image and stake out positions on issues that will enhance their chances of winning elections. Just as market entrepreneurs pursue profits, politicians pursue votes.

Political competition more or less forces politicians to pay primary heed to how their actions influence their electoral prospects. If a politician refuses to support policies that are vote-getters, perhaps because he thinks the policies are counterproductive or morally wrong, the politician runs an increased risk of being replaced by a competitor who is more strenuous in his search for votes. The requirements of electoral competition present even the most public-spirited politician with a strong incentive to base decisions primarily on political considerations. Just as neglect of economic profit is the route to market oblivion, so is neglect of potential votes the route to political oblivion.

While the politician's position is parallel to that of a producer in the marketplace, the voter's position is parallel to that of a consumer. Just as consumers use dollar votes to demand market goods, citizens use votes, lobbying, campaign contributions, and the like to demand political goods—that is, to try to bring political outcomes into line with personal objectives. Many elements may enter into a voter's decision concerning which legislative candidate to support. The television image, perceived honesty, communication skills, and experience of alternative candidates may, in varying degrees, influence the choices of voters. However, the basic postulate of economics indicates that voters, like consumers, will ask "What can you do for me and how much will it cost me?" Other things remaining constant, voters will tend to support those candidates whom they believe will provide them with the most political goods, services, and transfer benefits *net of personal costs.*

In making their choices, however, voters are likely, by and large, to be poorly informed. It is more likely that a voter will be struck by lightning on the way to the polls than it is that his vote will decide who is elected mayor or county commissioner, to say nothing of senator or congressional representative. Since one vote is not going to decide who is elected, why should an individual study the issues and research the position of alternative candidates? After all, the outcome will be unaffected regardless of whether a voter makes an informed choice or simply chooses on the basis of current knowledge and vague impressions. Voters have, at best, a weak incentive to invest the time and energy required to cast a well-informed vote. It is not surprising, then, that few voters are able to accurately identify their congressional representative, much less identify and understand the position of their representatives on issues like minimum wage legislation, tariffs, or agricultural price supports. The scanty information voters have on most political issues—a fact confirmed again and again by voter surveys—merely indicates that they are responding sensibly to the political incentive structure. Since it was first articulated by Anthony Downs in 1957, public choice theorists have referred to this phenomenon as the "rational ignorance effect."[4]

The political process can be visualized as a complex set of interrelationships among citizens, politicians, and bureaucrats. Public choice analysis seeks to understand and assess the outcomes that emerge from different political processes. Its cardinal presupposition, which was also held by the Founders of the American constitutional order, is that a properly functioning political order depends not on the generosity or the self-denying capacities of those who engage in political activity, but on the presence of a well-constructed constitutional order that channels the pursuit of self-interest into generally desirable directions.

For instance, when the people who pay for a public sector project are the same as those who desire or benefit from the project, democratic political processes generally work quite well. If a project generates more value than it costs, most citizens affected by the project are likely to gain, provided that taxpayers and beneficiaries are the same people. Predictably, politicians will be supportive of such productive projects. By the same reasoning, counterproductive projects that generate less value than costs will impose losses on most voters, so long as taxpayers and beneficiaries are the same people. Vote-seeking politicians have an incentive to oppose such projects. The general principle that emerges from this line of reasoning elaborated by public choice theory is that so long as government acts in a non-discriminatory manner, thereby avoiding "the violence of faction," the individual pursuit of self-interest within political processes will tend to be harmonious with the general or common welfare.[5]

Public Choice and Democratic Pathology

The theory of public choice has articulated with contemporary analytical techniques what was common knowledge among the Founders of our constitutional order: democratic political processes can, both through their police powers and their budgetary powers, become an instrument of discrimination that accommodates the plunder of some for the benefit of others.[6] One of the major subsets of public choice scholarship has come to be called the theory of rent-seeking, which is an examination of the various ways by which government can serve as an instrument of discrimination and plunder.[7] Rather than trying to build that proverbial better mousetrap, people might lobby for tariffs or quotas on imports, they might lobby a safety commission to ban lower cost, competitive mousetraps, or they might lobby to prevent people from making mousetraps at home. Rather than applying resources to the creation of wealth, rent-seeking uses resources to redistribute previously created wealth.

The incentive to engage in rent-seeking is directly proportional to the ease with which the political process can be used to transfer income and modify existing property rights. When the effective law of the land makes it difficult to take the property of others or to force others to pay for projects favored by you and your interest group, rent-seeking is unattractive. Because the benefits of rent-seeking are relatively low under such circumstances, few resources flow into rent-seeking activities. But when government becomes more involved in transfer activities and when it fails to link its expenditures with taxes, the payoff to rent-seeking expands and rent-seeking attracts resources away from socially productive activities.

When government gets more involved in doing good things for some people (for example, providing them with direct transfers or favored programs) by imposing bad things on others (forcing them to pay for benefits supplied to others), individuals and groups will invest more resources into efforts designed to shape political outcomes to their advantage. Resources that otherwise would be used to create wealth and generate income will be "invested" in rent-seeking. People will spend more time organizing and lobbying politicians and less time producing goods and services. The employment of lobbyists, "expert" witnesses, lawyers, accountants, and other political specialists capable of influencing public policy and/or the size of one's tax bill will expand. By contrast, engineers, architects, physical scientists, craft workers, machine operators and other workers involved in the creation of goods and services will decline as a share of the labor force. The size of the economic pie will decline (or expand less rapidly) as more and more resources are employed in rent-seeking activities rather than the creation of wealth. Fewer people will be engaged in seeking after that proverbial better mousetrap as more become engaged in such things as lobbying for tariffs or quotas on imported mousetraps or for regulations restricting the ability of new firms to compete with established producers.

As the size of the tax-transfer sector increases, the theory of rent-seeking indicates that more resources will flow into lobbying, which is the most visible manifestation of rent-seeking. The data are consistent with this view. Between 1976 and 1983 the number of lobbyists registered with the federal government rose from 3,420 to 6,500, an increase of 90 percent in 7 years. As recently as 1979 New York City had twice as many national trade associations as Washington, D.C. By 1983 the number of Washington trade associations exceeded New York's by nearly 20 percent. A recent study found that 65 percent of the chief executive officers of the top 200 Fortune firms are in Washington on business at least once every two weeks, up from 15 percent a decade ago.[8] When the political process makes transfers more likely, an increase in rent-seeking and a decrease in wealth creation are natural outcomes. Viewed in this light the economic stagnation in personal disposable incomes during the past two decades is not surprising. It is a man-made and not a "natural" occurrence.

Sources of Democratic Pathology

The democratic pathologies characterized by the theory of public choice arise out of some institutional features that distinguish political processes from market processes. Those features lead to a predominance of special over general or common interests, produce a shortsightedness within government, and promote waste through the bureaucratic form of organization.

In contrast with the situation when the benefits and costs of individual voters are closely linked, the political process goes awry when the two are disconnected and fiscal discrimination arises. Special interest issues—policies that provide substantial personal gain to a concentrated group of beneficiaries at a cost which is spread widely among voters—illustrate the troublesome features of fiscal discrimination, as a comparison of the political gains a vote-seeking politician can expect from supporting the special interest relative to the disorganized majority shows. Since the personal stake of the concentrated beneficiaries is substantial, they have a strong incentive to inform themselves and their allies and to let candidates (and legislators) know how strongly they feel about the issue. Many such beneficiaries—perhaps as illustrated by, among others, social security recipients or protected industries—will vote for or against politicians almost exclusively on the basis of whether those politicians support their interests. Such concentrated beneficiaries will also use financial assistance and work to support politicians who are receptive to their views and oppose those who are not.

By contrast, consider the probable political consequences a representative could expect from the support of the interests of the diffuse majority—the ordinary taxpayer if you like. Voters who have only a small *personal* cost imposed on them by special-interest measures will care little about the issue. Most likely, they will be rationally uninformed (remember the rational ignorance effect) since the time and energy necessary to examine the issue and figure out its impact will be more costly than it is worth, particularly if the issue is fairly complex. And even if the diffuse majority of citizens is informed on the issue, they will not feel very strongly about it because it exerts little impact on their personal welfare.

If you were a vote-seeking politician, what would you do? Clearly, you would gain little from supporting the interest of the largely uninformed and disinterested majority. An astute politician would almost surely support the special, concentrated interest over the general, diffused interest. Support of the special interest is capable of providing additional votes, campaign workers, and perhaps most importantly, campaign contributions. In turn, the finances supplied by the special interest can be used to buy media time and take other steps to win the support of other voters.

When the benefits are concentrated and the cost diffused, politicians will be led as if by an invisible hand to serve the purposes of the well-organized, concentrated beneficiaries.[9] This is true even if the project reduces the size of the economic pie. Much economic inefficiency emanates from this deficiency of the political process. For example, consider the case of the roughly 11,000 sugar farmers in the United States. The cost of producing sugar in the U.S. is three or four times higher than production costs in many other countries, particularly in the Caribbean. Nonetheless, Congress has instituted import restrictions and price supports which have pushed the U.S. price above 20 cents per pound compared to the 7 cents per pound price on the world market. As of 1986 the average U.S. resident pays approximately $6 more for sugar each year than would otherwise be the case, while the 11,000 sugar farmers gain $1.5 billion in gross income, approximately $130,000 per farm. Of course, the average ("rationally ignorant") voter is totally unaware that special interest policies have pushed up the price of sugar, while the sugar farmers are among the leading contributors to those politicians who exert a key impact on agricultural policy. As a nation we are poorer, because we could buy sugar cheaper than we can raise it. Nonetheless, the continuation of the program under both Republican and Democratic administrations indicates that catering to the concentrated interests of the sugar industry is "good politics" even if it is "bad economics."

The special interest effect helps to explain the presence of tariffs and quotas on steel, automobiles, textiles, and several other products. Regulations mandating that Alaskan oil be transported by the high cost American maritime industry reflect the industry's political clout, not its economic efficiency. Acreage restrictions and price supports on feed grains, tobacco, and peanuts generate waste and promote the adoption of inefficient production methods. Nonetheless, they survive in the political marketplace because agricultural pressure groups support such policies while most others are largely disinterested and uninformed. Federally-funded irrigation projects, subsidized grazing rights, subsidized loans, subsidies to airports—the list goes on and on. Policy in each of these areas is rooted in the special interest effect and not in sound economic doctrine. While each such program individually imposes only a small drag on our economy, in the aggregate they drain our resources, threaten our standard of living, and impair our liberty.

What happens prior to the next election is of crucial importance to incumbent politicians. Since issues of public policy are usually complex, it is often difficult for voters to anticipate *future* benefits and costs accurately. To the extent this is so, voters will tend to judge incumbents primarily on the basis of economic conditions around election day. Therefore, policies that improve the state of affairs prior to an election will be attractive to politicians, even if those policies are likely to have substantial negative consequences after the election. On the other hand, policies that impose costs now but whose benefits will emerge only after the next election will reduce the re-election prospects of incumbents. As a result, the political process is biased toward the adoption of shortsighted policies and against the selection of sound long-range policies.

Essentially, legislators can claim credit—whether rightly or wrongly is irrelevant—for benefits (for example, improvements in the economy) that accrue *prior* to the next election, but they have much less ability to claim credit for prospective benefits *subsequent* to the election. Unlike their market counterparts, who can borrow against anticipated future benefits to stay in business now, politicians have limited ability to capture prospective future benefits from wise decisions. As a result, politicians tend to exaggerate the importance of policy impacts prior to the next election and to discount excessively their post-election consequences.

This shortsightedness often leads to a conflict between good politics and sound economics. Even counterproductive policies can enhance the election prospects of politicians when the short-term results differ substantially from the effects over a longer time period. Unfortunately, this is often the case with economic issues. Examples abound. Financing government by monetary expansion is likely to stimulate employment and output in the short-run, even though inflation, uncertainty, and instability are side effects observable in the long run. Borrowing to finance short-term programs that benefit coveted voting blocks is attractive even though the long-term result will be higher real interest rates, less capital formation, and higher future taxes. Rent controls may reduce rental housing prices in the short-term, but at the price of housing shortages, black markets, and a deterioration in housing quality in the long run. In each case, the positive short-term effects strengthen the political attractiveness of policies that are generally detrimental in the long run.

The day-to-day functions of government are performed by bureaus, which derive most if not all of their revenues from the periodic appropriations of the legislature rather than from the direct sale of output to consumers. In effect, the legislative body supplies the bureau with a budget along with instructions for dealing with its assigned tasks. The function of the bureau is to transform the budget into public services.

If bureaucrats are pretty much like the rest of us, neither more nor less virtuous or self-interested, it is useful as a first approximation to view them as seeking to maximize the size of their bureau's budget.[10] A larger budget will enhance the opportunities and resources available throughout the bureau. As the bureau expands, the power, prestige, salary and other benefits to bureau managers will generally increase. At the middle and lower levels of employment, a larger budget and an expanding bureau will offer additional job security and possibilities for promotion. Larger budgets are also likely to generate additional funds for office space, furniture, travel, and other resources that improve the work environment of bureaucrats. Almost every bureaucrat can expect to gain something from the growth of the bureau; it is surely a rare bureaucrat who would lose as the result of an expansion in the bureau's budget. Therefore, the people who staff the bureau can be expected to develop and unite behind a strategy designed to increase the size of the bureau's budget.

Political competition might seem to provide legislators with an incentive to curb inefficient performance by public sector suppliers. However, there are several reasons why it will be extremely difficult for a legislative body to control the cost effectiveness of a bureau and promote operational efficiency, particularly when the bureau is a monopoly supplier. Bureaus do not have an easily identifiable "bottom line," analogous to the net income of a corporation, that might be used to judge the bureau's performance. The absence of a well-defined index of performance provides managers in the public sector with considerably more leeway to gloss over inefficiency and to pursue personal objectives than is available to their counterparts in the market sector. Neither do bureaus confront a mechanism, like bankruptcy in the private sector, capable of bringing inefficient projects to a halt. In fact, failure to meet objectives often generates pressure for larger appropriations in the public sector. If the crime rate is rising, crime prevention agencies will lobby for additional funds. If schools are plagued with discipline problems and low achievement scores, public school administrators and unions will demand more funds. If the Department of Defense is beset with cost overruns, you can bet that supplemental appropriations will be requested.

The major source of information with regard to the bureau's performance invariably comes from a biased source—the bureau itself. In addition, bureaucratic suppliers and their clients often constitute concentrated interests capable of influencing legislative action. All of these factors combine to reduce both the ability and the incentive of legislative overseers to control the cost of bureaucratic suppliers. It is important to note that the fault lies with the organizational structure and not with the character of public sector employees. On the whole there is no reason to think that government employees are less competent, less energetic, or less committed to their work than other workers. Nonetheless, given the incentive structure under which they toil, bureaucratic inefficiency is a predictable result.

Constitutional Implications of Public Choice

Both bad news and good news flow from public choice analysis. The bad news is that unconstrained democratic government is far from being a corrective device, and is rather itself a major source of economic waste and inefficiency. Unless somehow restrained constitutionally, democratic governments will often enact programs that waste resources and impair the general standard of living of their citizens. In the language of economics, the world is beset not only by "market failure" but also by "government failure." Therefore, we must understand how both market and political processes work before we can judge which is likely to be more consistent with economic efficiency and the general welfare. Merely because the market fails to meet someone's hypothetical idealized conditions for economic efficiency (what economists call pareto optimality), it does not follow that government intervention will improve the situation. In like manner, just because the market does not achieve what someone perceives as a fair distribution of income, it does not follow that the political process will do better.

In the aftermath of the public choice revolution, sound economics must be comparative economics. Economists who formulate optimizing solutions to market failure that are inconsistent with the operation of political organization might as well be spending their time working crossword puzzles. The real value of economics, at least with respect to questions of public policy, lies in its ability realistically to compare the properties of different institutional frameworks guiding the organization of economic activity. Expected outcomes under market organization (in its various forms) must be compared with expected outcomes under political organization (in its various forms). Unless we follow this approach, we are as George Stigler once stated, like the judge who after hearing the first contestant sing, immediately declared the second contestant the winner.

Fortunately, there is also good news arising from the public choice revolution: if the rules of politics are structured properly, which is a task for constitutional construction as the authors of *The Federalist* recognized, many of the adverse consequences of the political process can be limited. Public choice theory provides insights into how this might be accomplished—that is, how political institutions and rules can be designed in a manner which will direct the self-interest of political players to the furtherance of the general welfare.

The major problems of political organization emanate from two related characteristics: (1) centralization, and (2) lack of competition among governmental units. Both these factors strengthen the position of organized interest groups relative to the general taxpayer, weaken the incentive for efficiency in government, and enhance the likelihood that public sector action will be exploitative through fiscal discrimination.

What would a political structure designed to bring the self-interest of political players into harmony with the betterment of the general citizens look like? Interestingly, with regard to economic affairs it would encompass a number of the ideas emanating from Philadelphia 200 years ago. First, the primary function of the central government would be to protect the life, liberty, and property of its citizens from both foreign and domestic aggressors, including the government itself. Performance of these protective functions would require that government enforce contracts (U.S. Constitution, Article 1, Section 10) and prohibit the taking of private property without the granting of full compensation to the owner (Amendment V). Governments would also be prohibited from the fixing of prices or the barring of entry into the production of otherwise legal goods, both of which restrain trade and are indirect forms of taking property without compensation. Similarly, governments would be restrained from imposing discriminatory taxes and regulations designed to limit the movement of people or goods across the boundaries of governmental units.

Second, at the central government level, the primary beneficiaries of a program should be required to foot the bill for its cost. This would be accomplished if the central government were permitted only to undertake projects that provide widespread, general, or common benefits to citizens financed by general taxation. The U.S. Constitution, Section 8 states: "The Congress shall have power to lay and collect taxes, duties, imports and excises to . . . provide for the *common* defense and *general* welfare of the United States, but all duties, imposts and excises shall be *uniform* throughout the United States." This constitutional provision indicates that it was the intent of the Founders that uniformly levied taxes would be used only for the finance of expenditures yielding general benefits (the "common" defense and "general" welfare). Certainly there is nothing in the Constitution authorizing programs of the general nature that A and B enrich themselves at the expense of C (and possibly D and E as well). However, with the passage of time and erosion of the original intent, today a large share of federal expenditures are precisely of this type—they benefit a narrow segment of society at the expense of others.[11] In order to assure greater adherence to this substantive provision, tax and spending proposals at the central government level could be required to secure the approval of a supra-majority (for example three-fourths) approval of the legislative members. Such a procedure would constrict the scope for winning factions to practice fiscal discrimination.

Third, the size of the supra-majority required for legislative action could reasonably decrease at lower levels of government. For example, we might continue to permit local legislative bodies (city commissions, county commissions, regional authorities, etc.) to act with the approval of only a simple majority, while requiring a three-fifths majority for legislative action at the state level and a three-fourths majority at the federal level. The increasing majorities required for legislative action at higher levels of government would help remedy a deficiency of the current system: the tendency of public sector activities to move toward the central government, where government is least competitive and the potential for oppressive action is greatest. At the state and local level, citizens are better able to control government and to avoid being victimized by fiscal discrimination. If a decentralized governmental unit is operated inefficiently or being used to funnel resources to interest groups, citizens could at a relatively low cost move to governmental units which provide them more value for their tax dollar. In a decentralized setting, the tax base of inefficient governmental units would fall relative to local governments that are operated more efficiently. Much as the competitive process roots out inefficiency in the marketplace, competition among decentralized governmental units could be a useful weapon against public sector inefficiency.

Of course, public choice theorists are continuing to investigate the operation of alternative forms of political organization.[12] The challenge before us is to develop political institutions capable of bringing, to the fullest extent possible, the self-interest of politicians, bureaucrats, and voters into harmony with the general welfare of a society. In other words, public choice economists seek to design political structures and procedures capable of directing the political players to serve the general welfare just as Adam Smith's invisible hand directs market participants to serve the general welfare.

With regard to the achievement of this objective, one thing is certain: success rests upon our ability to develop and institute sound rules and procedures rather than on our ability to elect "better" people to political office. Unless we get the rules right, the political process will continue to be characterized by special interest legislation, bureaucratic inefficiency, and the waste of rent-seeking. The political incentive structure is like the law of gravity. Just as both Republicans and Democrats fall at 32 feet per second, so too do both engage in special interest politics and other socially wasteful political behavior when the political incentive structure encourages them to do so.

As James Buchanan has often stated, in a very real sense the roots of public choice analysis are found in the writings of the American Founders, particularly the contributions of James Madison in *The Federalist Papers*.[13] The Founders were designing a government for fallible men. As Madison stated in *Federalist* No. 51: "If men were angels, no government would be necessary."

How do you provide fallible men a government which necessarily possesses a monopoly on the use of force within society without simultaneously giving rise to a situation which will lead to the abuse of that force? This was the central issue at the time of our constitutional founding and it is still the central issue today. The Founders answered it with a constitution providing for a federal system, enumerated powers of the central government, substantive limitations on the taxing and spending authority of the federal government, a bicameral legislative system, and a division of power between three branches of government. As Madison explained, they sought to counteract ambition with ambition. Public choice theory suggests that they might also have provided procedural restraints such as the requirement of a supra-majority for legislative action at the federal level, which would have retarded the tendency toward the centralization of power which has undermined the American system during the last 50 years. Although public choice theory has developed new insights into the problems of self-government, it has also reaffirmed that the American Founders had the right idea. The Founders sought to design a government that would provide the legal framework and stability necessary for private sector cooperation while simultaneously limiting government, particularly the federal government, to activities where there was reason to believe its actions would be beneficial. In brief, they sought to structure government so that it would undertake beneficial activities and refrain from counterproductive actions. In a very real sense, their work reflected the objectives of modern public choice analysis.

NOTES

1. For a survey of Buchanan's scholarship with particular reference to its implications for constitutional order, see Richard E. Wagner, "James M. Buchanan: Constitutional Political Economist," *Regulation* 11 (February 1987), 13–17.

2. Adam Smith, *An Inquiry into the Nature and Causes of the Wealth of Nations* [1776] (New York: Modern Library, 1937), 14.

3. Contrary to the charges of some, this self-interest postulate does not imply that individuals are greedy materialistic money-grubbers who care only about themselves. People act for a variety of reasons, some selfish and some humanitarian. The basic economic postulate implies that the choices of *both* the humanitarian and egocentric individual will be influenced by changes in personal cost and benefits. For example, both will be more likely to support a policy that generates benefits for others (for example, farmers, the poor, or the elderly) when the personal cost of doing so is low than when it is high. Similarly, both the humanitarian and the egocentric will be more likely to discover and act upon opportunities to reduce costs the greater the personal payoff for doing so.

4. See Anthony Downs, *An Economic Theory of Democracy* (New York: Harper and Brothers, 1957).

5. On this property of non-discrimination, see W. H. Hutt, "Unanimity Versus Non-Discrimination (As Criteria for Constitutional Validity)," *South African Journal of Economics* 34 (June 1966), 133–47.

6. For a thorough survey of the Public Choice literature see William C. Mitchell, "Fiscal Behavior of the Modern Democratic State: Public Choice Perspectives and Contributions," in *Political Economy: Recent Views,* ed. L. Wade (Los Angeles: Sage, 1983), 69–114.

7. The seminal work on rent-seeking is Gordon Tullock, "The Welfare Cost of Tariffs, Monopolies, and Theft," *Economic Inquiry* (June 1967), 224–32. A survey of the literature is presented in Robert D. Tollison, "Rent-Seeking: A Survey," *Kyklos* 35 (March 1982), 575–602.

8. See David Boaz, "Spend Money to Make Money," *Wall Street Journal* (November 13, 1983, op-ed).

9. For additional discussion of this topic, see Gary Becker, "Public Policies, Pressure Groups, and Dead Weight Costs," *Journal of Public Economics* 28 (December 1985), 329–47, and James Gwartney and Richard Stroup (4th ed.), *Economics: Private and Public Choice* (New York: Harcourt, Brace, and Jovanovich, 1987), 696–700.

10. For additional information on the theory of bureaucracy, see William Niskanen, *Bureaucracy and Representative Government* (Chicago: Aldine-Atherton, 1970), and Gordon Tullock, *The Vote Motive* (London: The Institute of Economic Affairs, 1976), Chapter IV.

11. See Richard Epstein, *Takings: Private Property and the Power of Eminent Domain* (Cambridge: Harvard University Press, 1985) for a comprehensive analysis of why constitutional prohibitions on governmental activities of this type are crucially important for both economic efficiency and the preservation of a free society.

12. See, for example, many of the essays collected in James Gwartney and Richard E. Wagner, eds., *Public Choice and Constitutional Economics,* (Greenwich, CN: JAI Press, 1988).

13. For a detailed analysis of the contribution of Madison to the U.S. Constitution, see James Dorn, "Public Choice and the Constitution," *Public Choice and Constitutional Economics,* eds. Gwartney and Wagner.

Suggested Additional Readings

Buchanan, James M. *Constitutional Economics.* Chap. 3. Oxford: Blackwell, 1991.

Buchholz, Todd G. *New Ideas from Dead Economists.* Chap. 11. New York: Penguin Books, 1989.

Mitchell, William C. "The Old and New Public Choice: Chicago versus Virginia." In *The Elgar Companion to Public Choice,* ed. William F. Shughart and Laura Razzolini. Cheltenham, UK: Edward Elgar, 2001.

Mueller, Dennis C. "Public Choice Theory." In *Companion to Contemporary Economic Thought,* ed. David Greenaway, M. F. Bleaney, and Ian Stewart. London: Routledge, 1991.

Ordeshook, Peter C. "The Emerging Discipline of Political Economy." In *Perspectives on Positive Political Economy,* ed. James E. Alt and Kenneth A. Shepsle. Cambridge: Cambridge University Press, 1990.

PART II

Institutional Political Economy

Rent Seeking

Economists typically assume firm behavior is motivated by profit maximization. Scarce resources are used to create production to satisfy consumer wants, which generates profits, or rents, for the firms. The desire to amass the greatest profit possible ensures resources will be used efficiently. For social efficiency to prevail, competition must weed out the inefficient producers.

To protect itself from competition, a firm can engage in innovative research and development. Any product or production improvements that prove successful are likely to be copied by competitors, resulting in the first firm bearing the up-front costs while other firms are able to share the resulting benefits. Patents can be issued to protect the first firm's investment, giving that firm a monopoly on its innovation. Thus firms may use resources in the innovation process to secure the resulting monopoly rents. Since innovation and technological improvements are generally considered socially enhancing, this represents a socially beneficial use of scarce resources.

On the other hand, monopolies can be created for reasons other than innovation protection. For example, "natural monopolies" represent industries where economies of scale are so large that a single producer would operate in the downward-sloping portion of its average cost curve when supplying the entire market demand. Segmenting the market through competition would thus result in each firm producing at a higher average cost. To prevent this "inefficient" competition, governments may restrict access to the market to a single producer. The question then remains as to which firm is allowed to produce and capture the monopoly rents. Each firm now has an incentive to lobby government officials for the right to be the emergent monopolist. Lobbying, here, is socially inefficient since the (potential) firms are now using scarce resources not to create new production that would not otherwise exist but simply in an attempt to redistribute monopoly gains. If all firms are the same, then regardless of which firm ends up being selected, the same level of production and quality will occur. The resources used to gain the monopoly right are socially wasteful. Thus there is socially harmful competition to become the monopolist.

Consider, for example, cable television. The local government decides cable access is important for its residents but does not want lots of companies digging up the ground to lay their cable wires. It may be dangerous to have so many different wires in close proximity to each other, and since the main cost is the infrastructure, there is a large fixed cost but negligible marginal cost to hooking up each additional house. Thus the city council plans to limit the cable market to a single firm. Cable companies, anxious to enter this market free of any additional competition, hire marketing experts, lawyers, and so forth to make their pitch to the city council. The firms are now exhausting resources not to produce but rather for the right to produce. This would be socially beneficial if the lobbying were to convince the council to lift a total ban on cable so that cable can now exist where it otherwise would not. Resource use simply to distribute the monopoly cable rents, once the decision has been made to allow cable television, is socially wasteful. In order to protect its monopoly status, further socially harmful rent seeking can occur even after one firm is awarded the right to be the lone producer. Local cable companies may spend resources, for example, to convince legislators to ban satellite television or to pass legislation preventing the new satellite companies from including local channels, thereby making satellite less competitive to cable.

Governmental policies often have economic consequences. Those that can gain from certain policies have the economic incentive to lobby on their behalf. For policies that may cause them economic harm, those agents have an incentive to lobby against their passage. The rent seekers themselves may benefit, but society overall will be harmed when inefficient policies are passed or efficient policies are thwarted. Typically this is viewed in terms of policies that restrict competition, for example, domestic industry efforts to affect policies restricting free trade through tariffs and quotas. Conversely, resources can also be used to direct policy to encourage inefficient production, such as, for example, through farm subsidies.

Socially harmful rent seeking need not be limited to government policy. As a concrete example, consider the Super Bowl. Every year, the champions of the AFC and NFC meet in the Super Bowl to determine the championship. In the other major sports of baseball, basketball, and hockey, the championship series is played with games switching between the home stadiums of each team involved. In football, however, only a single game is played, so to prevent either team from having an unfair advantage, a neutral site is selected, typically a few years in advance. While this arrangement might appear to be fair, the question remains as to where to hold the game. Since the Super Bowl attracts a lot of visitors to the area, the selected city will benefit greatly from increased business in local hotels, restaurants, and tourist attractions and all the increased tax revenues. Potential cities spend a great deal of time, energy, and money to lobby the NFL commissioner's office to select their city as the monopoly host site. From a social standpoint, this resource use is wasteful. Even in the absence of lobbying (for example, if the NFL simply drew a lottery from all NFL cities) the Super Bowl would exist—the only question is which city in particular would reap the rewards. If for some reason the NFL was planning to eliminate the Super Bowl, and lobbying took place to create (hold) a Super Bowl, this resource usage could be socially beneficial (to the extent that people enjoy watching the Super Bowl), but resource use simply to decide who gets the monopoly rents is not.

How harmful is rent seeking? That is, how much would firms spend to secure or protect the monopoly right to production? Deadweight losses that occur from monopolies are simply a function of the reduced output and increased prices compared with the competitive equilibrium outcome. To these expected deadweight losses must be added the nonproductive use of resources, the rent seeking costs. One thought would be that each firm would be willing to spend up to the value of the monopoly rents so that all the monopoly profits are in essence a social cost as well. A firm competing with others faces an uncertain outcome as to which firm will win the right to become the monopolist, so the expected value of the rent-seeking investment is only a portion of the total rent, but all the firms in total could spend up to the total rent value. Decisions made under uncertainty depend on risk attitudes. Although most economic agents are thought to be risk averse, implying they would be willing to spend less than the expected value, rent seekers are entrepreneurs who are usually assumed to be risk takers, suggesting they may be willing to spend more than the expected value of the potential rents. Thus, social losses from rent seeking can be potentially very large indeed.

Rent seeking is arguably the principal component of public choice analysis. Tollison's "Is the Theory of Rent-Seeking Here to Stay?" is a survey of the evolution of the rent-seeking literature, where the main focus has been on interest groups and lobbyists wasting valuable time and resources to further their interests at the expense of others. The question remains: How large are the rent-seeking costs on society? Tullock's "Rent Seeking and Tax Reform" grapples with the proper definition of rent seeking, specifically whether to include only activities designed to redistribute existing wealth or also those activities that can promote new wealth as well. Tullock concludes with an application to public finance issues in terms of tax reform. In "Rent Extraction and Rent Creation in the Economic Theory of Regulation," McChesney explains how the politicians themselves engage in rent seeking by threatening the imposition of new costs or removal of protective regulations.

Is the Theory of Rent-Seeking Here to Stay?

Robert D. Tollison

Review Questions

1. How are the normal deadweight losses from a monopoly quantified? How are the rent seeking losses quantified?
2. What is meant by over- and under-dissipation of rents? Which does Tollison think more likely and why?
3. How does rent seeking affect the distribution of income?
4. How does the government structure affect rent seeking incentives?
5. What conclusions are drawn about the role of government in a rent seeking society?

1. Introduction

Government, as all students of public choice know, is not free. Yet until very recently the cost of government intervention in the economy has been underestimated. The reason for this is that the economic theory underlying such measurements was incomplete. In 1967, Gordon Tullock offered a picture of what a complete economic theory of the cost of government looks like when

Tollison, Robert D. "Is the Theory of Rent-Seeking Here to Stay?" In *Democracy and Public Choice,* ed. Charles K. Rowley, 143–57. Oxford: Blackwell Publishing, 1987.

he invented what has come to be called the theory of rent-seeking.[1] The purpose of this chapter is to assess the evolution of Tullock's idea in the literature, with special attention given to the problems and conundrums that presently dog rent-seeking theory.

There is, moreover, some market evidence that Tullock's concept of rent-seeking should be taken seriously. Using 1984 citation data, Tullock's 1967 paper, "The Welfare Costs of Tariffs, Monopolies and Theft," ties for second among his most cited works, and is the only article-length publication in his top five list (see table 1). I have not checked, but I would also guess that citations of this paper have greatly increased over the past several years. I am, therefore, not dealing with a backwater of Tullock's work, but rather a peak, and a growing peak at that.

The chapter proceeds as follows. Section 2 is definitional: in the simplest terms, what does rent-seeking mean? Section 3 further develops the theory of rent-seeking in the context of a government-created monopoly right. Section 4 examines the concept of equilibrium in rent-seeking contests. Section 5 introduces the concept of rent-protection. Section 6 discusses durable and nondurable monopolies and their welfare implications. Section 7 considers the possible links between income distribution and rent-seeking activities. Section 8 considers the relationship between political order and rent-seeking. Section 9 briefly introduces the positive economic side of rent-seeking theory. Section 10 concludes the chapter.

2. Rent-Seeking Defined

Economic rent is a familiar concept to economists. Simply, it is a return to a resource owner in excess of the owner's opportunity cost. Economic analysis has identified various categories of such returns (not all distinct one from the other)—quasi-rents, monopoly rents, inframarginal rents, and so on.

TABLE 1. Gordon Tullock's Five Most Cited Works—1984

Book or article	Number of 1984 citations*
The Calculus of Consent	49
The Politics of Bureaucracy	17
'The welfare costs of tariffs, monopolies, and theft'	17
Towards a Mathematics of Politics	10
Economics of Income Redistribution	7

* Citations to *The Calculus of Consent* are found under James M. Buchanan and are counted as 1.
Source: Social Science Citation Index, 1984.

Rent-seeking in the sense of seeking quasi- or temporary rents is nothing more than the normal profit-seeking incentive that motivates economic behavior. Such behavior is healthy for an economy; it allocates resources to their most highly valued uses, creates new products and values, and so on (Buchanan, 1980b). This behavior is not what Tullock's concept of rent-seeking means. Positive or negative temporary rents compel entry or exit, and hence impact on economic output. The economy gets something in return for temporary rents (more or less product).

Rent-seeking arises where output is given and fixed, as in the case of monopoly rents. Output cannot be augmented by definition, so expenditure to capture monopoly or contrived rents do not yield any additional products for the economy. It was such expenditures that Tullock categorized as wasteful.

Perhaps the most useful way to think about rent-seeking is in terms of using real resources to capture a pure transfer. Since expenditures to take a dollar from A and give it to B produce nothing, they are wasted from the point of view of the economy at large; they are zero-sum at best and are probably negative-sum (Tullock, 1980b). A lawyer, for example, employed to transfer a dollar from A to B has an opportunity cost in terms of the lawyer output he or she could have produced alternatively. This opportunity cost is the social cost of rent-seeking.

Rent-seeking is perhaps most usefully illustrated in the context of government interference in the economy to promote monopoly and economic regulation. The most efficacious way to promote monopoly rents in an industry is to pass a law to restrict output and to license entry. As individuals and firms seek government's favor to operate in the industry, rent-seeking occurs because such competition cannot expand output in the industry, which is fixed by law. It is not necessary, however, to have government to have rent-seeking. Private collusion among firms to fix prices, for example, has all the attributes of a rent-seeking game. Likewise the Mafia, competitive advertising by oligopolists, and the competition among siblings for inheritances are other possible examples of rent-seeking in a private context.[2]

Another definitional point is useful. Once government has intervened in the economy to create rents, the implications of rent-seeking behavior are difficult to escape (Buchanan, 1980b). Transfers will beget rent-seeking competition to capture them on some margin. If rents are created in the civil service, queues and "extra" educational investments will arise to dissipate them. Proffered tax reductions will induce entry into tax-favored classes. The same holds on the expenditure side of the budget. Basically, rent-seeking is a cost of government activity in general.

Finally, the theory of rent-seeking has positive and normative elements. The latter, which will occupy the bulk of this chapter, consists of devising theories of how the social costs of rent-seeking can be measured. This is the welfare economics part of rent-seeking theory. The former involves using the struggle to capture or to protect rents to explain the behavior of interest groups, legislators, regulators, voters, and other relevant actors in the political economy.

3. The Social Costs of Rent-Seeking

The purpose of this section is essentially to repeat the analysis of Section 2 in a slightly more complicated way. Hopefully, by the end of this discussion, we will be in a position to discuss the strengths and weaknesses of rent-seeking theory in more detail.

Following the above semantics, a useful way to analyze the social costs of rent-seeking is to consider the case where government promotes monopoly power in the private sector with a law or regulation (see figure 1).

At the original competitive equilibrium, P_cQ_c, consumer surplus in this industry is DBP_c. However, no one guarantees that consumers will get this real income; it is essentially up for grabs in the economic system. This being the case, let us assume that producers seek to capture part of the surplus by obtaining economic regulation of their industry. Price rises to P_m, as the regulatory program restricts industry output to Q_m. The marginal revenue curve is omitted to avoid cluttering the diagram.

In the old theory of monopoly (Harberger, 1954), producers succeeded in capturing P_mACP_c as a *transfer* from consumers (those who continue to buy the product at P_m). Consumers were made poorer to the same extent that the monopolist was made richer. Interpersonal judgments aside, the economy was seen as unaltered by such transfers. *ABC*, however, vanished from the economy as a result of the monopoly, and this real income was captured by no one. Hence, *ABC* was called the deadweight cost of monopoly or regulation. The fact that *ABC* was empirically small led to a complacency about monopoly and regulatory power in the economy, and to less interest among economists in the formal theory of monopoly (Mundell, 1962).

Tullock looked at this same type of analytical model, but posed the following question: what if P_mACP_c is not a simple transfer from consumers to producers? Suppose, instead, that those producers who aspire to be regulated have to spend real resources to capture the potential transfer of P_mACP_c? By asking such questions, Tullock was led to discover the concept of rent-seeking.

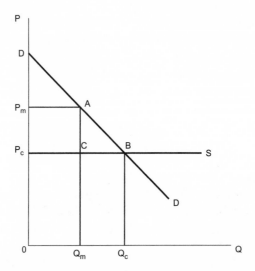

Figure 1. The basic welfare trade-off diagram

Let us suppose a simple rent-seeking game. There is a fixed number of bidders for a government monopoly right, say 20. The monopoly right has a known and fixed value of $100,000. All bidders are risk neutral. Thus, each person bids $5,000 for a one-in-twenty chance of winning the $100,000 pool of rents; at a social level, $100,000 is spent to capture $100,000. In this case, P_mACP_c is exactly or perfectly dissipated, and the social costs of the monopoly is a trapezoid, P_mABP_c, which consists of the Tullock or rent-seeking costs, P_mACP_c, and the Harberger or deadweight cost of monopoly, ABC. Tullock's invention thus provided a framework cost of monopoly, ABC. Tullock's invention thus provided a framework for increasing the social costs of monopoly and regulation by a significant amount, in the limit, the value of the monopoly profits at stake, making the theory of monopoly and regulation more interesting and richer to study as a result (Kreuger, 1974; Posner, 1975).

Of course, the stylized example here oversimplifies. For example, I did not say what happens to the payments made by the rent-seekers. They clearly flow to the public sector in some form. At an elementary level, each bidder may have spent $5,000 in taking regulatory officials out to dinner. Thus, the cost of rent-seeking in this case consists in the difference between the value of the in-kind transfer to the officials and its cash equivalent. In other words, not all of P_mACP_c is wasted; the officials place some value, though less than $100,000, on being taken out to dinner.

But this is a simple problem in rent-seeking theory. There are more interesting complexities that derive from this basic model, which I address in the sections that follow. Space does not allow a detailed elaboration of any of these issues. In each case, I endeavor to give the flavor of the problems at stake and to cite the relevant literature for those who would like to know more.

4. Equilibrium

The case where rents are exactly dissipated represents an example of competitive rent-seeking. With free entry and exit for bidders, the rent-seeking contest comes to reflect an equilibrium structure of bids and bidders. In the above example, rents are perfectly competed away with 20 bidders. Thus, even though the winner earns $95,000 on his or her bid, the game is presumably in equilibrium, and this prize is only a normal return investment in rent-seeking. If government, for example, were to seize the monopoly with no compensation, bidders would adjust their bids in the next round of rent-seeking.

Competitive rent-seeking is a popular equilibrium hypothesis in the literature (Posner, 1975). This is because it yields the exact dissipation result, which makes empirical work on the costs of rent-seeking easier. Rectangles and trapezoids are exact areas, which can be reasonably estimated. The exact dissipation model is thus like perfect competition; it is a useful, though not necessarily descriptive, analytical construct for increasing our understanding of how the world works.

This does not mean, however, that all rent-seeking contests are perfectly competitive in nature. Tullock (1980a) has offered classes of models where rent-seeking is imperfectly competitive in the sense that the competitive process for rents leads to over- or under-dissipation of the available rents. These cases are interesting, and they are obviously generated by assumptions about limitations on the number of bidders, imperfect information, and so on. They are not very popular, however, because imperfect dissipation makes the problem of deriving reduced-form equations with which to estimate rent-seeking costs much more difficult and case-specific (Fisher, 1985). One can no longer simply estimate the area of a trapezoid; rather, the task is to estimate the area of something more or less than a trapezoid that is a function of behavior in the economy. This is clearly a harder modeling task.

As between Tullock's analysis of over- and under-dissipation possibilities, I do not find the over-dissipation possibility to be very plausible. In this case, rent-seekers are somehow led to bid more than the value of the prize. While this is perhaps possible once, through the distortion of information to rent-seekers about their expected chances of winning, such behavior should not persist for long. The regulator/bureaucrat should only be able to lie once. In the next round of rent-seeking, bids will be adjusted to reflect "true" probabilities of winning; bureaucratic promises will be properly discounted.

Underbidding, where rent-seekers bid in the aggregate less than the value of the prize, is another matter. There are several plausible bases for under-bidding equilibria, including risk aversion (Hillman and Katz, 1984), comparative advantage among monopolizing inputs (Rogerson, 1982), and game-theoretic considerations (Tullock, 1980a, 1985). As stressed above, such considerations make the problem of analyzing the costs of rent-seeking more difficult and case-specific.

The point is that the concept of equilibrium is important in rent-seeking theory because it informs us as to how costly such behavior is likely to be in the real economy. Under-dissipation means less waste of rents (though as we shall see later, perhaps more monopoly). Theory is in its infancy in this area. At present, the literature (Corcoran, 1984; Higgins, Shughart, and Tollison, 1985) suggests that exact dissipation best describes the long-run tendency in games where the prize is fixed and there is free entry and exit of bidders. Tullock (1985) is quite adept, however, at undermining such results, and as he puts it, returning us to the bog of under-dissipation.

All this is to say that exact dissipation appears to be a good general conjecture about equilibrium in rent-seeking contests, but that this theory must be adapted to the circumstances of any particular case of rent-seeking. Like the model of perfect competition, the model of exactly dissipated rents is simply a vehicle and starting point for helping us to understand the real world.

5. Rent Protection

Not only do individuals use real resources to seek transfers, but they also are sometimes required to use real resources to protect their rents from encroachment by rent-seekers. This behavior is called "rent avoidance" in the literature; I choose to call it "rent protection." The basis for such behavior is clear. Not all "suppliers" of wealth transfers find it economically rational to allow their wealth to be taken away (why spend a dollar to save a dime?). Some will find it cost-effective to fight back (spend a dollar to save two dollars).

Let us use the simple example of an excise tax on a competitive industry to illustrate the potential of rent protection theory. Figure 2 illustrates. Here,

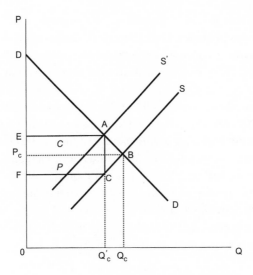

Figure 2. Rent-seeking in a heterogeneous market

as a result of an excise tax on the industry's product, industry supply shifts from S to S' The traditional analysis of this case stresses three basic results: (1) ABC is the deadweight cost of the tax; (2) $EACF$ is the tax revenue that is transferred to government; and (3) the incidence of the tax is split between consumers (C) and producers (P) as a function of the elasticities of demand and supply.

Enter rent protection. Assume that consumers (C) are unorganized and have no rational incentives to organize to resist the loss of consumer surplus that the tax imposes on them. However, let producers be organized and prepared to lobby against the tax. In the case at hand, producers may rationally spend up to their loss of producer surplus, P_cBCF, to resist the tax or to keep it from being higher than it is. This is the amount of wealth that the tax takes away from the industry. These expenditures are a rent-seeking (rent-protecting) cost in Tullock's terms, and so must be added to the traditional cost of the excise tax, ABC, to obtain the total social cost of excise taxation in this case. The total cost of the excise tax thus equals P_cBCF plus ABC.

Now the traditional or optimal taxation analysis is in a little bit of trouble. It is a mainstay of optimal taxation theory that the excess burden imposed by selective excise taxation (ABC) is minimized, for a given amount of revenue raised, when such taxes are placed on commodities with relatively inelastic demand curves. Unfortunately, this optimal taxation rule cannot stand up to the above analysis. It is quite easy to show that when P_cBCF is counted as part of the cost of excise taxation, taxing an industry with a more elastic demand curve, but no organized, rent-protecting opposition to the tax, is socially preferable. Moreover, considerations of monopoly only strengthen the analysis.[3]

In sum, then, the concept of rent protection can be brought into conventional economic analysis, perhaps to yield new and interesting insights about the way the world works. For example, the idea that excise taxes in the face of organized industry opposition are not a good idea undercuts the tax program of most countries with respect to such commodities as beer and cigarettes. Moreover, virtually all welfare analyses of monopoly and regulation ignore rent-protection activities of organized opponents of such governmental programs. A more general welfare analytics will include traditional deadweight costs, rent-seeking costs, *and* rent-protecting costs.[4]

6. Durability

The durability of monopoly rights poses some interesting issues for the theory of rent-seeking.[5] Consider the following limiting case. The monopoly right is granted forever, and all Tullock-type expenditures to capture the right are made *ex ante* by rent-seekers. In this situation, the Tullock costs are *sunk.* The economy is forever poorer by the amount of Tullock spending; abolishing the monopoly right cannot get the Tullock expenditures back.

Now consider the case where Tullock costs have not been completely capitalized. That is, the holder of the monopoly right must engage in some rent protection expenditures each period as there are threats to the political status of his or her monopoly. In this situation, *if,* for example, the monopoly is deregulated *permanently,* the ongoing Tullock expenditures can be returned to the economy.

The moral of this story about durability for anti-trust and regulatory reform efforts is clear. The gains from deregulation are greater where Tullock costs have not yet been capitalized. Others things being equal, the most cost-effective program of deregulation is to concentrate on industries that fight back, for here the social gains from deregulation are largest. There is less point in taking action with, say old, quiet monopolies.

Mind you, this is a point about social gains. Consumers, on the whole, could not care less whether monopoly rents have been capitalized. But still the logic of the argument is to point out where it is in the political economy that the gains from deregulation are potentially the highest. This is paradoxically where deregulation is fought the hardest. Such are the implications of rent-seeking for anti-trust and regulatory reform.

7. Rent-Seeking and the Distribution of Income

Pre-Tullock, the effect of monopoly on the distribution of income was clear: the monopolist got richer and consumers got poorer (Comanor and Smiley, 1975). In the rent-seeking approach, the impact of monopoly on income distribution is a murkier issue. Of the original formulators of the theory, only Posner (1975) relates his analysis to the distribution of income. He states: "There is no reason to think that monopoly has a significant distributive effect. Consumers' wealth is not transferred to the shareholders of monopoly firms; it is dissipated in the purchase of inputs into the activity of becoming a monopolist" (1975, p. 821).

Posner's argument seems logical. Rent-seeking dissipates monopoly rents, translating potential transfers into social costs. The effect of monopoly on the distribution of income in the rent-seeking society would thus appear to be nil. Unfortunately, this argument does not stand up.

Rent-seeking has a pronounced impact on the distribution of income— the winner of the monopoly right becomes wealthier. Using the simple example employed by Posner, suppose that there are $1 million in rents to be captured and ten risk-neutral bidders for a monopoly right. The allocative effects in the problem are clear. Each bidder bids $100,000 for the franchise; $1 million is spent to capture $1 million; at a social level the monopoly rents are exactly wasted. But Posner is incorrect to imply that the example does not embody a distributional consequence. Clearly, one of the ten bidders wins the competition, and receives a net return on his efforts of $900,000. The resulting income distribution is different than that which prevailed before the monopoly right was created, in this example significantly different. Simply, nine people are $100,000 poorer, and one is $900,000 richer.

Without more information, one cannot say in this stylized example whether rent-seeking increases or decreases the degree of inequality in the distribution of income. The winner in this case could, for example, have been poor relative to the nine losers, and his victory would have leveled the income distribution to some extent. It seems a little far-fetched, however, to think that rent-seeking generally promotes any leveling in the income distribution of an economy. Set in a world of tradition, class, privilege, power, and differential organization costs, rent-seeking most likely promotes more inequality in the distribution of income.

Perhaps even more realistically, there will not be an equal distribution of rent-seeking ability in a society. Thus, the mechanism by which rents are assigned is likely to affect the distribution of wealth to the extent that Ricardian rents are earned in rent-seeking. Consider a regulatory hearing mechanism for assigning rents, and suppose that some lawyers or economists earn inframarginal rents in rent-seeking. On average, these individuals will be wealthier than their marginal competitors and wealthier than they would be without a rent-seeking mechanism of the particular type that rewards their skills. The choice of such a transfer mechanism increases the demand for lawyers (and possibly economists) above that which would hold with (say) an auction mechanism for assigning monopoly rents. So, first of all, the mechanism will alter the distribution of wealth by occupation. Moreover, if the requisite talents of the favored occupation cannot be reproduced at constant costs, the inequality of wealth in society may be further affected. For example, suppose the qualities of a good businessman/speculator are more fungible among the population than the qualities of a good lawyer. Then, inframarginal rents will accrue to the best of the legal profession in regulatory hearing cases, whereas with an auction no Ricardian rents would be earned. The distribution of wealth would differ between these two societies as a consequence.

The main point, then, is that rent-seeking will affect the distribution of income. This is not an empirical chapter. Estimating the actual impact of rent-seeking on income distribution has not been done and would be a formidable task. Perhaps Posner is right. If anyone looked, the actual impact of rent-seeking on income distribution would be trivial. This seems doubtful, however, given the rather large role that government has assumed in the economy and the degree to which government largesse figures prominently in the circular flow of income.[6]

8. Rent-Seeking and the Political Order

What is the relationship between the political order and the amount of rent-seeking that it begets? There are no easy answers here; in fact, to my mind, there are no answers at present. Let me explain.[7]

Rent-seeking can be seen as a two-stage game. First, there is competition to control the political apparatus that creates, enforces, and assigns rent flows. This is related to issues such as who controls the legislature, or how monarchs are selected. Second, there is a rent-seeking behavior that we have been discussing thus far in the chapter, namely, the competition to capture the rents that inhere in particular instances of monopoly and regulation. These two stages are linked in the discussion that follows, presenting a problem of some importance for rent-seeking theory.

The problem is easy to exposit. At base, in a world where Tullock waste is exact and complete, there is no marginal incentive to create monopolies. Investments in monopoly creation lead only to a normal rate of return. Political entrepreneurs will seek higher return margins of political investment. There thus exist incentives to convert Tullock waste into transfers, which make the creators of monopoly rents better off. Better to receive a transfer than to see transfers wasted.

In this context, consider two types of worlds. In one, Tullock waste is exact and complete. Here, the incentive to create monopoly will be low because there are no excess returns from doing so, but the social cost per instance of realized monopoly will be high. In the other world, politicians have succeeded in converting rent-seeking costs into transfers. There are thus significant excess returns to monopoly creation; hence, there will be more monopolies in such a society. Returns to politicians are only transfers and not waste in this society, but this society will have more monopolies and more Harberger losses than the first society.

The dilemma is now clear—which society will be wealthier? There does not appear to be an *a priori* way to say: one society has less monopoly and more waste per monopoly; the other has more monopoly and less waste per monopoly. As I said at the outset, I write only to pose the issue. I do not know what the answer to the question is.

Indeed, the issue becomes murkier when we return to the first stage of rent-seeking discussed above. If there is a lot to be gained from controlling government, as in the second case above where rents are converted to transfers by political actors, then perhaps a lot is spent at the first stage of the contest to control the government. Alternatively, where there is not much to be made through monopoly creation, little effort may be expanded to capture the state. Of course, this is all quite *ad hoc*. For example, the divine right of monarchs with clearly defined rules of royal succession leads to a fairly low-cost means of transferring control of the state, even though the state may be fairly effective at using monopolies as a source of revenue (Ekelund and Tollison, 1981).

One can thus find odd combinations of first- and second-stage incentives. Majoritarian democracy, for example, appears to give away regulatory rents through in-kind auctions, which maximizes the incentive to create monopolies at the second stage, while allowing maximal dissipation to acquire legislative majorities at the first stage. One, almost perversely, gets lots of Tullock and

Harberger waste in such a case. The point is that rent-seeking takes place within a given political order and that this order impacts on the character and amount of rent-seeking that we subsequently observe. This is really a problem of constitutional political economy. (Buchanan, 1980a). Of course, the control of rent-seeking is not the only objective in designing or evaluating a state, but the issue clearly deserves to be on the menu of relevant considerations.

9. Positive Economics and Rent-Seeking

There is a positive economics of rent-seeking which, if I were to do justice to it, would take another chapter. Briefly, the literature which expounds it is driven by the idea that much of government activity can be explained in wealth-transfer terms. That is, government is about taking wealth from some people ("suppliers" of wealth transfers) and giving it to other people ("demanders" of wealth transfers), or put into the terms of this chapter, about rent-protection and rent-seeking.[8]

Most people are taken aback at such a starkly simple (and cynical) view of government. They wonder, well surely government is about something more than organized, legitimized theft? Surely government is about Truth, Beauty, Justice, the American Way, and the production of Public Goods?

And, of course, the rent-seeking theory has answers to these types of questions. Yes, government does produce things in the rent-seeking theory of these state, but these are mere by-products of the fundamental transfers at stake. We thus get our national defense, roads, schools, and so on as an unintended consequence of the competition for wealth-transfers. As stated at the start of the chapter, government is not free, and rent-seeking is the cost of government.

But more importantly, and more scientifically, the rent-seeking theory of government is an *empirical* theory. Not only is it on the front page of the newspapers every day, but there is scholarly empirical support for the theory which is strong and growing. This cannot be said about any other theory of government (such as the public-interest theory) of which I am aware. And it is this scientific hallmark (the testability) of the rent-seeking theory, which will make it harder and harder to avoid as the best available rational choice explanation of government (median-voter models to the contrary notwithstanding).

I shall cease and desist from reviewing positive developments in rent-seeking theory for want of time and space. Suffice it to say that there is a growing literature in this area, ranging from legislatures and legislators (McCormick and Tollison, 1981), to pressure groups (Becker, 1983), to regulation (Stigler,

1971; Peltzman, 1976), to the independent judiciary (Landes and Posner, 1975), to monarchies (Ekelund and Tollison, 1981), and so on, to virtually all aspects of government behavior. Perhaps another time I shall write a paper about this literature. The reader should be aware, however, that the statements in this section are not idle boasts. There is an important empirical theory of government extant, and it is the rent-seeking theory.

10. Conclusion: What Hath Tullock Wrought?

The theory of rent-seeking is here to stay. As I have observed in another context (Tollison, 1982), the most interesting thing about Tullock's ingenious insight is how simply he put it. Like Coase, he communicated his vision in terms that every lay economist could follow. This is a criterion by which greatness in science is measured. In economics, the Tullocks of our profession are more indispensable than ever. To wit, the scarcest thing in any science is a good idea, clearly communicated.

NOTES

1. There is a debate about what to call the behavior described by rent-seeking. The name is from Krueger's 1973 paper by the title, "The Political Economy of the Rent-Seeking Society." Bhagwati objects to the rent-seeking terminology, preferring instead the appellation, Directly Unproductive Activities (DUP) (see, for example, Bhagwati, Brecher, and Srinivasan, 1984). His interest in the relationship between the theory of second-best and rent-seeking is apparent in his preferred terminology. Others, such as North (1984), simply want to identify rent-seeking as economic behavior subject to constraints, that is, as an application of the maximizing paradigm of economic theory. I have no strong feelings about what we call the behavior at issue here, though "rent-seeking" does just fine so long as the analysis is spelled out and carried through properly.

2. The latter example is a matter of some dispute in the literature; see Buchanan (1983); and Anderson and Brown (1985). Also, one could argue that each of these examples of rent-seeking in a private setting are somehow related to government in the limiting case. Competitive advertising by oligopolists, for example, takes place because agreements among firms on such matters are illegal under the anti-trust laws. See DiLorenzo (1984).

3. For the basic analysis, see Lee and Tollison (1985).

4. See Baysinger and Tollison (1980) for an effort along these lines.

5. The following is adapted from McCormick, Shughart, and Tollison (1984). Also, see Landes and Posner (1975) for a positive theory of the durability of legislation.

6. For more discussion along these lines, see Higgins and Tollison (1985).

7. Again, see Higgins and Tollison (1985) for a more elaborate version of the argument in this section.

8. This is meant to be simplified. Obviously, individuals belong to many different

groups, sometimes as rent-protectors, sometimes as rent-seekers, and sometimes as quiescent rent-"suppliers" (why spend a dollar to save a dime?).

REFERENCES

Anderson, G. M. and Brown, P. J. (1985) 'Heir pollution: a note on Buchanan's "Laws of Succession" and Tullock's "Blind Spot." *International Review of Law and Economics,* 5, June, pp. 15–24.

Baysinger, B. and Tollison, R. D. (1980) 'Evaluating the social costs of monopoly and regulation,' *Atlantic Economic Journal,* 8, December, pp. 22–6.

Becker, G. S. (1983) 'A theory of competition among pressure groups for political influence,' *Quarterly Journal of Economics,* XCVII, August, pp. 371–400.

Bhagwati, J. N., Brecher, R. A. and Srinivasan, T. N. (1984) 'DUP activities and economic theory,' in D. C. Colander, (ed.) *Neoclassical Political Economy.* Cambridge: Ballinger, pp. 17–32.

Buchanan, J. M. 'Reform in the rent-seeking society,' in J. M. Buchanan, R. D. Tollison, and G. Tullock, (1980a) (eds.) *Toward a Theory of the Rent-Seeking Society.* College Station: Texas A & M University Press, pp. 359–67.

Buchanan, J. M. (1980b) 'Rent seeking and profit seeking,' in J. M. Buchanan, R.D. Tollison, and G. Tullock, (eds.) *Toward a Theory of the Rent-Seeking Society.* College Station: Texas A & M University Press, pp. 3–15.

Buchanan, J. M. (1983) 'Rent-seeking, noncompensated transfers, and laws of succession,' *Journal of Law and Economics,* 26, April, pp. 71–86.

Comanor, W. S. and Smiley, R. H. (1975) 'Monopoly and the distribution of wealth,' *Quarterly Journal of Economics,* 89, May, pp. 177–94.

Corcoran, W. J. (1984) 'Long-run equilibrium and total expenditures in rent-seeking,' *Public Choice,* 43, 1, pp. 89–94.

DiLorenzo, T. J. (1984) 'The domain of rent-seeking behavior: private or public choice,' *International Review of Law and Economics,* 4, December, pp. 131–5.

Ekelund, R. B. and Tollison, R. D. (1981) *Mercantilism as a Rent-Seeking Society.* College Station: Texas A & M University Press.

Fisher, F. M. (1985) 'The social costs of monopoly and regulation: Posner reconsidered,' *Journal of Political Economy,* 93, April, pp. 410–16.

Harberger, A. C. (1954) 'Monopoly and resource allocation,' *American Economic Review,* 44, May, pp. 77–87.

Higgins, R., Shughart, W. F. and Tollison, R. D. (1985) 'Free entry and efficient rent-seeking,' *Public Choice,* 46, pp. 247–58.

Higgins, R. and Tollison, R. D. (1985) 'Life among the triangles and trapezoids: notes on the theory of rent-seeking,' unpublished ms.

Hillman, A. L. and Katz, E. (1984) 'Risk-averse rent-seekers and the social cost of monopoly power,' *Economic Journal,* 94, March, pp. 104–10.

Kreuger, A. O. (1974) "The political economy of the rent-seeking society," *American Economic Review,* 64, June, pp. 291–303.

Landes, W. M. and Posner, R. A. (1975) 'The independent judiciary in an interest-group perspective,' *Journal of Law and Economics* 18, December, pp. 875–901.

Lee, D. R. and Tollison, R. D. (1985) 'Optimal taxation in a rent-seeking environment,' unpublished ms.

McCormick, R. E., Shughart, W. F. and Tollison, R. D. (1984) 'The disinterest in deregulation,' *American Economic Review,* December, pp. 1075–79.

McCormick, R. E. and Tollison, R. D. (1981) *Politicians, Legislation and the Economy: An Inquiry into the Interest-Group Theory of Government.* Boston: Martinus Nijhoff.

Mundell, R. A. (1962) Review of L. H. Janssen, 'Free trade, protection and customs unions,' *American Economic Review,* 52, June, p. 622.

North, D. (1984) 'Three approaches to the study of institutions,' in D. C. Colander, (ed.) *Necolassical Political Economy.* Cambridge: Ballinger, pp. 33–40.

Peltzman, S. (1976) 'Toward a more general theory of regulation,' *Journal of Law and Economics,* 2, August, pp. 211–40.

Posner, R. A. (1975) 'The social costs of monopoly and regulation,' *Journal of Political Economy,* 83, August, pp. 807–27.

Rogerson, W. P. (1982) 'The social costs of monopoly and regulation: a game-theoretic analysis,' *Bell Journal of Economics,* 13, Autumn, pp. 391–401.

Stigler, G. J. (1971) 'The theory of economic regulation,' *Bell Journal of Economics and Management Science,* 2, Spring, pp. 3–21.

Tollison, R. D. (1982) 'Rent seeking: a survey,' *Kyklos,* 35, (fasc. 4), pp. 575–602.

Tullock, G. (1967) 'The welfare costs of tariffs, monopolies, and theft,' *Western Economic Journal,* 5, June, pp. 224–32.

Tullock, G. (1980a) 'Efficient rent-seeking,' in J. M. Buchanan, R. D. Tollison and G. Tullock, (eds.) *Toward a Theory of the Rent-Seeking Society.* College Station: Texas A & M University Press, pp. 97–112.

Tullock, G. (1980b) 'Rent-seeking as a negative-sum game,' in J. M. Buchanan, R. D. Tollison and G. Tullock, (eds.) *Toward a Theory of the Rent-Seeking Society.* College Station: Texas A & M University Press, pp. 16–36.

Tullock, G. (1985) 'Back to the bog,' *Public Choice,* 46, 3, pp. 259–64.

Rent Seeking and Tax Reform

Gordon Tullock

Review Questions

1. How does Tullock define rent seeking?
2. Why is the distinction between harmful and beneficial rent seeking important? What are some examples of each?
3. How is it decided when rent seeking costs should or should not be included as a social cost? Do you agree with this procedure? What are the alternatives?
4. What is the advantage to direct, rather than indirect, subsidies?
5. What is the connection between general taxes, loopholes, and special interests?

I. Introduction

As some readers may know, I once was a Chinese expert, and rectifying terms was a main preoccupation of Confucian scholars. Let me begin, therefore, by briefly discussing the meaning of both tax reform and rent seeking. My personal definition of rent seeking essentially is using resources to obtain rents

Tullock, Gordon. "Rent-Seeking and Tax Reform." *Contemporary Policy Issues* 6 (1988): 37–47.

for people where the rents themselves come from something with negative social value. For example, if the automobile industry invests resources to get a tariff on Korean cars, then this makes Canadian citizens worse off. Hence, even though the automobile companies will gain, such investment of resources is rent seeking.

If, on the other hand, the automobile companies invest resources in developing a mechanical improvement on their automobiles, then I would not call it rent seeking. The cars would in fact be better. Note, however, that the benefit obtained from the mechanical improvement may in fact be less than its cost. Businessmen try to avoid such malinvestment, but it does happen. A rather crude distinction exists here. I would not call it rent seeking, even though society on the whole would have been better off had the investment not been undertaken.

Resorting to such a crude distinction is unfortunate, but it is the best we can do. We would prefer a general continuous function that includes both the benefit (or harm) and the costs of the activity. Unfortunately, because I have not yet been able to develop such a function, I am stuck with a crude distinction.

II. Advertising

Many cases exist in which expenditures that are privately beneficial have little or possibly no benefit for society as a whole, but at least they do no harm. As an obvious example, advertising often simply shifts customers back and forth among competing companies but has little other effect. The current arrangement of installing small signs directly on the shoulders of interstate highways is cheaper than, and presumably about as effective as, constructing large billboards.

Over the long term, the existence of competing advertising means that the product quality is subject to considerable improvement. Nevertheless, at any given point in time, cutting each company's advertising budget by 90 percent would save money and probably have no other significant effect. I do not think that such advertising should be called rent seeking. The same applies to research laboratories' investing in duplicative research in their efforts to win the patent race.

III. Tax Reform

The second term that must be rectified is "tax reform." The common technical meaning of tax reform is rearranging the tax code so as to meet some criterion—frequently a rather vague one—of efficiency. No implication of an increase or a reduction is necessary.

But that is the technical definition. I think that most ordinary citizens are not particularly interested in efficiency, and that they view tax reform as having two other characteristics. The first characteristic is that taxes go down, and the second—rather paradoxically—is that taxes on the very wealthy go up.

A sort of alliance exists here between the economic specialist and the ordinary unwashed citizen in that both oppose "loopholes." The common citizen thinks that the rich benefit greatly from loopholes and that if these loopholes were closed, then his own taxes would go down. The economic expert may also think that the rich have too many loopholes. However, the expert basically views the loopholes not as particularly favoring the rich but as distorting resource allocation.

IV. Loopholes

This, of course, raises the question of what exactly is a loophole. The most common single definition of a loophole is a legal provision under which someone does not pay taxes when I think he should. Tax codes are immense bodies of rules with immense numbers of both taxes and arrangements for non-taxes, i.e., provisions for not collecting taxes. Classifying as loopholes and "non-loopholes" the various provisions that permit the private citizen to keep at least some of his money is inherently rather arbitrary.

As an obvious example, most income taxes are at least moderately progressive. That people in lower tax brackets are not required to pay as high a percentage of their incomes as are people in the upper brackets is not classified as a loophole. This is, of course, a clear case in which one category of taxpayers is treated differently from another.

The usual assumption is that some kind of a general tax exists and that special interest groups have secured arrangements under which one of their particular activities is exempted from taxation or one of their particular expenditures is regarded as a business expense and hence not part of income. I should point out that loopholes also exist in revenue measures other than income tax. The U.S. Supreme Court, for example, once had to determine whether a tomato was a fruit or a vegetable since tariffs were different on the two categories of food products.[1]

Let us turn to income tax under which most of these problems arise. First, people listing the loopholes normally treat the deduction of interest on a home mortgage in a rather bizarre way. They include it in the data on the absolute size of the total loopholes in the tax code. Indeed, this deduction makes up more than half of total loopholes. On the other hand, when these people get around to listing loopholes and considering their elimination, this deduction rarely is mentioned. Some have suggested, however, that the deduction be withdrawn for second or third homes.

I suppose that the political reasons for this treatment are fairly easy to understand. Nevertheless, it clearly is an arbitrary distinction. Another arbitrary distinction is that many economists feel an expenditure tax would be better than an income tax since it would encourage investment. I have never heard any of these economists refer to this idea as a loophole for savings.

Nevertheless, I now introduce a rather artificial definition of loopholes that reflects the viewpoint of what one may call traditional public finance. I call a loophole any provision in a quite general tax rate that will exempt some particular matter. The reason for this is simply that such loopholes tend to lower economic efficiency. General taxes that are hard to evade—the true income tax, sales tax, value-added tax, real estate tax, etc.—do not much change resource allocation among different uses except in so far as they remove resources from the private sector. They may, of course, reduce the work incentive or savings incentive. (If the money is spent on genuine public goods, then the result of the whole package may be to increase such incentives.) The depletion allowance loophole in the U.S. income tax, however, did lead to an overinvestment in oil exploration. Most special provisions have similar characteristics.

V. Desirable Loopholes

Note that loopholes that switch resources may have a constructive purpose. For example, our maintaining—for military reasons—some particular industry that could not support itself without a subsidy may be desirable. As another wide example, the U.S. tax code grants exemptions for money contributed to a large variety of charitable organizations. Apparently, the American people feel that these institutions should be subsidized but mistrust Congress's ability to decide which particular charity should receive which particular subsidy. This system permits individual citizens, rather than Congress, to allocate the subsidies. This is not an ideally efficient system, but clearly one may argue that it is desirable.

Aside from these cases, the bulk of such special provisions result from lobbying by special interest groups. Indeed, that probably is also true of the charitable exemptions—at least in the U.S. Most special interest groups would argue that the production of milk, gloves, etc. should be subsidized by the government—and hence that the exemption is desirable. I was particularly intrigued by the lengthy treatment of racehorse breeding in the former U.S. income tax law.

VI. Lobbying

Suppose, then, that a well-organized lobby proposes to get the taxes lowered on some special industry. According to our earlier definition of rent seeking, whether or not this is rent seeking depends on both the tax side and the expenditure side.

The first consideration, of course, is whether reducing this particular tax will lead to a shift of resources that results in the economy as a whole being worse off. To keep this particular case pure, suppose the result of the loophole is not only that some particular industry—e.g., glove manufacturing—is exempted from tax, but that the rest of the tax structure is raised so that all other industries have a slightly higher tax. Clearly, this would make society as a whole worse off.

But suppose that when this loophole is generated, the government cuts back expenditures instead of raising other taxes. Then the question of whether or not this is desirable turns on where the money is saved. Some distortion in the manufacturing industry still will occur, but it easily could be a minor factor compared with the impact of the expenditure cut. Suppose, for example, that the necessary saving is made by abolishing the British Columbia Egg Board. (The Egg Board is self-supporting, but the amounts that it now charges egg producers could be retained for some other purpose while the Egg Board itself were terminated.) The distortion of the economy caused by exempting the glove industry from taxation would not likely be as great as the distortion relieved by abolishing the Egg Board.

As an equally extreme example on the other side, suppose that the expenditures reduction cut Environmental Protection Agency funding so that the amount of air pollution rose considerably. In this case, the damage that the loophole causes could be quite considerable. First, it would distort the manufacturing industry, and second, it would increase air pollution. I clearly would classify this act as rent seeking.

Note that from the standpoint of those organizing the lobby, this distinction simply is irrelevant. They are trying to make money by manipulating the government. They don't care about the secondary consequences, and yet I am classifying their activity as either rent seeking or non-rent seeking solely in terms of those secondary consequences.

Lobbyists sometimes lobby for things of general benefit. Some years ago, I read an article in the *Washington Post* dealing with what that newspaper called the "Christmas tree" committee of Congress. To the indignation of the *Washington Post*, the committee with jurisdiction over tariffs was listening to various industry representatives and then doing what they asked. But the intellectual climate of opinion had changed since the 1920s, and these industries now were asking for reductions in tariffs. Generally, they wanted to eliminate the tariffs on their raw materials or components.

The *Washington Post* was correct in identifying this as perfectly ordinary lobbying activity by special interest groups—indeed, the lobbyists were standard industrial lobbyists. But even if the net effect of these tax cuts was less desirable than simply abolishing the protective tariff as a whole, the net effect still was desirable. Loopholes in a bad tax code may be better than no loopholes in a bad tax code. That is particularly so in this case since practically no revenue effect was involved. Of the tariffs about which they complained, most had been set so high that nothing was being imported under them anyway.

VII. Special Interests

When I wrote "Problems of Majority Voting" (Tullock, 1959)—the tiny acorn from which *The Calculus of Consent* (Buchanan and Tullock, 1962) sprang—I ended by pointing out not only that special interest expenditures are funded by general taxation but that special interest loopholes could be funded by reducing general interest expenditures. The model that I presented can best be seen by considering figure 1. A continuous tendency exists to use revenues from general taxation for special interest expenditures and to relieve special interest groups of their taxes, i.e., to "fund loopholes." Similarly, the general interest type of government expenditure is continuously attrited by transferring funds to expenditures that benefit special interests and to tax loopholes that reduce the total amount of money available.

Of course, not all special interest tax exemptions are undesirable on general grounds (e.g., charitable exemptions maybe), and not all special interest expenditures cost much more than they are worth. But virtually all special expenditures for limited groups of people and virtually all tax loopholes affecting special interests result from lobbying. In some cases, however, this lobbying conveys a positive benefit—or at least does no harm—to the citizenry. Therefore, following my crude distinction between rent-seeking and non-rent-seeking activities, I can identify rent seeking in only some of these cases.

As most economists, I would like the government to shift to a general tax

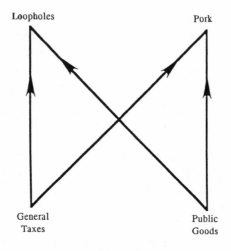

Figure 1

system with no loopholes except possibly for industries in which special subsidies genuinely are desirable. Even then, I would prefer that the subsidies be direct rather than indirect. I also would like the government to discontinue the large range of activities—the British Columbia Egg Board is a clear-cut example—that actually lower the efficiency of the economy. This not only would abolish the present tax loopholes and a great many government expenditures, but would result in a much lower but quite general tax level.

Clearly, most representatives of special interests would be delighted with such reform provided that it would not affect their particular special interests. They want reform to affect all others. The special interest groups that object to true reform—and they are quite numerous—generally are engaging in straightforward rent seeking. Unfortunately, these groups also are engaging in what is likely to be politically successful activity.

VIII. General Agreements

For a long time, Public Choice scholars have pointed out that getting rid of individual loopholes or individual pork-barrel government expenditures is very difficult. However, because on the whole such loopholes and pork-barrel expenditures hurt everyone, a general agreement to abolish all of them not only would be in the public interest but also might pass. Problems are twofold. First, because the public simply is not well informed on this or any other matter, dealing with a single all-or-none reduction—as opposed to a series of small steps—is politically difficult. Second, the special interest groups all are well informed and will fight intensely for their own particular special interests.

If the automobile industry could get repealed all tariffs and quotas on everything except automobiles, then this would serve its interest greatly. The industry would be even better off if all tariffs, together with all pork-barrel legislation, were repealed. But here we have the classic prisoner's dilemma. The automobile industry's best possible strategy is to get everything else repealed and to retain its own special privilege. If everybody tries that, then we likely will end up in the less than socially optimal lower right-hand corner (rational action without collusion) instead of in the socially optimal upper left-hand corner (rational action with collusion) of the prisoner's dilemma matrix.

That President Reagan was able to get through a rather general change in the U.S. tax code, in the direction that I have discussed above, is encouraging. As enacted, of course, the bill was a long way from perfect, and various special interests indeed were protected. One reason the bill went through may be that because the U.S. currently is depending so heavily on deficit financing, no lobbies favoring particular expenditures were worried about taxes to support those expenditures.

That the 1984 Democratic presidential candidate campaigned in favor of increasing taxes probably was not entirely a coincidence. Although favoring a tax increase was a very un-Democratic view, it perhaps was intended to rally all of the pork-barrel lobbies on the candidate's side. But it failed.

We are approaching a situation in which those people who want to cut taxes—either the economists seeking general reductions or the special interest groups seeking loopholes—are being thrown into a fairly direct conflict with those who want expenditures increased or at least held constant. On the expenditure increase side, once again, are the pork-barrel expenditures and the more general expenditures.

The tendency that I have described above—for things to go from the general to the particular—would seem to indicate that expenditures for items such as improving the U.S. military machine are apt to be dropped in favor of expenditures for special interest groups. I should emphasize, by the way, that a very important special interest group is the officer corps and the civil servants of the Department of Defense. The U.S. has one officer—mainly field-grade and up—for every seven enlisted men and one admiral on service in Washington for every single deep draft vessel that the United States owns. Firing three-quarters of all field-grade and flag officers surely would improve the U.S. military establishment while simultaneously saving money. Unfortunately, this is one case where well-organized special interest groups will not only fight but no doubt win.

IX. Charitable Expenditures

One area where an interest group exists, but where it seems ineffective, is in aid to the poor. Clearly, the poor are interested in this and tend to use whatever political assets they have to get such aid. In practice, however, they do rather badly. As one example, people in the second decile from the bottom receive larger transfers than do those in the bottom decile (see Tullock, 1983, p. 94). As another example, the poor were doing relatively as well during the middle of the 19th century as they are doing now, according to Lebergott's (1976, p. 57) study.

The apparent explanation for this is that the poor are poor because they are not very competent people. In some cases, their lack of competence comes from perfectly genuine organic illness. In any event, this lack of competence apparently carries over into the political sphere. They are relatively inept as special interest groups, and I think that the money they do receive largely reflects charitable impulses of the upper income groups. In any event, whether the poor engage in any significant amount of lobbying is not clear. Of course, various middle-class civil servants and social workers lobby in the name of the poor, but little money actually gets to the poor.

X. Ideal Taxes

Perhaps I should deviate a bit here and discuss what one might call the economist's ideal of taxation. First, in a new country—and I should point out that large parts of British Columbia still are unsettled—confiscatory taxation of land site values has much to commend it. One wants the land value to be confiscated by the state since no excess burden exists there. Also, one wants the land speculator to retain full return on his investment of talent. This is hard to do in areas that already are settled. But in areas that have not yet been occupied, selling land at auction—while including some kind of agreement as to what type of land taxes will be collected in the future—suits these conditions.

Second, most economists favor taxing things that, if left to themselves, would be overproduced. Air pollution is an obvious example. In this case, provided the tax is calculated properly, there is not only no excess burden but actually an excess benefit.

Unfortunately, in both of the above cases, resources may be invested to create inefficient institutions. For example, people may wish to receive the land free since from their personal standpoint, the land's highest value is as a place where they may occasionally go on camping trips. Similarly, people may invest resources to establish pollution taxes that are either too high or too low.[2]

Such nearly costless taxes, unfortunately, are insufficient to support most modern governments. This leaves two other types of taxes—one of them very general—that comprise the classical areas in which loopholes occur and to which economists refer when they discuss tax reform.

XI. User Taxes

Before turning to those areas, however, I must mention one other very important area. The impact of many government activities is quite widespread—but not spread over the entire population. In such cases, the obvious solution is a user tax. But arranging such a tax may be difficult. For example, the weather bureau is far more important for people proposing to fly and for farmers than it is for office workers. However, taxing the beneficiary groups without taxing others would be difficult if not impossible.

In this area, one first should examine the possibility of taxing the users. In the U.S., the road system is paid for partly by gasoline taxes and partly by real estate taxes that local governments impose. As a rough rule of thumb, the major highways are paid for by gas taxes and the local feeder roads are paid for by real estate taxes. This arrangement may not even approximate an ideal allocation, but it clearly is far from pathological.

However, for those services for which this type of funding is difficult to implement, relying on general taxes may prove economically desirable. After all, over their lifetimes, most people benefit about as much from these things as they would be harmed if the whole bundle of such services were taken away.

But this is an economic judgment and not a political one. If special services for special groups are funded out of general taxation, then rent seeking by those special groups will likely lead to overexpenditure. Many years ago, James Buchanan suggested a solution: The U.S. could select—perhaps at random—some other group of people about the same size as the benefitted group and could put the tax on them. Thus, two lobbying groups would be opposing each other and the outcome presumably would be improved.

XII. Budget Reform

One way to implement this solution would be to change the present budget procedures to those of a more traditional system. If we go back in history, we usually find that no such thing as a government budget existed. Individual government services were paid for by allocating specific taxes or parts of specific taxes to fund those services. The Lord High Admiral of Spain, for example, collected one gold guinea from every ship that called at a Spanish port. The only way to increase his revenue was either to encourage more shipping to call into Spanish ports or to fight it out with other government bureaus for a share of their taxes.

One can easily imagine similar arrangements, under present circumstances. Taxes could be allocated to individual bureaus, and the large tax sources could be broken up. The Department of Defense, for example, might receive, say, 75 percent of the personal income taxes or, possibly, all income taxes collected from people whose income is in the top one-third of the distribution pyramid.

This means that individual bureaucracies and the rent-seeking groups would, in essence, find their success dependent on dealing with somewhat similar-sized opposing groups. I think that this would lead to a more efficient allocation of resources than does our present method, but I certainly would not argue that it would be optimal in any theoretical sense. The objective would be to set lobbyists and special interest groups against each other. I should note that whether or not the lobbyists would be considered rent seekers would depend, more or less, on which side they were on and possibly would vary from budget year to budget year.

Suppose, for example, that in the middle of a major war, the upper-income taxpapers—who, by our proposed system, are paying the entire cost of the armed forces—were lobbying for reduced expenditures while the military suppliers, including the officer corps, were lobbying for increased expenditures. One might well argue that the upper-income people are the rent seekers in this case. As soon as the war is over, and assuming that the U.S. wins, cutting back sharply the size of the army would become desirable. Then the U.S. would begin listing the defense suppliers and the officer corps as rent seekers and would stop calling the wealthy taxpayers rent seekers. This is the result of the crude distinction given above. Again, I hope that somebody can improve the distinction.

All of this has been a digression on optimal taxation. Optimal taxation will not likely exist, of course. When contemplating tax legislation, one usually sees a good deal of effort to make the tax system less efficient and to spend whatever money is derived in wasteful ways. Obviously, this is clear-cut rent seeking.

If the U.S. attempts to put a special tax on the beneficiaries of some services—for which the externality is genuine—but not on the entire population, then one may expect defensive rent seeking. One may expect rent-seeking activity to open holes in general taxes for special groups and to divert the revenues of special and general taxes to special expenditures. Only when the rent seekers desire a loophole and the revenue lost by that loophole is compensated by a wasteful expenditure's being discontinued can one regard lobbyists' activity as other than rent seeking. Mainly, rent seeking in tax reform is as undesirable as it is in other areas.

Indeed, when lobbyists engage in an effort to create loopholes, whether or not their effort is rent seeking depends on how the money would have been spent had they not created the loopholes. We favor special interest groups that seek to save themselves from taxation by reducing government expenditures if such reduction itself is desirable. When this is not so, we call it rent seeking and condemn it. To reiterate a theme underlying the bulk of this paper, the concept of rent seeking is a crude one. At the moment, however, it is the best that we have.

XIII. Conclusion

In summary, tax reform is very difficult. If successful, however, it can reduce greatly rent seeking and other kinds of government waste. Unfortunately, rent seekers have motives to prevent this type of "reform." Fortunately, their opposition is not necessarily decisive. A general bargain in which everyone loses special privileges is apt to benefit everyone. With sufficient political ingenuity and work, this sometimes is possible.

NOTES

1. A distant relative of mine who was a scientist specializing in brewing techniques once spent much time and energy developing something that tasted like wine but technically was beer. The advantage, of course, was in the tax.

2. Dales (1968) has suggested tradable pollution rights, i.e., certificates permitting certain amounts of pollution, which would be issued probably by sale to individual companies and which could then be resold. They would have less susceptibility to rent-seeking activity than do pollution taxes.

REFERENCES

Buchanan, J. M., and G. Tullock, *The Calculus of Consent,* University of Michigan Press, Ann Arbor, 1962.

Dales, J. H., *Pollution, Property and Prices,* University of Toronto, Toronto, 1968.

Lebergott, S., *The American Economy,* Princeton University Press, Princeton, N.J., 1976.

Tullock, G., "Problems of Majority Voting," *Journal of Political Economy,* December 1959, 571–579.

———, *Economics of Income Redistribution,* Kluwer, Boston, 1983.

Rent Extraction and Rent Creation in the Economic Theory of Regulation

Fred S. McChesney

Review Questions

1. What are the different ways in which politicians reduce private rents? What implications arise from threatening to remove these rents? Why is it in the regulators' self-interest to threaten removal of existing rents rather than offering to artificially create new rents?
2. How are social losses measured in the traditional (Stiglerian) model of regulation? How does the potential forbearance of reducing rents affect estimates of the social costs of regulation?
3. Why are incumbents less likely to end protective regulation? What does this imply regarding election contributions to incumbents and their challengers?
4. Under what conditions would firms prefer regulations that raise their costs? Why don't they simply impose these costs on themselves if it is beneficial?

McChesney, Fred S. "Rent Extraction and Rent Creation in the Economic Theory of Regulation." *Journal of Legal Studies* 16 (1987): 101–18.

I. Introduction

The economic theory of regulation has advanced considerably since Stigler's seminal piece explained government's ability to create rents by cartelizing private producers.[1] Because political action can redistribute wealth generally, it is now seen that private interest groups other than producers also have an incentive to organize, both to obtain the gains and to avoid the losses from a whole menu of government enactments.[2] The configuration of winners and losers depends on many factors, and it changes as the underlying demands for and costs of regulation shift. New technology, for example, may render existing government regulations undesirable to their prior beneficiaries or make current regulations useful to groups previously not benefited. Finally, "government" itself has come to be treated, not as a unit, but as a complicated network of individuals, each with an incentive to maximize his own interest.

The original economic theory of regulation thus has evolved into a more complex description of the various ways government regulatory power can be turned to private ends. Two limitations of the current economic model are noteworthy, however. First, despite the growing realization that "government" is not a monolith, the role of the politician has not been integrated satisfactorily into the model. The politician has remained a "mystery actor,"[3] a passive broker among competing private rent seekers.[4] Second, the economic theory, even in its post-Stiglerian form, remains one of rent creation. Observers note that creation of rents does not seem to explain many of the regulatory statutes that legislators have enacted.[5] But the opportunities for political gains from activities other than rent creation have not been considered.

This article focuses specifically on politicians. It views them, not as mere brokers redistributing wealth in response to competing private demands, but as independent actors making their own demands to which private actors respond. The conceptual reversal of roles in turn forces consideration of the ways other than rent creation that politicians can gain from private parties. A model is developed to show how politicians reap returns first by threatening and then by forbearing from extracting private rents already in existence. These private rents, as opposed to politically created rents, represent returns to their owners' entrepreneurial ability and firm-specific private investments.[6]

Political office confers a property right, not just to legislate rents, but to impose costs. A politician can gain by forbearing from exercising his right to impose burdensome restrictions on private actors. The passage of sharply focused taxes and regulations will reduce the returns that private capital owners receive from their skills and investments. In order to protect these returns, private owners have an incentive to strike bargains with legislators, as long as the side payments to politicians are lower than the expected losses from compliance with the threatened law. (The payments need not be bribes; they might be contributions to political campaigns or in-kind donations of service and property, for example.)

A politician thus can gain by forbearing—for a price—from exercising his right to impose costs on private actors that would reduce rents from capital they have created or invested themselves. Though the strategy has not been recognized heretofore, one in fact observes private producers being compelled to pay legislators to prevent private rents from being extracted. In a static sense the payments might seem to be simple transfers. But the transfers required to protect returns to private investments create disincentives to invest in valuable specific capital in the first place. The short-run view ignores the longer-run adverse consequences of threatened rent extraction for overall levels of wealth. In the end, the article suggests, existing estimates of the welfare costs of government regulation overlook the costs of inducing government *not* to regulate.

II. Rent Extraction and the Economic Theory of Regulation

A. Legislative Creation of Political Rents

The original (Stiglerian) interpretation of regulation is the traditional cartel model, but one in which government imposes and enforces the anticompetitive restrictions. If expected political rents net of the costs of organizing and procuring favorable legislation are positive, then producers will demand—pay for—regulation. Deadweight consumer loss is measured by the welfare triangle. Producers stand to gain the rent rectangle, but political competition for it produces additional social loss from rent-seeking.[7]

Industry-wide cartelization is not the only way politicians can create rents. More recent theoretical[8] and empirical[9] contributions have noted that regulation can create Ricardian (inframarginal) rents if it raises costs of some firms more than those of others. This "cost-predation" strategy differs from Stiglerian cartelization in that only some firms in the industry gain while others lose. Industry cooperation to obtain rents for all firms is replaced by rivalry among industry subgroups to benefit some firms at others' expense.

The cooperation and rivalry models of regulation are the same, however, in that both focus on private purchase of rents. Politician-brokers respond to private demands for rents with a supply of regulation but do not actively enter the market for rents with their own demands.[10] This is perhaps in keeping with the consumer-sovereignty model of private markets, but the applicability of that model to the political market is questionable. Clearly, a politician himself actively seeks votes, campaign contributions, and other forms of recompense, contracting to receive a supply of goods or services from private parties in response to his own demands.[11]

Modeled just as a broker among competing private demands, the politician has not been well integrated into the economic theory of regulation. His role thus far has been "subsumed,"[12] with little explicit consideration given to the ways in which the politician himself benefits from private individuals.

A politician has alternative ways to engage private parties in exchange. He may demand votes or money and offer the rent rectangle as consideration, as in the orthodox economic theory of regulation. But a politician may also make his demands on private parties, not by promising benefits, but by threatening to impose costs—a form of political blackmail. If the expected cost of the act threatened exceeds the value of the consideration that private parties must give up to avoid legislative action, they will surrender the tribute demanded of them. With constant marginal utility of wealth, a private citizen will be just as willing to pay legislators to have rents of $1 million created as he will to avoid imposition of $1 million in losses.

Once the politician is seen as an independent actor in the regulatory process, his objective function cannot be treated as single valued. He will maximize total returns to himself by equating at the margin the returns from votes, contributions, bribes, power, and other sources of personal gain. All these, in turn, are positive functions not only of private benefits he confers but also of private costs he agrees not to impose.

The political strategy of cost forbearance can assume several forms. Perhaps most obvious is the threat to deregulate an industry previously cartelized. Expected political rents created by earlier regulation are quickly capitalized into firm share prices. If politicians later breach their contract and vote unexpectedly to deregulate, shareholders suffer a wealth loss. Rather than suffer the costs of deregulation, shareholders will pay politicians a sum up to the amount of wealth threatened to have them refrain from deregulating. In fact, one routinely observes payments to politicians to protect previously enacted cartel measures.[13]

Subsequent payments to avoid postcontractual opportunism by politicians must be distinguished from contractual payments to guarantee rent permanence ex ante. Both politicians and rent recipients gain when the durability of regulation is increased by holding legislators to longer contracts. But new arrivals on both sides succeed to the interests of the original contracting parties. A legislator not party to the original bargain has less incentive to abide by the political rent-creation deal struck by his predecessors unless he too is compensated. Guaranteed rent durability is thus impossible. Among firm owners, subsequent purchasers of shares with expected rents capitalized into their prices are vulnerable to rent extraction on the part of opportunistic politicians. Payments to political newcomers to secure performance of previously negotiated contracts earn no rents. Rather, they protect against windfall losses that new legislators could otherwise impose.

B. Political Extraction of Private Rents

The durability problem for politically created rents has been discussed elsewhere[14] and is not the focus of this article. But recognition of the rent-extraction opportunities that capitalized cartel rents represent to politicians suggests that similar strategies may offer gains to politicians when other sorts of rents exist. In particular, it leads one to focus on the capital value of privately created rents and predictable political responses to their existence.

1. THE MODEL

Figure 1 depicts an industry in which producers have differing amounts of entrepreneurial capacity or some firm-specific, fixed-cost asset. The industry supply curve in the absence of regulation (S_0) thus is upward sloping. Returns to entrepreneurship and specific assets come as rents out of producers' surplus, $0AD$. Regulatory measures could be identified that would increase costs for all firms, but more for marginal firms, moving the industry supply curve to S_1.[15] To inframarginal producers regulation is advantageous (that is, they would pay politicians to effect it) as long as there is a net increase in rents. In Figure 1, area I is greater than area II ($CDEF > ABC$): the gains from higher prices exceed the losses due to fewer sales. The capitalized value of the increased rent flow defines the maximum payment producers would make to politicians in return for regulation.[16]

But rent creation by a governmentally mandated shift from S_0 to S_1 is not the only option open to politicians. *Existing* private rents rewarding specific assets are greater than the rents that can be created by regulation: $0AD >$ $CDEF$ (area I). Regulatory measures can also be identified that would expropriate the producers' surplus, as explained below. Once such regulation is

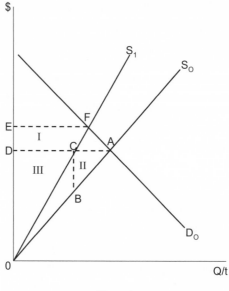

Figure 1

threatened, the price that producers would pay politicians in return for governmental nonaction would exceed any payment for rent-creating regulation.

Faced, then, with a choice between the two strategies, a regulator would maximize the benefits to himself by threatening to expropriate the existing private rents rather than by creating new political rents.[17] As with threatened deregulation of government cartels, payments must be made to protect rents. But unlike the cartel case, where rents were created by government itself, a legislator threatening to expropriate private rents is paid to let firms earn returns on capital they have created or invested for themselves. "Milker bills" is one term used by politicians to describe legislative proposals intended only to squeeze private producers for payments not to pass the rent-extracting legislation. "Early on in my association with the California legislature, I came across the concept of 'milker bills'—proposed legislation which had nothing to do with milk to drink and much to do with money, the 'mother's milk of politics.' . . . Representative Sam, in need of campaign contributions, has a bill introduced which excites some constituency to urge Sam to work hard for its defeat (easily achieved), pouring funds into his campaign coffers and 'forever' endearing Sam to his constituency for his effectiveness."[18] Milked victims describe the process simply as blackmail and extortion.[19] The threats are made quite openly. One reads, for example, that "House Republican leaders are sending a vaguely threatening message to business political action committees: Give us more, or we may do something rash."[20]

The producers' surplus compensating firm-specific capital is inframarginal, but this does not mean that its potential expropriation by politicians has no allocative consequences. Even if politicians eventually allow themselves to be bought off, their minatory presence reduces the expected value of entrepreneurial ability and specific-capital investments. The possibility that government may reduce returns to their capital unless paid off reduces firms' incentives to invest in the first place. It also induces inefficient shifts to investment in more mobile or salvageable (that is, less firm specific) forms of capital as insurance against expropriation. In either event, the allocative losses from politicians' ability to extract the returns from private capital are measured by investments that are never made in the industry threatened.

In effect, an important similarity between capital expropriations in less-developed countries and "mere" regulation in developed nations has been overlooked. In both cases the very presence of a threatening government will reduce private investment.[21] The resulting welfare losses would be measured by the value of specific capital and other investments that firms would have made, but for the fear of subsequent expropriation and the cost of purchasing protection from politicians. The consequences are like those of ordinary theft: "One way of minimizing loss by theft is to have little or nothing to steal. In a world in which theft was legal we could expect this fact to lead to a reduction in productive activities."[22]

Rent extraction can succeed only to the extent that threats to expropriate private rents are credible. With any given firm or industry, producers and politicians may be locked in a "chicken" game: since legislators seemingly gain nothing if they actually destroy private capital, capital owners may be tempted to call politicians' bluff by refusing to pay. But a politician's demonstrated willingness actually to expropriate private rents in one situation provides a lesson for other firms or industries that will induce them to pay in their turn. To make credible expected later threats to destroy others' capital, politicians may sometimes have to enact legislation extracting private rents whose owners do not pay.[23] (And as discussed below, legislators can always enact status now and sell repeal later.)

The credibility and thus the political attraction of rent-extraction strategies also depend on the strength of constitutional rules that protect private property and contract rights against governmental taking. Legislative threats to expropriate returns to private capital will elicit fewer payments to politicians the more likely it is that capital owners later can have any legislation voided constitutionally in the courts. The level of constitutional scrutiny of legislative expropriations involving private contract and property rights has declined throughout the twentieth century.[24] The scope for credible legislative threats against private capital has expanded apace. In effect, as courts have retreated from affording constitutional protection against legislative takings, potential private victims have been forced to employ more self-help remedies by buying off politicians rather than submit to rent-extracting regulation.

2. PRIVATE RENT EXTRACTION VERSUS POLITICAL RENT CREATION

Extraction of private rents and creation of political rents need not be mutually exclusive; maximum gains to politicians may involve a combination of the two. In Figure 1, for example, politicians could create rents in area I (*CDEF*) by imposing regulation while threatening at the same time to expropriate the remaining producers' surplus in area III (*0DC*). The maximum private payment forthcoming from this combined tactic, I + III (*0EF*), would exceed that from merely threatening rent expropriation without regulation (*0AD*). But a combined strategy of rent creation and rent extraction is not necessarily optimal to politicians. Political rent creation (of either the Stiglerian or the inframarginal sort) requires restriction of output, which itself reduces the current stock of expropriable producers' surplus. Ceteris paribus, greater rent creation therefore means more forgone rent extraction. Particularly because the political processes of creating or extracting rents are not costless to legislators, the gains may justify using only one or the other strategy in a particular market.

The relative gains from the two strategies, and thus the optimal political mix of created and extracted rents, will depend on industry supply and demand conditions. The more inelastic industry demand is, the greater the relative attraction of political rent creation. Likewise, if industry supply is perfectly elastic, there is no producers' surplus and so no opportunity for rent extraction. On the other hand, when industry demand is perfectly elastic, extraction of private rents is the only plausible political strategy. Similarly, a large stock of specific (nonsalvageable) capital increases the relative attraction to politicians of private rent extraction. Of course, producers themselves would rather buy new rents than pay to protect their own existing rents. But in some markets, rent-creation opportunities may be slight as compared to the opportunities for extraction of returns to entrepreneurship and private capital. For example, ease of new entry into an industry may make rent-creating cartelization futile. At the same time, the presence of large specific-capital stocks would make the same industry vulnerable to rent extraction.

Information concerning demand and supply elasticities, entry costs, and the size and mobility of capital stocks is costly to politicians. The specter of rent extraction naturally will induce private owners of expropriable capital to try to hide the size of their capital stocks, which increases the costs to politicians of discovering how much producers would pay to avoid expropriation.[25] But political threats to act have the effect of instituting an auction market among private parties. "[L]egislatures work on the presence or absence of opposition. Legislation for which the claim can be made that some group will benefit, if only modestly, and which induces no opposition is almost certain to pass. Thus, introduction of a milker bill which does not generate the expected opposition to its passage, as evidenced by resources devoted to lobbying for its defeat, indeed will pass. By contrast, milker bills which generate the anticipated opposition will fail. Contrasting these outcomes usually makes an effective case for generating the lobbying resources."[26] An auction not only drives competitive bids for legislative favors higher but also reveals which firms stand to gain and which to lose and the magnitude of the respective effects.

The auction thus provides valuable information whether regulatory action or inaction will be more lucrative to politicians themselves; it helps to identify the likely payors and to set the amounts of the compensation to be paid. Particularly since legislators may not know the size of the rents potentially expropriable, they may prefer to make good their threat in order to elicit bids revealing the true size of the private capital stock. Actual enactment of legislation raises to unity the probability of rent-destroying measures being imposed, unless firms buy legislative repeal. Legislation that would destroy rents can be enacted with a delayed effective date to allow firms to mobilize and bid to remove or alter the statute.[27]

Because the maximum gains to legislators depend on knowledge of elasticities and the size of private rents, there may also be gains from specialization in identifying industries with expropriable producers' surplus and in determining how best to extract it. If so, legislators predictably would delegate cost-imposing functions to specialized bureaucratic agencies. By threatening or actually imposing costs, these outside agents create a demand for politicians to mitigate the costs. Use of specialized agencies to impose costs has a second advantage to politicians. While they may act at the behest of elected officials, bureaucrats will be perceived by at least some rationally ignorant voters as independent. Information about the regulatory process is costly to obtain, and so it may appear that misguided agencies rather than politicians themselves are responsible for the costs threatened.[28] Designation of institutions like the Federal Trade Commission (FTC) and the Securities and Exchange Commission as "independent agencies" may further the perception in some voters' eyes that politicians are less responsible for their activities.[29]

C. Methods of Extracting Private Rents

Having located private capital stocks whose returns will come out of producers' surplus, how can legislators extract that surplus? Two general strategies represent threats to private producers: reductions in price and increases in cost.[30]

1. LEGISLATIVE THREATS TO REDUCE PRICES

Consider, for example, firms' fixed-cost investments in brand-name capital or reputation.[31] All firms may produce otherwise equivalent products, but some will have incurred greater costs in past periods (for example, by advertising) to make their names and quality familiar to consumers. Advertising creates a capital stock, returns from which are taken over time.[32] Once created, the capital is specific to the firm and enables the firm in a later period to incur lower costs to guarantee the quality of the goods or services that it sells. Rival firms without brand-name capital must incur higher costs in that same period to make their names and product quality as well-known and trustworthy to consumers.

This is shown in Figure 2 for two representative firms. Industry supply and demand (from Figure 1) establish the equilibrium price, $0D$. Firm X has been in business and advertised for years; firm Y has just started business. Both firms provide identical products of equivalent quality at the same production cost ($MC_X = MC_Y$). But customers cannot evaluate product quality prior to purchase; hence there is uncertainty. Both firms guarantee quality, but in different ways. Firm X relies on its investment in brand-name capital in prior periods, its customers paying a premium for the credible guarantee of quality that the reputation capital provides. To offer an equivalent guarantee, firm Y must incur other fixed costs in the current period, such as having an independent laboratory test its product quality and publicize the fact that it is just as good as X's, making its average costs higher ($AC_Y > AC_X$). The premium (AB) that firm X's customers pay for the reputational guarantee earns rents ($ABCD$).

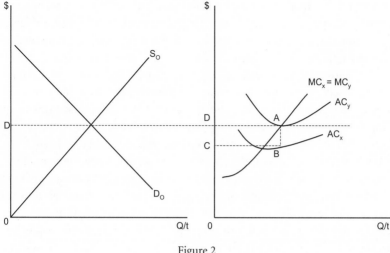

Figure 2

But X's rents can be reduced or destroyed by government intervention. Politicians can pass legislation to have administrative agencies guarantee quality or truthful information by imposing minimum quality standards or mandatory information-disclosure regulations. Government agents then would police the market for quality and truth, substituting both for the brand-name capital invested earlier by firm X and for the current testing that firm Y would have commissioned to guarantee quality. To the extent it substitutes for private reputation capital, government regulation destroys the premium value of firm X's private capital while relieving the nonreputational firm, Y, of the need to incur new costs to warrant its own quality.

The threatened government intervention would lower price and increase the elasticity of industry supply, eradicating the producers' surplus available to compensate firms for their earlier fixed-cost investments. Rather than have politicians depreciate their capital stock, firm X would pay up to *ABCD* per period for nonintervention in the market. Even if regulation "only" substitutes for activities currently provided privately, it reduces the expected returns to private-reputation investments and so over time the amount of investment. Note also that in the new equilibrium firm Y would earn no rents from the regulation and so would offer politicians nothing for it. The only gains to politicians in this case come from threatening to extract X's rents.

The history of the FTC's "Used Car Rule" provides an example of the gain to politicians from threatening this type of regulation and later removing the threat for a fee. In 1975, Congress statutorily ordered the FTC to initiate a rulemaking to regulate used-car dealers' warranties.[33] The FTC promulgated a rule imposing costly warranty and auto-defect disclosure requirements, creating the opportunity for legislators to extract concessions from dealers to void the burdensome measures. In the meantime, in fact, Congress had legislated for itself a veto over FTC actions.[34] On promulgation of the rule, used-car dealers and their trade association descended on Congress, spending large sums of money for relief from the proposed rule's costs.[35] When the concessions were forthcoming, Congress vetoed the very rule it had ordered.[36]

It is noteworthy that conditions in the used-car industry conform closely to those hypothesized as conducive to a strategy of rent extraction. As Stigler himself notes,[37] cartelization of the used-car industry would be difficult: start-up costs are low; there are no entry barriers (for example, licensing requirements); and units of the product have different qualities, making enforcement of cartel pricing difficult. By comparison, the industry is susceptible to a strategy of rent extraction. Quality uncertainty (the risk of getting Akerlof's "lemon")[38] is a problem, leading sellers to invest in reputation capital.[39] By requiring and policing seller disclosure of warranty and defect information, government would have substituted for sellers' investments in quality-assuring reputation. Rather than suffer the capital losses that regulation would entail, firms predictably would—and did—compensate legislators not to intervene.

2. LEGISLATIVE THREATS TO RAISE COSTS

Just as proposals to institute price-lowering regulation imperil private rents, so do regulations that threaten to increase costs. Consider the situation portrayed in Figure 3, in which legislators threaten to impose an excise tax or other per-unit cost of $0C$. Rather than suffer a net loss in producers' surplus, area I − area II ($0AEC − BDFE$), firms earning rents will offer to compensate legislators to refrain from imposing the costs.

There are many examples of payments to politicians to purchase governmental inactivity in taxation.[40] Recently, the excise tax on beer has generated substantial revenue for legislators in return for their inactivity.[41] Of course, excise taxes are just one cost that politicians can threaten to impose on private firms. Other recent threats include proposals to require financial institutions to start costly reporting and withholding of taxes from depositors' interest and dividends (a measure that was passed and then repealed) and proposals to impose "unisex" premiums and benefit payments on insurance

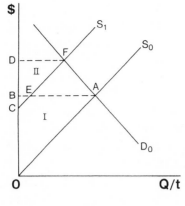

Figure 3

firms. Both episodes are difficult to explain using the standard economic model, as they consumed considerable political time but ended with no regulation at all being imposed. But even if the regulation was never actually imposed, each measure would be attractive politically as a device that might ultimately elicit private payments to legislators *not* to impose the threatened costs—which in fact each one did.[42]

III. Conclusion

This article extends the economic theory of regulation to include the gains available to elected politicians from alleviating costs threatened or actually imposed on private actors by legislators themselves and by specialized bureaucratic agencies. Status as a legislator confers a property right not only to create political rents but also to impose costs that would destroy private rents. Their ability to impose costs enables politicians credibly to demand payments not to do so. Even when politicians eventually eschew intervention, the mere threat and the payments required to remove it distort private investment decisions.

The model of rent extraction set out here in no way undermines the orthodox model of rent-creating regulation; rather it supplements it by recognizing alternative sources of political gains. Indeed, Stigler's original article foreshadowed a complementary rent-extraction model: "The state—the machinery and power of the state—is a potential resource *or threat* to every industry in the society. With its power to prohibit or compel, *to take* or give money, the state can and does selectively help *or hurt* a vast number of industries. . . . Regulation may be actively sought by an industry, *or it may be thrust upon it*" (emphasis added).[43] Conditions that make political rent creation relatively unattractive to politicians make private rent extraction more attractive. The relative attraction of rent extraction has also increased as constitutional protection of private rights has diminished.

Many of the insights from the rent-creation model of regulation will doubtless prove useful in further explorations of rent extraction. For example, the problem of double-dealing by opportunistic politicians that was discussed above in connection with deregulation raises equivalent issues for contracts with legislators not to extract private rents. As with rent creation, the rent-extraction model will be enriched by consideration of the need to assemble coalitions to obtain rent protection, the problems created by changes in coalitions' composition and power, and similar issues that arise once "government" is recognized as a collectivity of rational, maximizing individuals.

For the moment, however, it is sufficient to note that the problems of political opportunism and the imperfections in private-capital protection create disincentives for capital owners to buy off legislators. Yet several instances have been presented here in which private actors in fact have paid significant sums to induce government not to impose costs. Despite the political impediments to contract, then, the evident willingness of capital owners to purchase protection indicates that appreciable capital stocks are credibly imperiled by regulations that are never actually enacted.

If so, one cost of government regulation has been missed. Heretofore, the economic model has identified several different costs of government regulation: deadweight consumer loss, resources expended as private parties seek rents,[44] costs of compliance with regulation,[45] and diversion of resources to less valuable but unregulated uses.[46] To these should be added the costs of protecting private capital even when politicians ultimately are persuaded not to regulate. There is no such thing as a free market.

NOTES

1. George J. Stigler, The Theory of Economic Regulation, 2 Bell J. Econ. 3 (1971).

2. Sam Peltzman, Toward a More General Theory of Regulation, 19 J. Law & Econ. 211 (1976); Gary S. Becker, A Theory of Competition among Pressure Groups for Political Influence, 98 Q. J. Econ. 371 (1983).

3. Robert D. Tollison, Rent Seeking: A Survey, 35 Kyklos 575, 592 (1982).

4. For example, Robert E. McCormick & Robert D. Tollison, Politicians, Legislation, and the Economy (1981).

5. "The 'consumerist' measures of the last few years . . . are not an obvious product of interest group pressures, and the proponents of the economic theory of regulation have thus far largely ignored such measures." Richard A. Posner, Theories of Economic

Regulation, 5 Bell J. Econ. 335 (1974). Migué also discusses regulations that are "difficult to reconcile with the economic theory of regulation." Jean-Luc Migué, Controls versus Subsidies in the Economic Theory of Regulation, 20 J. Law & Econ. 213, 214 (1977).

6. Technically, some of the returns to private individuals are true economic rents (for example, the returns to entrepreneurial capacity), while others are more properly termed "quasi rents" (the returns to any fixed-cost investment). See Milton Friedman, Price Theory: A Provisional Text 115–18 (1962). Often, however, the differences are of little operational significance. See, for example, Donald N. McCloskey, The Applied Theory of Price 294 (1985) ("Producers' Surplus Is Economic Rent Is Quasi-Rent Is Supernormal Profit"). It is not the type of rent but its source that is of interest in this article. For expositional clarity, therefore, all profits created politically are described here as "political rents," while the returns to private capital are referred to as "private rents." Also, the term "capital" is used here to refer to both human (including entrepreneurial) and other types of capital.

7. Gordon Tullock, The Welfare Costs of Tariffs, Monopolies, and Theft, 5 W. Econ. J. 224 (1967); Richard A. Posner, The Social Costs of Monopoly and Regulation, 83 J. Pol. Econ. 807 (1975).

8. For a diagrammatic presentation of the theory, see Fred S. McChesney, Commercial Speech in the Professions: The Supreme Court's Unanswered Questions and Questionable Answers, 134 U. Pa. L. Rev. 45, 74–100 (1985).

9. For example, Howard P. Marvel, Factory Regulation: A Reinterpretation of Early English Experience, 20 J. Law & Econ. 379 (1977); R. H. Coase, Payola in Radio and Television Broadcasting, 22 J. Law & Econ. 269 (1979): Michael T. Maloney & Robert E. McCormick, A Positive Theory of Environmental Quality Regulation, 25 J. Law & Econ. 99 (1982); B. Peter Pashigian, The Effect of Environmental Regulation on Optimal Plant Size and Factor Shares, 27 J. Law & Econ. 1 (1984); Ann P. Bartel & Lacy Glenn Thomas, Direct and Indirect Effects of Regulation: A New Look at OSHA's Impact, 28 J. Law & Econ. 1 (1985).

10. "Regulation is . . . an instrument of wealth transfer—the extent of which is determined in a political market—where interest groups demand regulation and politician-regulators supply it." Migué, *supra* note 5, at 214.

11. For one of the few models based on political demands being made of private individuals, see William P. Welch, The Economics of Campaign Funds, 17 Pub. Choice 83, 84 (1974) ("[t]he politician demands funds in exchange for political influence").

12. Robert E. McCormick, The Strategic Use of Regulation: A Review of the Literature, in The Political Economy of Regulation: Private Interests in the Regulatory Process 14 (Robert A. Rogowsky & Bruce Yandle eds. 1984).

13. Dairy interests pay handsomely for the continuation of congressional milk-price supports. Larry J. Sabato, PAC Power: Inside the World of Political Action Committees 133, 137 (1984). Physician and dentist "political action committees" (PACs) contribute large sums for continuation of self-regulation. *Id.* at 134–35.

14. Since more durable rent contracts are in the interest of both private parties and politicians, the intervention of third-party institutions predictably would be sought to hold legislators to their deals. The judiciary, for example, may help guarantee congressional rent-creation contracts, since courts can overrule legislators' attempted revisions

of earlier contracts by holding the changes unconstitutional. William M. Landes & Richard A. Posner, The Independent Judiciary in an Interest-Group Perspective, 18 J. Law & Econ. 875 (1975); Robert D. Tollison & W. Mark Crain, Constitutional Change in an Interest-Group Perspective, 8 J. Legal Stud. 165 (1979). Executive veto of attempted changes in legislative deals is another way to increase the amounts private parties would spend for rent creation. W. Mark Crain & Robert D. Tollison, The Executive Branch in the Interest-Group Theory of Government, 8 J. Legal Stud. 555 (1979). But neither guarantee system is perfect "since there will be some expectation that an independent judiciary will not support all past legislative contracts," Tollison & Crain, *supra*, at 167, and because newcomers to both the legislature and the executive office have less stake in continuing bargains made by their predecessors, Crain & Tollison, *supra*, at 561–66.

15. For an empirical demonstration of the harm to marginal firms from minimum-wage and union-pay increases, for example, see David E. Kaun, Minimum Wages, Factor Substitution and the Marginal Producer, 79 Q. J. Econ. 478 (1965); and Oliver E. Williamson, Wage Rates as a Barrier to Entry: The Pennington Case in Perspective, 82 Q. J. Econ. 85 (1968). For discussion of other regulatory measures with different effects on firms, see the sources cited in note 9 *supra.*

16. Maximizing payments to politicians would require, inter alia, that all producer beneficiaries be induced to pay and that consumer-voters exert no counterinfluence on the amount of regulation imposed. Relaxing these assumptions would not alter the fundamental implications of the rent-extraction model proposed here. See, for example, Becker, *supra* note 2; and Peltzman, *supra* note 2.

17. The conditions under which rent extraction is politically preferable to rent creation are explored further below.

18. W. Craig Stubblebine, On the Political Economy of Tax Reform 1, 2 (paper presented at the meeting of the Western Economic Ass'n 1985).

19. One PAC director describes congressional "invitations" to purchase tickets to political receptions as "nothing but blackmail." Sabato, *supra* note 13, at 86. Likewise, "[t]he 1972 reelection effort for President Richard Nixon included practices bordering on extortion, in which corporations and their executives were, in essence, 'shaken down' for cash donations." *Id.* at 5.

20. Brooks Jackson, "House Republicans Are Pressing PACs for Contributions," Wall St. J., June 27, 1985, at 36, col. 2. Further instances of how politicians pressure PACs for money are given in Sabato, *supra* note 13, at 111–14.

21. The effects of Third World government expropriations of private capital in diminishing the amount of investment made are analyzed in Jonathan Eaton & Mark Gersovitz, A Theory of Expropriation and Deviations from Perfect Capital Mobility, 94 Econ. J. 16 (1984).

22. Tullock, *supra* note 7, at 229 n. 11.

23. The situation is thus a form of the "Samaritan's dilemma," in which a politician must convince private producers that he is willing to suffer losses in the short run in order to reap longer-run gains whose present value exceeds that of any immediate losses. See James M. Buchanan, The Samaritan's Dilemma, in Altruism, Morality, and Economic Theory 71 (Edmund S. Phelps ed. 1975). Of course, to the extent that the political threats are convincing, private parties are more likely not to call a legislator's bluff, and he therefore will not actually suffer any short-run loss.

24. Richard A. Epstein, Takings: Private Property and the Power of Eminent Domain (1985); Terry L. Anderson & P. J. Hill, The Birth of a Transfer Society (1980).

25. See J. Patrick Gunning, Jr., Towards a Theory of the Evolution of Government, in Explorations in the Theory of Anarchy 22 (Gordon Tullock ed. 1972).

26. Stubblebine, *supra* note 18, at 2.

27. This was the pattern observed, for example, with the amendments to the Clean Air Act in the early 1970s, when the Department of Transportation repeatedly delayed and altered standards on auto emissions in response to auto-firm lobbying.

28. The rent-extraction model thus sheds light on the recurring controversy whether bureaucratic agencies "run amuck," free of congressional or other constraints. The most recent study of the Federal Trade Commission (FTC), for example, concludes that "the Commission remains largely unconstrained from without." Kenneth W. Clarkson & Timothy J. Muris, Commission Performance, Incentives and Behavior, in The Federal Trade Commission since 1970: Economic Regulation and Bureaucratic Behavior 282 (1981). But Weingast and Moran present evidence of systematic congressional influence over FTC actions. Barry R. Weingast & Mark J. Moran, Bureaucratic Discretion or Congressional Control? Regulatory Policymaking by the Federal Trade Commission, 91 J. Pol. Econ. 765 (1983). The rent-extraction model suggests that neither view may fully capture the essence of Congress-agency relations. A politician has less incentive to monitor specialized agencies ex ante while they consider and adopt cost-imposing measures more cheaply than Congress itself could. There is more incentive for legislative surveillance of agency action ex post, in order to locate opportunities for alleviating those costs (for a fee). For a discussion and evidence of politicians' intervention to remove the costs imposed by bureaucrats' antitrust investigations and prosecutions, see Roger L. Faith, Donald R. Leavens, and Robert D. Tollison, Antitrust Pork Barrel, 25 J. Law & Econ. 329 (1982).

29. Further, the appearance may not be purely illusory. Congressional monitoring of agencies is costly. See Isaac Ehrlich & Richard A. Posner, An Economic Analysis of Legal Rulemaking, 3 J. Legal Stud. 257 (1974). Some of what agencies do, therefore, will not be known to a legislator until constituents bring it to his attention.

30. The purpose here is to illustrate how politicians acting collectively can induce private payments not to extract rents. This admittedly leaves unaddressed public-choice problems of achieving collective political action: how to assemble political coalitions when each politician maximizes his own interest, how to divide the gains from rent extraction among individual politicians, the role of the committee system in rent extraction, and so forth.

31. Benjamin Klein & Keith B. Leffler, The Role of Market Forces in Assuring Contractual Performance, 89 J. Pol. Econ. 615 (1981); L. G. Telser, A Theory of Self-enforcing Agreements, 53 J. Bus. 27 (1980).

32. See, for example, Yoram Peles, Rates of Amortization of Advertising Expenditures, 79 J. Pol. Econ. 1032 (1971); Robert Ayanian, Advertising and Rate of Return, 18 J. Law & Econ. 479 (1975).

33. The Magnuson-Moss Warranty–Federal Trade Commission Improvement Act of 1975 included an order to the FTC to initiate within one year "a rulemaking proceeding dealing with warranties and warranty practices in connection with the sale of used motor vehicles." 15 U.S.C. §2309(b). For the FTC's initial rule, see 16 C.F.R. § 455 (1982).

34. Since Congress has always been able to annul any agency rule or regulation statutorily, the question arises why it would want a veto. Statutes to change agency action require the president's signature. If the president must sign the statute, he then is able to exact payment for his participation in rent-protecting legislation, lowering the payments available to Congress. In eliminating the executive role, the legislative veto is hardly a check on agency action. It is an attempt to avoid splitting fees with the executive. Indeed, if Congress has a veto, it then has an incentive to fund even more rent-threatening activities by independent agencies, ceteris paribus.

35. One study, cited in Sabato, *supra* note 13, at 134, found that, "[o]f the 251 legislators who supported the veto resolution and ran again in 1982, 89 percent received contributions from NADA [National Auto Dealers Association], which averaged over $2,300. This total included 66 legislators who had not been backed by NADA at all in 1980, before the veto resolution vote. Just 22 percent of the 125 congressmen who voted against NADA received 1982 money, and they averaged only about $1,000 apiece."

36. See the FTC announcement of the veto published at 47 Fed. Reg. 24542 (June 7, 1982). When the Supreme Court later invalidated the legislative veto, INS v. Chadha, 462 U.S. 919 (1983), and thus Congress's overruling of the FTC's rule, Process Gas Consumers Group v. Consumer Energy Council, 463 U.S. 1216 (1983), the FTC recalled its proposed rule and essentially gutted it. See 16 C.F.R. § 455 (1985).

37. Stigler, *supra* note 1, at 9–10.

38. George A. Akerlof, The Market for "Lemons": Quality Uncertainty and the Market Mechanism, 84 Q. J. Econ. 488 (1970).

39. "Both intuition and empirical data suggest that the used-car market attracts lemons. . . . A number of market mechanisms serve to alleviate these problems. The most visible solutions take the form of dealer guarantees and warranties, which recently have been beefed up with extended coverage backed by national insurers. Indirectly, dealers invest in brand-name maintenance (local television ads, for instance), which makes it more costly for them to renege on a reputation for quality. The reputation of the parent automakers is also laid on the line. All four domestic car manufacturers have certified the quality of the better used cars sold by their dealers. Two generations of Chevrolet dealers, for example, have designated better used cars with an 'OK' stamp of the dealer's confidence in the car's marketability." Can Regulation Sweeten the Automotive Lemon? Reg., September/December 1984, at 7, 8.

40. "[M]embers of the tax-writing committees nearly tripled their take from political action committees during the first six months of this year, to $3.6 million, compared to the like period in the past two-year election cycle. . . . [T]he money is pouring in from . . . insurance companies that want to preserve tax-free appreciation of life insurance policy earnings, from horse breeders who want to keep rapid depreciation of thoroughbreds, from drug companies seeking to keep a tax haven in Puerto Rico, and from military contractors seeking to retain favorable tax treatment of earnings from multiyear contracts." Brooks Jackson, Tax Revision Proposals Bring Big Contributions from PACs to Congressional Campaign Coffers, Wall St. J., August 9, 1985, at 32, col. 1.

41. One report notes that "there hasn't been an increase in the 65-cent-a-case federal tax on beer since the Korean War, and nobody is seriously proposing one right now." Yet the industry has organized a coalition of brewers and wholesalers to compensate key members of Congress anyway: "Members of House and Senate tax-writing committees

regularly drop by the coalition's monthly meetings to talk about budget and tax trends, [and] pick up $2,000 appearance fees." Though new beer taxes "haven't . . . generated much interest in Congress," the president of the brewers' trade association says they "want to be prepared." Brooks Jackson, Brewing Industry Organizes Lobbying Coalition to Head off Any Increase in U.S. Tax on Beer, Wall St. J., July 11, 1985, at 48 col. 1.

42. The banking industry contributed millions of dollars to politicians in 1982 to obtain repeal of the statutory provision requiring banks to withhold taxes on interest and dividends. There are no precise figures on contributions to politicians to stop legislation banning gender-based insurance-rate and benefit schedules, but their magnitude may be inferred from the American Council of Life Insurance's media budget of nearly $2 million in 1983 and 1984 to defeat the legislation. Sabato, *supra* note 13, at 125.

43. Stigler, *supra* note 1, at 3.

44. Posner, *supra* note 7. See also Franklin M. Fisher, The Social Cost of Monopoly and Regulation: Posner Reconsidered, 93 J. Pol. Econ. 410 (1985); W. P. Rogerson, The Social Costs of Monopoly and Regulation: A Game-theoretic Analysis, 13 Bell J. Econ. 391 (1982).

45. Tullock, *supra* note 7.

46. James Alm, The Welfare Cost of the Underground Economy, 24 Econ. Inquiry 243 (1985).

Suggested Additional Readings

Coffman, Richard B. "Tax Abatements and Rent-Seeking." *Urban Studies* 30 (1993): 593–98.

Dougan, William R., and James M. Snyder. "Are Rents Fully Dissipated?" *Public Choice* 77 (1993): 793–813.

Flowers, Marilyn R. "Rent Seeking and Rent Dissipation: A Critical View." *Cato Journal* 7 (1987): 431–40.

Hartle, D. G. "The Theory of 'Rent Seeking': Some Reflections." *Canadian Journal of Economics* 16 (1983): 539–54.

Hoffman, Elizabeth, and Gary D. Libecap. "Political Bargaining and Cartelization in the New Deal: Orange Marketing Orders." In *The Regulated Economy: A Historical Approach to Political Economy,* ed. Claudia Goldin and Gary D. Libecap. Chicago: University of Chicago Press, 1994.

Laband, David N., and John P. Sophocleus. "The Social Cost of Rent-Seeking: First Estimates." *Public Choice* 58 (1988): 269–75.

McChesney, Fred S. *Money for Nothing: Politicians, Rent Extraction, and Political Extortion.* Cambridge: Harvard University Press, 1997.

Rowley, Charles K., Robert D. Tollison, and Gordon Tullock (eds.). *The Political Economy of Rent-Seeking.* Boston and Dordrecht: Kluwer Academic Publishers, 1988.

Tollison, Robert D. "Rent-Seeking." In *Perspectives on Public Choice: A Handbook,* ed. Dennis C. Mueller. Cambridge: Cambridge University Press, 1997.

———. "The Rent-Seeking Insight." In *Public Choice Essays in Honor of a Maverick Scholar: Gordon Tullock,* ed. Price V. Fishback, Gary D. Libecap, and Edward Zajac. Boston: Kluwer Academic Publishers, 2000.

Tullock, Gordon. "The Transitional Gains Trap." *Bell Journal of Economics* 6 (1975): 671–78.

———. "Back to the Bog." *Public Choice* 46 (1985): 259–64.

Wittman, Donald. *The Myth of Democratic Failure: Why Political Institutions Are Efficient.* Chicago: University of Chicago Press, 1995.

Advanced Readings

Becker, Gary S. "A Theory of Competition among Pressure Groups for Political Influence." *Quarterly Journal of Economics* 98 (1983): 371–400.

Buchanan, James M., Robert D. Tollison, and Gordon Tullock (eds.). *Toward a Theory of the Rent-Seeking Society.* College Station: Texas A&M University Press, 1980.

Nitzan, Shmuel. "Modeling Rent-Seeking Contests." *European Journal of Political Economy* 10 (1994): 41–60.

Rice, Edward M., and Thomas S. Ulen. "Rent Seeking and Welfare Loss." *Research in Law and Economics* 3 (1981): 53–65.

Tullock, Gordon. *The Economics of Special Privilege and Rent Seeking.* Boston: Kluwer Academic Press, 1989.

Collective Action

There are situations when blind pursuance of self-interest can actually make everyone worse off. These situations are generally referred to, in game-theoretic terminology, as a prisoner's dilemma. For example, products that are inexcludable in nature, where property owners are unable to prevent others from making use of their goods, give individuals the incentive to free ride on someone else's purchase. People seek to save themselves the costs of purchase without sacrificing the benefits. Such free riding is individually beneficial as long as someone else makes the product or service available. There are equity issues involved, but from a social standpoint, efficiency is not harmed by such free riding. Social efficiency is harmed when everyone attempts to free ride and no one makes the product available. All the individuals are worse off than if they had shared the costs.

Consider two roommates renting a house, each with a car in the garage. They attend different schools and must drive themselves to class. A heavy snowfall the night before covers the driveway, but none of their classes is canceled. Both roommates want to drive to their schools, but they need to first shovel out the driveway. Each would prefer, however, the other to do the shoveling. Once the driveway is cleared, both cars can leave regardless of who did the actual work. In this way, clearing the driveway yields inexcludable benefits. If they both got up early in the morning, the driveway could be cleared in less than an hour. Instead, each sleeps in, expecting the other to get up and

73

do all the shoveling. Neither one shovels, and they remain stuck in the house, losing the benefits of their professors' fascinating lectures.

The benefits to shoveling may not be equal. Suppose one person has an exam scheduled for early that morning. Most students feel attending class on exam day is far more crucial than for any run-of-the-mill lecture. Although the student with the exam would certainly appreciate help in shoveling the driveway, she would still find it worthwhile to do it all by herself to ensure she doesn't miss the exam. The other roommate can count on this and be confident the driveway will be shoveled in time for her to get to class as well.

There are several reasons to believe the roommates may be able to overcome their free riding tendency. They can meet in the hallway and simply agree to go outside together. Since they live together, they will interact on a daily basis, and a certain degree of cooperation will naturally result. Since another snowfall may occur later on, cooperation on shoveling the current snow accumulation will signal a willingness to help on future shoveling endeavors. There are many situations in which free riding can occur, and over time they should come to realize that mutual cooperation makes them better off. Free riding by one person can result in free riding by the other person later on, in a tit-for-tat response. Their friendship can also be taxed if one person feels the other is not doing her fair share.

The situation would become more dire once the cars got to the road. It is a long way to drive to campus, and not feasible for any one person to shovel all the roads, and difficult to coordinate each person in town shoveling a small portion of the road. It would also be more efficient to have a snowplow move the snow to the roadside, but purchasing the plow is too expensive for any one person. There are enough people that sharing the cost would impose minimal financial difficulty on any one person. The townsfolk, however, face the same collective action problem as the two roommates. Each person believes his or her contribution is not necessary, because there are enough other people to buy the plow, and thus is tempted to free ride on everyone else's contribution. If too many people free ride, however, not enough money is collected and the plow is not purchased. To avoid this problem, the town citizens have agreed to an enforcement mechanism whereby each is forced to contribute. One way to establish this is to have the township purchase the plow and tax each person (household). Because the taxes are legally binding, this eliminates the free riding problem. The size of the tax is small enough that everyone decides it is worthwhile.

Government provision of these types of public goods and services can lead to some potential problems. Once the government is established for this purpose, other goods may also be created that everyone is forced to contribute to through taxation that some or many or all decide is not worth their individual cost. In a private market, consumers are free to purchase or pass on the available products when they compare the benefit to the cost. In a public market, such freedom is not allowed (specifically to prevent free riding behavior), with the consequence that taxpayers may be forced to pay for products they do not desire. Public production may or may not be socially efficient, but even if it is, certain individuals can still be made worse off. The private market suffers from underprovision of inexcludable goods, whereas the public market suffers from overprovision of goods.

The main distinction between the roommates and the general townspeople is the size of the group involved. Free riding is more likely to occur the larger the group size. Each person in a small group may recognize how important his or her contribution is to getting the good he or she desires. As the size of the group grows, the individual contribution of any one person becomes less critical, and free riding behavior is less noticed. Thus, we are more likely to see small groups work together than large groups.

Group cooperation is not always beneficial to society overall. Since small groups, by definition, contain only a small segment of the overall population, their goals may differ from the general public's. They represent particular, or special, interests. For example, an industry trade group would benefit from reduced foreign competition, even though society as a whole (consumers and other firms that rely on these products for their inputs) would be worse off. It is easier for firms in one industry to form a group and lobby for protectionist policies than for all the consumers to group together to fight such policies. Not only will free riding be more prevalent among the larger group of general consumers, but each person individually will have very little at stake from any one particular tariff. Tariffs targeted at specific import products yield a very concentrated benefit toward a small group of domestic firms, so each firm has a strong incentive to contribute to the industry trade organization to help passage of the tariff. Meanwhile, the social losses that accrue, as large as they may be, are spread out over a very large group, so each person individually loses just a small amount and finds it not worth his or her time and money to care very much. In the aggregate, however, each person does stand to lose a great deal as more and more small special interest groups form to curry governmental favors. Larger, or more encompassing, groups have a greater incentive to promote the social well-being but are more subject to the collective action problem. The longer the special interest groups exist, the more skilled they become at generating special favors. Over time, then, more resources get devoted to creating socially inefficient redistribution, rather than socially enhancing new production. Economic growth prospects become diminished.

Once this process is set in place, it is difficult to reverse. Major changes to the economic structure of society would be needed, in the form of changing the policy institutions or the special interest groups themselves. The power of successful special interest groups will naturally blossom rather than shrink, and wholesale institutional changes are rare. While there is some degree of complacency in social and political stability, institutional upheaval can serve the purpose of breaking special interest domination of policy. Such upheavals can occur, for instance, due to civil and other wars that destroy the economic infrastructure of interest groups or lead to replacement of the current form of government. It will then take time for new groups to form and to learn how to ply the new government structure to their advantage. In the interim, the economy can be expected to grow faster compared to other economies with otherwise similar levels of endowments and institutional structures. These upheavals, as harmful as they may be to the social fabric, may also have the unexpected benefit of destroying harmful politico-economic special interests and their avenues for socially inefficient redistribution.

Theories of collective action have most often been applied to the highly visible international setting of treaties and alliances. Oneal extends the analysis in "The Theory of Collection Action and Burden Sharing in NATO." In his presidential address to the Southern Economic Association, entitled "The South Will Fall Again: The South as Leader and Laggard in Economic Growth," Olson outlines his thesis on group formation overcoming the free rider effect, and details the logical conclusion of special interest groups using resources to distribute wealth rather than promote new growth, and explains how over time these groups will form in a stable democratic society and limit future growth possibilities. This lecture combines the most important elements of his two most influential books, *The Logic of Collective Action* and *The Rise and Decline of Nations*, and discusses evidence relating to comparative growth rates across regions of the United States.

The Theory of Collective Action and Burden Sharing in NATO

John R. Oneal

Review Questions

1. Why does "exploitation of the great by the small" occur?
2. In what ways do alliances among sovereign states typically fit the assumptions of the theory of collective action? What are some examples that violate these assumptions?
3. Early studies of the NATO alliance showed a strong relationship in accordance with the exploitation theory. How was this determined? What explanations were given for why this relationship eroded over time? What arguments are presented against these explanations?
4. What private goods were NATO nations pursuing? How does this impact the exploitation hypothesis? Why did cooperation within the alliance increase over time? How is this shown?
5. What is a "uniquely privileged" group? Does NATO fit this description?

Mancur Olson's theory of collective action has frequently been applied to the behavior of nations in alliances, particularly the North Atlantic Treaty

Oneal, John R. "The Theory of Collective Action and Burden Sharing in NATO." *International Organization* 44 (1990): 379–402.

Organization (NATO). Although the theory could account for much of the variance in the defense burdens of the NATO allies in the early years of the Cold War, the association between economic size (gross domestic product, or GDP) and defense burden (the ratio of military expenditures to GDP) has declined to insignificant levels over the postwar period. In this article, I review early applications of Olson's theory to the NATO alliance, briefly critique previous efforts to account for the theory's declining explanatory power, and then propose an alternative explanation: the diminished success of the theory is attributable both to the pursuit of private goods by Greece, Turkey, and Portugal and to increasing cooperation among the other European allies. Using data for the period 1950–84, I test these hypotheses and then attempt to clarify the process by which European cooperation has increased. In doing so, I show that the theory of collective action continues to provide important insights into the behavior of the NATO allies and, in particular, the central role of the United States.

Early Applications of the Theory of Collective Action to NATO

Olson first published *The Logic of Collective Action* in 1965.[1] There he noted the distinction between a private good and a public good and showed why the behavior of rational, self-interested actors differs in response to the two types of benefits. If it is infeasible to exclude anyone from consuming a good, even an individual who does not help provide it, and if its consumption by one does not reduce its availability to others, a public or collective good is involved. In this case, Olson demonstrated that individuals acting independently will not promote their common interest optimally, since each person has an incentive to enjoy the goods created by others without contributing to them. It is especially difficult for large groups to act collectively. For small groups, the same tendency for free (or cheap) riding operates, but the situation is more complex.

The behavior of members of small groups is more difficult to predict because the actions of each individual are more easily observed by others and communication is facilitated. These characteristics of the group increase the opportunities for strategic interaction and explicit bargaining. As a result, collective action is more likely to occur, but groups with few members will still tend to produce less of a public good than is jointly desired. In addition, as Olson pointed out, there is "a surprising tendency for the 'exploitation' of the *great* by the *small*."[2] Those who would benefit most from a public good and have the greatest means to provide it will bear a disproportionate share of the costs, while "smaller" members of the group will bear a burden that is less than their share of benefits and resources.

The theory of collective action has been used to explain a wide variety of social behavior,[3] but one of its most frequent applications has been to the study of cooperation among nations. The association of sovereign states in alliances intended to deter war seems to fit closely the assumptions of the theory:[4] the actors are likely to be rational and self-interested; they cooperate in institutions generally characterized by limited authority; and, when successful, the peace that results has the characteristics of a public good.

Some alliances do not satisfy these conditions, of course. The Warsaw Pact's enforcement of the Brezhnev doctrine against Czechoslovakia in 1968, for example, is inconsistent with the assumption of independent, voluntary behavior. And it must be possible for the armed forces of one nation to be substituted for those of an ally if a public good is to be produced.[5] Finally, an offensive alliance victorious in war will gain many spoils that are private, not public, in nature. But the North Atlantic alliance seems to meet the requirements upon which the theory depends, as Olson himself concluded.[6]

Indeed, Olson and Richard Zeckhauser were the first to apply the theory of collective action to NATO.[7] They reasoned that a nation's gross national product (GNP) was a good measure of the benefits it derives from collective security and its ability to provide for it; therefore, contributions to the alliance, measured by national defense burdens, were expected to be correlated with GNP.[8] Data from the 1960s were consistent with this prediction;[9] but Bruce Russett soon noted that the explanatory power of the theory declined over time.[10] Later, Todd Sandler and John Forbes showed that the association between gross domestic product (GDP) and the ratio of military expenditures to GDP, though always in the predicted direction, was not statistically significant after 1966.[11] The relationship has remained slight, especially if the United States is excluded from the analysis, as the first two rows in Table 1 show.[12]

Previous Attempts to Explain the Declining Association between Economic Size and the Defense Burden

The trivial association between GDP and defense burden over the last two decades suggests that NATO no longer satisfies the assumptions of Olson's theory. In a series of influential articles, Todd Sandler, Jon Cauley, John Forbes, and James Murdoch have argued that this is due to a change in the nature of the good produced by the alliance. As the Soviet Union gained parity with the United States in strategic nuclear weapons, NATO was forced to

TABLE 1. Variance of Defense Burden Explained by Gross Domestic Product (GDP)

Group	Year[a]														
	1950	1953	1956	1959	1962	1965	1968	1971	1974	1977	1980	1982	1984
All NATO allies	9%	57%*	43%*	55%*	44%*	37%*	44%*	25%	11%	7%	16%	17%	20%
NATO allies excluding the United States (1950–84)	28%*	39%*	28%*	35%*	17%	19%	5%	2%	2%	2%	7%	4%	5%
NATO allies excluding Greece and Turkey (1974–84) and Portugal (1964–75)	9%	57%*	43%*	55%*	44%*	49%*	63%*	46%*	49%*	32%*	34%*	47%*	49%*
NATO allies excluding the United States (1950–84), Greece and Turkey (1974–84), and Portugal (1964–75)	28%*	39%*	28%*	35%*	17%	36%*	21%	15%	46%*	27%*	27%	31%	36%*

[a]Statistical significance: * $p \leq .05$.

shift from a strategy of deterrence to one of defense in providing for the security of the North Atlantic region. Under the doctrine of flexible response adopted in 1966, the allies, they suggest, no longer enjoy a pure public good but are partly rivals for the benefits provided increasingly by actual war-fighting capabilities.[13]

This distinction between deterrence, which is a relatively pure or inclusive public good, and defense, which is impure or exclusive, is important if not exaggerated.[14] In fact, the retaliatory threats upon which deterrence rests must remain credible as deterrence is extended, so for this good, too, allies may be partly rival. Nor does the addition of territory always reduce the defensive capabilities of an alliance and increase rivalry among its members, even if the ratio of forces to the area defended is reduced, because the new territory may confer a tactical advantage. The creation of interior lines of communication or a more defensible perimeter, for example, may more than offset the thinning of forces.

But did NATO really shift from deterrence to defense? Elsewhere, Mark Elrod and I have discussed several reasons for doubting this hypothesis.[15] The most important arguments can be briefly summarized. First, the deployed military capabilities of the alliance relative to those of the Warsaw Pact actually declined from 1967 until at least 1978, as NATO itself and others have noted.[16] If the European countries had thought it necessary to provide their own defense, for fear of being excluded from the deterrence provided by the United States, as Sandler and his colleagues suggest, they would have had to improve the balance of forces in central Europe. But, apparently satisfied with NATO's capacity for deterrence, they reduced their defense burdens even as the Soviet Union was increasing the proportion of its economy devoted to the military. As a consequence, the ratio of NATO Europe's defense expenditures to those of the Soviet Union declined sharply in the late 1960s and declined more slowly, but steadily, thereafter until 1977. Second, NATO Europe did not seek a truly defensive capability in the late 1960s or at any other time, despite American urgings, because most Europeans have never believed that such a course of action is either feasible or desirable.[17] The French withdrawal from the integrated military command in 1966 has been the most dramatic indication of these doubts; but the other European allies, too, have consistently favored a strategy of deterrence rather than defense.[18] For most Europeans, flexible response, by raising the stakes of aggression and providing time for consultation and negotiation, was a way of reestablishing the credibility of America's extended deterrence, not a substitute for it.[19] Indeed, there are good reasons for believing that deterrence does rest on a firm foundation.[20]

An Alternative Explanation

If the declining association between defense burden and GDP shown in the first two rows of Table 1 is not the result of a significant change in the nature of the good produced by NATO, how can it be explained? Elrod and I have suggested two other possibilities.[21] First, the military expenditures of some countries in recent years may have been determined primarily by the pursuit of private benefits. The association between defense burden and economic size hypothesized by Olson and Zeckhauser would decline if smaller countries increased their defense budgets in order to gain private goods, such as the maintenance of domestic order, perceived economic gains, or influence in conflicts independent of the confrontation between NATO and the Warsaw Pact. Second, the declining association may have resulted from the assumption of more equal burdens by the allies or a large subgroup of them. In the limiting case, where the defense burden would be the same for all nations, the correlation with GDP would, of course, be zero.

Theoretically, defense burdens might converge because nations became less rational, less self-interested, or less independent. The first two possibilities seem unlikely and need not be seriously considered. Of course, governments are not perfectly rational, strictly speaking; their decisions are seldom objectively optimal. Instead, they "satisfice" on the basis of incomplete information, inconsistent goals, and other cognitive and organizational limits on rationality.[22] And nations may on occasion and to a degree act altruistically. But it seems safe to assume that most countries most of the time "satisfice" egoistic objectives at a high level of aspiration. The third possibility, that the allies have become less independent in setting their defense expenditures, is not implausible, however.

Greater cooperation in sharing the costs of collective security could be either voluntary or the result of coercion. As Duncan Snidal has noted, powerful states may not allow the weak to act independently and free ride on the public goods they provide.[23] Instead, weak nations may be forced to contribute to collective action or even to pay tribute in excess of its costs. Alternatively, independent action may give way to coordinated behavior as nations, perceiving themselves linked by a network of interdependent relations, pursue their interests in far-sighted fashion. Such "rational altruism" may be reinforced by explicit linkage to other issues.[24]

Interdependence in effect constitutes a midpoint between independence and union. When states are independent, free riding should be prevalent; when united, contributions to collective action can be authoritatively fixed and compliance enforced.[25] As interdependence increases, cooperation should also grow, and the burden of creating public goods should be more equally distributed.[26]

Given the political, economic, and cultural ties that link the NATO allies, cooperation among them might be thought more likely than free riding. Certainly, movement toward a more equal distribution of the costs of collective security, whether coerced or voluntary, would be facilitated by the small size of the alliance, its existing organizational structure, and the importance of the good being produced.[27]

Testing the Alternative Explanation for the Declining Association between Economic Size and the Defense Burden

The Pursuit of Private Goods

Table 2 sheds light on the possibility that the pursuit of private goods by some countries explains at least part of the declining association between defense burden and GDP. There the ratio of military expenditures to GDP for each ally is compared to the alliance-wide average during representative years from 1950 to 1984. Specifically, each country's defense burden was first divided by the ratio of total NATO defense spending to the sum of the GDPs of the NATO countries. This is algebraically equivalent to dividing each nation's share of total defense spending by its share of the NATO countries' combined GDPs. Then the relative burdens were standardized to create an index that permits comparisons through time.[28] A score less than 1.0 in Table 2 indicates that a nation is bearing a relatively light burden: the smaller the value, the greater is the nation's free riding. A score greater than 1.0 means that a nation is being exploited, in the sense that its share of the costs of providing the public good exceeds its share of the benefits.[29]

As shown in the last column of Table 2, only the United States has had a defense burden greater than average over the whole period. But three other countries—Greece, Turkey, and Portugal—had average burdens greater than 1.0 for the years after 1967, when the association with GDP became negligible for the NATO allies excluding the United States (second row, Table 1). For each of these countries, private benefits that account for this departure from theoretical expectations can easily be identified. The dramatic increase in Greek and Turkish defense expenditures after 1974 can be traced to the Turks' invasion of Cyprus, while the unusually large defense outlays of Portugal were the result of its military operations in Angola and Mozambique from

TABLE 2. NATO Allies' Defense Burdens as Fractions of Weighted NATO Average

Country	Year													Period averages		
	1950	1953	1956	1959	1962	1965	1968	1971	1974	1977	1980	1982	1984	1950–67	1968–84	1950–84
United States	1.03	1.34	1.28	1.31	1.32	1.27	1.40	1.33	1.23	1.17	1.20	1.24	1.25	1.30	1.25	1.27
Britain	1.34	1.00	1.02	0.92	0.84	0.91	0.75	0.85	1.01	1.04	1.10	0.98	1.03	0.96	0.97	0.96
Greece	1.18	0.50	0.74	0.65	0.58	0.60	0.72	0.89	1.24	1.69	1.34	1.47	1.50	0.66	1.27	0.96
France	1.17	0.94	1.03	0.94	0.90	0.91	0.76	0.76	0.83	0.94	0.95	0.88	0.86	0.92	0.86	0.89
Portugal	0.79	0.41	0.54	0.61	0.99	1.04	1.13	1.40	1.64	0.85	0.83	0.73	0.68	0.72	1.04	0.88
Turkey	1.26	0.53	0.69	0.68	0.74	0.85	0.70	0.86	0.86	1.39	1.01	1.10	0.92	0.73	1.02	0.87
Netherlands	0.94	0.54	0.73	0.53	0.66	0.65	0.53	0.62	0.70	0.80	0.74	0.68	0.67	0.64	0.69	0.66
Germany	0.89	0.36	0.44	0.57	0.69	0.74	0.55	0.65	0.81	0.81	0.77	0.72	0.68	0.57	0.73	0.65
Norway	0.49	0.52	0.47	0.51	0.52	0.65	0.55	0.65	0.68	0.75	0.68	0.64	0.59	0.51	0.67	0.59
Belgium	0.52	0.49	0.47	0.50	0.48	0.51	0.45	0.55	0.63	0.78	0.80	0.72	0.67	0.49	0.67	0.58
Italy	0.72	0.35	0.43	0.43	0.33	0.52	0.42	0.51	0.57	0.58	0.57	0.55	0.56	0.45	0.54	0.50
Canada	0.48	0.68	0.69	0.56	0.55	0.46	0.37	0.39	0.39	0.43	0.39	0.40	0.41	0.58	0.39	0.49
Denmark	0.35	0.34	0.40	0.36	0.44	0.48	0.42	0.46	0.51	0.55	0.58	0.52	0.48	0.39	0.51	0.45
Luxembourg	0.23	0.25	0.21	0.21	0.17	0.21	0.13	0.14	0.15	0.22	0.24	0.23	0.20	0.21	0.19	0.20
Iceland	0.00	0.00	0.00	0.00	0.00	0.00	0.00	0.00	0.00	0.00	0.00	0.00	0.00	0.00	0.00	0.00

the early 1960s until Angolan independence in 1975.[30] It seems plausible, then, that the pursuit of private benefits by these three allies explains part of the decline in the predictive power of Olson's theory.

This can be confirmed by regressing NATO defense burdens on GDP with the three exceptional cases excluded in the years for which private benefits are most evident: Greece and Turkey from 1974 to 1984 and Portugal from 1964 to 1975. The results are reported in the third and fourth rows of Table 1 to permit comparison with the earlier findings. The improvement is apparent. The amount of variance explained by GDP for NATO allies excluding Greece, Turkey, and Portugal increases an average of 22 percent after 1964; and the results for all years except 1950 are now significant ($p < .05$). When the United States and these three countries are excluded, the variance explained increases an average of 22 percent per year, and the results for seven additional years in the period 1950–84 are statistically significant.

Increased Cooperation among the Allies

The calculations reported in Table 2 also suggest that cooperation has increased within the alliance, since there has been a modest decrease in the exploitation of the United States over the period considered. This can be seen by comparing the average values for 1950–67 and 1968–84. This change is significantly associated with the decline in the economic position of the United States relative to its allies.[31] As the theory of collective action suggests, a hegemon should be less willing to bear a disproportionate burden in providing a public good if its preponderant position erodes.[32] Evidently the United States has been able to shift some of the burden of collective security to the other members of NATO.

Yet the most striking fact shown in Table 2 is that there are few countries other than the United States with scores greater than 1.0 in any year. This provides strong support for Olson's theory: free riding has been prevalent among America's allies throughout the postwar period. Indeed, the data in Table 2 are consistent with the view that NATO is a "uniquely privileged group" seeking a relatively pure public good.

A group is said to be uniquely privileged when there is one member very much larger than the others who can profitably provide the good acting alone.[33] In the extreme case, the preponderant member would pay virtually the full cost of a public good. Is NATO such a group? Without a better measure of the benefits the allies receive from collective security, this question cannot be answered definitively. But even in 1984, after decades of relative economic decline, the GDP of the United States was still 4.5 times that of West Germany, the second largest ally; 22 times that of the Netherlands, the median member of the alliance; and nearly 700 times that of Luxembourg, NATO's smallest member. It is not surprising, then, that from 1950 to 1984 the United States devoted an average of 8.6 percent of its GDP to the military, while the defense burden of the other NATO allies averaged 4.7 percent.

Certainly, the central role of the United States in the alliance and the prevalence of free riding among the other countries revealed in Table 2 are unlikely to have occurred by chance. Two measures suggest just how improbable it is. If it were equally likely for each NATO member to free ride or be exploited, the mean for the last column in the table would equal 1.0. The actual figures reported would be expected only 12 times in 10,000. With the same assumption, the probability that the United States alone would be exploited is 1 in 32,768 (2^{15}).

Since the U.S. defense burden relative to the NATO average has changed little over the years, this cannot account for much of the decline in the association between defense burden and GDP reported in the first row of Table 1. However, there may have been a greater increase in cooperation among a subgroup of states. The obvious possibility is that the growth of European integration—represented institutionally by the European Community, the Council of Europe, the Rhine Commission, and other regional international organizations—has had a spillover effect on NATO. In fact, there are several European groups whose explicit objective is to increase cooperation in the military realm, the most important of these being the Western European Union and, within NATO, the Eurogroup and the Independent European Programme Group.

A simple measure of cooperation in providing for collective security is the standard deviation of the allies' defense burdens.[34] If this statistic declines over time, the allied nations are bearing more equal burdens in providing the public good—prima facie evidence that cooperation among them has increased. Two groups of allies can be compared: NATO as a whole and the European allies alone (NATO Europe). Greece, Turkey, and Portugal have been excluded from both groups in all years in this and subsequent analyses because, as shown earlier, the defense burdens of these exceptional cases have been strongly influenced by the pursuit of private interests.[35] For the alliance as a whole, the standard deviation has declined since the early 1950s. This is consistent with the diminished exploitation of the United States indicated in Table 2, and the results are very significant statistically.[36] By the same test, there is also strong evidence of increased cooperation among the European countries. But these results should perhaps not be unexpected, given the dramatic reductions in the portion of the allies' economies devoted to defense since the peak of the Cold War. Declining standard deviations may simply be an artifact of the smaller mean of allied defense burdens.

A more discriminating test for coordination of national defense policies is the coefficient of variation: the standard deviation divided by the mean.[37] As before, decreasing values through time suggest increasing cooperation in sharing the burden of collective security. For NATO as a whole, the North American states included, the regression coefficient is again negative and statistically significant ($t = -2.40$; $p = .02$; $R^2 = .15$). For NATO Europe, the decline in the coefficient of variation is still more evident ($t = -3.16$; $p = .004$; $R^2 = .24$). Apparently, cooperation has increased more within NATO Europe than between the Europeans and the North American members of the alliance.

The growth of European cooperation in defense affairs can be confirmed by means of the graphical technique proposed by Martin McGuire and Carl Groth.[38] The proof they provide for identifying the process by which a group allocated its resources for a public good is easily grasped. Consider Figure 1. There the x-axis represents members' resources, and the y-axis their contributions to the collective effort. If individuals act independently, the assumption of Cournot behavior, free riding will predominate among the smaller members of a group, while those with greater resources will bear a disproportionate share of the costs. This is the essence of Olson's theory of collective action. In such situations, the regression line that best describes the group will have a steep positive slope and a positive x-intercept, indicating that the contributions of members increase sharply with size and that below a threshold of resources individuals do not contribute to the public good. The more negative the y-intercept and the greater the slope, the greater is the exploitation of those whose resources are substantial. This situation is shown in Figure 1 as line A.

Line B in Figure 1 represents the contrasting case, a group whose members allocate resources to the public good, contrary to the theory of collective action, by a Lindahl or cooperative process. As can be seen, the regression line for the Lindahl process passes through the origin and has a smaller slope than that for the Cournot process. This indicates that Lindahl behavior involves no free riding or exploitation: smaller members of the group contribute the same percentage of their income to the collective effort as those with greater resources.

Knowing the graphical representation of the two ideal types, we can analyze the behavior of the allies to see if the level of cooperation has increased

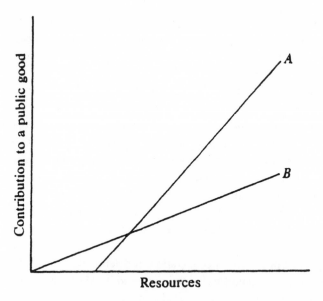

Figure 1. Two processes by which a group may allocate resources for a public good: the Cournot process (A) and the Lindahl process (B)

within NATO as a whole and within NATO Europe as a subgroup. As Glenn Palmer has shown, however, it is necessary to control for changes in the absolute level of resources when comparisons are made across time;[39] therefore, the following regression model was estimated for each year from 1950 to 1984:

$$MErel_i = \beta_0 + \beta_1 {}^*GDPrel_i$$

where $MErel_i$ are the military expenditures of nation i relative to the total for the group (nation i's defense spending/the group's total defense spending) and $GDPrel_i$ is the gross domestic product of nation i relative to the total for the group (nation i's GDP/combined GDPs of the group's members).

An increase in cooperation is marked by a decreasing slope (β_1) and an intercept (β_0) that approaches zero. The individual regression lines could be plotted, but it is easier to look at just the coefficients and intercepts through time. As before, two groups are to be considered: (1) NATO Europe excluding the exceptional cases of Greece, Turkey, and Portugal during all years (1950–84) and (2) NATO excluding the same three exceptional cases.[40] It is hypothesized that cooperation in sharing the defense burden has increased more among the European allies than in NATO as a whole.

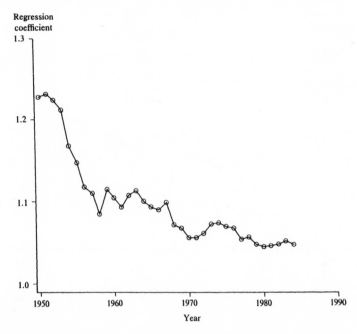

Figure 2. Regression coefficients for NATO Europe excluding Greece, Turkey, and Portugal (1950–84)

Figure 2 shows the regression coefficients for NATO Europe excluding the three exceptional cases, and Figure 3 gives the intercepts for the same group of countries. As expected, both curves indicate a transition from a Cournot to a Lindahl process: the coefficient declines sharply from its peak in 1951 through most of the 1950s and then more moderately to the 1980s, and the intercept approaches zero. Interestingly, the statistical significance of the intercept of the regression line declines from .15 in 1950 to .76 in 1984. Thus, there is less than a 1 in 4 chance that the intercept is *not* the origin by the end of the period.

Two additional features of Figures 2 and 3 are worth emphasizing. First, the coefficient never goes below 1.0, indicating that the larger European nations' shares of NATO's military expenditures have always been greater than their shares of NATO's combined GDPs. There has been, then, throughout the postwar period a degree of noncooperation among the European allies, which is consistent with the theory of collective action. Second, noncooperation was greatest when it would be most expected: at the height of the Cold War, when free riding had its greatest value.

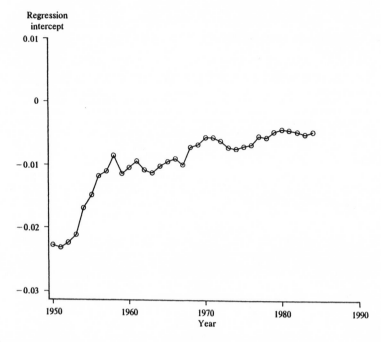

Figure 3. Regression intercepts for NATO Europe excluding Greece, Turkey, and Portugal (1950–84)

Figures 4 and 5 indicate that the growth in cooperation has been predominantly among the European nations and not within the alliance as a whole. Figure 4 gives the values of the regression coefficients for NATO and NATO Europe, with both groups excluding Greece, Turkey, and Portugal. As expected, there is no decline in the coefficients for NATO as a whole, and its curve is above that for the European allies for all years except the first. Regressing NATO's coefficients on time reveals that the curve for the alliance has actually increased slightly over the period analyzed, even if 1950 is dropped.

In Figure 5, the same results are revealed: an increase in cooperation is apparent for the European nations but not for the whole alliance. Indeed, the graphical analysis indicates that the costs of collective security were less evenly distributed after 1981 than in several years between the Korean and Vietnam wars. In contrast to the intercept for NATO Europe, the intercept for NATO is always significantly different from the origin ($.01 < p < .03$) except for 1950 ($p = .51$).

The distinctive character of 1950 in both Figures 4 and 5 is worth underscoring. It should not be surprising that 1950 is unusual, because military ex-

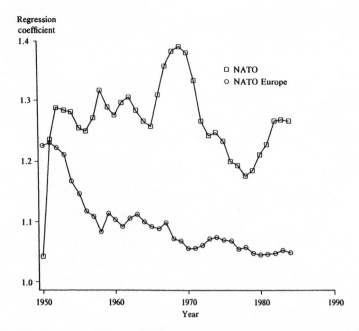

Figure 4. Regression coefficients for NATO and NATO Europe, with both groups excluding Greece, Turkey, and Portugal (1950–84)

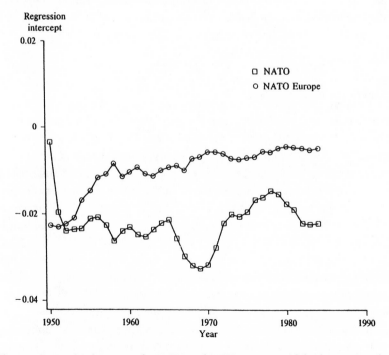

Figure 5. Regression intercepts for NATO and NATO Europe, with both groups excluding Greece, Turkey, and Portugal (1950–84)

penditures for that year were set before the attack on South Korea. That event was clearly an important *démarche* in allied relations; or, to put it differently, by increasing dramatically the value of free riding, the start of the war caused the underlying, theoretically expected relations to be revealed. Nor should it be surprising that cooperation within the alliance as a whole was least during the Vietnam war or that the war did not interrupt the process of European integration.

The apparent inverse relationship between the variance in defense burdens explained by the theory of collective action (Table 1) and the level of cooperation among the Europeans indicated by McGuire and Groth's graphical technique (Figures 2 and 3) can be confirmed. Regressing the annual variance of NATO defense burdens accounted for by Olson's theory (with the United States, Greece, Turkey, and Portugal excluded)—given in row four of Table 1—on either the coefficients or intercepts for NATO Europe excluding the exceptional cases reveals a statistically significant association ($t = 2.32$; $p < .03$; $R^2 = .14$). The European allies have moved toward a common defense burden; consequently, the ability of the theory of collective action to predict the contributions to the alliance of individual members of this group has declined. The fact that the mean of the Europeans' defense burdens is substantially less than that of the United States is, as noted earlier, consistent with theoretical expectations for a uniquely privileged group.[41]

Attempts to Clarify the Process by Which European Cooperation Has Increased

As noted earlier, cooperation is more likely if there are other important ties among the members of a group; and there are for the European countries, of course. Karl Deutsch lists fourteen regional organizations that include among their members at least some of the European NATO allies, and Stanley Sloan cites two others.[42] In an attempt to clarify the evolution of European cooperation in security affairs, I performed several regression analyses in which individual countries' contributions to the results were weighted according to their membership in various international organizations. If institutional links have contributed importantly to the evolution of European cooperation, this should be revealed in the movement of the intercept and coefficient of the resulting regression lines: the two curves in the weighted analyses should approach the x-axis more closely than those in the unweighted analysis.

The European Community (EC) is unquestionably the most important European regional organization. To see if membership in the EC promoted

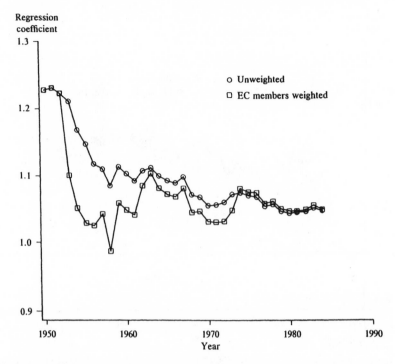

Figure 6. Regression coefficients for NATO Europe unweighted and for NATO Europe weighted on the basis of EC membership, with both groups excluding Greece, Turkey, and Portugal (1950–84)

military cooperation in NATO Europe, each country was first given a weight of 1 in each year when it was not a member of the EC and a weight of 2 in each year when it was. Greece, Turkey, and Portugal were again excluded for all years because they were presumed to be pursuing private goods in several years. The resulting coefficients and intercepts were then compared to those for the same countries unweighted in all years. The two curves for the regression coefficients are shown in Figure 6, and the weighted and unweighted intercepts are given in Figure 7. As can be seen, the EC does seem to have had a positive effect on military cooperation in its early years, especially before 1962; but in later years, the difference between the weighted and unweighted analyses is slight and in the wrong direction.

The effect of several other regional organizations on cooperation among the European countries of NATO was also examined. The Western European Union, the Eurogroup, the Independent European Programme Group, and

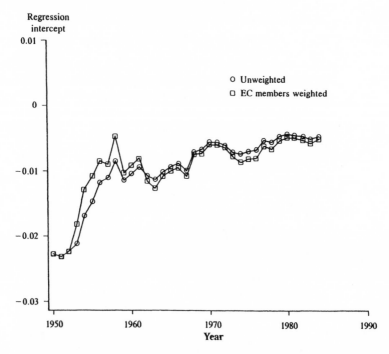

Figure 7. Regression intercepts for NATO Europe unweighted and for NATO Europe weighted on the basis of EC membership, with both groups excluding Greece, Turkey, and Portugal (1950–84)

the formalization of "political cooperation" within the EC were considered; but none seemed particularly associated with the improvement in cooperation in the security realm detected among the European allies.

Conclusions

In 1989, NATO celebrated its fortieth anniversary. The most obvious enduring feature of the alliance over the years has been the central role played by the United States: collective security in the North Atlantic region in the 1980s, as in preceding decades, rested largely on U.S. capabilities for deterring war. As the theory of collective action predicts, the relative economic decline of the United States did result in a shift of some of its defense burden to the other allies; but the adjustment to America's declining preponderance has thus far been modest. NATO still seems in essence a uniquely privileged group providing a relatively pure public good.

The theory of collective action is less able to account for the individual allocations to defense of America's allies in recent years than in the early postwar period, although the relationship between defense burden and GDP has always been in the predicted direction. The reduced explanatory power of the theory is not the result of a fundamental change in the nature of the alliance associated with the strategy of flexible response, as others have argued, however. Rather, two other influences seem important: an increase in the pursuit of private goods by Greece, Turkey, and Portugal and greater cooperation among the other countries of NATO Europe. Increasing coordination among the European countries in the military realm is plausibly a consequence of their growing economic, political, and cultural ties. As might be expected, the EC seems to have played a significant role in this process, especially before 1962. If the European countries continue to integrate their economies and move toward a common political identity, as the Single European Act indicates, their defense burdens should converge further; but greater integration in Europe may have more profound consequences for the alliance.

The logic of collective action indicates that the United States should bear a disproportionate share of allied defense expenditures as long as it believes that its security depends upon NATO, allows its allies to act independently, and is economically preponderant—that is, as long as the alliance is uniquely privileged. But movement toward economic and political union in Europe undermines these conditions and raises the prospect of a more fundamental change in Atlantic relations. America's willingness to bear a disproportionate defense burden should diminish substantially if its transatlantic allies are perceived not as several relatively small states but, rather, as constituents of a unified Europe whose economic size is equal to its own. As Olson and Zeckhauser noted, the unification of small states increases their incentive to contribute to collective action.[43] Continued progress in European integration is also apt to raise expectations in the United States that the Europeans will indeed make greater contributions to the alliance.

NOTES

1. See the more recent edition: Mancur Olson, *The Logic of Collective Action,* rev. ed. (Cambridge, Mass.: Harvard University Press, 1971).

2. Ibid., p. 3.

3. Russell Hardin, *Collective Action* (Baltimore, Md.: Johns Hopkins University Press, 1982).

4. Bruce M. Russett and John D. Sullivan, "Collective Goods and International Organizations," *International Organization* 25 (Autumn 1971), pp. 845–65.

5. Wallace J. Thies, "Alliances and Collective Goods," *Journal of Conflict Resolution* 31 (June 1987), pp. 298–332.

6. Mancur Olson, "Increasing the Incentives for International Cooperation," *International Organization* 25 (Autumn 1971), pp. 866–74.

7. Mancur Olson and Richard Zeckhauser, "An Economic Theory of Alliances," *Review of Economics and Statistics* 48 (August 1966), pp. 266–79.

8. There is an extensive literature on whether defense spending as a percentage of either GNP or GDP is a valid measure of the contribution the allies make to collective security. Nations vary in the efficiency with which they produce military capabilities; prices for military equipment are often not set by markets; and some contributions to collective security, such as the full value of conscripted personnel, are not reflected in defense budgets. In addition, not all of the military forces of several allies are deployed in or even dedicated to the defense of the North Atlantic region, and those that are may be used for purely national objectives. Regarding this last point, however, Allen and Diehl note that "NATO members have generally agreed to count all of a nation's military forces, regardless of mission or deployment, as a contribution to NATO. The rationale is that the strengthening of defense and deterrence anywhere in the world indirectly contributes to European security." See Christopher S. Allen and Paul F. Diehl, "The Defense Issue in West Germany," *Armed Forces and Society* 15 (Fall 1988), p. 96. For discussions of the defense burden as a measure of a nation's contribution to the alliance, see José Lello, "Draft Interim Report on Burden-Sharing in the Alliance," North Atlantic Assembly, Brussels, November 1988; U.S. Department of Defense, "Report on Allies Assuming a Greater Share of the Common Defense Burden," Report to the U.S. Congress by the Secretary of Defense, Washington, D.C., February 1989; and Paul F. Diehl and Gary Goertz, "Measuring Military Allocations," *Journal of Conflict Resolution* 30 (September 1986), pp. 553–81. Even Knorr, who provides one of the most complete critiques, concludes, however, that the defense burden is the "least unsatisfactory" measure available. See Klaus Knorr, "Burden-Sharing in NATO," *Orbis* 29 (Fall 1985), pp. 517–36.

9. See Olson and Zeckhauser, "An Economic Theory of Alliances"; Jacques M. van Ypersele de Strihou, "Sharing the Defense Burden Among Western Allies," *Review of Economics and Statistics* 49 (November 1967), pp. 527–36; Frederic L. Pryor, *Public Expenditures in Communist and Capitalist Nations* (Homewood, Ill.: Irwin, 1969); and Francis A. Beer, *The Political Economy of Alliances* (Beverly Hills, Calif.: Sage, 1972).

10. Bruce M. Russett, *What Price Vigilance?* (New Haven, Conn.: Yale University Press, 1970).

11. Todd Sandler and John F. Forbes, "Burden Sharing, Strategy, and the Design of NATO," *Economic Inquiry* 18 (July 1980), pp. 425–44.

12. All tables and figures are based on data from the following sources: The defense expenditures of the NATO allies in current prices and national currencies are published annually in the *NATO Review*, usually the January issue. Germany's expenditures are counted as contributions to the alliance from 1950, though it did not become a member until 1954. This is NATO's convention. The alliance's data are preferable to national statistics because they conform to a common accounting standard. A serious problem that remains, however, involves conscripted personnel, whose value is greater than their pay because of the coercive character of the draft. To increase further the comparability of the data on defense spending, the expenditures of allies that did not rely on volun-

teers were increased by 10 percent to reflect the monetary value of conscription. See John R. Oneal and Mark A. Elrod, "NATO Burden Sharing and the Forces of Change," *International Studies Quarterly* 33 (December 1989), pp. 435–56; and van Ypersele de Strihou, "Sharing the Defense Burden."

Soviet defense expenditures for the years 1963–84 are from the U.S. Arms Control and Disarmament Agency (ACDA), *Yearbook of World Armament and Disarmament* (Washington, D.C.: Government Printing Office, 1978 and 1987). ACDA's estimates were extrapolated back to 1950 on the basis of data from the Stockholm International Peace Research Institute, *Yearbook of World Armament and Disarmament* (New York: Humanities Press, 1970).

The GDPs of all countries are from Robert Summers and Alan Heston, "A New Set of International Comparisons of Real Product and Price Level Estimates for 130 Countries, 1950–1985," *Review of Income and Wealth* 34 (March 1988), pp. 1–26. These estimates are based on purchasing power parities (PPPs), which are not only more stable than exchange rates in the years after the Bretton Woods system but are also theoretically preferable because they indicate the amount of a foreign currency required to buy the quantity of goods and services that can be purchased in the United States for one dollar. Specifically, the chain index of real domestic product (1980 base year) was used because the index number problem is least severe with its use. The military expenditures of the NATO countries were converted into U.S. dollars using the PPPs associated with this index. Ideally, PPPs specifically for military goods would have been used; but these are not available except for a few countries in a few years. See United Nations, *Reduction of Military Budgets*, UN General Assembly Report A/40/421, 40th Session, New York.

13. See Todd Sandler and Jon Cauley, "On the Economic Theory of Alliances," *Journal of Conflict Resolution* 19 (June 1975), pp. 330–48; Sandler and Forbes, "Burden Sharing, Strategy, and the Design of NATO"; James C. Murdoch and Todd Sandler, "A Theoretical and Empirical Analysis of NATO," *Journal of Conflict Resolution* 26 (June 1982), pp. 237–63; James C. Murdoch and Todd Sandler, "Complementarity, Free Riding, and the Military Expenditures of the NATO Allies," *Journal of Public Economics* 25 (November 1984), pp. 83–101; and Todd Sandler and James C. Murdoch, "Defense Burdens and Prospects for the Northern European Allies," in David B. H. Denoon, ed., *Constraints on Strategy: The Economics of Western Security* (Washington, D.C.: Pergamon-Brassey, 1986), pp. 59–113.

14. For a theoretical discussion of the difference between inclusive and exclusive public goods, see Olson, *The Logic of Collective Action*, pp. 36–43.

15. See Oneal and Elrod, "NATO Burden Sharing and the Forces of Change."

16. See NATO, *Texts of Final Communiques*, vol. 2, *1975–1980* (Brussels: NATO Information Service, n.d.); U.S. Congressional Budget Office, *Assessing the NATO/Warsaw Pact Military Balance* (Washington, D.C.: Government Printing Office, December 1977); International Institute for Strategic Studies (IISS), *The Military Balance* (London: IISS, 1968, 1971, and 1977); and Thomas Cusack, "The Evolution of Power, Threat, and Security," *International Interactions*, vol. 12, 1985, pp. 151–98.

17. See Bernard W. Rogers, "The Atlantic Alliance," *Foreign Affairs* 60 (Summer 1982), pp. 1145–56; Robert McNamara, "The Military Role of Nuclear Weapons," *Foreign Affairs* 62 (Fall 1983), pp. 59–80; Karl Kaiser, "Nuclear Weapons and the Preservation of Peace," *Foreign Affairs* 60 (Summer 1982), pp. 1157–70; Alois Mertes, "What

Should Be Done to Change NATO," *Atlantic Community Quarterly* 22 (Summer 1984), pp. 122–29; Stanley Hoffmann, *Janus and Minerva* (Boulder, Colo.: Westview, 1987), pp. 251–57; and Theo Sommer, "Through German Eyes," *The National Interest*, no. 10, Spring 1988, pp. 3–12.

18. See Geoffrey Williams, *The Permanent Alliance* (Leyden: A. W. Sijthoff, 1977), p. 75; Thomas A. Callaghan, Jr., "Can Europe Be Defended?" *Atlantic Community Quarterly* 21 (Summer 1983), pp. 110–17; and Steven Canby and Ingemar Dorfer, "More Troops, Fewer Missiles," *Foreign Policy*, no. 53, Winter 1983, pp. 3–17.

19. Seymour J. Deitchman, *Military Power and the Advance of Technology* (Boulder, Colo.: Westview, 1983), pp. 187–98.

20. See Steven J. Brams, *Superpower Games* (New Haven, Conn.: Yale University Press, 1985); Bruce M. Russett, "The Mysterious Case of Vanishing Hegemony; Or, Is Mark Twain Really Dead?" *International Organization* 35 (Spring 1985), pp. 845–65; and John R. Oneal, "Measuring the Material Base of the East–West Balance of Power," *International Interactions*, vol. 15, 1989, pp. 177–96.

21. Oneal and Elrod, "NATO Burden Sharing and the Forces of Change."

22. Herbert A. Simon, "Human Nature in Politics," *American Political Science Review* 79 (June 1985), pp. 293–304.

23. Duncan Snidal, "The Limits of Hegemonic Stability Theory," *International Organization* 39 (Autumn 1985), pp. 579–614.

24. See Martin C. McGuire and Carl H. Groth, Jr., "A Method for Identifying the Public Good Allocation Process Within a Group," *Quarterly Journal of Economics* 100 (Supplement 1985), pp. 915–34; and Robert O. Keohane and Joseph Nye, *Power and Interdependence* (Boston: Little, Brown, 1977).

25. Olson and Zeckhauser, "An Economic Theory of Alliances."

26. Equal defense burdens are the most obvious and perhaps the most important sign of cooperation among allies; but cooperation can, of course, take other forms, notably in the standardization of equipment or specialization of contributions and roles according to comparative advantage. For discussion of the progress and continuing shortcomings of NATO in these areas, see U.S. Department of Defense, "Standardization of Equipment Within NATO," Report to the U.S. Congress by the Secretary of Defense, Washington, D.C., 1988; and NATO, "Enhancing Alliance Collective Security," Report by the Defence Planning Committee, Brussels, 1988.

27. See Thomas E. Borcherding, "Comment: The Demand for Military Expenditures," *Public Choice*, vol. 37, 1981, pp. 33–39; Richard Cornes and Todd Sandler, "The Theory of Public Goods: Non-Nash Behavior," *Journal of Public Economics* 23 (April 1984), pp. 367–79; and Robert O. Keohane, *After Hegemony* (Princeton, N.J.: Princeton University Press, 1984).

28. Standardization was necessary because the sum of the unstandardized scores for any country and for all others as a group is not a constant; therefore, only comparisons within a single year would be strictly accurate. To permit comparisons through time, the burden of each ally relative to the NATO average each year was divided by the mean of the score for the United States and the score for all other countries combined.

29. Olson, *The Logic of Collective Action*, p. 3.

30. See Kevin Forbes, George Korsun, and Martin McGuire, "Defense, Growth, and Allocation Behavior in the Alliance," in Denoon, *Constraints on Strategy*, pp. 114–51;

and Peter Calvocoressi, *World Politics Since 1945,* 4th ed. (London: Longman, 1982), pp. 181–95 and 413–14.

31. Oneal and Elrod, "NATO Burden Sharing and the Forces of Change."

32. See Snidal, "The Limits of Hegemonic Stability Theory"; and Mancur Olson, "A Theory of the Incentives Facing Political Organizations," *International Political Science Review* 7 (April 1986), pp. 165–89.

33. Olson, *The Logic of Collective Action,* pp. 28–30 and 49–50.

34. Russett, *What Price Vigilance?* p. 110.

35. The three exceptional cases have been excluded in all years because they were unusually influenced by private interests during much of the postwar period. Although most significant after 1974, the rivalry between Greece and Turkey predated the invasion of Cyprus, of course; and Portugal's defense spending was skewed by its colonial obligations before 1964 and by its military governments after 1975. Excluding these countries in all years also ensures comparability in analyses across time.

36. Throughout this study, regression analyses have been corrected for an AR(1) autocorrelation process using the method recommended by Hibbs. See Douglas A. Hibbs, Jr., "Problems of Statistical Estimation and Causal Inference in Time-Series Regression Models," in Herbert L. Costner, ed., *Sociological Methodology, 1973–1974* (San Francisco: Jossey-Bass, 1974), pp. 252–308.

37. Theodore Hitiris, "Convergence and the Relationship Between the Members of the European Community," in Douglas Dosser, David Gowland, and Keith Hartley, eds., *The Collaboration of Nations* (New York: St. Martin's Press, 1982), pp. 42–60.

38. McGuire and Groth, "A Method for Identifying the Public Good Allocation Process."

39. Glenn Palmer, "Guns, Vacations, and GNP: The Elasticity of Defense Spending," paper presented at the annual meeting of the Southern Political Science Association, Atlanta, 1988.

40. Including Greece, Turkey, and Portugal would exaggerate the results of the tests for cooperation, since their increased expenditures on private goods in later years adds to their defense burdens and thereby raises the lower end of the regression line. It is particularly important to recognize this distorting influence because it is *rivalry* between Greece and Turkey that has caused their defense spending to be so high.

41. These results have been corroborated by pooled cross-sectional and time-series regression analyses. See John R. Oneal, "Testing the Theory of Collective Action: NATO Defense Burdens, 1950–1984," *Journal of Conflict Resolution* 34 (September 1990).

42. See Karl W. Deutsch, *The Analysis of International Relations,* 3d ed. (Englewood Cliffs, N.J.: Prentice-Hall, 1988), p. 255; and Stanley R. Sloan, *NATO's Future* (Washington, D.C.: National Defense University Press, 1985), pp. 173–82.

43. Olson and Zeckhauser, "An Economic Theory of Alliances."

The South Will Fall Again: The South as Leader and Laggard in Economic Growth

Mancur Olson

Review Questions

1. What are "selective incentives," and how do they impact collective action? How does the size and composition of the group affect its ability to engage in selective incentives?
2. Why are organizations more likely to engage in activities that focus on distributional aspects rather than social efficiency?
3. It is proposed that wars and revolutions destroy distributional coalitions. What does this imply about economic growth for countries that have recently suffered through wars or for those that have enjoyed a long time of internal stability?
4. How is this theory applied to different regions within the United States? What is the evidence in favor of the theory, and how is the theory modified to better explain growth in the South?
5. What limited the South's economy between the Civil War and World War II, and why did it grow so rapidly following World War II? What other ex-

Olson, Mancur. "The South Will Fall Again: The South as Leader and Laggard in Economic Growth." *Southern Economic Journal* 49 (1983): 917–32.

planations were offered, and why are they considered to be less convincing? Why is it surmised the South's higher growth rates will not be maintained?

I.

It is well known that since World War II, and especially since the early 1960s, the South has enjoyed more economic growth than the United States as a whole, and very much more than the declining Northeast and older Middle West. In this short period the South shed its almost century-old reputation as the poorest region of the country and one which continually suffered a substantial emigration of its people to other regions, and gained fame for leading the pace of economic advance and attracting a substantial net immigration from other parts of the country. Why has the South grown so much more rapidly than most of the rest of the country in recent decades? This is a question of some importance, among other reasons because there is no way of making an informed judgement about whether this advance will continue until we know its causes.

My answer to this question grows out of the theory set forth in a book I have just published on the rise and decline of nations and regions in general.[1] Since the answer is not meaningful without some impression of at least one aspect of the theory set forth in that book, it will be necessary to describe one feature of the theory, though only in a brief and unrigorous way.

The theory begins with organizations or groups that lobby for favorable legislation and administrative rulings or act cartelistically to influence prices or wages. The governmental favors and the monopolistic or monopsonistic prices or wages obtained by combination are, analytically speaking, public or collective goods, in that the benefits automatically go to every firm or individual in some group or category; a tariff or tax loophole favors every firm in some industry or group, and cartelization raises the price or wage for every seller in the relevant market. It follows that any sacrifice an individual makes to support a lobby or cartel for his group will benefit others as much as himself; if the group in question is large, the individual will get only a minuscule share of the benefits of any action he takes in the interest of his group. In view of the "external economy" of individual action in the group interest, there will normally be less than a group-optimal level of activity, and in very large groups there is usually no incentive for an individual to provide any amount of the collective good at all. Collective action to lobby or cartelize therefore requires, at least for large groups, "selective incentives" or punishments and rewards that are applied to individuals according as they do or do not act in the group interest. Empirical investigations show that large groups that engage in collective action are in fact normally motivated by such selective incentives. Small groups may sometimes organize without such selective incentives, but then difficult bargaining is required to obtain group-optimal levels of collective action.

Collective action is accordingly difficult and problematical. Some large groups are not in a position to obtain selective incentives and cannot organize. Such groups as consumers, taxpayers, the unemployed, and the poor are, for example, so spread out that coercive picket lines are not feasible, and such groups are not organized for collective action in any society. Even those groups that are small or that have access to selective incentives will usually be able to organize only if they have favorable circumstances and good leadership. Coercion is difficult to organize and likely to be resisted, and it is difficult to find any surplus from which positive rewards for those who act collectively can be obtained. Even the bargaining needed for group optimal action by small groups may be difficult to work out.

It follows that no society will achieve that comprehensive organization of all common interest groups that would make it possible for the leaders of all groups to bargain with one another until an efficient, core allocation of resources for the society is obtained. As time goes on in stable societies, however, more of those groups that have the potential to organize will have enjoyed the favorable circumstances and good leadership needed to get organized. Since organizations that succeed in obtaining the selective incentives needed to survive rarely disband or collapse, stable societies (which do not destroy organizations through violence or repression) will accumulate more organization for lobbying and cartelization as time goes on.

Most organizations for lobbying or cartelization have no incentive to strive to make the society in which they exist more efficient or prosperous; the members of the organization will normally get only a minute fraction of the society's gains from greater efficiency, but will bear the whole cost of any effort to increase social efficiency. Normally these organizations can best serve their memberships by seeking a larger share of the social output for their members by distributional struggle—they will be coalitions concerned about distribution rather than production. If, as is always the case in the United States, they are small in relation to the whole society, they will rationally persist in distributional struggle even if the excess burden or loss to society should much exceed the amount won; an organization that represents one percent of the income-earning capacity of the country will bear on average only one percent of any losses in social efficiency, but will obtain the whole amount redistributed to its membership, so its clients will gain from any redistribution unless the excess burden is a hundred times or more greater than the amount redistributed.

One testable implication of the theory is that societies in which distributional coalitions have been destroyed through totalitarianism, war, or revolution, if they can after the institutional devastation create a stable framework suitable for growth, should for a time grow more rapidly than comparable countries. The rapid growth of West Germany and Japan after World War II is consistent with this implication. A further implication of the theory is that a country that has enjoyed stability for an unusually long time should tend to grow less rapidly than comparable countries, and the relatively slow growth of Great Britain in recent times is consistent with this implication. When the argument that has been described impressionistically in the foregoing paragraphs is developed and combined with familiar and generally accepted microeconomic theory, it is able to explain the most anomalous examples of economic growth and decline since the Middle Ages, to account for involuntary unemployment and business cycles, and to illuminate a variety of social rigidities arising from castes, classes, and racial discrimination. If this general theory is consistent with the relatively rapid growth in the South in the last quarter century, and with the general pattern of regional growth in the United States, then discussions of the changing fortunes of the South need no longer be mired down in a morass of conflicting ad hoc explanations.

II.

At least at a superficial level, the aforementioned theory does explain the general pattern of regional growth in the United States since World War II and in particular the rapid growth of the South. Consider first the non-southern states. For these states, the number of years since they achieved statehood gives a reasonable approximate measure of the time they have had to accumulate special interest organization. If one regresses the years since statehood in these states against recent rates of economic growth, one finds a strong, statistically significant *negative* relationship. The more recently settled and more westerly states are on the whole growing much more rapidly than the northeastern and older middle western states that have had a longer time to accumulate special interest organization. Though the frontier is conventionally supposed to have closed at the end of the last century, this pattern might just conceivably be due to lingering frontier disequilibria, and this makes the pattern in the South all the more interesting. The southeastern states are about as long removed from frontier status as any parts of the country, but the defeat and turbulence these states have suffered have given them far less time to accumulate distributional coalitions than those in the Northeast and older Middle West. But the southern states as a whole, and even those of them that have been settled the longest, tend to be growing faster than most of the rest of the country. This is clearly consistent with the theory. A variety of regressions, in which the length of time a state has had both settlement and stability is used to predict growth rates by state, uniformly support the theory, and a variety of statistical tests also suggest that none of the familiar alternative explanations of southern and regional growth fit the facts nearly as well.[2]

Not long ago the account of southern and regional growth given in the foregoing paragraph seemed convincing to me, but I now believe it is seriously oversimplified. One problem with the account I have just given is that it does not specify well enough just when the South should have experienced its rapid growth. The South's history was turbulent and often violent from its defeat in the Civil War until relatively recently, but it is not clear just how much organization was destroyed or repressed and just how this affected the rate and timing of Southern growth. The account also suffers from a lack of specificity about just how different types of special-interest organizations influence regional growth, on the one hand, and national growth, on the other. So a somewhat deeper and more precise analysis of the matter seems to be needed.

III.

The key to a better analysis of the matter now seems to me to be the very different effects that some types of distributional coalitions can have on regional and national growth. On reflection, it is obvious that some special-interest groups that are harmful to national efficiency and growth are at the same time helpful to the growth of the region, state, or locality in which they are located. Consider an industry that is confined by natural resources or climate to one section of the country and is organized in a lobby or a cartel. Any governmental favors or monopoly prices this industry then receives will normally increase not only the income of the industry but also that of the section of the country in which it is located. In general, taxpayers throughout the country must bear the burden of any subsidies or tax loopholes the industry obtains, and consumers throughout the country or the world must pay the higher prices that any cartelization makes possible. But, so long as the industry is restricted by natural resources or climate to one section of the country, that section of the country is likely to gain from whatever prosperity lobbying or mo-

nopoly prices bring to a local industry; at the least the specialized local resources the organized industry uses must rise in value. Except in certain
anomolous "second-best" situations, the gains of the local area will be less
than the nation's losses, but the local gains may nonetheless be considerable.
Price supports for cotton and peanuts, for example, may well have added to
the prosperity of the South, however uneconomic they were for the nation as
a whole.

Now let's turn to the opposite extreme, and suppose that the labor force or
the professions in a particular area become cartelized, and that we have footloose industry that is not constrained in its locational decisions by natural resources or the location of markets. If cartelization of labor or the professions
raises wages or other costs of production in a locality, the footloose industry
will, at least when the time comes for it to construct new factories, have an incentive to move to other communities where wages are lower and where work
practices may be changed without time-consuming negotiations. In such a
situation cartelization (or lobbying for local and state government regulations that are harmful to business) will tend to reduce local income and
growth rates. The losses to the locality or region will also exceed the costs to
the nation, since the internal migration of business will reduce the extent of
the nation's loss. As firms migrate to uncartelized or less cartelized areas,
some labor will also migrate in search of jobs, so population as well as per
capita income will tend to grow at above average rates in the areas to which
the firms migrate.

The emphasis in any study of regional growth and decline within a country with free mobility of factors should therefore be particularly on the
cartelization of the labor force. Ideally, one should also consider the impact
of local and state government policies harmful to business and the ways that
the local level of organization of professions such as medicine, law, and ar-
chitecture, or organizations of retail businesses, can raise the costs of living
and doing business in the community. Any analysis of national growth must,
of course, have a much broader perspective on distributional coalitions, and
not focus exclusively or overwhelmingly on labor unions. Indeed, for many
analyses of the growth of whole economies labor unions will not be relevant
at all. In Adam Smith's time, for example, the main sources of inefficiency
were probably merchants (and perhaps "masters" or manufacturers); Smith
called the system of protection, subsidy, and cartelization in his day "mercantilism" because he believed it was inspired in large part by merchants. He
also argued that businessmen were more likely than other classes to conspire
against the public interest, and the argument earlier in this paper that small

groups can organize with less difficulty than large ones offers support for Smith's hypothesis; the firms in an industry, being usually less numerous than the workers, can overcome the obstacles to collective action more readily. So we must not assume that cartelization of labor is the main source of inefficiency in economies, even as we give it the leading role in the analysis of regional growth and decline.

IV.

Now that we have distinguished the effects of different types of special-interest organizations on regional and total growth, the timing of the southern advance is easily explained. The single period of greatest growth in labor union membership and power in the history of the United States was from 1937–1945, and especially during World War II. The Wagner Labor Relations Act, which greatly facilitated the organization of unions, was passed in 1937, and the fear of strikes during World War II enabled organized labor to obtain special "maintenance of membership" rules which made union membership more or less compulsory for a wide set of workers. Many unions were not able to consolidate or exploit their full power until some time after World War II. So it is only since World War II that unions have been at all pervasive in any parts of this country, and it is only since World War II that the *differential* in union membership across states could have had a massive significance on the location of economic activity. And it is, of course, precisely in the postwar period that the South has been converted from being much the poorest region of the country with a substantial outflow of people into being an unusual dynamic part of the American economy that attracts a considerable net inflow of migrants.

There is some corroboration of this explanation of the timing of Southern growth in the fact that economic growth in more recently settled Western states tended to speed up at the same time. These states also had lower levels of union membership than the northeastern and older middle western states. Throughout the United States, moreover, the percentage of a state's nonagricultural labor force that is unionized has a strong *negative* association with rates of growth of the state's economy.[3]

V.

Since the book in which I offered the foregoing explanation of rapid southern growth went to press, interesting new evidence has been gathered. Charles

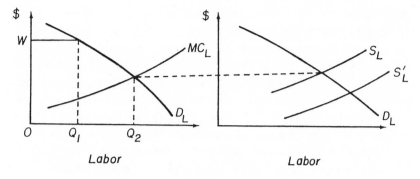

Figure 1

Hulten and Robert Schwab have developed estimates of productivity growth in U.S. manufacturing in each of the nation's regions.[4] Their estimates are full of paradoxes that are utterly inconsistent with any standard neoclassical story. They find that the marginal product of labor was greater in the Northeast and the older Middle West than in the South and other (western) regions that grew relatively rapidly, but that the marginal product of capital was higher than in the latter regions; the wage-rental ratio was of course also considerably higher in the Northeast and older Middle West than in the South and West. If unfettered markets were tending toward equilibrium, this would lead us to expect that capital would flow to the South and similar regions and that labor would flow to the higher wage regions, or at least that the declining regions would lose much less labor than capital to the South. In fact, there is a vast flow of labor *out* of the northeastern and older middle west sections; little if any of such growth in output as they achieve is due to any increased input of labor. The labor moves *away* from the high wage regions to the relatively low-wage South and other growing regions in large quantities; a large part of the growth of these regions is due to increases in employment. Labor, in other words, moves to the regions where its marginal product is *lower*. Capital, on the other hand, moves as conventionally predicted to the South and to other growing areas with a relatively higher marginal product of capital, but not to such a dramatic degree; the amount of growth in the South and other rapidly growing areas that is due to additional inputs of capital is only moderately greater than in the Northeast and older Middle West.

Why would workers go through the costs and upheaval of migration to move from where wages were high to where they were low? If there had been no cartelization and free entry in the labor markets of the Northeast and the older Middle West the workers could in general have enjoyed higher wages by staying at home. But if, as has been argued here, there were cartelized supra-competitive wage levels in the older and long-stable regions of the country, employers would not want to take on many of the workers who would have liked employment with them, so these workers had no choice but to move to the South or other growing regions to take lower-paying jobs. This is depicted in Figure 1, where the quantity OQ_2 minus OQ_1 of labor shifts from the cartelized region to the uncartelized region to accept jobs at the competitive wage there (which is however somewhat lower than it would otherwise have been because of the influx of labor). Some capital also moved to the rapidly growing regions, but this movement was less striking because the high wage-rental ratio in the Northeastern regions provided an incentive for more capital-intensive production there. Other features of Hulten's and Schwab's estimates also appear to be consistent with the argument offered here and difficult to explain in other ways.[5]

VI.

Though the explanation that has been offered here fits the data very well, there is still one more aspect of the matter than must be explained before we can be confident about this (or any other) explanation. We should also have an explanation of why the Southern economy failed to catch up with the rest of the country in the long period from the end of the Civil War until World War II. The South's disproportionately rapid growth occurred when the theory here says it should have—just after the *differential* in cartelization of the labor market first became important during World War II, and at the same time that other parts of the country that benefited from the same differential also grew. But it would also be nice to have an explanation of the failure of the South to catch up earlier with the rest of the country. Even though the South did not have the special institutional advantage discussed here before World War II, we must still ask why it did not catch up with the rest of the country for other reasons. In particular, why did not the combined effect of the outmigration of labor and the inmigration of firms seeking lower wage rates eliminate the differentials in wage rates long before World War II? A substantial outmigration of labor, both black and white, occurred, but the inflow of capital in response to the lower wage rates between the Civil War and World War II did not proceed rapidly enough to reduce significantly the great gap in levels of industrialization between the North and the South. Something kept the rapid industrialization that occurred after World War II from happening earlier, and we should not be completely confident of *any* explanation of postwar southern growth until we know what it was.

Unfortunately, although there is a substantial literature on the matter, no persuasive explanation of the South's failure to catch up with the North appears to have been offered. One of the most common explanations of the retardation of Southern development before World War II was that the South had a "colonial" economy, and its growth was in some way suppressed by the imperial power of corporations or other interests in the North. Usually those who subscribe to this explanation do not spell out why the northern capitalists' desire for profit did not induce them to come in and exploit the low wage workers, thereby eliminating the gap in levels of development. It is possible that northern cartels, such as the one that led to the "Pittsburgh plus" pricing system in steel, could have blocked some new Southern enterprises from entering certain industries, but it is hard to see how this could have prevented development in many industries, in part because in most cases the firms in the cartels would often still have had an incentive to produce in the South if that was more economical than remaining in the North. The imperial repression is often alleged to have taken the form of discriminatory freight rates, but detailed investigation reveals that the differentials were often illusory and in any event could not have had great quantitative significance.[6]

More generally, it is not even certain that colonial status is bad for economic growth and imperial status good for it. The colony of Hong Kong has one of the most impressive records of economic growth in all the world, but its imperial master Great Britain has at the same time done relatively poorly. Great Britain first began to fall behind other developed democracies in relative growth rates at the very time its empire was the largest the world has ever seen. Some of the newly-independent countries are now surely less prosperous than they would have been had they remained colonies. There is an emotional incentive in every relatively backward area to explain the area's backwardness in terms of the actual or alleged colonialism of more prosperous areas, and we should be skeptical about the many inadequately documented efforts to blame the South's long period of retardation on regions that were at that time more successful. And we should insist that those who offer a "colonial" explanation of the South's long retardation explain why that retardation ended at a time when the South was apparently still in what they would have to call a "colonial" status—when the nation as a whole was imposing some of the most sweeping changes in institutional arrangements, such as the Civil Rights and Voting Rights acts, upon the South.

The low per capita incomes in the South in the three-fourths of a century after the Civil War are sometimes also traced to southern agriculture. It is clear that secular declines in cotton prices at times reduced southern incomes, and no doubt there were diverse shortcomings in southern agriculture as well. Yet these agricultural problems probably cannot explain the slow pace of southern industrialization, since low incomes in agriculture meant that labor was available to industry at a lower wage.

The formerly slow pace of southern development is sometimes also ascribed to the absence of air conditioning and the postwar growth to its presence. Surely air conditioning has been a significant factor, but any wide-ranging examination of the evidence shows that it is only one part of a much larger story. At the same time that manufacturing expanded in the South it also grew in some of the more recently settled northwestern plains and mountain states, many of which were cooler than the northeastern and older middle western states that were in relative decline. The international differences in postwar growth rates into which the pattern of southern growth fits so nicely certainly cannot be ascribed to air conditioning. We must also remember that cold winters in the North also often raise production costs, especially in construction industries, and that the world's most advanced civilizations have often been in areas as hot as the American South, such as Mesopotamia, the Nile and Indus valleys, and the area around the Mediterranean Sea. The later dominance of the civilizations of Northern Europe might argue that northern climes had the economic advantage, but the advance of these civilizations began when even castles had no more than fireplaces, and in such circumstances it is by no means certain that a cold climate was preferable. If one looks at the wide range of climates in which economic advance has taken place in the past, before either air conditioning or central heating became widespread, and at either the nationwide or world-wide pattern of development today, it is difficult to see how air-conditioning by itself could have been the dominant influence on the development of the South.

VII.

Another explanation of the long retardation of Southern development was offered by William H. Nicholls in a presidential address to this association twenty three years ago, and later elaborated in a well-known book on *Southern Tradition and Regional Progress.*[7] Nicholls argued that agrarian values, a rigid social structure, an undemocratic political structure, conformity of thought and behavior, and an irresponsible neglect of public education were principal obstacles to southern development. To assess Nicholls's argument we must answer at least three questions. First, were there organizations, coalitions, or other instrumentalities that could propogate agrarian values, discourage dissent, and maintain the barriers to entry that would sustain exclusive social and political structures? An argument that purports to explain some phenomena in terms of culture or national or regional character is not really an adequate explanation unless it also explains how the culture or tradition came to exist; it only provides a label for the pattern of behavior that is observed. And no account of social or political exclusiveness can be complete unless it specifies the interests and the mechanisms by which the exclusion was accomplished. Second, how would economic development and the influx of outside capital and labor affect the interests embodied in any such coalitions? Third, is Nicholls's argument consistent with the timing of both the retardation of southern growth in the past and also the exceptional progress of recent times?

There is some indirect evidence about whether there was an organizational or coalition structure that could sustain the pattern of culture and behavior that Nicholls observed in *The Strange Career of Jim Crow*[8] by the famous southern historian C. Vann Woodward. Woodward found that the rigid patterns of racial segregation that characterized much of the South until relatively recently usually did not date back to the Civil War or to the end of Reconstruction. The Jim Crow legislation and the rigid patterns of segregated behavior they required were more often than not established quite some time after the end of Reconstruction, and it was well into the twentieth century before the system achieved its full extent and rigor. A careful set of state-by-state and community-by-community studies is needed to determine exactly what interests brought about this system of segregation and white supremacy and how these interests were organized. There is also a need for more study to see what relationships there were between the Jim Crow system and the poll taxes and other limitations on voting that greatly reduced rates of voting among whites while almost completely disenfranchising blacks.[9] The slow and gradual emergence of this pattern of white supremacy with a restricted franchise is, however, exactly what reflection about the logic of collective action would lead us to expect. Racial segregation and a restricted franchise were collective goods to those who wanted such arrangements, and the organization of the coalitions or associations that would bring them about was not prompt or automatic. Admittedly, small associations are not so difficult to establish as large ones, and the Jim Crow system was established on a courthouse-by-courthouse or state-by-state basis that would not usually require massive organization, but even so the frameworks for collective action could emerge only gradually.

The next question is, how would the interests that obtained the segregation and franchise limitations be affected by economic development, and especially by industrialization with the influx of capital and the outside management, skilled labor, and new ideas that often came with it? Here we surely must have a complex and mixed picture. No doubt many retailers in southern towns and cities were sincerely and even intensely interested in increasing the population and incomes in their communities and thus the number of their customers. Property owners in such towns and cities would tend to realize capital gains if the size of the community increased because of economic development. Presumably there were also some workers and small farmers in the ruling coalitions that would welcome the additional employment opportunities that economic development would bring. There must have been many who traced the South's defeat in the Civil War to the greater industrialization of the North and who coveted industrialization as a means to modernity and power. Owners of plantations and other employers naturally also saw immigration as a source of an increased supply of labor. Thus it is by no means surprising that from the end of the Civil War onward there have been innumerable pleas for economic development and efforts to attract outside capital and sometimes also immigrants from the North and from foreign countries. Many southern leaders emphasized in speech after speech that industrialization was the key to southern progress, and many organized industrial expositions and state offices designed to attract industry and immigrants. There can be no question that many southern leaders all along had a genuine interest in economic development.

It is also true that the owners of plantations and existing firms were not anxious to have an influx of outside business bid up the wages they had to pay. Nor was there much enthusiasm in the ruling coalitions for changing local customs to help attract the professional and skilled labor that was more plentiful in the North. For a long time there was probably no intense desire to educate the labor force to the extent that would have most encouraged economic development, and certainly no desire to educate the black part of the labor force to that extent. There were also chauvinistic prejudices against foreigners and Yankees; by World War I there came to be strong opposition to foreign immigration in the South, and Ku Klux Klan and other opposition to Catholics and Jews, even though the South had experienced incomparably less immigration than most of the rest of the country.[10] Many of the southern ruling coalitions were also anything but hospitable to nonconformity and to the new ideas that must play a large role in economic advance. The "agrarians" that William Nicholls confronted at Vanderbilt University were not advocates of capitalistic agricultural enterprise, but more nearly devotees of the feudal, anti-industrial, anti-capitalistic mentality that was more in keeping with the myths attached to the antebellum plantation than with the ideas needed for modern economic progress.[11] The attitudes of the agrarians were not of course typical of the South, but were they not an extreme and literary manifestation of attitudes that were especially well represented in the South? And were not many of the ruling coalitions aware that a massive influx of outside industry, expertise, and labor would at least endanger the established patterns of white supremacy and segregation? And were they not capable of realizing that their own political dominance would be threatened by the drastic changes and the influx of new people and new ideas that rapid industrialization would bring with it?[12]

In short, one may wonder whether the support of the governing southern coalitions for outside industry, immigration, and economic development was as unanimous, intense, and single-minded in the days of Jim Crow as it is has been recently. This is a question that cannot be answered definitely without a colossal amount of new research, but perhaps we can get some tentative impressions by turning to the third question about William Nicholls's argument on *Southern Tradition and Regional Progress,* the question of whether the timing of Southern industrialization, and the timing of the most aggressive campaigns to bring industry to the South, were consistent with the argument.

VIII.

Before the civil rights and voting rights legislation of the mid-sixties was passed, it was often argued that legislation could not quickly change the racial folkways of the South, and if federal legislation that was fundamentally incompatible with these folkways passed there would be a period of instability and turmoil that would interrupt economic and social progress; ancient customs and patterns of behavior could not easily or quickly be changed by legislation. This argument was not only used by opponents of civil rights and voting rights legislation, but was also accepted (as I can testify from memory and personal experience) by some who were nonetheless ardent advocates of such legislation.

We now know that this view was wrong. The South's lead in economic growth widened at the very time the civil rights and voting rights legislation first took effect. That lead had, moreover, emerged in the very period when the New Deal, World War II, and Supreme Court decisions began to undo the Jim

Crow system. And in how many fields, if any, did Southern accomplishments diminish in this period?

The rapid and relatively peaceful change in the institutions concerning race in the South, and the rapid economic growth that occurred at the same time, provide indirect support for C. Vann Woodward's contention that the Jim Crow system did not spring up immediately after Reconstruction; those folkways were not really so ancient as they were sometimes supposed to be. There also had to have been strong forces for change within the South itself. The rapid southern adjustment to the voting rights and civil rights legislation also supports what is sometimes called the economic view of discrimination; that is, the view that in a free market discrimination is costly to any firms and individuals that engage in it, that such costs limit the extent of discrimination, and that at least the most severe patterns of discrimination must be enforced by governments or cartels. The Jim Crow system had for the most part not been the automatic and natural consequence of southern folkways, but had been established largely by force. At first and in part the force was extra-legal, but most of it came to be codified in legislation. What was imposed by legislation could be ended by legislation, and economic growth could at the same time continue and even increase.

What does the fact that southern leadership in economic growth emerged at the same time the political and social system of Jim Crow was dismantled tell us about whether the old ruling coalitions were in any way harmful to economic growth? I have in this paper already offered another explanation of why the South has grown more rapidly than the Northeast and the older Middle West in the postwar period. Since that other explanation also accounts for growth in recently settled western states that had never been under the Jim Crow system, there is some reason to argue that the association in time between the dismantling of the Jim Crow system and the emergence of the southern lead in economic growth was purely coincidental. Nonetheless, we must still explain why the South failed to industrialize or catch up with the rest of the country in the long period before Word War II, and face up to the fact that the "colonial" excuse is certainly not sufficient to do this. This is a matter that is not adequately understood and that cries out for further research. That research should certainly not overlook the possibility that the dominant coalitions of Jim Crow and the system they established were not in every respect favorable to economic growth.

This possibility is made somewhat more significant by the fact that from 1860 to 1870, before the Jim Crow system had begun to form, there was (despite immense dislocations resulting from the South's defeat and the costs of the transition from slavery to other systems of organization of labor and of agriculture) a 64 percent increase in the number of manufacturing establishments in the South. This was the largest percentage increase in the 19th century.[13] The fact that the Southern industrialization that did occur during the Jim Crow period occurred mostly in the areas of the South in which that system was less significant—in the mainly white areas, such as the Piedmont textile regions, rather than in the black belt areas—argues in the same direction.

So does the timing of the most aggressive campaigns to attract Northern and foreign business to the South. Though there were certainly earlier efforts to attract outside industry, it appears that the really ardent campaigns to attract outside industry emerged after World War II, when many Southern communities began to offer substantial subsidies to attract outside firms to locate in their communities. The intensity and extent of these efforts, which began with Mississippi's Balance Industry with Agriculture act in 1936, are fully documented in James C. Cobb's *The Selling of the South: The Southern Crusade for Economic Development, 1936–1980.*[14] One must ask why the really serious campaign to attract enterprise emerged when it did. No doubt such campaigns are more likely in periods when they have greater chances to succeed, and I have offered one important reason why such campaigns could succeed in the postwar period earlier in this paper. One must nonetheless wonder whether the New Deal, World War II, and the postwar court decisions and legislation about civil rights did not also make a contribution. It appears, at least at first glance, that the effort to attract and subsidize firms from afar became really intensive at the very time it became evident that the Jim Crow system was in any case likely to be destroyed.

When one takes all this together, and focuses on industrialization and economic growth, it is tempting to argue that World War II and the years that followed were perhaps more portentous for the South than the Civil War and Reconstruction, and conceivably even that they led to the greater emancipation. An historian has learnedly and seriously argued that World War II was more important for the South than the Civil War.[15]

IX.

There is another reason why the South did not succeed in industrializing before World War II that is probably more important than any other, yet somehow has been seriously neglected in the literature. This is the secular change in the cost of transportation. In the analysis of cartelization I emphasized that it was only footloose industry, or at any event industry that was not tied down completely by transportation costs to natural resources, markets, or transportation switching points, that could move in response to variations in labor costs. For unskilled labor, at least, there were some wage differentials even before World War II. In rural areas of the South, particularly, labor was available at significantly lower cost than in great cities of the North. It might be objected that the inferiority of the southern school systems in the nineteenth and early twentieth centuries, at least, counterbalanced the wage differential, but this might not matter for many unskilled jobs, and in any case it is by no means clear that the education in the South was inferior to that possessed by most of the immigrants that staffed much of the industry in the North, many of whom had never received any schooling and who often did not know English. So we must find out why much of northern industry didn't move to the South, and particularly to rural areas of the South, as it has since World War II.

In trying to determine whether higher costs of transportation costs in earlier periods could explain this, I discovered that there is amazingly little knowledge about how changing transportation costs have affected the location of the industry. None of several leading location economists I have consulted knew of a good quantitative study of this issue, and historians of the South have also neglected it.

There does, however, appear to be one way of finding out whether transportation costs have fallen in real terms since the last century. We know that important new modes of transportation have been developed in the present century, such as the truck and the airplane. Since these modes of transportation have come to be widely used, we know that for the many purposes for which these models are used they must on balance be more advantageous to the shipper than the mode of transportation they have replaced, which is mainly the railroad. Transportation costs could nevertheless have risen, because it is possible that the costs of railroads could have increased in real terms, and that much of the switch to other modes may have been due to this. The railroad industry has surely been a badly regulated industry and one with a lot of labor cartelization and featherbedding, and it is hard to imagine that it has attracted the most innovative managers in the economy. But if, despite this, the cost of railroad transportation has fallen in real terms we can be confident that aggregate transportation costs have fallen. If shippers were switching to other modes even when rail costs were falling, it must mean that for the relevant commodities and distances the new modes were even more advantageous.

Happily, there is enough information on railroad costs and charges to arrive at a qualitative judgement. For the years between 1899 and 1946 Harold

Barger's study of *The Transportation Industries, 1889–1946* for the National Bureau of Economic Research provides the needed data, and for the postwar years there are unpublished implicit price deflators for railroad transportation from the Bureau of Economic Analysis. Barger found that in 1939 the railroads had about the same number of employees as in 1899, but twice as much output. Output per worker, he estimates, increased rather steadily at about 1.9 percent per annum, and output per manhour somewhat faster than that. By looking at the data on the stock of equipment, Barger is also able to conclude that "output per equipment unit rose at roughly the same speed as output per worker."[16] These advances Barger attributes to a variety of technological advances in railway equipment in this period, such as more powerful locomotives (even before diesel locomotives were introduced, mainly after 1946), to larger cars, to chemically treated ties, to improved ballast and tie plates, automatic block signaling devices, etc. Barger's conclusion that railroad productivity was increasing steadily throughout this period seems compelling.

The Bureau of Economic Analysis's implicit price deflator for railroad transportation is given along with the GDP deflator in Table 1. The South had already long surpassed the rate of growth of the North by 1972, the base year for these figures. Between 1946 and 1972 the costs of railroad transportation in nominal terms had increased from 61.8 to 100, whereas the GDP deflator had risen from 49.5 to 100, so that the relative or real costs of transportation declined. Even if we include the years after the oil price increases in the

TABLE 1. Gross Product by Sector or Industry of Origin (Dollars in Millions: Indexes, 1972 = 100.0)

	Railroad Transportation—SIC 40			Gross Domestic Product		
	Current Dollars	Implicit Price Deflator	Constant Dollars	Current Dollars	Implicit Price Deflator	Constant Dollars
1947	7,340	61.8	11,877	231,815	49.5	467,847
1950	8,278	79.3	10,439	284,839	53.6	531,771
1955	8,942	81.8	10,932	397,288	60.8	652,970
1960	8,079	83.4	9,687	502,943	68.7	732,020
1965	8,645	73.3	11,794	685,186	74.4	921,422
1970	9,713	84.4	11,508	985,425	91.4	1,077,597
1972	10,330	100.0	10,330	1,175,022	100.0	1,175,023
1975	11,521	118.7	9,706	1,531,898	125.8	1,217,798
1980	18,399	184.9	9,951	2,587,035	178.7	1,447,886
1981	20,237	215.7	9,382	2,888,536	195.5	1,477,236

Source: Donald Eldridge, Bureau of Economic Analysis, U.S. Department of Commerce (Unpublished data)

1970's, railroad transportation costs have still risen less since 1947 than the general price level. Separate data on ton miles hauled per train, distances traveled per day, and other data support the impression drawn from the BEA price deflator.

With this reduction in the real cost of railroad transportation, and at the same time a rapid shift to other modes, there has to have been a large reduction in transportation costs. With the growing importance of trucks and the creation of the interstate highway system, the cost of transportation to smaller rural communities must have dropped dramatically. This is confirmed by John Kendrick's and Kendrick's and Grossman's estimates of total factor productivity by industry. These estimates show that since 1889 total factor productivity has increased more rapidly in transportation than in the economy as a whole.[17] Since these estimates, like most others, do not take account of the gains from shifting from one mode of transportation to another, they probably even understate the reduction in the real costs of transportation.

Perhaps the most important reason why the South did not industrialize faster between the Civil War and World War II, then, is that transportation costs were too high, at least in the earlier part of this period. Transportation costs were not crucial for industries like textiles, and the textile industry and some others like it had in fact moved South earlier than other industries. Industries that needed to be near the larger markets, which were not in the South, or which needed to be near raw materials, often could not move South, and especially not to rural parts of the South, to take advantage of lower wages. By the 1930's transportation costs had already fallen significantly, but there was naturally very little investment in new plants anywhere during the depression.

X.

The advantage in economic growth which the South has enjoyed since World War II because of the differential in levels of cartelization cannot last forever. Now that it has about the same institutional arrangements as the rest of the country, it will, however slowly and gradually, probably accumulate much the same level of cartelization as the Northeast and the older Middle West. Some of the differential has already been eliminated. Similarly, any advantage in economic growth rates due to wage differentials arising from other causes is rapidly being eliminated, if it has not been eliminated already.

Thus the South will eventually lose its position as a leader in American economic growth. In that sense, the South will fall again. In another sense, it will not only fall, but even fall out of sight. With a per capita income similar to the rest of the country, with institutional arrangements and racial policies much the same as those in the nation as a whole, and with rapid and inexpensive transportation linking it with the rest of the country, the South is losing its regional peculiarities. Southerners, like people elsewhere, will no doubt continue to have special attachments to their communities, perhaps even their states. But the South as an utterly distinctive region with its own sense of nationhood—the South of the old evils and the old romance—is already disappearing, and becoming one with the nation as a whole.

NOTES

1. *The Rise and Decline of Nations: Economic Growth, Stagflation, and Social Rigidities.* New Haven: Yale University Press, 1982.

2. *Ibid.,* pp. 94–117.

3. *Ibid.,* pp. 102–108.

4. Charles R. Hulten and Robert M. Schwab, "Regional Growth in U.S. Manufacturing, 1951–1978," *American Economic Review,* vol. 74 (1984), pp. 152–62.

5. The pertinence of other aspects of the Hulten-Schwab estimates to the present argument will be apparent if we first reflect briefly about the patterns of productivity of different factors of production that might be expected in different circumstances. If the disproportionate postwar growth of southern manufacturing were due to innovations that occurred only in the South, or to some shift in the pattern of demand that favored industries in which the South had a comparative advantage, this should be reflected in a more rapid growth of total factor productivity for a time in the South; the new technology or pattern of demand would make southern resources produce a larger quantity of output or more valuable outputs than before and should raise the productivity of southern factors of production, at least until such time as resources from outside migrated into the region and diminishing returns set in. The growth in total factor productivity outside the South would also tend for a time to be slower than in the South. If the innovations or changes in demands favored labor-intensive products or activities, the wages of labor would rise in the South relative to the North until a new equilibrium emerged; if the changes by contrast favored capital, the returns to capital in the South would increase disproportionately.

Hulten and Schwab did not find any tendency for total factor productivity to increase faster in the South or other rapidly growing regions than in the Northeast and older Middle West. This seems puzzling, but it is consistent with the model offered here. To see this, consider how the firms that had to pay supra-competitive wages in the cartelized and declining regions could survive in the long run. Firms in the rapidly growing regions could get labor at lower cost, and capital is available at approximately the same cost in all regions of the country. If the argument offered here is correct, some of these firms could not survive, or could not survive unless they too moved to the low wage areas, and there were of course both firms that failed and firms that migrated from the high-wage to the low-wage regions. But firms in the Northeast and older Middle

West that had been enjoying sufficient rents could survive. If these rents grew out of proximity to natural resources or markets or other location-specific advantages, the firms also would be constrained from moving to the South or to other growing regions. This leads to the prediction that the diminished share of the nation's manufacturing that both survived and remained in the Northeast and older Middle West had something else going for it—it was productive enough to sustain itself even with higher wages. The demise or migration of less productive establishments to the growing regions would raise total factor productivity in the declining regions as only firms with higher productivity remained.

As Hulten and Schwab found, total factor productivity grew at the same rate in the declining as in the expanding regions. Partly this was due to the high and increasing marginal productivity of labor in the declining regions, which must be higher than in other regions simply because high and increasing wage rates insure that profit-maximizing employers continue limiting the employment of labor until the marginal product of labor rises enough to equal the wage. (Inefficient work rules due to bargaining costs in the cartelized industries will diminish the rate at which the marginal productivity of labor schedule shifts up as technological progress occurs, but I assume that this is not enough to offset the effect of the wage differential on marginal productivity.) In part, I hypothesize, the similar rate of growth of total factor productivity in the declining and expanding regions was due to the higher productivity that must typify firms or activities that continue in their customary locations when their labor costs are higher and their capital costs no less than those of competing firms in other regions. As I argued above, if the growth of the South and comparable regions had been due to local innovations or to shifts in the pattern of demand that favored southern firms, total factor productivity would have tended to have grown more rapidly than in the Northeast and the older Middle West.

The tendency of labor to migrate in the opposite direction from that suggested by wage differentials and the high level of labor productivity and total factor productivity in the declining regions are then both consistent with the argument offered here.

6. Calvin B. Hoover and B. U. Ratchford, *Economic Resources and Policies of the South*. New York: Macmillan, 1951. Pp. 78–85.

7. Chapel Hill: University of North Carolina Press, 1960: Nicholls's address was entitled "Southern Tradition and Regional Economic Progress," and is in *The Southern Economic Journal*, January 1960, 187–98. For interesting arguments that minimize the significance of Nicholls's thesis, see William Laird and James Rinehart, "Exogenous Checks on Southern Development," *South Atlantic Quarterly*, vol. 65 (1966), pp. 491–508; "Post-Civil War South and the Great Depression: A Suggested Parallel," *Mid-America*, vol. 48 (1966), pp. 206–20; and "Deflation, Agriculture, and Southern Development," *Agricultural History*, vol. 42 (1968), pp. 115–24.

8. Third Rev. Edition, New York: Oxford University Press, 1974.

9. See J. Morgan Kousser's useful book, *The Shaping of Southern Politics*. New Haven: Yale University Press, 1974.

10. Rowland T. Berthoff, "Southern Attitudes Toward Immigration, 1865–1914." *The Journal of Southern History*, vol. 17 (1951), 328–60.

11. Twelve Southerners, *I'll Take My Stand: The South and the Agrarian Tradition*. New York: Peter Smith, 1951.

12. On the persistence of planter interests and their lack of zeal for policies favorable to industrial development, see Jonathon M. Weiner, *Social Origins of the New South.* Baton Rouge: Lousiana State University Press, 1978. For more recent examples of established business and agrarian interests that were detrimental to economic development, see Abt Associates, *The Southern Rural Areas* (Economic Development Admin., U.S. Dept. of Commerce, 1968), pp. 115–24.

13. Gavin Wright, "The Strange Career of the New Southern Economic History," *Reviews in American History,* vol. 10 (1982), pp. 164–80. I have also been greatly helped by several of Wright's other writings.

14. Baton Rouge: Louisiana State University Press, 1982.

15. Morton Sosna, "More Important than the Civil War?: The Impact of World War II on the South," in James C. Cobb and Charles R. Wilson (eds.), *Perspectives on the American South: An Annual Review of Society, Politics and Culture,* vol. 4 (1987), pp. 145–61.

16. New York: National Bureau of Economic Research, 1951. Pp. 63–111.

17. John W. Kendrick, *Productivity Trends in the United States* (Princeton: Princeton Univ. Press for NBER, 1961), pp. 133–70 and 507–56; John W. Kendrick and Elliot S. Grossman, *Productivity in the United States* (Baltimore: Johns Hopkins Univ. Press, 1980), pp. 31–50.

Suggested Additional Readings

Azfar, Omar. "The Logic of Collective Action." In *The Elgar Companion to Public Choice,* ed. William F. Shughart and Laura Razzolini. Cheltenham, UK: Edward Elgar, 2001.

Chan, Steve. "Growth with Equity: A Test of Olson's Theory for the Asian Pacific-Rim Countries." *Journal of Peace Research* 24 (1987): 135–49.

Dougherty, Keith L. "Public Goods and Private Interests: An Explanation for State Compliance with Federal Requisitions, 1777–1789." In *Public Choice Interpretations of American Economic History,* ed. Jac C. Heckelman, John C. Moorhouse, and Robert Whaples. Boston: Kluwer Academic Press, 1999.

Gray, Virginia, and David Lowery. "Interest Group Politics and Economic Growth in the U.S. States." *American Political Science Review* 82 (1988): 109–31.

Hardin, Russell. *Collective Action.* Baltimore: Johns Hopkins University Press, 1992.

Heckelman, Jac C., and Dennis Coates (eds.). *Collective Choice: Essays in Honor of Mancur Olson.* Berlin: Springer, 2003.

Kwon, Gi Heon. "Retests on the Theory of Collective Action: The Olson and Zeckhauser Model and Its Elaboration." *Economics and Politics* 10 (1998): 37–62.

Mitchell, Robert C. "National Environmental Lobbies and the Apparent Illogic of Collective Action." In *Collective Decision Making: Applications from Public Choice Theory,* ed. Clifford S. Russell. Baltimore: Johns Hopkins University Press, 1979.

Mueller, Dennis C. (ed.). *The Political Economy of Growth.* New Haven, CT: Yale University Press, 1983.

Olson, Mancur. *The Logic of Collective Action.* Cambridge: Harvard University Press, 1965.

———. *The Rise and Decline of Nations.* New Haven, CT: Yale University Press, 1982.

Reisman, David A. *Theories of Collective Action.* New York: St. Martin's Press, 1990.

Stroup, Richard L. "Free Riders and Collective Action Revisited." *Independent Review* 4 (2000): 485–500.

Van Bastelaer, Thierry. "The Political Economy of Food Pricing: An Extended Test of the Interest Group Approach." *Public Choice* 96 (1998): 43–60.

Wade, Robert. "The Management of Common Property Resources: Collective Action as an Alternative to Privatization or State Regulation." *Cambridge Journal of Economics* 11 (1987): 95–106.

Advanced Readings

Chamberlin, John R. "A Diagrammatic Exposition of the Logic of Collective Action." *Public Choice* 26 (1976): 59–74.

Quiggin, John. "Testing the Implications of the Olson Hypothesis." *Economica* 59 (1992): 261–77.

Sandler, Todd. *Collective Action: Theory and Applications.* Ann Arbor: University of Michigan Press, 1992.

Sandler, Todd, and Keith Hartley. "Economics of Alliances: The Lessons for Collective Action." *Journal of Economic Literature* 39 (2001): 869–96.

Stigler, George J. "Free Riders and Collective Action: An Appendix to Theories of Economic Regulation." *Bell Journal of Economics* 5 (1974): 359–65.

Bureaucracy

The alternative to private market production is production by the government. While firms are expected to behave in a profit-maximizing way, the government is not. This raises the question as to what the government's objective function looks like. We might expect government officials to directly pursue social efficiency, thereby escaping perceived private market failures. This means the size of the budget, paid for through taxes, should be just equal to the total costs at the optimal level of production. Even if legislation is drafted requiring the socially efficient level of some product to be produced, there are reasons to suspect it still will not occur.

Firm owners pursue profits because they retain the profits themselves. The net benefits to public production, though, are kept by the consumer-taxpayer citizens. Public choice models typically suggest the same motivation characterizes bureaucratic incentives as for private incentives: that is, the desire to capture as much of the net benefits as possible. Specifically, one model posits that bureaucrats attempt to maximize the size of their budget. Heads of bureaus prefer having larger budgets to work with, rather than smaller budgets.

One problem elected government officials face is determining the socially optimal level of output. This point occurs where the marginal social benefit is just equal to the marginal social cost, because the benefit from additional production does not justify the added costs. The legislators are not likely to have good information on either dimension and may rely on the experts in charge of carrying out government production and services. If the bureaucrats' goals differ from the legislators', the principal agent problem inherent in many forms of organization may be present. Bureaucrats can use their informational advantage to fool the legislature into sponsoring a higher budget than it otherwise would.

First, bureaucrats may attempt to make the case that the benefits they produce are larger than generally perceived. This can be done either through direct lobbying of the legislators or by "educating" the general public into demanding more. Second, they can attempt to inflate their costs.

A legislator interested in social efficiency would never allocate a budget larger than the social benefits. Thus the largest budget attainable would be equal to the maximum social benefits. The legislature in return, though, would expect a large output to justify such a budget. For directly measurable output, such as highway miles constructed or number of clients served by the public defender's office, the goals might not be able to be met given the true cost structure. Thus cost information would need to be manipulated in such a way as to require not as great a level of output (and corresponding budget). For services that are not tangible or are in some way difficult to directly measure, such as public safety or quality of service, the legislature would not as easily be able to determine if the goals have been met or not, which allows more flexibility for the bureau to attain the greatest budget possible. In either case, output exceeds socially efficient levels; the only question is by how much. Taxes are imposed that are necessary to fund the bureaucracy, but at a greater than optimal size.

An alternative strategy for the bureau to pursue would be focusing not on the size of the budget itself but rather on the size of the discretionary budget, that is, attaining a budget larger than necessary for the output that is required. The surplus budget can then be spent on the bureau chief's personal desires, such as unnecessary trips, glamorous offices, or a bloated workforce to direct. Bureaucratic output may be optimal, but again taxes are assessed at a higher than necessary level.

There are several potential ways out of this dilemma. One involves greater oversight of the bureau to better estimate the true costs. Oversight itself has social costs that somewhat limit the net benefits to this approach. Alternatively, competition itself can reveal costs and limit the bureau's ability to take advantage of its informational advantage since its monopoly position is eliminated. However, competition among bureaus involves redundancy and other potentially negative consequences as bureaus come to see other agencies as competitors. Private markets can exist along with the governmental service.

In the extreme, privatizing public services eliminates public bureaucracies altogether but potentially leads back to private market failures. Where both private firms and bureaucratic production exist, it is possible to compare the two to determine the relative degree of inefficiencies. Predominantly, studies suggest public production is more inefficient, entailing greater costs for comparable output. This lends credence to the notion of privatization as a way to reduce social inefficiency.

Blais and Dion survey the theoretical literature on bureaucracies and review the empirical evidence in "Are Bureaucrats Budget Maximizers? The Niskanen Model and Its Critics." Breton and Wintrobe's "The Equilibrium Size of a Budget-Maximizing Bureau: A Note on Niskanen's Theory of Bureaucracy" provides an early important extension to the basic model in which there is oversight of the bureau but the monitoring is not costless, in which case the socially optimal degree of oversight is where marginal benefit equals marginal cost. The implication then is that bureau size will fall in between the socially optimal size and the size resulting from an unmonitored, pure budget-maximizing bureau.

Are Bureaucrats Budget Maximizers?
The Niskanen Model and Its Critics

André Blais & Stéphane Dion

Review Questions

1. Why would a bureaucrat seek to maximize the agency's budget? What might be some alternative goals?
2. What is the evidence for each assumption or implication of the bureaucratic model? Which tests are more persuasive?
3. Why don't the bureau sponsors limit the budgets they give to the bureaus? What are the arguments against this idea?
4. Why might a bureau maintain an informational advantage over its sponsor? How can the sponsor overcome this hurdle?

The public choice model is distinguished from other models in public administration in its view of civil servants, called bureaucrats, as biased in favor of their own sector, the public sector. This incisive argument has made the model one of the most debated in the field. The major book written from this perspective is William Niskanen's *Bureaucracy and Representative Govern-*

Blais, André and Stéphane Dion. "Are Bureaucrats Budget Maximizers? The Niskanen Model and Its Critics." *Polity* 22 (1990): 655–74.

ment.[1] Authored by a former bureaucrat and immediately acclaimed as a breakthrough, the book provides the economic theory of bureaucracy with its key concept: the budget-maximizing bureaucrat. We accept the Niskanen model as an important one and believe that it is time for a comprehensive assessment of its merits and limits. To this end, we will summarize the model, review the debate around it, and assess the empirical evidence relevant to the major propositions of the model. Our analysis is presented in two sections, corresponding to the two central hypotheses of the model: that bureaucrats *attempt to* and that they *succeed* in maximizing their budgets.

I. Do Bureaucrats Attempt to Maximize Their Budgets?

The Model

The bureaucrat is assumed to maximize his utility. This utility is derived from rationality and survival arguments. Niskanen lists a certain number of variables that enter the bureaucrat's utility function: salary, perquisites, reputation, power, patronage, output, ease of making changes, and ease of managing the bureau. He argues that all these variables, except the last two, are a positive monotonic function of the total budget. The bureaucrat also maximizes his budget in order to survive. Niskanen contends that the bureaucrat's tenure depends critically on the employees of the bureau. They influence his tenure through the performance of the bureau, as they can be more or less cooperative and efficient. Their own interest in a larger budget is similar to that of the bureaucrat: greater opportunities for promotion, more job security, etc.

The Critique

Two major objections have been raised against the budget-maximizing utility hypothesis. The first is that the bureaucrat is not motivated primarily by his personal interests; the second questions the link between the budget and the bureaucrat's personal interest.

THE BUREAUCRAT AND THE PUBLIC INTEREST

Maurice Kogan[2] and Julius Margolis[3] contend that the Niskanen model is seriously flawed because the senior bureaucrat is a different type of human being than the one assumed in *Bureaucracy and Representative Government*. In this view, the typical bureaucrat is a professional deeply committed to the task he is performing and pursues primarily what he perceives to be the public interest.

Niskanen acknowledges that some bureaucrats "undoubtedly try to serve (their perception of) the public interest."[4] Yet, he argues, the concept of public interest is a fuzzy one and is likely to be defined subjectively. The bureaucrat will tend to give greater weight to his narrow field of expertise. The bureaucrat committed to a mission will therefore give higher priority to his own field and attempt to maximize his budget in a way that is consistent with his partial view of the public interest. Moreover, a bureaucrat who does not wish to maximize his budget may be driven to do just that in order to survive: "The nature of a bureaucrat's relations with both the bureau's employees and sponsor are such that bureaucrats who do not maximize their budget will have an unusually short tenure."[5]

It would seem unreasonable to argue that bureaucrats are not concerned with their own personal material interest. Indeed, some data clearly indicate that they have such concerns: for instance, when the relative wage in the public sector increases, the queue for public sector jobs gets longer; and when the wage decreases, the queue gets shorter.[6] The basic question is not whether the bureaucrat is egocentric or altruistic since the issue so defined becomes intractable (how are we to measure egocentrism and altruism?). The Niskanen model predicts that the bureaucrat's personal utility is a function of the budget and that bureaucrats attempt to maximize their budgets. These are testable propositions that can be dealt with whatever one's view of the deeper motivations of bureaucrats.

THE BUREAUCRAT'S INTERESTS AND BUDGETS

The proposition that it is in the bureaucrat's interest to maximize budgets has been widely debated. It is argued either that the bureaucrat's maximand is something else or that interests are extremely varied so that budget maximization cannot be considered as the central motive of the whole bureaucracy.

Before considering these two objections, the logic of the proposition needs to be clarified. The hypothesis can be put in static or dynamic terms. The static hypothesis is that bureaucrats are better off in large-budget bureaus than in small-budget ones. The dynamic hypothesis is that bureaucrats are better off in rapidly growing bureaus than in slower growing or declining ones. This key distinction is not made in any consistent way by Niskanen nor by his critics and that is unfortunate as it introduces confusion in the debate.

The literature has dealt mainly with the static hypothesis. Albert Breton and Donald Wintrobe note that in the Canadian government, "the salaries (and also, one observes, the power and prestige) of senior bureaucrats in the Department of Finance and the Treasury Board are higher than those of their counterparts in other larger bureaus such as Health and Welfare."[7] The objection is valid. The size of a bureau is not the sole or even the most crucial factor in the bureaucratic utility function. In our view, however, the dynamic hypothesis—that bureaucrats gain from increased budgets—is the more interesting proposition. This is the hypothesis that will be discussed in the remainder of this essay.

The most direct challenge to the Niskanen model is the one that proposes substitutes to the budget as the bureaucrat's maximand. One such challenge is the view that bureaucrats are more concerned with security and stability than with trying to maximize budget increases. Guy Peters[8] argues for a more satisfactory model of bureaucratic politics in which the major objective is the preservation of the status quo and the prime value to be maximized is security. Peters acknowledges, however, that some budget maximization takes place: "In general, we can expect agencies to attempt to get as large a share of the budgetary pie as possible."[9] The bureaucrat may well be too prudent a person to be totally committed to budget maximization, but that should not prevent him from trying to obtain substantial budget increases, and there are likely to be some less risk-aversive individuals who will aim for very large increases. Moreover, budgetary cuts are probably perceived as the worst outcome and the bureaucrat will do his best to prevent or resist them. In short, bureaucrats attempt to maximize both budgets and stability. Their strategy might be more appropriately labeled budget "maximin." That strategy, however, entails requesting substantial budget increases.

Jean-Luc Migué and Gérard Bélanger[10] suggest that bureaucrats are primarily concerned with managerial discretion and that it is therefore the discretionary budget that is being maximized. They point out, however, that discretionary resources depend on a large budget. Their model departs from Niskanen's in predicting that budget increases will be allocated to inefficient production rather than to overproduction. Later on, Niskanen[11] admits that a higher budget may lead to either output or slack, but that is in some sense irrelevant. In both cases, it is in the bureaucrat's interest to get a higher budget.

The most frequent criticism of the Niskanen model is that bureaucratic interests are essentially heterogeneous and that budget maximization is only one of many strategies pursued. This position is developed by Breton and Wintrobe, who note that many objectives have been imputed to bureaucrats (size, budgets, discretion, prestige, self-preservation, security, secrecy, leisure, patronage). They argue that "one cannot build a generally applicable theory of bureaucracy on a specific objective function."[12] That bureaucrats have many motivations is hardly disputable. The point is acknowledged by Niskanen, who contends however that most of these objectives are dependent on a higher budget.[13] It is not enough, therefore, to point out the great variety of bureaucratic motivations; it has to be shown also that these other motivations do not require higher budgets.

A similar though more nuanced and carefully drafted argument is made by Patrick Dunleavy.[14] He develops six propositions, each of which points out a potential flaw in the Niskanen model. His first four propositions can be considered as amendments to the budget-maximizing model. Dunleavy suggests that the link between the bureaucrat's utilities and the budget varies across agencies, ranks, and components of the budget and is probably non-monotonic, i.e., bureaucrats maximize budgets up to an optimal level. There is undoubtedly much validity in each of these points, but their relevance, we contend, is of limited value, as they do not question the existence of a positive relationship, on the whole, between bureaucratic interests and an increased budget.

Dunleavy then goes on to argue that top bureaucrats are more concerned with the intrinsic character of their work than with pecuniary considerations and hence focus on a "bureau-shaping strategy designed to bring their bureau into a progressively closer approximation to 'staff' (rather than 'line') functions, a collegial atmosphere and a central location."[15] It may be so. This, however, does not affect the Niskanen survival argument, since bureaucrats at the bottom are still motivated by pecuniary considerations and "a bureaucrat's life is not a happy one . . . unless he can provide increasing budgets for his subordinate bureaucrats."[16] Moreover, the bureau-shaping strategy implies increased budgets. Bureaus "may want to export troublesome and costly low-grade tasks to rivals" but they "always defend the scope of responsibilities."[17] The strategy calls for the government to take on new "important" mandates which inevitably require a larger budget.

Finally, according to Dunleavy, the biggest blow to the Niskanen model pertains to the form of state growth: "If bureaucrats maximize budgets then state growth should have produced a progressive expansion of large bureaucracies—in fact, a rare pattern in liberal democracies."[18] The argument is not compelling once it is acknowledged that bureaucratic utility is related not to a large budget (the static Niskanen proposition) but to an increased one (the dynamic proposition) and that the bureaucrat's interest is well served by organizational change. The latter point is documented by Meyer, et al. They show, in their study of municipal agencies having finance functions in Chicago, Detroit, and Philadelphia, that "for each new department added (or lost), the size of the city finance function increases (or decreases) 10.6 percent beyond the normal rate of growth."[19] The fragmentation of the state may well favor increased budgets for each bureaucratic responsibility.

In short, Dunleavy provides compelling reasons to believe that the budget-maximizing strategy is not an all-encompassing one, that it is less pervasive in some contexts than in others. It is possible, however, to agree with many of his points and still to contend that budget-maximization is a crucial aspect of bureaucratic behavior.

How can we tell whether this is the case or not? What is the empirical evidence on this question? The model predicts that bureaucrats *want* and *benefit* from increased budgets. The first is easier to test. With top bureaucrats, one may examine their behavior and attitudes, the simplest and most straightforward test of which is to determine whether they request substantial budget increases. Surprisingly, we do not have much information on this simple fact. Aaron Wildavsky notes that "it is usually correct to assume that department officials are devoted to increasing their appropriation."[20] This observation is of course consistent with the Niskanen model. Unfortunately, the many studies which have dealt with budget requests and appropriations[21] do not report what is probably the most crucial data, which is the average increase requested. There is one interesting exception. Lance Leloup and William Moreland[22] analyzed 500 cases of appropriation requests for the 36 agencies of the U.S. Department of Agriculture that were in existence for at least three years between 1941 and 1971. They report that the mean request is for a 41 percent increase. This is strong support for the Niskanen model. Bureaucratic attitudes can also be surveyed. Lee Sigelman[23] reports that the median response of high-level state administrators to questions about whether and how much the "level of programs, services and expenditures provided by their agency should be expanded and increased" is a 10–14 percent growth. Sigelman interprets that figure as indicating that bureaucratic support for truly major expansion is not extremely widespread. We believe it is more significant that 80 percent do want some expansion and that, among the four degrees of expansion suggested in the questionnaire (0–4, 5–9, 10–14, 15 +), the modal response is the fourth and the median the third. Bureaucrats are reasonable persons who do not want to appear overly demanding, but they do want larger budgets.

The Niskanen model also predicts that bureaucrats of all ranks will be more favorable to the growth of the state and will tend to support parties which favor greater state intervention. These predictions, it should be pointed out, are not related as directly to the model as those we just reviewed. Bureaucrats may be concerned solely with the budget of their own bureaus rather than with the overall budget. Still, one may suppose that the greater the increase in the total budget the better the chances are that a given bureau will obtain a large increase. We should thus expect differences in the political behavior and attitudes of public and private sector employees. The empirical evidence shows that there is a public/private sector cleavage of the type predicted by the Niskanen model, but the cleavage is a weak one: public sector employees are more likely to support parties of the left and to endorse state intervention.[24]

The Niskanen model, finally, assumes that bureaucrats benefit from increased budgets. Christopher Hood, et al.,[25] examine the assumption, and point out that the substantial increase in government spending in Britain between 1971 and 1982 did not lead to staff or pay increases over that period. They also show that the increase in a department's share of central government budget is not necessarily associated with an increase in the share of total staff or civil service chiefs. They conclude that the budget utility model cannot be dismissed entirely but that the link between budgetary increases and bureaucratic utility is not universally applicable.

This is a most interesting study. The fact that the growth in government spending did not lead to an increase in staff or pay tends to invalidate the theory. Staff and pay are, however, affected by many other factors (education, productivity, party in power) besides the bureaucratic drive assumed by Niskanen, and these other factors should be controlled for when it comes to establishing the independent impact of budget increases. What is needed is a systematic analysis of the determinants of public sector salaries and of the specific effect of government growth on these salaries.

But it is clearly the more disaggregated aspect of the analysis, that dealing with departments, which is crucial. Hood, et al., examine ten departments and look at the correlations over the 1971–1982 period between share of central government budget, on the one hand, and share of total staff and total "chiefs," on the other. Of the 20 correlations resulting from the analysis, ten are positive and statistically significant, thus confirming the Niskanen model. The authors do not report other correlations but do say that they are not statistically significant. This is unfortunate. Because the analysis is based on very few cases (12 years), it is quite difficult to get any significant result (in fact correlations must be equal to or higher than .6), and it would be more appropriate to consider the general pattern (what is the proportion of positive correlations?). What we know is that the median correlation is close to .6 and in our view, this should be construed as supporting the Niskanen model.

Burke Grandjean examined the evolution of salaries for a sample of white-collar U.S. federal employees from 1963 to 1977. He finds that "the steadily growing agencies . . . enjoyed a fairly consistent salary advantage."[26] He concludes that the hypothesis that organizational growth creates opportunities for career advancement is incomplete, as it cannot account for the pattern observed in some specific agencies, but it is useful.[27] This is again consistent with the Niskanen model.

A central proposition of the Niskanen model is that bureaucrats want and benefit from increased budgets. From this proposition can be derived testable hypotheses. Unfortunately the actual empirical tests are rare. The few results available, however, tend to vindicate the model. It seems that agencies request substantial budget increases. In surveys, senior public administrators express a desire for a moderate expansion of their programs. Public sector employees are slightly more likely to be favorable to the growth of the state and to support parties of the left than their private sector counterparts. Finally, bureaus that obtain a larger share of the total budget tend to increase their share of staff and chiefs, and bureaucrats in steadily growing agencies enjoy larger salary increases. The evidence is still rather thin and we need many more tests of these propositions. It is also likely that bureaucrats attempt merely to increase, rather than maximize, their budget. All in all, however, the basic idea that bureaucrats want increased budgets looks plausible.

II. Do Bureaucrats Succeed in Maximizing Their Budgets?

The Model

Niskanen assumes not only that bureaucrats adopt budget-maximizing strategies but also that their strategies succeed. This second assumption raises the whole question of the power of bureaucrats and, more specifically, of the relationship between the bureau and its sponsor. The officers of the sponsor organization "review the bureau's proposed activities and budget, approve the budget, monitor the methods and performance of the bureau and, usually, approve the appointment of the bureau head."[28] It has the authority to block the bureau's budget-maximizing strategy. Niskanen believes that it does not exercise that authority and is therefore a basically passive actor for two reasons.

First, the sponsor lacks the incentive to use its political power. Secondly, even if and when it has the incentive, it does not have the capacity because of a lack of information.

The first argument is that the sponsor does not have much incentive to resist bureaucratic demands for increased budgets. The officers of the sponsor organization cannot "appropriate as personal income part of the difference between the budget they would be willing to grant and the budget they in fact do grant to the bureau,"[29] because the organization is not a profit-seeking one. Politicians, for their part, are mainly concerned with reelection. That motivation is likely to be "only weakly related to the total net benefits generated by the services financed by the organization."[30] Furthermore, they will pay greater attention to those bureaus whose services they find more important. This division of labor supports bureaucratic demands. Ministers will attempt to maximize their department's budget. Parliamentary committees will be made out of those legislators most favorable to a bureau's output.

Niskanen acknowledges that the bureau and the sponsor have conflicting interests: the latter, for instance, "prefers that the output be efficiently produced."[31] He hastens to add, however, that politicians have time constraints, pay greater attention to outputs they want to be increased, and just hope that others will watch over budgetary restraint.

The second argument is that the sponsor is handicapped by a lack of information. One difficulty stems from the bureau's monopsonistic position. The absence of competition prevents the sponsor from determining the most efficient production processes. The bureaucrat, for his part, has precise information about the sponsor "from previous budget reviews, recent changes in the composition of the sponsor organization, and recent constituent influences on these officers."[32] He knows more about production processes than do the officers of the sponsor organization. As a consequence, it is easier for the bureaucrat to exploit his position as a monopoly supplier than it is for the sponsor to exploit its position as a monopoly buyer.

The Critique

Niskanen's assumption of a passive sponsor is an extreme one. The basic idea is that the sponsor usually lacks the motivation and the capacity to resist the bureau's demand for an increased budget so that the bilateral monopoly relationship is tilted to the advantage of the bureau. The objections to the model can be distinguished as to whether they address the sponsor's motivation or his capacity to control the budget.

THE SPONSOR'S MOTIVATION

It has been argued that Niskanen's view of the budgetary process is myopic, that it does not take into account the fact that American institutional arrangements are specific to that country.[33] He seems to assume, for instance, the presence of strong independent legislative committees and the absence of a unified executive. Certainly this assumption does not make sense outside the U.S. Even with respect to the U.S., Niskanen is silent about the role of the President, who is not faced with the free rider effect that may afflict legislators, and who does care about the size of the total budget.[34]

That the model suffers from a narrow American perspective is indisputable. Indeed, the American executive is weaker than the executive in parliamentary democracies and the processes and strategies described in *Bureaucracy and Representative Government* may therefore be less pervasive in other nations. Yet, there are good reasons to believe that the same pattern prevails everywhere. In cabinets, most ministers are likely to defend *their* budget. As one of them admits candidly, "ministers are judged by how much money they can spend and how well they can extract money from the system for their projects."[35]

Everywhere, however, top decision makers (presidents, prime ministers, finance ministers, chairmen of the treasury board, their political and administrative staffs) have to adopt a broader perspective and will be induced to resist bureaucratic demands. Their absence in the Niskanen model should be reckoned as a major failure. Yet that absence does not invalidate the whole argument. The willingness to control is concentrated in a small group and that group is faced with a battery of demands for larger budgets.

It has also been suggested that the Niskanen model is predicated on a pattern that was dominant in the period in which it was written but may not be applicable to other times.[36] During that period, heavily influenced by the Keynesian doctrine, bureaus dealt with sponsors inclined to believe that "the money was always there" and that "the State was the universal provider."[37] Since then, of course, the Keynesian orthodoxy has been shivered and some parties have been elected on an anti-state platform. This new state of affairs corresponds to Niskanen's normative preferences but does not fit well with his model.

How can we tell whether the motivations ascribed to politicians by the Niskanen model are valid? It seems to us that the basic approach should be the same as that followed with respect to bureaucratic strategies. The model raises a crucial question: Do politicians want and benefit from increased budgets? In other words, do they have a particular ideology or interest with respect to the budget? Let us deal first with ideology. To the extent that people tend to seek jobs in areas they perceive to be interesting and important, those more favorably disposed toward the state would feel more attracted to a career in politics. There is some support for that proposition. Herbert McClosky and John Zaller[38] report that in the U.S., the elite, including politicians, even though it is divided along party lines, is twice as likely as the general public to express strong support for the welfare state. This suggests that politicians tend to have a more positive view of the state than the mass public and that they may be less motivated to resist bureaucratic demands for increased budgets.

The politicians' interest with regard to the size of the budget is more ambiguous. On the one hand, politicians, like bureaucrats, gain from an increased budget: the larger the budget, the more powerful they can be, the higher their salaries and perquisites.[39] On the other hand, they can be hurt by the tax increases that larger budgets may entail. Niskanen himself has presented evidence that "a 10% increase in real per capita tax revenues appears to reduce the popular vote for the candidate of the incumbent party by around 1.4% of the total vote."[40] Neither Gerald Pomper[41] nor Bruno Frey,[42] however, finds any correlation between expenditures or taxation and electoral results or government popularity. The evidence is therefore unclear on this question and more research is needed on the consequences of spending and tax increases on the popularity of governments. As the empirical findings are inconsistent, we are inclined to infer that politicians have some motivation, albeit not a strong one, not to increase taxes. Their strategy will be one of maximizing revenue while minimizing political costs,[43] i.e., of relying on buoyant taxes which have high income or inflation elasticities and can generate greater revenues without tax rate or base increases. That strategy is different from the one assumed by Niskanen, but the outcome is similar. Politicians will try to accommodate bureaucratic demands, but only to the extent that they do not entail tax increases. As a consequence, budget increases will be modest and incremental, much less substantial than the Niskanen model leads us to believe. But increases are still what the game is about.

Niskanen argues that politicians are not strongly motivated to resist bureaucratic demands. He fails to take into account top decision makers, some of whom will fiercely oppose the budget-maximizing strategy. Bureaucrats and politicians, moreover, do have conflicting interests. Politicians want increased outputs and improved efficiency and are reluctant to increase taxes, whereas bureaucrats are more concerned with the intrinsic character of their work, power, salaries, and perquisites. These conflicting interests act as constraints on bureaucratic influence. This being said, governments deeply concerned with budgetary restraint are likely to be the exception rather than the rule.

THE SPONSOR'S CAPACITY

According to Niskanen, the major factor responsible for the sponsor's incapacity to control the bureau is lack of information. The sponsor lacks the necessary information that would enable it to assess the bureau's performance. The absence of profit deprives it of a precise criterion for evaluation that is available in the private sector. The absence of competition deprives it of a benchmark, as it is impossible to tell whether the bureau's performance is superior to or inferior to that of other bureaus. Hence the information flux is biased to the advantage of the bureau and to the disadvantage of the sponsor.

It has been argued that Niskanen overstates the bureau's capacity to manipulate information. As L. L. Wade puts it, "there are limits to dissimulation, incompetence and monopoly power."[44] Gary Miller and Terry Moe concede that the bureau has an informational advantage, since "the budgetary process tends to reveal more reliable information to the supplier than to the committee," but they add that "it is much easier for the committee to know what the supplier is maximizing than for the supplier to know what the committee is maximizing, and this gives the committee a strategic advantage."[45] It is indeed difficult to dispute the fact that Niskanen exaggerates the power of bureaucrats, yet we find it revealing that, in the end, Miller and Moe acknowledge that "it is reasonable to think that bureaucrats may have some advantages in the budgetary bargaining game [even though] these advantages are unlikely to be very dramatic."[46]

Jonathan Bendor, et al.,[47] also acknowledge that the bureau has informational advantages but contend that politicians anticipate the bureau's strategic behavior and establish a monitoring system to counteract it. Such monitoring is imperfect but reduces the bureau's deception of the legislature, especially in the case of a risk-averse bureau chief and with respect to perquisites. Furthermore, it may be in the interest of a bureaucrat not to distort information so as to build a good reputation, that reputation being itself a crucial resource for obtaining increased budgets over the long haul. Again, one can hardly disagree with these observations. But it is telling that, in the end, the authors adopt a position not that far from Niskanen's:

"Budgets are supraoptimal . . . the final consumption preferences of bureaucrats matter: they shape how much budget they seek and the output they
produce . . . it is possible for informational asymmetries between politicians
and bureaucrats to persist."[48]

Another point of contention concerns the role of competition. Breton and
Wintrobe assert that "the world of bureaucracy is essentially a world of competition"[49] and that "competition among bureaucrats for positions has a dev-
astating impact on the Niskanen model."[50] This holds, however, only to the
extent that different bureaus can provide the sponsor with the same or substitute products. Moreover, competition among bureaus makes the budget-
maximizing strategy even more compelling. Each bureau anticipates that
other bureaus will request greater resources and that the sponsor will accept
only a fraction of all requests, including its own; it is led to participate in the
struggle for increased budgets.

A final objection is that the monitoring problems with which sponsors are
faced are basically similar in the public and private sector. In the private sector,
one may know the firm's overall profitability but this is of no help in assessing
the contribution of a specific bureau to that profit. In both sectors "performance evaluation is a complex matter involving . . . subjective judgment."[51]
Moreover, there is an adequate measure of overall performance in the public
sector, the equivalent of profits in private firms: government popularity.[52]

It is a useful reminder that things are not as simple and neat in the private
sector as we may be inclined to assume. And indeed there is a great need for
careful comparative analyses of the budgetary process in public and private
organizations. We are unaware of any such study. There are good reasons to
suppose, however, that performance is more difficult to assess in the public
sector, because the outputs of government are more diverse than those of a
private firm and because each output is typically related to many, sometimes
conflicting objectives. Businessmen are quite clear and explicit in stating that
profit is their bottom line. The link between politicians and popularity is a
more ambiguous one.[53]

In short, the critiques of the Niskanen model have failed to undermine
what is one of Niskanen's most interesting and original arguments: in the
bargaining process between the sponsor and the bureau, the latter has an informational edge that is used to further its interest in an increased budget.
The critics have, however, scored a point in challenging the implications of
that advantage. It does not follow that the sponsor is powerless, since it has
the final authority and is quite capable of imposing budgetary cuts however

ill-advised these cuts may be. Of course, the mere fact that the spending limits are more or less arbitrary makes them less appealing to politicians who will use them only as a last resort. The informational edge is an important resource, but it does not confer automatic power.

This raises the question of what concrete empirical hypotheses can be derived from that aspect of the model. If Niskanen's extreme claim that the sponsor is completely passive were true, it follows that the budget would not be affected by the sponsor's characteristics, for it would be determined entirely by bureaucratic demands. The evidence that public spending is related to the partisan composition of government[54] and is influenced by the electoral cycle[55] clearly indicates that politicians exert some control and that, therefore, the extreme claim should be dismissed.

It remains to be clarified how one can empirically demonstrate the power of bureaucrats to obtain increased budgets. The most frequent approach has been to examine the potential link between the size of bureaucracy and the growth of government spending. Other studies have looked at the impact on policy outputs of organizational structure, i.e., its complexity and fragmentation, and/or of the professionalism of the bureaucracy. The results of these studies are mixed; some confirm the Niskanen model,[56] others do not.[57] Many of them, however, are seriously flawed.[58] The basic problem concerns simultaneous causation between government spending and the size and structure of bureaucracy. Until that problem has been solved, these types of studies will remain inconclusive.

Another approach has been to examine the potential implications of the Niskanen model. It has been argued, for instance, that in a bureaucratically-controlled organization, the demand for public services is price elastic, that a dollar of lump-sum aid generates more than a dollar extra expenditure and that lump-sum and matching aid have the same expenditure effect.[59] These predictions have been tested with mixed results,[60] yet these tests are not really persuasive. If bureaucratic power is not complete, which is bound to be the case, these conditions do not necessarily apply. Paul Gary Wyckoff[61] suggests that the best way to gauge the extent of bureaucratic distortion is to compare the price elasticities of voters and government demand through survey and expenditure studies respectively. If bureaucratic power is present, the price elasticity revealed by expenditure data will be greater than elasticity of voter demand. This new test, however, is still unsatisfactory, because the difference in elasticities may result from political as well as bureaucratic distortion.

Given the difficulty of the task, there is a need for good qualitative studies on the role of bureaucrats in the budgetary process. The most fruitful case studies, when it comes to testing that aspect of the model, would be those looking at situations where politicians and bureaucrats have clearly opposite objectives, such as the coming to power of a government committed to reducing government spending.

Conservative governments, therefore, provide a critical test of the Niskanen model. The leaders of conservative governments are usually convinced that the bureaucrat is a budget-maximizer, and they are determined to reward budget-minimizing bureaucrats. The Niskanen model predicts that these governments will fail to implement a policy aimed at undermining bureaucratic influence and reducing budgets. The model also predicts that the few bureaucrats who play the budget-minimizing game will be rejected and despised by the bulk of the bureaucracy, which will identify them as close allies of the party in power.

The most interesting study from this perspective is the one by Christopher Hood, et al.,[62] of the Fraser and Thatcher governments in Australia and the United Kingdom. They first show that spending as a proportion of Gross Domestic Product remained about constant under these two governments. This, of course, tends to support the Niskanen model. One should take into account, however, the fact that government expenditure and revenues have increased much more in other countries during the same period (the mean percentage increase in tax revenues in OECD countries is 3.1 percent over the 1976–1983 period and 3.9 percent over the 1979–1986 period).[63] Conservative governments have managed to stop budget increases. They have also made substantial cuts in many areas: in its first five years, the Thatcher government reduced spending in about one-third of the departments. Moreover, the budgetary changes made by these two governments reflect their ideological preferences: "both governments increased real spending on defense and law and order, and both governments singled out housing programs for heavy real spending cuts."[64] Clearly, governments strongly determined to reduce the size of the state are able to cut spending in some crucial areas.

The success of conservative government in cutting back the size of the bureaucracy is even more spectacular. Hood, et al. report that the ratio of civil servants in relation to the population has declined by 19 percent and 13 percent under the Thatcher and Fraser administrations.[65] Furthermore, it was the topmost ranks in the bureaucracies which suffered the greatest proportionate cutbacks. The recent experience of conservative governments, therefore, demonstrates that governments with strong convictions are quite able to resist bureaucratic requests for budget increases. There is, however, a political cost involved. Attempts to cut spending and staff are vehemently denounced by the bureaucracy and public sector unions. Conservative governments thus run the risk of having to work with a hostile bureaucracy short on loyalty to its political master and not motivated to improve its productivity.[66] As a consequence of bureaucratic resistance, as well as other factors, these governments only partially achieve their objective of rolling back the state.

Niskanen's assumption about the sponsor's incapacity to control bureaucrats is the weakest link in his whole argument. The extreme view that the sponsor is completely passive is simply wrong. Studies on the impact of parties on public expenditure have shown that politicians make a difference and thus are far from being passive. The success of recent conservative governments in cutting the size of the budget and of the bureaucracy is a clear sign that politicians committed to reducing government spending have the ability to do so. This, however, does not at all imply that bureaucrats do not have an informational edge in the budgetary process and that they do not have some political leverage.

III. Conclusion

Great ideas stimulate great debates. The debate on the Niskanen model is a rich one, as objections have been raised about each of its major arguments. Great ideas are not necessarily true, however, and it is imperative to confront Niskanen's ideas with hard data in order to assess their usefulness. This is why we believe it is important to review the empirical evidence on the model and to point out its major merits and limits in light of the empirical findings.

Though the debate on the model is a wide-ranging one, there have been relatively few studies designed to test its hypotheses. This is a most unfortunate state of affairs. As a consequence, it would be inappropriate to come to any firm conclusion on the validity of the model. It is possible, however, to offer a tentative assessment, especially if, as has been done here, one takes into account the findings of studies on bureaucrats and/or budgets, which are directly relevant to the Niskanen model without necessarily being inspired by it.

Our review of the available evidence suggests the following. First, the idea that bureaucrats want increased budgets appears eminently credible. Second, the hypothesis that bureaucrats benefit from increased budgets also seems to be confirmed, though the evidence on this is still thin. Third, politicians are not as passive as they are depicted in the model. Niskanen is probably right to assume that few governments are deeply concerned with budgetary restraint; they are, however, reluctant to raise taxes and will try to accommodate only those bureaucratic requests that do not require tax increases. Finally, even though bureaucrats enjoy an informational edge in the budgetary process, governments strongly committed to reducing spending are quite capable of doing so.

What does this tell us about the overall usefulness of the model? One might argue that the evidence supports a budget-boosting strategy but not a budget-maximizing one, that it refutes the assumption of a passive sponsor and that the model therefore should be rejected. This is not our position. The available evidence shows that the basic strategy of budget increases imputed to bureaucrats is credible. Furthermore, even though the idea of a passive sponsor must be dismissed, there is evidence that bureaucrats exercise substantial influence, as governments are usually not strongly motivated to resist bureaucratic requests and do not have precise information to assess these requests. What we know about budgets and bureaucrats suggests that there is a kernel of truth in the budget-maximizing bureaucrat model and that it would be unwise at this stage to reject it.

What we need, however, is less in the way of theoretical or ideological discussion of the model and much more in the way of systematic testing of its major hypotheses. In particular, we need to know whether senior bureaucrats who obtain substantial budget increases benefit in terms of promotion, staff, etc.; whether politicians are punished when they raise taxes; and how successful governments are when they attempt to tame the bureaucracy. These are important questions that the Niskanen model appropriately signals as crucial areas of inquiry.

NOTES

1. William A. Niskanen, *Bureaucracy and Representative Government* (Chicago: Aldine Atherton, 1971).

2. M. Kogan, "Comment on Niskanen Bureaucracy," in *Bureaucracy: Servant or Master?* ed. William A. Niskanen (London: Institute of Economic Affairs, 1973).

3. Julius Margolis, "Comment on Niskanen 'Bureaucrats and Politicians,'" *Journal of Law and Economics,* 18 (December 1975): 645–59.

4. Niskanen, *Bureaucracy,* p. 39.

5. Ibid., p. 41.

6. Alan B. Krueger, "The determinants of queues for federal jobs," *Industrial and Labor Relations Review,* 41 (July 1988): 567–81.

7. Albert Breton and Donald Wintrobe, "The Equilibrium Size of a Budget-Maximizing Bureau: A Note on Niskanen's Theory of Bureaucracy," *Journal of Political Economy,* 83 (February 1975): 204.

8. Guy Peters, *The Politics of Bureaucracy: A Comparative Perspective* (New York: Longman, 1978), p. 175.

9. Ibid., p. 174.

10. Jean-Luc Migué and Gérard Bélanger, "Towards a General Theory of Managerial Discretion," *Public Choice*, 17 (1974): 24–43.

11. William A. Niskanen, "Bureaucrats and Politicians," *Journal of Law and Economics*, 18 (December 1975): 617–44.

12. Albert Breton and Donald Wintrobe, *The Logic of Bureaucratic Conduct* (New York: Cambridge University Press, 1982), p. 27.

13. Niskanen, *Bureaucracy*, p. 38.

14. Patrick Dunleavy, "Bureaucrats, Budgets and the Growth of the State: Reconstructing an Instrumental Model," *British Journal of Political Science*, 15 (July 1985): 299–328.

15. Ibid., p. 322.

16. Niskanen, *Bureaucracy*, p. 40.

17. Dunleavy, "Bureaucrats," p. 323.

18. Ibid., p. 300.

19. Marshall W. Meyer, with William Stevenson and Stephen Webster, *Limits to Bureaucratic Growth* (Berlin: Walter de Gruyter, 1985), p. 177.

20. Aaron Wildavsky, *The Politics of the Budgetary Process* (Boston: Little, Brown, 1964), p. 19.

21. See for instance, Mark C. Kamlet and David Mowery, "Budgeting Side Payments and Government Growth: 1953–1968," *American Journal of Political Science*, 27 (November 1983): 636–64.

22. Lance T. Leloup and William B. Moreland, "Agency Strategies and Executive Review: The Hidden Politics of Budgeting," *Public Administration Review*, 38 (May–June 1978): 232–39.

23. Lee Sigelman, "The Bureaucrat as Budget Maximizer: An Assumption Examined," *Public Budgeting and Finance*, (Spring 1986): 50–59.

24. André Blais and Stéphane Dion, "Les Employés du Secteur Public sont-ils Différents?" *Revue française de science politique*, 37 (février 1987): 76–97; André Blais, Donald Blake, and Stéphane Dion, "The Public-Private Sector Cleavage in North America," *Comparative Political Studies* 23 (1990): 381–404.

25. Christopher Hood, Meg Huby and Andrew Dunsire, "Bureaucrats and Budgeting Benefits: How British Central Departments Measure Up?" *Journal of Public Policy*, 4 (Fall 1984): 163–79.

26. Burke D. Grandjean, "History and Career in a Bureaucratic Labor Market," *American Journal of Sociology*, 86 (March 1981): 1081.

27. Ibid., p. 1088.

28. Niskanen, *Bureaucracy*, p. 24.

29. Ibid., p. 29.

30. Ibid.

31. Ibid., p. 159.

32. Ibid., p. 29.

33. Ronald Rogowski, "Rationalist Theories of Politics: A Midterm Report," *World Politics*, 30 (January 1978): 311.

34. Julius Margolis, "Comment on Niskanen 'Bureaucrats and Politicians,'" *Journal of Law and Economics*, 18 (December 1975): 652.

35. Jean Chrétien, *Straight from the Heart* (Toronto: Key Porter, 1986), p. 72.

36. Breton and Wintrobe, *Logic of Bureaucratic Conduct,* p. 28.

37. Geoffrey Fry, "The British Career Civil Service Under Challenge," *Political Studies,* 34 (December 1986): 542.

38. Herbert McClosky and John Zaller, *The American Ethos: Public Attitudes toward Capitalism and Democracy* (Cambridge, MA: Harvard University Press, 1984).

39. Gary M. Anderson and Robert D. Tollison, "Legislative Monopoly and the Size of Government," *Southern Economic Journal,* 54 (October 1987): 529–46.

40. William A. Niskanen, "Economic and Fiscal Effects on the Popular Vote for the President," in *Public Policy and Public Choice,* ed. Douglas W. Rae and Theodore J. Eismeier (Beverly Hills, CA: Sage, 1979), p. 111.

41. Gerald M. Pomper, *Elections in America* (New York: Dodd, 1978).

42. Bruno Frey, "The Political Business Cycle: Theory and Evidence" in *The Economics of Politics,* ed. W. M. Buchanan, et al. (London: Institute of Economic Affairs, 1978).

43. Richard Rose, "Maximizing Tax Revenue while Minimizing Political Costs," *Journal of Public Policy,* 5 (Fall 1985): 289–320.

44. L. L. Wade, "Public Administration, Public Choice and the Pathos of Reform," *The Review of Politics,* 41 (July 1979): 344–74.

45. Gary Miller and Terry M. Moe, "Bureaucrats, Legislators and the Size of Government," *American Political Science Review,* 77 (June 1983): 308.

46. *Ibid.,* p. 310.

47. Jonathan Bendor, et al., "Bureaucratic Expertise versus Legislative Authority: A Channel of Deception and Monitoring in Budgeting," *American Political Science Review,* 79 (December 1985): 1041–60.

48. Ibid., p. 1056–57.

49. Breton and Wintrobe, *Logic of Bureaucratic Conduct,* p. 9.

50. Ibid., p. 99.

51. Ibid., p. 117.

52. Ibid., p. 94.

53. J. A. Schlesinger, "On the Theory of Party Organization," *Journal of Politics,* 46 (May 1984): 369–401.

54. Francis G. Castles, "The Impact of Parties on Public Expenditure," in *The Impact of Parties: Politics and Policies in Democratic Capitalist States,* ed. Francis G. Castles (Beverly Hills, CA: Sage, 1982).

55. Edward Tufte, *Political Control of the Economy* (Princeton, NJ: Princeton University Press, 1978); André Blais, Ken McRoberts, and Richard Nadeau, "Budgets and Electoral Cycles in two Canadian Provinces" (Montréal: mimeo, 1989).

56. A. Edwin Amentha and Bruce J. Carruthers, "The Formative Years of U.S. Social Spending Policy: Theories of the Welfare State and the American States during the Great Depression," *American Sociological Review,* 53 (October 1988): 661–78; James C. Garand, "Explaining Government Growth in the U.S. States," *American Political Science Review,* 82 (September 1988): 837–52.

57. Kenneth V. Green and Vincent Monley, "Generating Growth in Public Expenditures: The Role of Employee and Constituent Demand," *Public Finance Quarterly,* 7 (January 1979): 92–110; D. J. Storey, "The Economics of Bureaux: The case of London Boroughs, 1960–76," *Applied Economics,* 12 (June 1980): 223–34.

58. For a critical review, see George A. Boyne, "Bureaucratic Power and Public Policies: A Test of the Rational Staff Maximization Hypothesis," *Political Studies,* 35 (March 1987): 79–104.

59. Thomas McGuire, "Budget Maximizing Governmental Agencies: An Empirical Test," *Public Choice,* 36 (1981): 313–22.

60. Ibid; John H. Beck, "Budget Maximizing Bureaucracy and the Effect of State Aid on School Expenditures," *Public Finance Quarterly,* 9 (April 1981): 158–82.

61. Paul Gary Wyckoff, "A Method for Measuring Bureaucratic Power Using Survey and Expenditure Data," paper presented at the Public Choice Society Meetings, San Francisco, 1988.

62. Christopher Hood, Andrey Dunsire and Lynne Thomson, "Rolling Back the State: Thatcherism, Fraserism and Bureaucracy," *Governance,* 1 (July 1988): 243–71.

63. OECD, *Revenue Statistics of OECD Countries, 1967–1987,* (Paris, 1988).

64. Hood, Dunsire and Thompson, "Rolling Back the State," p. 257.

65. Ibid. The same pattern seems to hold in the U.S.; see Edie N. Goldenberg, "The Permanent Government in an Era of Retrenchment and Redirection," in *The Reagan Presidency and the Governing of America,* ed. Lester M. Salomon and Michael S. Lund (Washington, DC: The Urban Institute Press, 1984).

66. David C. Dillman, "Personal Management and Productivity Reform: Taming the Civil Service in Great Britain and the United States," *International Journal of Public Administration,* 8 (December 1986): 345–67.

The Equilibrium Size of a Budget-maximizing Bureau: A Note on Niskanen's Theory of Bureaucracy

Albert Breton and Ronald Wintrobe[1]

Review Questions

1. What are the two main assumptions of the Niskanen model? What objections are raised, and how are these assumptions modified?
2. It is stated bureaus can supply an output level up to twice as much as the competitive outcome. Why does this limitation hold?
3. How do politicians act to constrain bureaucratic monopoly power? What are some examples of control devices?
4. How is "control-loss" measured? How much control-loss results in Niskanen's model and in the modified model presented here? When will they be the same? In general, why is not all control-loss eliminated?
5. What conclusions are drawn regarding bureaus engaging in oversupply or X-inefficiencies?

Breton, Albert and Ronald Wintrobe. "The Equilibrium Size of a Budget-Maximizing Bureau: A Note on Niskanen's Theory of Bureaucracy." *Journal of Political Economy* 83 (1975): 195–207.

I

William Niskanen, elaborating on a hypothesis initially formulated by Parkinson (1962) and Tullock (1965), has recently developed a formal and elegant model of bureaucratic supply of public output (1967, 1971) which implies that a central and characteristic feature of the public sector is oversupply of output and not inefficiency in the narrow sense of output provided at more than minimum cost.[2] Niskanen's model rests on two central assumptions. One is that bureaucrats maximize the size of their budgets and the other that bureaucrats are in effect simple monopolists who are able to impose their own preferences on the governing political party. In this note we would like to raise questions about the two assumptions and suggest that neither of them is acceptable. For that purpose, in the next section, we first restate what we take to be the core of the model in order to bring out some implications which Niskanen overlooks. Then we abandon the assumption that bureaucrats are simple monopolists and replace it with one that allows a role to politicians, but we retain the hypothesis of budget maximization. We show that the model so modified can account for some features of the real world which the pure Niskanen model is unable to explain. In the third section, we go further and suggest that a number of other important facts appear to be inconsistent with the assumption of budget maximization itself. We conclude by arguing that an alternative hypothesis is needed which would be more general, in the sense that it would be capable of providing an explanation for the facts that appear consistent at least with the modified version of the Niskanen model adumbrated here, but which could also explain those facts which seem to be beyond the capacity of even the modified model.

II

Niskanen begins by characterizing the relationship between a bureau and its sponsor as one of bilateral monopoly, since he assumes that a public bureau is a monopolistic supplier of a service facing a single buyer—the governing political party. But Niskanen goes on to assert that "although the nominal relation of a bureau and its sponsor is that of a bilateral monopoly, the relative incentives and available information, under most conditions, give the bureau the overwhelmingly dominant monopoly power" (1971, p. 30).

The central motivational hypothesis of Niskanen's model is that bureaucrats maximize the size of the budget under their control. This is justified on two main grounds: first, on utility-maximizing ground, since it is asserted

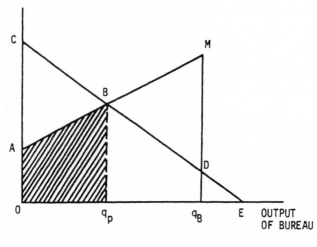

Figure 1

that income, prestige, power, emoluments, and other amenities are a positive monotonic function of budget size; and second on survival ground, since pressure from subordinates for larger budgets on the one hand and from executive and legislative committees on the other[3] is said to ensure the survival of budget-maximizing bureaucrats only in the same way that competition among firms dictates the survival of profit maximizers only.

The sponsor's preferences are represented by the marginal valuation curve labeled CE in figure 1. Since the preferences of governing politicians are assumed to accurately reflect the preferences of all citizens, CE can be taken to portray correctly the sum of the citizens' marginal valuations of the services of the bureau. It follows from the assumption that bureaus are monopolists that they will obtain the budget they prefer, subject only to the constraint that the total costs of supplying the particular service must not exceed the maximum available budget.[4]

The equilibrium rate of output is therefore at the point where the marginal valuation of output is zero—that is, at E in figure 1—and the equilibrium budget is equal to the entire area under the "demand" curve, unless the minimum cost of that output exceeds the maximum budget (OCE), in which case the bureau is said to be in the "budget-constrained" region. In this region, the equilibrium rate of output is at the point where total cost (the area under the marginal cost, or AM, curve) and total budget are equal. This latter case is shown in figure 1: equilibrium output is q_B with a budget of $OAMq_B$ ($= OCDq_B$).

It follows that a bureau can supply an output which is up to two times as large as would be the rate of output of a competitive firm or industry facing the same demand and cost conditions.[5] Since all bureaus have to be assumed to behave in the same way and to be endowed with the same monopoly power, the size of the public sector and hence the amount of taxes paid by citizens will be up to two times the social optimum, and, consequently, most—if not all—citizens will be in a state of disequilibrium. Now, if there is an idea that is central to economics, especially after the work of Coase (1960), it is that individuals will react to a disequilibrium situation, whatever its origin, as long as the marginal benefit exceeds the marginal cost of doing so.

We would then have to conclude that at the occasion of the first election the governing political party would be defeated, since the electorate would seek to reduce both the quantity of public goods it receives and the amount of taxes it pays. However, in the nature of the case, the newly elected political party has to be assumed to be unable to exercise its power vis-à-vis the bureaucracy and therefore be unable to implement the promises to cut taxes and public expenditures that have led it to be elected in the first place. That party would also consequently be defeated at the next election. That process would continue without end, one party replacing the other at each election. This does not seem to be a very interesting theorem and does not appear to be supported by the facts.

Building on an idea of Tullock, Oliver Williamson (1967) has recently shown that an inverse relationship between the size of a profit-maximizing organization and the degree of control exercised by its managers over its employees will set a limit to the optimum size of a firm. If, as Niskanen suggests, a bureau's employees can "indirectly influence a bureaucrat's tenure . . . through the real and perceived performance of the bureau" (1971, p. 40), then clearly the advantages of the bureau's manager of larger size will similarly be offset by increasing loss of control over the bureau, and there will be a point beyond which an income- or prestige-maximizing bureaucrat would not seek further budget increases.

The basic flaw in the assumption that bureaus are simple monopolists is really in the counterpart assumption that sponsors are completely passive. Politicians interested in their reelection will obviously attempt to exploit their position as monopsony buyers of the bureau's output. This would seem to leave us in the well-known indeterminacy of bilateral monopoly, but this need be the case only if the problem is formulated to make it that way. Let us examine the kind of results that we get by holding to the hypothesis of budget maximization, but dropping the simple monopoly one.

Consider instead that: (1) bureaucratic managers are subject to the exercise of direct hierarchical controls—rewards and sanctions—by the governing political party; a bureau may be a monopoly, but individual bureaucrats are not monopolists, and the careers of senior bureaucrats at least are tied to the sponsor's evaluation of their performance; (2) the limited "power" of a public bureau over its sponsor does not stem from its position as a monopoly supplier of a service, but rather from its control of information. To see this, imagine that information about the minimum costs of a bureau's services is costlessly available to its sponsor. Then if the sponsor constrained the bureau to supply the optimal output at minimum cost, the bureau would have to do so; a bureau head who did not would be replaced, so that the preferences of bureaucrats would be irrelevant in the determination of public output.

The bilateral monopoly framework therefore can easily obscure the fact that the bargaining power of a bureau depends on its ability to distort or conceal information from the sponsor. The problem for governing politicians in controlling this type of behavior is the same as that of the head of any organization in which the interests of subordinates differ from those of superiors, and governing politicians—like other managers—have a battery of techniques at their disposal to help them in that task. Some of these have been described and examined by Downs (1967), including direct monitoring, overlapping bureaus, duplication of services, and the purchase and acquisition of information from alternative sources, including sources at lower levels in the bureau itself.

The general problem of ensuring that subordinates act in the interests of superiors is referred to in the literature on organization theory as the problem of control. Tullock (1965) has invented the term "control-loss" to refer to the cumulative discrepancy between the actions or results of the actions of subordinates and the desires of superiors. In the following discussion, this control framework will be exploited to provide an alternative theory of the equilibrium size of a budget-maximizing bureau.

To that effect, assume that the governing party attempts to maximize the probability of its reelection. In order to isolate the role of bureaucratic preferences in the analysis, assume further that the rules governing the election of politicians are "optimal," in the particular sense that the victorious political party is always motivated to supply public goods to the point where the sum of the marginal benefits to all citizens is exactly equal to the marginal cost of supplying the good. (See n. 10 below, where this assumption is modified.) At that point, total consumers' surplus is maximized.[6]

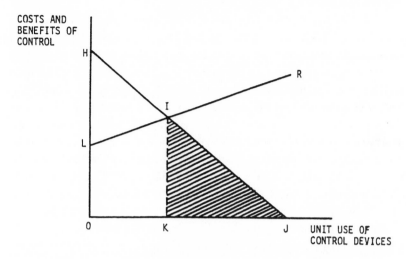

COSTS AND
BENEFITS OF
CONTROL

Figure 2

In figure 1, politicians therefore desire an output of q_P supplied at minimum cost, implying a budget of $OABq_P$. The bureau, on the other hand, will attempt to supply an output of q_B to have a budget of $OCDq_B$. The difference between the budget that the bureau succeeds in obtaining and that desired by politicians is the amount of consumers' surplus appropriated by the bureau and is therefore a measure of control-loss.

Let us now assume that antidistortion or "control" devices are available to politicians at a cost. The cost of the incremental use of these devices is portrayed in figure 2 as the LR curve. Controls have many uses, including that of serving to control costs and as a deterrent against distortion of information. Their value to politicians in all uses, however, is simply the reduction in the excess budget of bureaus which their use makes possible.

In figure 2, JH is a marginal "revenue" curve which shows the benefits to politicians (and hence to citizens) of a reduction in a bureau's budget brought about by operating control machinery at different levels. The area OHJ in that figure is equal in monetary terms to area ACB in figure 1, that is, it is equal to the total loss in consumers' surplus if control processes are unavailable.[7]

The sponsor will incur control expenditures up to the point at which marginal benefits—measured along the HJ curve—are equal to marginal cost, that is up to point K in figure 2. In equilibrium, total control costs are equal to $OLIK$, and the reduction in the budget of the bureau, using as a starting point the budget desired by the bureaucrats, is $OHIK$. The equilibrium size of the bureau's budget, given the availability and use of antidistortion devices, is therefore equal to the money value of $OABq_P$ in figure 1 plus the money value given by KIJ in figure 2—that is, to the sponsor's optimum budget plus the excess which it does not pay him to eliminate. Note that it is the amount of excess budget given by the area KIJ, and not literally the area KIJ, which is added to the sponsor's desired budget $OABq_P$. Changing the units in which control processes are measured would change the literal size of KIJ relative to $OABq_P$, but it would not of course change the sum of money represented by KIJ.

Alternatively, the equilibrium budget is equal to $OCDq_B$ in figure 1, minus $OHIK$ in figure 2—that is, to the bureaucrats' optimum budget minus the excess which it pays the sponsor to eliminate.[8]

There are two limiting cases which deserve special interest. If control devices are so costly that it does not pay to use them (in fig. 2, LR lies entirely above HJ), then our results coincide with Niskanen's, and the bureau appropriates the entire consumers' surplus for itself.[9] On the other hand, one could rationalize the traditional assumption about the neutrality of public servants as an assumption that control devices are costless and therefore the excess budget is always zero. Of course, the traditional assumption is not one about the costs of control, but about the motivation of bureaucrats; it is interesting, however, to note the equivalence of costless controls and selfless bureaucrats![10]

The equilibrium output is not depicted in figure 1. To be able to represent that level of output, we have to clear up an additional problem. The extent to which output will exceed q_P will depend on whether the bureau prefers to take the excess budget in the form of larger output or in the form of higher costs on the inframarginal units of output. The extent to which bureaus will adopt one or the other alternative will depend on the relative effectiveness of control procedures in reducing two sources of inefficiency: excess supply and use of inefficient production techniques.

To see this, assume initially that the cost of control devices is prohibitive and that the bureau is initially budget constrained so that the entire consumers' surplus is appropriated through oversupply of output. Assume now a technological change that makes costless the use of the antidistortion devices that pertain to the flow of information, but does not change the prohibitive cost of supervising and hence of altering the use of inefficient production techniques, so that sponsors can now—as a result of the technological change—monitor actual costs but are still unable to monitor the relation between these costs and the true minimum cost function.

To put it still differently, the sponsor knows the bureau's actual costs, but he has no idea of how efficient the bureau actually is. In such circumstances the best strategy for the bureau is to decide not to operate efficiently and to pretend that its marginal real-resource cost curve is the sponsor's marginal valuation curve but instead to use expensive production processes with declining marginal costs so that its *actual* cost curve shifts upward until it is identical to the sponsor's marginal valuation curve. In equilibrium, the bureau will produce q_P with a budget of $OCBq_P$ and the size of the budget will have been reduced from $OCDq_B$ to $OCBq_P$, but the loss *in terms of consumers surplus* is unchanged from what it was before the reduction in the budget, and the benefits from using control devices are zero.

A necessary condition for control devices to be useful, therefore, is that they be effective to some extent against both sources of inefficiency: the optimal level at which the two types of control mechanisms should be operated is where their marginal productivities are proportional to their respective marginal costs.

A model which takes account of the sponsor's potential use of control processes has at least one implication which is different from that of the Niskanen model: that implication relates to whether oversupply of output or X-inefficiency is the likely source of inefficiency in bureaucratic supply. To eliminate overproduction, the sponsor needs only to acquire information about the bureau's actual cost curve; to reduce X-inefficiency, he needs that information plus an estimate of the true minimum cost of supplying the service. Since it is costlier to police X-inefficiency than to police oversupply, the implication is that the major source of inefficiency in bureaucratic supply is X-inefficiency and not oversupply of output.

The modified model of bureaucratic supply presented above is capable of accounting for some empirical facts which the pure Niskanen model—which has no rule for control devices—cannot explain. Since there is no reason to think that the productivity of control instruments is uniform across bureaus, we could hypothesize that in controlling bureaus performing relatively routine tasks, the sponsor's information requirements would be lower, *ceteris paribus*, than in controlling the bureaus involved in more complex or nonroutine tasks, at least in that the information acquired in a particular period retains its usefulness longer as a deterrent to distortion in routine-task than in non-routine-task bureaus. We would therefore expect the equilibrium use of control instruments to be greatest in bureaus performing relatively nonroutine tasks and using relatively specialized personnel. This hypothesis is consistent with the evidence presented in numerous sociological studies (Blau 1968; Blau, Heydebrand, and Stauffer 1966; Meyer 1968; Woodward

1962) that the ratio of control personnel to direct labor in both firms and government agencies does vary systematically in this fashion.

As we have shown, the monopoly assumption implies that instruments of control are not used because they are too costly to justify their use. Evidence not only that they are used in a wide class of organizations, but that their employment is not haphazard but varies in a systematic and predictable way, is especially difficult to reconcile with this assumption and in particular is difficult to reconcile with the view that sponsors are completely dominated by the bureaucrats. Indeed, the systematic and rational use of control devices implies that the preferences of sponsors, and possibly those of citizens, are reflected in the supply of public output.

Another piece of evidence, admittedly much more impressionistic, supports the view that control devices are used by sponsors to control bureaus and indicates that the supply of public output is not completely at variance with the preferences of politicians and of the public.

Much of the recent interest in the role of the bureaucracy in political decision making was stimulated by the search for an explanation of U.S. involvement in the Vietnamese war. An influential thesis—propounded by, among others, the historian Arthur Schlesinger, Jr. (1967), and the political scientist Richard Barnet (1972) and which Daniel Ellsberg has termed the "quagmire myth" (1972)—is that U.S. military escalation was inadvertent, largely unintended, and prompted by the exaggerated claims and self-interested distortions of evidence by the military to show that each small additional escalation would guarantee success.

Niskanen does not take a position on this issue, but he does specifically cite the conduct of the U.S. military in Vietnam as an example of the workings of the monopoly assumption (1971, p. 76), and furthermore the thesis is surely broadly consistent with his own.

Internal documents and memoranda released as the Pentagon Papers have largely demonstrated this explanation to be false, as Ellsberg has shown (9) and Schlesinger himself has accepted (1971). Estimates prepared by the CIA, the systems analysis branch of the Defense Department, and the federally funded Institute for Defense Analysis were used by the Johnson administration to contradict the exaggerated claims of the military, and the administration's overall estimates of the likely effectiveness of various escalations were surprisingly accurate. If the military budgets were too large, it would not seem to be because the executive branch could not utilize competition between bureaus, redundant sources of information, and other instruments of control to evaluate effectively the claims of the military. It is presumably because such budgets reflected the preferences of the executive, and possibly those of a segment of the public.

III

Finally, we would like to raise a few objections to the assumption that bureaucrats act in such a way as to maximize the size of their budget. As we have already stated, and as Niskanen himself recognizes, such a maximand can only be used if "salary, perquisites of the office, public reputation, power, patronage, output of bureau . . . are a positive monotonic function of the total budget of the bureau during the bureaucrat's tenure in office" (1971, p. 38). While it seems consistent with casual observation and reasonable to assume that a positive monotonic function between the size of budgets and the salary and other amenities of office exists within a given bureau, the same kind of casual empiricism indicates that such a relationship does not exist between bureaus.

To put it differently, the salary of bureaucrats, as well as the other benefits of office, may be larger in some bureaus with smaller budgets than in others with larger ones. The absence of a positive monotonic relationship across bureaus is not of itself catastrophic for Parkinson-Tullock-Niskanen-type models, but when we take into account the additional facts that mobility among bureaus in governmental organization is large, and that heads of bureaus often improve their salaries and other amenities of office by moving from a position at the head of a relatively large bureau to one at the head of a smaller one, this would seem to indicate that a different objective function is being maximized.

In the Canadian government, for example, the salaries (and also, one observes, the power and prestige) of senior bureaucrats in the Department of Finance and the Treasury Board are higher than those of their counterparts in other, much larger bureaus such as Health and Welfare, and a bureaucrat in Health and Welfare could be promoted to Finance at the same time as the size of the budget under his control is reduced.

Another empirical observation which is implied by the assumption of mobility, but which is inconsistent with the hypothesis of budget maximization, is that bureaucrats sometimes cut budgets as a means to further advancement. For example, the present secretary of defense in the United States, James Schlesinger, made his reputation while head of the CIA in part by substantially reducing the agency's personnel![11]

We suggest, therefore, that careful empirical work would reveal that a

positive monotonic relationship between budget size and the flow components of a bureaucrat's wealth across bureaus does not exist. Combined with
what appears to be a large amount of mobility among the various bureaus of
governmental organization, the implication is that there is a great deal of observable bureaucratic behavior which is inconsistent with the hypothesis of
budget maximization.

An additional difficulty with the budget-maximization hypothesis is that
it is critically dependent on a much more precise definition of a bureau than
what Niskanen or anyone else who has used the hypothesis—including Breton, Breton, and Wintrobe (1972)—has provided to date. The problem is that
it is difficult to define a bureau in a way that does not automatically involve
something essential about the size of its budget, so much so that if one adopts
a particular definition of a given bureau its budget will be large and even
growing, while on a different definition it will be small and possibly falling.
To be sure, falling budgets are consistent with budget maximization as much
as falling profits are consistent with profit maximization, but then it is imperative that the consequence of falling budgets be spelled out as they are in
the standard theory of the firm.

However, a still more difficult problem for the hypothesis comes from the
fact that preoccupation with analytical models of bureaucracy originate in an
age when government revenues (and expenditures) have been growing very
rapidly as a result of the existence of progressive income taxation coupled with
large price increases and rapid economic growth. These three factors, even in
the absence of tax illusion, but in the presence of decision rules to elect representatives that are in effect compound simple-majority rules and thus imply
the holding of office with the support of only a subset of the electorate, would
be sufficient to explain much of the increase in public revenues—and expenditures—that we have observed over the recent half-century. In other words,
we are saying that it is not clear what the behavior of bureaucrats would be
and what kind of models we would be churning out if government revenues
were not increasing automatically.

Although the existence of transfer payments blurs the picture, a look at the
behavior of bureaus at the provincial and local level would be rewarding, because these levels of government have not experienced the same automatic increase in their revenues as have central governments. Indeed, the so-called centralization of government expenditures analyzed by Peacock and Wiseman
(1967) and also by Bird (1970)—but much more skeptically—may simply be
the product of the different elasticities of the tax bases of central and local gov-

ernments. A good theory of bureaucracy would have to be one that is capable of explaining the behavior of bureaucrats whether at the national, provincial, or local level. We suggest that a comparative study of bureaucrats at these different levels of government would find much that can be imputed to the different elasticities of tax bases and much less to the budget-maximization hypothesis.

IV

In this note, we have formulated a model of bureaucratic behavior based on the assumptions that bureaucrats maximize the size of their budgets and that politicians are able to enforce their own preferences by the use of control devices, and it appears that such a model is capable of accounting for not unimportant aspects of the real world of bureaucracy. On the other hand, we have suggested observations and empirical tests that would seem harmful to the budget-maximization hypothesis. One way out of this dilemma would be to recognize that although the hypothesis of budget maximization is not, as we believe, a useful one to employ in general, it may be applicable in certain contexts. We would expect to observe the kinds of behavior associated with budget maximization only where mobility is relatively restricted, which may be the case for the managers of relatively specialized bureaus such as the military. A more satisfactory alternative to the multiplication of models, each valid only in particular contexts, would be to abandon the assumption of budget maximization entirely and to replace it with the assumption that bureaucrats maximize wealth, as the other agents in economic theory are usually assumed to do. Breton (1974) constructed a theory of bureaucratic supply using this assumption in which the constraint on bureaucratic wealth maximization is provided by the sponsor's use of control instruments, as it is in the present formulation. That theory yields a number of interesting empirical implications, including those developed in Sections II and III of this note. It does not, however, provide us with a theory of the equilibrium size of a bureau's budget, as we have attempted to do here using the stronger assumption that bureaucrats maximize the size of their budgets. It is the natural course of progress in economic theory to derive empirical propositions under successively weaker and less restrictive assumptions about human behavior. We hope that the present analysis, which modifies Niskanen's model, contributes to that progress in the economic approach to bureaucracy and will stimulate the interest of others in the subject.

NOTES

1. Wintrobe's contribution to this note is based on his doctoral dissertation.

2. The latter type has been called X-inefficiency by Leibenstein (1966).

3. It is claimed that in the political system of the United States, legislative committees at least wish and expect bureau managers to request larger-than-required budgets so that they will themselves be capable of performing their own roles.

4. The constraint implies that the output of public bureaus is always measurable; otherwise a bureau could obtain a larger budget by promising more than it intends to deliver, and the constraint would not be binding. In some cases (e.g., Defense, External Affairs), it is difficult to define the output, let alone measure it, as Niskanen recognizes (1971, pp. 20–22). Breton, Breton, and Wintrobe (1972) deal with this problem at length.

5. The socially optimal rate of output in fig. 1 is q_p; it is also the rate desired by politicians under the assumption in the text. As stated, a bureau in the budget-constrained region produces twice this output. It is perhaps easier to see this conclusion algebraically. Following Niskanen's approach, let the bureau's total cost function be

$$TC = cq + dq^2. \tag{1}$$

The sponsor's preferences are represented by a budget-output function, which gives the maximum budget the sponsor will grant for a specified output.

$$B = aq - bq^2. \tag{2}$$

The constraint specifies that $B \geq TC$. The bureau's optimum in the budget-constrained region is where $B = TC$. Solving for q from the equality of (1) and (2) gives

$$q_B = \frac{a - c}{b + d}.$$

The sponsor's optimum is where the marginal benefit from output equals its marginal cost. Differentiating (1) and (2),

$$MC = c + 2dq, \tag{3}$$

$$MV = a - 2bq. \tag{4}$$

Solving for q_P from the equality of (3) and (4),

$$q_P = \frac{1}{2} \frac{a - c}{b + d},$$

which is $\frac{1}{2}q_B$.

6. That point is unique only if we possess a social welfare function or some other device that will determine the distribution of income—it is hoped a "just one"—for us.

7. In fig. 1, the bureau is in the "budget-constrained" region, and hence the loss is due entirely to excess production and not to excess costs of production. Whatever the source of the loss, it must be equal to ABC under Niskanen's assumptions. As we make clear later on, in our framework control procedures are assumed to be effective against both sources of inefficiency, but not necessarily equally so.

8. It might appear that the optimum output should take control costs into account so that sponsors would simply equate the marginal benefits of output to the marginal

costs of output plus those of control. This is not the case, however, since control costs are not a function of output, but of consumers' surplus that would be lost if the costs were not incurred. Hence, they are like fixed costs in that they cannot be imputed to specific units of output.

9. Where the cost of controls is high, the sponsor may be expected to look for substitutes. The importance of "loyalty" in bureaucracies may be explained in this fashion; where formal control devices are costly, it may be more efficient to hire even less competent but loyal bureaucrats whose careers are tied to the sponsor's rather than to the bureau, and who may therefore be trusted not to distort information in order to obtain a bigger budget. Of course, similar considerations apply not only between sponsors and senior bureaucrats, but between any two levels of the hierarchy where subordinates have some monopoly power over information.

10. If we remove the assumption that the system of political representation is optimal, the demand curve in fig. 1 (*CE*) may be taken to represent the preferences of governing politicians, but not the sum of citizen's demands for the bureau's output. The analysis in figs. 1 and 2 is unchanged, but q_P is no longer the optimum output from the point of view of the citizenry. For example, if, as Niskanen contends, review committees in the U.S. Congress are biased toward oversupply and the Congress simply follows their recommendations, *CE* would lie to the right of the sum of citizen's demands, and there would be oversupply of output at q_P. On the other hand, if citizens suffered from "tax illusion" or for other reasons vote for a smaller quantity of public output than they in fact prefer, their true demand would be understated by the political process and q_P would be too small. In both cases, of course, the inefficiency is due to the structure of political representation and cannot be attributed to the bureau, a point which Niskanen's formulation obscures. A nonoptimal system of political representation may allow governing politicians some freedom to pursue their own objectives at the public's expense, but there is no reason why they would cede this freedom to the bureau. Hence, the analysis of figs. 1 and 2 always holds.

11. *Time,* February 20, 1974.

REFERENCES

Barnet, R. *Roots of War.* Baltimore: Penguin Books, 1972.

Bird, R. M. *The Growth of Government Spending in Canada.* Toronto: Canadian Tax Found., 1970.

Blau, P. M. "The Hierarchy of Authority in Organizations." *American J. Soc.* 73 (January 1968): 453–67.

Blau, P. M.; Heydebrand, W.; and Stauffer, R. "The Structure of Small Bureaucracies," *American Soc. Rev.* (April 1966).

Breton, A. *The Economic Theory of Representative Government.* Chicago: Aldine, 1974.

Breton, A.; Breton, R.; and Wintrobe, R. "A Theory of Public Bureaus." Mimeographed. 1972.

Coase, R. H. "The Problem of Social Cost." *J. Law and Econ.* (October 1960).

Downs, A. *Inside Bureaucracy.* Boston: Little, Brown, 1967.

Ellsberg, D. *Papers on the War.* New York: Simon & Schuster, 1972.

Leibenstein, H. "Allocative Efficiency vs. X-Efficiency." *A.E.R.* (June 1966).

Meyer, M. W. "Expertness and the Span of Control." *American Soc. Rev.* (December 1968).

Niskanen, W. A., Jr., "The Peculiar Economics of Bureaucracy." *A.E.R.* (May 1967).

———. *Bureaucracy and Representative Government.* Chicago: Aldine-Atherton, 1971.

Parkinson, C. N. *Parkinson's Law and Other Studies in Administration.* Boston: Houghton Mifflin, 1962.

Peacock, A. T., and Wiseman, J. *The Growth of Public Expenditure in the United Kingdom.* London: Allen & Unwin, 1967.

Schlesinger, A. M., Jr. *The Bitter Heritage: Vietnam and American Democracy, 1941–1966.* Boston: Houghton Mifflin, 1967.

———. "Eyeless in Indochina." *New York Review of Books* (October 21, 1971).

Tullock, G. *The Politics of Bureaucracy.* Washington: Public Affairs Press, 1965.

Williamson, O. E. "Hierarchical Control and Optimum Firm Size." *J.P.E.* 75, no. 2 (April 1967): 123–38.

Woodward, J. *Industrial Organizations.* London: Oxford Univ. Press, 1962.

Suggested Additional Readings

Acheson, Keith. "Bueaucratic Theory: Retrospect and Prospect." *European Journal of Political Economy* 4 (1988): 17–46.

Bennett, James T., and Manuel H. Johnson. "Tax Reduction without Sacrifice: Private Sector Production of Public Services." *Public Finance Quarterly* 8 (1980): 363–93.

Benson, Bruce L. "Understanding Bureaucratic Behavior, Implications from the Public Choice Literature." *Journal of Public Finance and Public Choice* 8 (1995): 89–117.

Benson, Bruce L., Iljoong Kim, and David W. Rasmussen. "Estimating Deterrence Effects: A Public Choice Perspective on the Economics of Crime Literature." *Southern Economic Journal* 61 (1994): 161–68.

Blais, André, and Stéphane Dion (eds.). *The Budget Maximizing Bureaucrat: Appraisals and Evidence.* University of Pittsburgh: Pittsburgh Press, 1991.

Boyes, William J., William S. Mounts, and Clifford Sowell. "Monetary and Fiscal Constitutions and the Bureaucratic Behavior of the Federal Reserve." *Public Finance Review* 26 (1998): 548–64.

Carroll, Kathleen A. "Industrial Structure and Monopoly Power in the Federal Bureaucracy: An Empirical Analysis." *Economic Inquiry* 27 (1989): 683–703.

Garand, James C. "Explaining Government Growth in the U.S. States." *American Political Science Review* 82 (1988): 837–52.

Lindsay, Cotton M. "A Theory of Government Enterprise." *Journal of Political Economy* 84 (1976): 1061–77.

McGuire, Thomas G. "Budget-Maximizing Government Agencies: An Empirical Test." *Public Choice* 36 (1981): 313–22.

Moe, Terry M. "The Positive Theory of Public Bureaucracy." In *Perspectives on Public Choice: A Handbook,* ed. Dennis C. Mueller. Cambridge: Cambridge University Press, 1997.

Niskanen, William A. "Bureaucracy." In *The Elgar Companion to Public Choice,* ed. William F. Shughart and Laura Razzolini. Cheltenham, UK: Edward Elgar, 2001.

Shughart, William F., Robert D. Tollison, and Brian L. Goff. "Bureaucratic Structure and Congressional Control." *Southern Economic Journal* 52 (1986): 962–72.

Toma, Mark, and Eugenia F. Toma. "Bureaucratic Responses to Tax Limitation Amendments." *Public Choice* 35 (1980): 333–48.

Volden, Craig. "Delegating Power to Bureaucracies: Evidence from the States." *Journal of Law, Economics and Organization* 18 (2002): 187–220.

Weingast, Barry R. "The Congresional Bureaucratic System: A Principal Agent Perspective (with Application to the SEC)." *Public Choice* 44 (1984): 147–91.

Advanced Readings

Bendor, Jonathon. "Formal Models of Bureaucracy." *British Journal of Political Science* 18 (1988): 353–95.

Borcherding, Thomas E. (ed.). *Budgets and Bureaucrats: The Sources of Government Growth.* Durham, NC: Duke University Press, 1977.

Dearden, James A., and Thomas A. Husted. "Do Governors Get What They Want? An Alternative Examination of the Line-Item Veto." *Public Choice* 77 (1993): 707–23.

Holtz-Eakin, Douglas. "The Line Item Veto and Public Sector Budgets: Evidence from the States." *Journal of Public Economics* 36 (1988): 269–92.

Miguel, Jean-Luc, and Gerard Belanger. "Toward a General Theory of Managerial Discretion." *Public Choice* 17 (1974): 27–43.

Niskanen, William A. "Bureaucrats and Politicians." *Journal of Law and Economics* 18 (1975): 617–44.

Wintrobe, Ronald. "Modern Bureaucracy Theory." In *Perspectives on Public Choice: A Handbook,* ed. Dennis C. Mueller. Cambridge: Cambridge University Press, 1997.

Wyckoff, Paul G. "The Simple Analytics of Slack-Maximizing Bureaucracy." *Public Choice* 67 (1990): 35–47.

Elections and the Economy

Electoral fortunes can turn with the economy. Headlines trumpet changes in unemployment, inflation, and growth. Political popularity for incumbents rises as the economy prospers, and they find it easier to get reelected in such an environment. Surveys suggest that, among other factors, incumbent popularity is partially dependent on economic conditions. Voters favor those politicians who are able (or thought to be able) to reduce unemployment and inflation and increase output and income. A cottage industry has developed to predict election outcomes and vote shares. Traditionally, political scientists have relied on such factors as candidate ideology and personal charisma, but economists have shown that economic variables are also important. Evidence suggests this holds true across many different types of elected offices.

Given such emphasis by the voters, politicians naturally are sensitive to current economic conditions. This is especially true near an election when they need voter support to retain their jobs. The state of the economy is less important early in a politician's term if voters have short memories. Macroeconomic theory suggests it may be possible to use monetary and fiscal stimulus to help the economy grow, but such effects are only temporary. When policy changes are anticipated, the beneficial effects may not appear at all.

The notion of "political business cycles" refers to the incentive for incumbent politicians to manipulate the economy over the course of their term in order for short-term favorable economic conditions to exist at the time of the next election to help them get reelected. An unexpected policy stimulus shortly before an election, such as increased governmental spending or an easy monetary policy, will create inflation but also enable the economy to grow. As workers and businesses adjust to the new policies, the economy will eventually return to its natural rate after the election, but with potentially even higher inflation. Tighter policies to curtail the resultant inflation will slow the economy further, potentially creating a recession. Later in the term as the next election draws near, stimulus can be used to end the recession but starts the inflation spiral again.

While such policy cycles are harmful to long-term growth, well-timed cycles where the short-term growth and reductions in unemployment occur close to elections can benefit the incumbents when voters are unaware of the long-term harm and intentional manipulations. Thus, one cost of democracy is the creation of business cycles solely to help reelection prospects. In parliamentary nations, the current government determines when to hold a new election, subject to constitutional limits. Given that popularity is closely tied to the state of the economy, the incumbent government's decision as to when to hold the next election may depend in part on the prevailing economic conditions, to give itself the best chance of retaining power.

Although all incumbents are typically rewarded by the voters for low unemployment and inflation, it is difficult to achieve both at the same time. Blue-collar workers, the backbone of left-wing parties, have less job security and, given a trade-off between unemployment and inflation, are more concerned with the former. White-collar workers with more job security, who tend to favor the small-government philosophy of right-wing parties, will find their real wealth reduced when inflation erodes the value of their assets. Thus, to placate their respective constituencies, leftists in power generate expansionary policies to keep unemployment low, while conservatives in power favor contractionary policies that help keep inflation low.

As stated before, current macroeconomic theory predicts that unemployment will deviate from its natural rate only in the short run, and such deviations can occur only due to unexpected shocks to the economy. Changing government policy can represent such a shock. When an election is approaching, if it is not clear which party will be victorious, it is unclear whether expansionary or contractionary policies will be enacted. This creates difficulties for economic agents constructing their long-term contracts, which may not end up properly reflecting prevailing price conditions after the election. Since the new policies put in place shortly after the election are not fully accounted for by the current contracts, the economy will not be at its natural rate. As contracts come due and wages and prices are once again able to change, further adjustments will be made, eventually returning the economy to its natural rate, until the next election approaches and uncertainty reappears.

Soh outlines the development of the political business cycle literature in "National Elections and Policy Induced Business Cycles: A Historical Perspective on the Literature." Arguably the most famous empirical model in public choice is Fair's representation of presidential vote shares, which uses macroeconomic indicators to predict election outcomes. "Econometrics and Presidential Elections" represents a recent iteration and presents the evolution of his model. Case uses a Fair-type model in "Taxes and the Electoral Cycle: How Sensitive Are Governors to Coming Elections?" to show how economic conditions affect gubernatorial election outcomes and how incumbent governors respond to these incentives through tax policy.

National Elections and Policy Induced Business Cycles: A Historical Perspective on the Literature

Byung Hee Soh

Review Questions

1. What are the three sets of relations found in the circular flow model of the politico-economic system? How do these relations impact each other? Which directly affect each other, and which are only indirectly related?
2. What factors mark the development of different periods of political business cycle analysis? How do rational expectations affect the traditional political business cycle approach?
3. Summarize the evidence for political business, monetary, and budget cycles. How is this evidence interpreted?
4. What suggestions are made for further development of this area of study?

> Cycles are not like tonsils, separable things that
> might be treated by themselves, but are, like the
> beat of the heart of the essences of the
> organism that displays them.
> —Joseph Alois Schumpeter (1939, p. v)

Soh, Byung Hee. "National Elections and Policy Induced Business Cycles: A Historical Perspective on the Literature." *Seoul Journal of Economics* 7 (1994): 53–75.

I. Influence of Elections on Economic Policy Formulation

In shaping economic policy, political considerations play important roles, especially in a democratic society where the political figures, who influence and determine economic policies, are at the mercy of the voters for holding on to the political power. As early as the 1930s and 40s political scientists, sociologists, and economists observed that economic conditions have an important influence on election outcomes of incumbent officials. Some argued that the incumbent government would try to manipulate the economy in order to have at least a minor boom near an election.

Various factors affect voters' voting decisions for a political candidate. Not only the personality and ideology of the candidate, but also his actual achievements and future potentials are important factors that influence the voting decisions. In so far as an elective office, whether it is the Presidency or a senatorship, is considered to have powerful influence on formulating economic policies, the economic conditions in election years are likely to be an important factor in the evaluation of an incumbent candidate.

The President, in his capacity as the chief executive, is expected to exercise a powerful influence on formulating and implementing economic policies. Thus, a President is more likely to be blamed or praised than a senator or a congressman for the state in which the nation's economy finds itself. Recognizing the effect of economic conditions on national elections, the incumbent president seeking reelection may try to manipulate economic policies to achieve a desired state of the economy.

According to Lindbeck (1976, p. 12), three sets of relations of political behavior have to be specified in politically motivated economic policy models. Firstly, a "popularity function" or "voting function" should be specified. Secondly, a "target-preference function" of the government should be specified. Thirdly, "how the government can influence the economy through the maximization of the target-preference function should be described, and the economic constraint within which such influence takes effect" should be specified.

For each numbered box in Figure 1, there are three inputs and one output. In box (1), economic conditions manifested in the policy-induced business cycle are an input for voters, popularity or voting function. In addition, there are the indirect (denoted by the broken arrow) effect of election related institutional constraints and voters' own subjective factors. Popularity indices are the output or signal to the government. Institutional constraints may include the political system, the period of election, the party system, the terms of eligibility, the power of incumbency, and the like. It is assumed that these

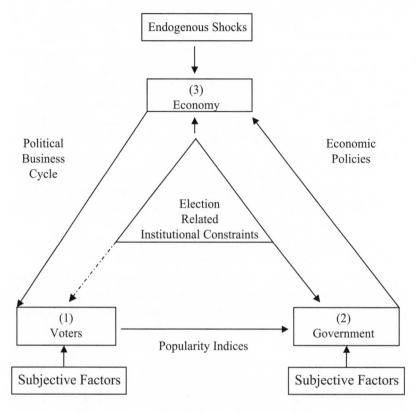

Figure 1. Circular Flow in the Politico-Economic System

institutional constraints influence the government directly, but the voters and the economy only indirectly. The subjective factors for an individual voter can be party loyalty, certain preference structure based upon his ideological inclinations, his perception of the personality of the incumbent, and so forth. The subjective factors that influence an elected government official in box (2) may be, among other things, his subjective perception and evaluation of the popularity index signal, his ideological goal, his desire to get reelected, his confidence in himself, and so forth.

The reelection-minded government in box (2) receives three sets of inputs for its target-preference function or reaction function. They are the popularity index signal from voters in box (1), the election related institutional constraints, and its own subjective factors. From these sets of inputs, its decision regarding economic policy implementation is formulated. The economy in box (3) is affected by the economic policies implemented by the reelection-minded government and by some exogenous shocks.

The structural and behavioral specifications of the economic state and policy variables are assumed to be similar to those in any standard macroeconomic policy analyses. What is new and interesting in this kind of "politico-economic" model is that the government policy is itself a function of the popularity function which is, in turn, influenced by the economy. This amounts to a built-in feedback mechanism of the government policy instruments. In the standard theories of macroeconomic policy since Tinbergen (1952), the economic policy is usually assumed to be exogenously determined. There have been some models of endogenized economic policy as in the dynamic stabilization policy models since Phillips (1954, 1957), and in the optimal control policy models since Theil (1958, 1964). However, in those models, economic policy is endogenized or policymaker's utility is maximized with neither any political motives nor any political implications. In politico-economic models, the economic policy is determined by the built-in feedback from voters' voting decisions through the changes in the economic conditions.[1] That is, economic policies are endogenized as a function of the economic conditions. It is possible that the economy thus run by endogenous economic policy implementations may display a unique pattern of economic fluctuations.

If the government can maintain good economic conditions throughout its entire electoral term, needless to say, it would be the best. If it cannot do so due to some inherent economic constraints and exogenous shocks, it has to become "strategic."[2] When the government must be strategic, the information about voting decision process becomes valuable to the government. That is because, with this information, it can plan its strategy of when to use the contractionary policies and when to use the expansionary policies in accordance with the voters' preferences.[3] The economic fluctuations due to this strategic manipulation of the economic policies by the reelection-seeking government are the "political business cycles (PBCs)."

II. Distinct Stages of Development in the Literature

There have been several surveys of the literature on the interdependence between the economic conditions and political events. Brief surveys of earlier studies can be found in Kramer (1971), Frey and Schneider (1975), and D. Mueller (1976). Frey (1978a) is a survey of mostly empirical studies of politico-economic interactions. Paldam (1981b, sec. 6) briefly surveys the empirical findings of the patterns of the PBCs and Paldam (1981a) covers a more broad range of literature on popularity and voting functions including most of the studies which appeared in European journals. Surveys of the literature on voting theories in political science can be found in Page (1977), Monroe (1984), and Kiewiet (1983, Chapter 2). Locksley (1980) surveys the theoretical development.

Since there are already quite a number of survey papers, the present paper is not intended to be an exhaustive survey of the literature but a concise presentation of a rather broad and general historical perspective on the development of the literature on PBCs which are induced by politically motivated policies, and somewhat closer examination of a few important studies. The development of the literature on the effect of national elections on the economic conditions and vice versa can be divided into six periods of distinctly different characteristics.

The earliest study (known to the author) about the influence of economic conditions on the outcome of elections is Tibbitts (1931). In the 1930s and 40s, there were several studies in this vein. The first economist to use the term "political business cycle" was Kalecki (1943). According to Kalecki, big business leaders and the rentier class in a capitalist economy would form a powerful bloc to oppose a continued government deficit undermining a long lasting boom and full employment lest the workers should "get out of hand." When the slump follows, the government would increase the deficit and the economy would again reach a boom. But then, the big business would again make sure that the boom would not last, and so on. Thus, the first theory of a PBC was born.

The concept of a PBC in relation to national elections as is used nowadays, can be found a few years later in Akerman (1947, p. 107). He looked at the political events as "primarily a function of the economic pattern." He examined the share of the percentage of the Republican votes in U.S. Presidential elections in relation to some economic indicators. He found some evidence of the "political economic cycle." He wrote, "in the United States the Presidential elections as a rule involve a change in party control when the votes are cast during a depression and maintenance of the party in office when the votes are cast during periods of prosperity. Sixteen out of twenty elections between 1865 and 1945 follow this routine." To be sure, Akerman was not the first one to examine the influence of macroeconomic variables on voting behavior. In the 1930s and 40s, a few studies by political scientists and sociologists painted a mixed picture of the importance of economic conditions on election outcomes.[4] This incipient period was characterized by new insights regarding the interaction between economic conditions and national elections.

The appearance of Tibbitts (1931) marked the beginning of the first period and the publication of Downs (1957) signified a new period of a more settled accommodations of earlier insights of politico-economic interactions in the analyses of economic and political decision making processes. There were three influential studies which attempted to apply economic theories to the analyses of political behavior. They were Downs' (1957) analysis of the government as a self-interested rational decision making unit, Buchanan and Tullock's (1962) theory of collective choice, and Olson's (1965) theory of interest groups. These periods of insights and accommodations, from the 1930s through the 1960s, served as the building block for the research in the 1970s.

Although economists are rapidly catching up with them, traditionally, political scientists have always been more active in the research of politico-economic interactions, especially in relation to voting behaviors and political systems of governments. The third period of rekindled interests opened with studies mostly by political scientists. Goodhart and Bhansali (1970) and J. Mueller (1970) tested the relationship between popularity of government and economic variables. Kramer (1971) and Arcelus and Meltzer (1975) examined the effect of economic variables on the outcome of Congressional elections with more statistical rigor. Often quoted comments by Bloom and Price (1975) and Goodman and Kramer (1975) followed.[5]

Kramer's (1971) study, which used modern statistical techniques, indicated the importance of real personal income, but not the changes in the rates of unemployment and inflation, in the outcomes of the U.S. Congressional elections from 1896 to 1964. His results were contested by a subsequent study by Stigler (1973). Stigler, who corrected some of Kramer's data and modified his statistical methods, claimed that economic conditions were not an important factor in the outcomes of national elections. This controversy drew serious attentions of economists to this provocative field of politico-economic interaction.

Kramer and Stigler may have improved on the methodology, but the basic concept and theory were not much different from the earlier studies. Their analyses were incomplete and static in the sense that only the relationship between voting behavior and the state of the economy was investigated rather than the whole circular flow of the interrelationships among voters, government, and the economy. That is, the dynamics of the complete circular flow, which runs from the influence of the state of the economy on voting decisions to the government's reaction in implementing economic policies, and finally to the consequent policy induced business cycles, was not analyzed.

Although Frey and Lau's (1968) analysis was a theoretical development in such a dynamic direction, it was Nordhaus' (1975) seminal work on the "PBC" that triggered rather active research by economists in politico-economic interaction models in the late 1970s and early 1980s. Nordhaus' (1975) social welfare function was based on the unemployment-inflation tradeoff relationship. Voters were assumed to have a quasi-concave utility function based on their well-behaved ordinal preference orderings over economic variables. It was also assumed that they have the same subjective standard for a tolerable level of economic conditions. This subjective standard sets the acceptable level of performance of the incumbent. Individual voter votes for the incumbent or against the incumbent depending on whether the ratio of his utility derived from the current economic conditions to his utility from his subjective standard of economic conditions is greater than or less than 1 respectively. If the ratio equals to 1, no vote is added to either candidate. By assuming that the expected level of economic performance remains the same, Nordhaus justifies the use of a quasi concave voting function.

He makes two crucial assumptions. One is that the "decaying memory" of voters represented in the "backward-looking" discount rate. That is, voters are assumed to forget past events rather quickly. The other is "myopic" voter assumption encompassed in the integral over the length of only the current electoral period.

Fair (1978) and Frey and Schneider (1978a, 1978b) presented supporting evidence for the influence of economic conditions on election outcomes, and the influence of the government's political goal of reelection on its economic policy implementation. MacRae's (1977) empirical study verified the PBC hypothesis while McCallum's (1978) rational expectations model found no such evidence.

MacRae (1977) assumed the vote loss as a function of inflation and unemployment. The government's objective is to minimize the loss in votes (accumulated over the past years since the last election) subject to an economic constraint. The solution to this optimization problem yields an optimal decision rule for the government which is to choose the unemployment rate subject to an inflation-unemployment tradeoff relationship of a Phillips curve. The presence of "strategic" voters, who vote rationally and strategically in the short run so that the government may promote the long run optimum policies, modifies the vote loss function. By comparing the prediction errors of the unemployment rates predicted by the two hypotheses with the corresponding values of Theil's inequality coefficients, MacRae concluded that "the myopic hypothesis does a better job during the Kennedy-Johnson and Johnson administrations while a strategic hypothesis holds better in the second Eisenhower and Nixon administration" (p. 262).

McCallum (1978) tested the rational expectations hypothesis against Nordhaus-MacRae type PBC model through an empirical examination of the unemployment rates of the U.S. quarterly data between 1949 and 1974. The unemployment rate was assumed to be generated by a covariance-stationary stochastic process that may be expressed in an autoregressive form. He set out to test if an additional explanatory variable such as the phase of the electoral cycle could provide additional explanatory power. To test their correlations with the residuals, first, ARMA models were estimated. Then, residuals from the chosen ARMA models were regressed on the various electoral variables. Both seasonally adjusted and unadjusted unemployment data were tried, and again, the results showed that the electoral variables were not significant. The hypothesis of the PBC did not seem to withstand the test of rational expectations. An unfavorable result was also obtained by Beck (1982) who investigated if there were changes in the unemployment and inflation series near election day by using Box-Tiao intervention analysis.

In this fourth period of endeavor, the number of articles of politico-economic interaction models published in economic journals rose substantially. In fact, the number of monographs and articles in economic journals which were published between 1975 and 1983 was more than fifty.[6] This showed a remarkable increase from less than twenty monographs and articles in economic journals on the same subject in the preceding three decades. However, after a short period of a renewed enthusiasm, a period of set-back in this line of research followed immediately.

This fifth period of slow-down and modification of research in PBCs may be attributed to the following three factors. Firstly, the findings of empirical tests yielded less than definite evidence for PBCs. Secondly, the bulk of the literature in the preceding period used to be empirical studies with various specifications, methodologies, and sample periods for various countries. And soon, the feasible variety and ingenuity in empirical tests of PBCs became almost exhausted. Thirdly, on the theoretical front, the emerging predominance of rational expectations models in macroeconomics forced the politico-economic models, which were based on the usual assumptions of myopic voters with adaptive expectations, to be not only rather naive and uninteresting but also out of fashion.

The implications of the policy ineffectiveness and the advocation of rules over discretion in the rational expectations models (Sargent and Wallace 1975; Kydland and Prescott 1977; Barro and Gordon 1983) rendered seeming absurdity to the PBC hypothesis according to which the myopic voters with adaptive expectations are fooled by the conniving policymaker repeatedly.

With such influence of the new classical macroeconomics, beginning with McCallum (1978), studies which incorporated rational expectations into PBC models sprouted here and there until they almost completely displaced the earlier Keynesian PBC models in the 1990s.

This sixth and current period since the late 1980s may be called the period of rational expectations critique. Some studies attempted to incorporate rational expectations with an information gap in the voting behavior and to set the interplay between the policymaker and the voters (Backus and Driffill 1985; Cukierman and Meltzer 1986; Rogoff and Sibert 1988) or between two political parties (Alesina 1988) in a game-theoretic framework. Most recent studies reject the PBC in economic state variables such as output and unemployment. Yet some concede that there are some indications that fiscal and/or monetary policies might have been manipulated in accordance with PBC hypothesis resulting in political "budget" cycles (Beck 1987; Grier 1987; Alesina 1989; Rogoff 1990; Alesina, Cohen and Roubini 1993).

III. Formulation of Policy and Resulting Business Cycles

A. Endogenization of Political Factors into Formulation of Policy

What is new and interesting in the politico-economic models is that the economic policy formulation is endogenized as a function of voting decisions which are, in turn, influenced by the economic conditions. According to these models, economic policy formulation amounts to a built-in feedback mechanism of the reelection-seeking government's reaction to voters' preferences. The government, as a unit of collective decision making, can be looked upon as a maximizer of its own utility instead of that of the entire society (i.e., social welfare). An elected government could be inclined to maximize its chances of getting reelected even at some cost of the welfare of its people if necessary. If that is the case, the utility of the government will depend more heavily on the prospect of reelection rather than on the general welfare of the people. If the government is indeed a utility maximizer and values its own reelection above anything else, then the economic policies implemented by such a government will have distinct features arising out of its effort to appease the voters. Maximizing the utility of the reelection-seeking government is equivalent to maximizing the number of votes through manipulating economic conditions.

The manipulation of the economic conditions, however, may be subject to some economic as well as political constraints. The government is essentially under two kinds of pressure according to Frey and Lau (1968). Internal pressure may arise from the government officials or party leaders who have specific interests of their own, but are, at the same time, united by a "common interest to stay in power." External pressures stem from the fact that the government must obtain the majority of votes in each upcoming election. The outcome of an election, thus, would depend on how much "goodwill" the government has been able to accumulate in the past. The internal pressure is encompassed in government's ideology function, and the external pressure is expressed in the approval function of the voters. The government's utility depends on these two functions.

To the extent that the government succumbs to such internal and external political pressures, economic policy formulation may depend "on the future electoral gains of accommodation weighed against the future electoral losses of resistance" (Gordon 1975, p. 835). Lindbeck (1976, p. 11) also notes the importance of the role of government policies in economic fluctuations:

> It is obvious that macroeconomic fluctuations today are so intimately connected with government policies that realistic explanations and forecasts of macroeconomic fluctuations require that government behavior be analyzed as an integral part of the fluctuations.

As a result of such politically calculated economic policy implementations, the economy may display a unique pattern of policy induced business cycles in close tune with the intervals of national elections. If so, by disregarding the possibility of politically calculated economic policy implementations, the traditional non-political macroeconomic models may be foregoing an opportunity for improving their predictive power.

When the political factors were endogenized in Frey and Schneider's (1979) model, its predictive power proved to improve over a traditional non-political econometric model. The influence of the reelection constraint, not only on fiscal policy but also on monetary policy, was investigated by Maloney and Smirlock (1981) and Laney and Willett (1983).

Frey and Schneider's (1979) work is essentially an extension of their two previous studies (1978a, 1978b). By incorporating political variables into an existing econometric model (Bonn Version V2 Model by W. Krelle) for West Germany, they empirically investigate the hypothesis that if the economic policies are endogenized, the predictive power of the model must increase. The political variables in the economic policy instrument function are the squared popularity surplus term and an ideology term.

In the estimation of the popularity function, the dummy variables for right-wing, left-wing and a coalition government are included. The regression equation for the policy instrument included government tax receipts reflecting the influence of the budget constraint, and a dummy variable indicating how many years there are until the next election for the government to take action. The lagged policy variable is included in order to capture the bureaucratic and legal obligation of maintaining the policy action at least at the level of the preceding year. They claim that their politico-economic model yields in almost every year better forecasts than the pure economic model. The policy instruments used were government expenditures, government transfers to wage earners, the wage rate of government employees, and employment in the government sector.

Maloney and Smirlock (1981) look at both fiscal and monetary policies. The fiscal policy instrument is nondefense government expenditures. Its economic constraint is real net tax receipt, and its political constraint is "politically optimal unemployment rates" derived from a popularity function. Monetary policy instrument is the real value of free reserves in the system. Its economic constraint is the short term interest rate which represents the opportunity cost of holding excess reserve. The political constraint is the same as that of the fiscal policy. Their empirical results from the period 1957:1–1976:4 show that "politically optimal unemployment rate" is significant in both fiscal and monetary policies. They claim it as an indication that the stabilization policies are being used to achieve political goals.

Laney and Willett (1983) set out to test whether the election cycle has influenced the behavior of the money supply. They distinguish two channels of such influence. One is a direct linkage in which the Fed caters to the desire of the party. The other is an indirect effect of partisan politics which may affect the variables to which the Fed responds in a non-partisan manner. In particular, they hypothesize that "to the extent that fiscal deficits tend to be partially accommodated by monetary expansion—for example, in order to limit the associated rise in interest rates—then an election cycle in fiscal policy would induce an election cycle in monetary policy also, even if the Fed were entirely apolitical in partisan sense" (p. 54).

The direct influence of electoral cycle was investigated through the use of dummy variables for election effects. They found no dummy variables to be significant, and conclude that there has been no such direct influence. In order to see the indirect influence of the PBC through the government deficit which was found to be a very significant variable in the regression of money supply, the cyclically adjusted government deficit was regressed on political variables. Besides the electoral cycle variables, Democratic power variable, changes in the ratio of total federal government consumption to nominal gross national product, and dummy variables for special years such as 1967 for Vietnam War spending were added.

From the regression result, the coefficient for the electoral cycle (significant at 5% level) was multiplied to the electoral cycle dummy variable to form an "election-induced component" of the federal deficit. The "election-adjusted component" of the deficit is defined simply as the government deficit minus the election-induced component. In place of the plain electoral cycle dummy variable and high employment deficit variable, these two components are entered into the original regression equation. The results show that coefficients are statistically significant. The coefficient of the election-induced component is about 1.5 times that of the other components. Their outcomes suggest that "the Fed may have created more money to accommodate the politically induced component than the remainder of the deficit" (p. 66).

Grier (1987) detected an electoral monetary cycle in the U.S.A. which was confirmed also by Beck (1987). However, claiming that the monetary cycle disappears when one controls for fiscal policy, Beck conjectures that the Fed may be passively accommodating fiscal business cycles rather than actively pursuing such monetary policy. Pre-election deficits for signalling purposes occur in the equilibrium PBC model of Rogoff and Sibert (1988). They postulate that the incumbent reduces taxes and/or increases spending before elections to appear competent assuming voters prefer a competent government to a less competent one. Even though pre-election deficits are monetized, the effects of monetization on inflation and on the seignorage tax are perceived by the voters only with a lag after the election. Hence, pre-election deficits for signalling purposes can still take place even if the voters are rational and aware of the policymaker's political incentives in Rogoff and Sibert (1988). Budget cycles take the form of distortions in the allocation of public spending programs in Rogoff (1990).

Somewhat weak qualitative evidence of the existence of budget cycles in OECD countries is reported in Alesina (1989). Alesina, Cohen and Roubini (1993) empirically test autoregressive models of monetary base and fiscal deficit separately with election and country dummy variables and political cohesion variables. Since PBC hypothesis indicates that the base money growth is higher immediately before the election, the election dummy takes the value of 1 the last three or five quarters of the election. The political cohesion variable in the budget deficit model tests the effects of political instability of a coalition government on budget deficits. The degree of the political cohesion is measured by assigning the value of 0 to a one-party parliamentary government or a presidential government, the value of 1 to a two-party coalition government, and 2 to a parliamentary government with three or more coalition partners.

They conclude that the existence of monetary cycle cannot be ruled out even though the evidence is not very strong. No evidence of cycles on GDP and unemployment is found. However, some evidence of the electoral cycles on inflation and on monetary and fiscal policy instruments is found. Thus, even though Nordhaus formulation of the PBC is rejected, the rational political budget cycle is not rejected. They interpret these results as follows: "although the politicians may not have enough control over economic outcomes, they still try to avoid restrictive monetary and fiscal policies in election years, and occasionally are openly expansionary." (p. 21)

In most of the models of politically formulated economic policies discussed above, some policy instrument variables are usually regressed on some economic state variables or autoregressive policy variables and on some election related political variables without much theoretical justifications. In these studies, the electoral cycle dummy variables are assumed to capture such reelection seeking government's prior knowledge about the voting function. They implicitly assume that the government has at least some knowledge of voters' utility function or popularity function even though the function itself may not be known to the researchers. In these studies, all that is necessary is that the government tries to maximize the chance of reelection by expansionary economic policies. This kind of assumption is most frequently employed in the empirical studies of the PBCs.

To the reelection seeking government, the voting function serves as a criterion for its policy formulation. In order to have an effective and realistic policy reaction function, the government must have the following three capabilities: (i) The government must have prior and exact knowledge of the voters' response in the form of a popularity or a voting function. (ii) It must have thorough knowledge of the workings of the economic system and the effect of policy variables on the economy. (iii) It must have absolute control over available policy instruments, if not in absolute terms, then at least to within a certain manageable range.

Even with all these three capabilities, the effect of the government's economic policies can still be uncertain if we consider politico-economic models with rational expectations. If voters had all the information available to them, they would not be fooled by the government's repeated manipulation of economic conditions to win elections. If the voters' expectations are rational, then the government's expectations of the effect of manipulating economic policies for popularity must also become rational. If the voters reward the honest government for maintaining economic stability, then the government has no other choice but to become honest and to stop manipulating economic policies for the political gain. In that case, the introduction of rational expectations would effectively eliminate the PBC as shown in the studies of Cukierman and Meltzer (1986), Rogoff and Sibert (1988), and Rogoff (1990).

B. Patterns of Resulting Political Business Cycles

If we detect no evidence of the PBC, then, does this mean that both the government and voters are rational? Or does it simply mean that only the hypothesis of the PBC is refuted? On the other hand, if we see any evidence of the PBC, does it mean that voters are not rational? Or could it be that, even though the voters are perfectly rational, an irrational government, in its desperate quest for reelection, just cannot feel safe until it tried everything within its power? If the implementation of such policies are affected by stochastic elements, we may still observe a PBC even within the rational expectations framework. Brittan (1978, p. 169) notes that "it is only because manipulation is irregular and sparingly used, that the election cycle has lasted as long as it has." If the government has manipulated the economy by deviating from the announced policy rules in the past, then a credibility gap may be created. The public's skepticism could induce the policymaking into "the kind of circularity which is generally characteristic of games of strategy" as Fellner (1976, p. 116) warns.

What most of the studies of the PBC try to do is to see if there exists a nontrivial relationship between the realized fluctuations of the important economic variables and the timings of national elections. They tend to become a description of how certain economic variables exhibit cyclical patterns in consort with the electoral cycles. While a few studies (MacRae 1977; McCallum 1978) try to test some theoretical models, many other studies (Paldam 1979; Dinkel 1981; Amacher and Boyes 1982; Beck 1982; Soh 1986) simply examine the changes in the most visible economic conditions for indications of the PBC without much theoretical development.

Finding no conclusive evidence for PBC, Hibbs (1977, 1987) presents a partisan theory of business cycles which argues that the Democratic party prefers higher inflation and less unemployment than the Republican. This suggests that if PBC exists at all, the partisan difference must be taken into consideration for the study of policy-induced business cycles. Chapell and Keech's (1986) study of the impact of unexpected monetary shocks on the changes in unemployment showed similar partisan differences even though it did not support PBC hypothesis. However, assuming this kind of systematic partisan difference in implementing monetary policies and using the post-World War Two data in the U.S.A., Alesina and Sachs (1988) found some evidence for PBC in the partisan aspect.

With the rational expectations models, the key factor for the existence of PBC is the asymmetry in information between the policymaker and the voters which makes the voters perceive the effects of the policy with a lag, i.e., after the election. However, the rationality of the voters and their awareness of the political motivation of the incumbent politician exert a subduing effect on the resulting PBCs which will be more short lived and less regular than the adaptive expectations PBC models.

In contrast to the somewhat ambiguous evidence concerning the influence of national elections on the fluctuations of economic conditions, most empirical studies of the effect of national elections on economic policy formulation show that the economic policy variables are indeed influenced by the electoral variables. Still, much more theoretical development is needed. For example, it has not been shown clearly how the fluctuations in popularity indices would be reflected in the government's policy reaction function. Although the findings of the studies of the popularity and voting functions are utilized in the formulation of the government's reaction function, there is virtually no research done on how the endogenous economic policies may generate the PBC, not to mention the research on the complete circular flow of the three sets of interrelationships among the voters, the government and the economy.

Even though one cannot readily detect a known pattern of the PBC by examining the raw economic data, the stronger evidence in the politically manipulated economic policy models supports the existence of the PBC at least in the policy formulation. It is not entirely implausible that the recent studies may have looked for the wrong signs or incorrectly hypothesized pattern of the PBC thereby obtaining seemingly weak evidence of its existence. For instance, in the case of the United States, it is not inconsistent with the hypothesis of the PBC if the data do not follow the anticipated pattern during the second term of a President who is prohibited by the 22nd Amendment to seek a third term in the office.

IV. Conclusions and Thoughts for Further Research

The study of the politico-economic models as a specialized area of economics is still at a developing stage. The shortcomings of the current research can be the starting point for the future research. In the literature, it is still not very clearly modeled how the information on the popularity or voting function influences government's policy formulation. More theoretical development on how the voters' preferences concerning economic conditions are fed back into the government's economic policy formulation may be desirable. In addition, more empirical tests of the predictability of the macroeconometric models in which the economic policies are endogenized, for example, as in Frey and Schneider (1982), may be stimulating. It may be interesting to incorporate the reelection constraint into a standard macroeconomic model as in Fassbender (1981) or Borooah and Ploeg (1983). It may be essential to construct multiperiod dynamic models of endogenous economic policies which generate PBCs.

Instead of the usual PBC corresponding to one electoral period, perhaps a cycle which corresponds to two consecutive electoral periods may be worthwhile to investigate. Since most of the existing empirical studies examine the traits of the PBC in isolation from the other two sets of relationships, namely voters' response and the government's reaction, the characteristics of the PBC are not theoretically well defined. Some theoretical characterization of the PBC generated by the reelection seeking government's economic policy implementations may be necessary before we can empirically pin down the precise pattern of the PBC.

The empirical findings do not appear to endorse the existence of the PBC unequivocally. Given this inconclusive evidence for the existence of the PBC, the "isolation" of the influence of the election cycle from other influences may still be one of the important tasks ahead. According to Frey (1978b, p. 103), "the only way to isolate electoral cycles from other influences is to construct carefully formulated theoretical models which specify exactly in what way the government is envisaged to create political cycles."

The characteristics of the realized PBC would depend very much on institutional factors. For an extreme example, if any elected government official is prohibited to run for reelection, we may not be able to see any business cycle that is attributable to the reelection-seeking behavior of the government. Such reelection-free government may conscientiously choose to maximize the welfare of the public. One implication of the PBC hypothesis is, then, elections are costing the public economic stability and thereby reducing its economic welfare.[7] It means that there can be a certain dead-weight welfare loss associated with the PBC. The welfare cost of the PBC to the economy in terms of lost economic stability has rarely been investigated.

In the similar vein, we could examine whether the election is a public good or a public bad. We could also derive some implications for institutional changes such as the optimal length of the electoral period as in Keech and Simon (1983) and the undesirability of the incumbent's candidacy with the implication of some constitutional change as in Wagner (1977). The study of the interaction between the government and the electorate in a game theoretic framework could be challenging. The incorporation of uncertainty and stochastic elements into the politico-economic models could be rewarding.

Overall, further research is needed for the illumination of the linking mechanisms for the three sets of relationships among voters, government, and the economy. The construction of an integrated dynamic model which can account for the whole circular flow in the politico-economic system could be crucial. One always has to keep in mind that the PBC is neither the sole nor the most powerful explanation of the economic fluctuations. Although one should be wary of attributing too much to the political aspect of the business cycle when there are more essential and inherently economic causes, the inclusion of political factors in the analysis of the macroeconomic policymaking and the resulting dynamic changes in the economy will undoubtedly prove fruitful in the end.

NOTES

1. For an overview and discussions of the economic policies in a politico-economic system, see Frey (1983).

2. The very notion of the political business cycle implies that the government will "strategically" manipulate its economic policies in the short run so that it will be reelected in the next election. If its goal is to get reelected continuously, its strategy will have to be different as Frey and Lau (1968) suggested. It may well turn out that the more ambitious long run goal of continuous reelection may not be compatible with the short run maximization of the probability of getting reelected in the next election in which case a rational government would concentrate on the short run or myopic strategy even if it is not optimal for the long run.

3. For cited evidence of the influence of political considerations on the formulation of economic policies in the United States, see Chapter 2 in Tufte (1978).

4. Kramer (1971) offers an excellent survey and summary of these earlier studies. He points out that these early empirical studies were based on "rather simple statistical methods such as tabulations or simple correlations, and in almost every case no indication given of the stability or statistical significance of the results obtained." (p. 133).

5. Hibbs (1977) made a comprehensive international comparison of the dependency of economic policies (manifested in the rates of unemployment and inflation) on the ideology of the governing parties.

6. This is based on a few monographs and the relevant articles listed under headings 011, 025 and 131 in the (old version) subject index of articles in current periodi-

cals in the *Journal of Economic Literature*. The articles (mostly by political scientists) published in the journals of political science are not counted.

7. This may open up a host of questions ranging from the most optimal length of the term of an elected office to the philosophical, ethical and legal justification of the democracy and the search for the best form of government. Although these are very important questions, they are beyond the scope of this paper.

REFERENCES

Akerman, Johan. "Political Economic Cycles." *Kyklos* 1 (1947): 107–17.

Alesina, A. "Credibility and Policy Convergence in a Two Party System with Rational Voters." *American Economic Review* 78 (No. 4 1988): 796–805.

———. "Politics and Business Cycles in Industrial Democracies." *Economic Policy* 8 (1989): 54–98.

———, and Sachs, J. "Political Parties and the Business Cycles in the United States, 1948–1984." *Journal of Money, Credit, and Banking* 20 (1988): 63–82.

———, Cohen, G. D., and Roubini, N. "Electoral Business Cycle in Industrial Democracies." *European Journal of Political Economy* 9 (1993): 1–23.

Amacher, R. C., and Boyes, W. J. "Unemployment Rates and Political Outcomes: An Incentive for Manufacturing a Political Business Cycle." *Public Choice* 38 (No. 2 1982): 197–203.

Arcelus, F., and Meltzer, A. "Effects of Aggregate Economic Variables on Congressional Elections." *American Political Science Review* 69 (No. 4 1975): 1232–9.

Backus, D., and Driffill, J. "Rational Expectations and Policy Credibility Following a Change in Regime." *Review of Economic Studies* 52 (No. 2 1985): 211–21.

Barro, Robert J., and Gordon, D. B. "Rules, Discretion, and Reputation in a Model of Monetary Policy." *Journal of Monetary Economics* 12 (1983): 101–21.

Beck, N. "Does There Exist a Political Business Cycle: A Box-Tiao Analysis." *Public Choice* 38 (No. 2 1982): 205–9.

———. "Elections and the Fed: Is There a Political Monetary Cycle?" *American Journal of Political Science* 31 (1987): 194–216.

Bloom, H. S., and Price, H. D. "Voter Response to Short Run Economic Conditions: The Asymmetric Effects of Prosperity and Recession." *American Political Science Review* 69 (No. 4 1975): 1240–54.

Borooah, V., and van der Ploeg, R. *Political Aspect of the Economy.* Cambridge: Cambridge University Press, 1983.

Brittan, S. "Inflation and Democracy." In F. Hirsch and J. Goldthrope (eds.), *The Political Economy of Inflation.* Cambridge: Harvard University Press, 1978.

Buchanan, J. M., and Tullock, G. *The Calculus of Consent.* Ann Arbor: The University of Michigan Press, 1962.

Chapell, H., and Keech, W. "Party Differences in Macroeconomic Policies and Outcome." *American Economic Review* 76 (May 1986): 71–4.

Cukierman, A., and Meltzer, A. H. "A Positive Theory of Discretionary Policy, the Cost of Democratic Government and the Benefits of Constitution." *Economic Inquiry* 24 (1986): 367–88.

Dinkel, R. "Political Business Cycles in Germany and the United States: Some Theoretical and Empirical Considerations." In Hibbs and Fassbender (1981): 209–30.

Downs, Anthony. *An Economic Theory of Democracy.* New York: Harper and Row, 1957.

Fair, Ray C. "The Effect of Economic Events on Votes for President." *Review of Economics and Statistics* (May 1978): 159–73.

Fassbender, H. "From Conventional IS-LM to Political-Economic Models." In Hibbs and Fassbender (1981): 153–68.

Fellner, W. J. *Towards a Reconstruction of Macroeconomics: Problems of Theory and Policy.* Washington, D.C.: American Enterprise Institute, 1976.

Frey, Bruno S. "The Politico-Economic System: A Simulation Model." *Kyklos* 27 (1974): 227–54.

———. "Politico-Economic Models and Cycles." *Journal of Public Economics* 9 (1978): 203–20. (a)

———. "The Political Business Cycle: Theory and Evidence." In Institute of Economic Affairs, *The Economics of Politics.* Lancing, West Sussex: Gordon Pro-Print Co. Ltd., 1978: 93–108. (b)

———. *Modern Political Economy.* New York: John Wiley & Sons, 1978. (c)

———. *Theory of Democratic Economic Policy.* Oxford: Martin Robertson & Co. Ltd., 1983.

———, and Lau, L. J. "Toward a Mathematical Model of Government Behavior." *Zeitschrift fuer Nationaloekonomie* 28 (1968): 355–80.

Frey, Bruno S., and Schneider, F. "On the Modelling of Politico-Economic Interdependence." *European Journal of Political Research* 3 (1975): 339–60.

———. "An Empirical Study of Politico-Economic Interaction in the United States." *Review of Economics and Statistics* (May 1978): 174–83. (a)

———. "A Politico-Economic Model of the United Kingdom." *Economic Journal* 88 (1978): 243–53. (b)

———. "An Econometric Model with an Endogenous Government Sector." *Public Choice* 23 (1979): 29–43.

———. "Central Bank Behavior: A Positive Empirical Analysis." *Journal of Monetary Economics* 7 (No. 3 1981): 291–315.

———. "Politico-Economic Models in Comparison with Alternative Models: Which Predict Better?" *European Journal of Political Research* 10 (1982): 241–54.

Goodhart, C. A. E., and Bhansali, R. J. "Political Economy." *Political Studies* 18 (1970): 43–106.

Goodman, S., and Kramer, G. "Comment on Arcelus and Meltzer." *American Political Science Review* 69 (No. 4 1975): 1255–65.

Gordon, Robert J. "The Demand for and Supply of Inflation." *Journal of Law and Economics* (December 1975): 807–36.

Grier, K. B. "Presidential Elections and Federal Reserve Policy: An Empirical Test." *Southern Economic Journal* 54 (1987): 475–86.

Hibbs, Douglas A., Jr. "Political Parties and Macroeconomic Policy." *American Political Science Review* 71 (No. 4 1977): 1467–87.

———, and Fassbender, H (eds.). *Contemporary Political Economy.* New York: Elsevier North-Holland Inc., 1981.

———. *The American Political Economy.* Cambridge: Harvard University Press, 1987.

Kane, E. J. "Politics and Fed Policymaking: The More Things Change the More They Remain the Same." *Journal of Monetary Economics* 6 (1980): 199–211.

Kalecki, Michal. "Political Aspects of Full Employment." *Political Quarterly* 14 (1943): 322–31.

Keech, W. R., and Simon, C. P. "Inflation, Unemployment, and Election Terms: When Can Reform of Political Institutions Improve Macroeconomic Policy?" in Monroe, K. R. (ed.) *The Political Process and Economic Change.* New York: Agathon Press, 1983.

Kiewiet, D. Roderick. *Macroeconomics and Micropolitics: The Electoral Effects of Economic Issues.* Chicago: The University of Chicago Press, 1983.

Kramer, Gerald H. "Short-Term Fluctuations in U.S. Voting Behavior, 1896–1964." *American Political Science Review* 65 (March 1971): 131–43.

Kydland, F., and Prescott, E. "Rules Rather Than Discretion: The Inconsistency of Optimal Plans." *Journal of Political Economy* 85 (No. 3 1977): 474–93.

Laney, L. O., and Willett, T. D. "Presidential Politics, Budget Deficits, and Monetary Policy in the U.S.: 1960–1976." *Public Choice* 40 (No. 1 1983): 53–69.

Lindbeck, Assar. "Stabilization Policy in Open Economies with Endogenous Politicians." *American Economic Review* (May 1976): 1–19.

Locksley, G. "The Political Business Cycles: Alternative Interpretations." In Whiteley (1980): 177–98.

MacRae, C. D. "A Political Model of the Business Cycle." *Journal of Political Economy* 85 (April 1977): 239–63.

Maloney, K. J., and Smirlock, M. L. "Business Cycles and the Political Process." *Southern Economic Journal* 48 (October 1981): 377–92.

McCallum, Bennett T. "The Political Business Cycle: An Empirical Test." *Southern Economic Journal* 44 (January 1978): 504–15.

Mises, Ludwig von. *Human Action: A Treatise on Economics.* 3rd revised ed., Chicago: Henry Regnery Company, 1966.

Monroe, K. *Presidential Popularity and the Economy.* New York: Praeger, 1984.

Mueller, D. C. "Public Choice: A Survey." *Journal of Economic Literature* 14 (No. 2 1976): 395–433.

Mueller, J. E. "Presidential Popularity from Truman to Johnson." *American Political Science Review* 64 (No. 1 1970): 18–34.

Nordhaus, William D. "The Political Business Cycle." *Review of Economic Studies* (April 1975): 169–90.

Olson, M. *The Logic of Collective Action.* Cambridge: Harvard University Press, 1965.

Page, Benjamin I. "Elections and Social Choice: The State of the Evidence." *American Journal of Political Science* 21 (No. 3 1977): 639–68.

Paldam, M. "Is There an Electional Cycle? A Comparative Study of National Accounts." *Scandinavian Journal of Economics* 81 (1979): 323–42.

———. "A Preliminary Survey of the Theories and Findings on Vote and Popularity Functions." *European Journal of Political Research* 9 (No. 2 1981): 181–99. (a)

———. "An Essay on the Rationality of Economic Policy: The Test-Case of the Electional Cycle." *Public Choice* 37 (No. 2 1981): 287–305. (b)

Phillips, A. W. "Stabilization Policy in a Closed Economy." *Economic Journal* 64 (1954): 290–323.

————. "Stabilization Policy and the Time Form of Lagged Responses." *Economic Journal* 67 (1957): 265–77.

Rogoff, K. "Equilibrium Political Budget Cycles." *American Economic Review* 80 (March 1990): 21–36.

————, and Sibert, A. "Equilibrium Political Business Cycles." *Review of Economic Studies* 55 (January 1988): 1–16.

Sargent, T., and Wallace, N. "Rational Expectations, the Optimal Monetary Instrument, and the Optimal Money Supply Rule." *Journal of Political Economy* 83 (1975): 214–54.

Schumpeter, Joseph A. *Business Cycles: A Theoretical, Historical, and Statistical Analysis of the Capitalist Process.* New York: McGraw-Hill Book Co. Inc., 1939.

Soh, B. H. "Political Business Cycles in Industrialized Democratic Countries." *Kyklos* 39 (No. 1, 1986): 61–76.

Stigler, George J. "Micropolitics and Macroeconomics: General Economic Conditions and National Elections." *American Economic Review* (May 1973): 160–80.

————. "The Process and Progress of Economics." *Journal of Political Economy* 91 (No. 4 1983): 529–545.

Theil, H. *Economic Forecasts and Policy.* Amsterdam: North-Holland, 1958.

————. *Optimal Decision Rules for Government and Industry.* Amsterdam: North-Holland, 1964.

Tibbitts, C. "Majority Votes and the Business Cycle." *American Journal of Sociology* 36 (1931): 596–606.

Tinbergen, J. *On the Theory of Economic Policy.* Amsterdam: North-Holland, 1952.

Tufte, Edward R. *Political Control of the Economy.* Princeton: Princeton University Press, 1978.

Wagner, R. E. "Economic Manipulation for Political Profit: Macroeconomic Consequences and Constitutional Implications." *Kyklos* 30 (1977): 395–410.

Whiteley, Paul (ed.). *Models of Political Economy.* London: SAGE Publications Ltd., 1980.

Econometrics and Presidential Elections

Ray C. Fair

Review Questions

1. What economic factors are important in determining presidential vote shares? How is this determined?
2. How does the economic model for voting get updated each election? What specific changes were made after the 1992 election and why?
3. How is success of the models judged?
4. Which version of the model does Fair prefer? Do you agree?

At the beginning of the 1970s, Kramer (1971) wrote an influential paper on voting behavior, which concluded that votes depend on economic events in the year of the election. My interest in this topic was piqued when Orley Ashenfelter in June 1971 used a Kramer-type equation and my then-current prediction of the 1972 growth rate of real output to predict that Nixon would win the U.S. presidential election with a little over 60 percent of the vote. Nixon actually received 61.8 percent.[1] I began work on a model of how economic events affect voting behavior that I argued encompassed the theories of Kramer (1971), Stigler (1973), who believed that well-informed voters

Fair, Ray C. "Econometrics and Presidential Elections." *Journal of Economic Perspectives* 10 (1996): 89–102.

would look back more than a year, and the earlier theory of Downs (1957). This work was eventually published in Fair (1978).

The general theory behind the model is that a voter evaluates the past economic performances of the competing parties and votes for the party that provides the highest expected future utility. Within the context of the model, one can test both how far back voters look in evaluating the economic performances of the parties and what economic variables they use in their evaluations. Many tests were performed in Fair (1978) using data on U.S. presidential elections. The results supported the view that voters look only at the economic performance of the current party in power, not also, for example, the performance of the opposition party the last time it was in power. Furthermore, the most important economic variable was the growth rate of real per capita output in the year of the election, suggesting that voters look back only about a year.[2]

The equations in Fair (1978) were estimated through the 1976 election, and I have updated the equation after each election since (Fair, 1982, 1988, 1990, 1996). This paper reviews the voting equation, with particular emphasis on the update made after the 1992 election. For a complete discussion of everything that was tried for the 1992 update and the reasons for the final choices, see Fair (1996). Forecasts of the 1996 election are also made, conditional on a forecast of the economy. All the data used for the estimation and forecasts are presented in Table A in the Appendix. The focus here is on the empirical specifications; the reader is referred to Fair (1978) for the details of the theory.

The main interest in this work from a social science perspective is how economic events affect the behavior of voters. But this work is also of interest from the perspective of learning (and teaching) econometrics. The subject matter is interesting; the voting equation is easy to understand; all the data can be put into a small table; and the econometrics offers many potential practical problems. In fact, Ashenfelter developed an interest in this area in part because he needed a problem assignment that had both economics and politics in it for an econometrics class he was teaching at Princeton University. Thus, this paper is aimed in part at students taking econometrics, with the hope that it may serve as an interesting example of how econometrics can be used (or misused?). Finally, this work is of interest to the news media, which every fourth year becomes fixated on the presidential election. Although I spend about one week every four years updating the voting equation, some in the media erroneously think that I am a political pundit—or at least they have a misleading view of how I spend most of my days.

A Review of the Voting Equation

The task of the equation is to explain the Democratic party's share of the two-party vote. The sample period begins in 1916.[3] Two types of explanatory variables are used: incumbency variables and economic variables. Until the 1992 changes, the basic equation was as follows:

$$V = \alpha_1 + \alpha_2 t + \alpha_3 I + \alpha_4 DPER + \alpha_5 g \cdot I + \alpha_6 p \cdot I + u$$

where t is a time trend that takes a value of 8 in 1916, 9 in 1920, and so on; I is 1 if the Democrats are in the White House at the time of the election and -1 if the Republicans are; $DPER$ is 1 if the president himself is running and is a Democrat, -1 if the president himself is running and is a Republican and 0 otherwise; g is the growth rate of real per capita GDP over some specified period prior to the election; and p is the absolute value of the inflation rate over some specific period prior to the election. Whenever "growth rate" is used in this paper, it always refers to the growth rate of real, per capita GDP at an annual rate. Likewise, "inflation rate" refers to the absolute value of the growth rate of the GDP price index at an annual rate.

Table 1 presents four versions of this equation: the original and three updates. The 1976 equation is in Fair (1978, Table 2, equation 4), the 1980 equation in Fair (1982), the 1984 equation in Fair (1988) and the 1988 equation

TABLE 1. Previous Versions of the Voting Equation

Eq. Name: Sample:	1976 1916–1976	1980 1916–1980	1984 1916–1984	1988 1916–1988
cnst	.401	.418	.4073	.4021
	(6.45)	(10.08)	(11.73)	(11.70)
t	.00474	.00346	.0033	.0036
	(1.29)	(1.52)	(1.80)	(1.97)
I	.0043	.0147	.0049	.0053
	(0.16)	(0.81)	(0.29)	(0.34)
$DPER$	.0485	.0415	.0449	.0424
	(1.69)	(2.00)	(2.69)	(2.74)
$g \cdot I$	.0088	.0098	.0102	.0104
	(2.12)	(3.50)	(4.99)	(5.30)
$p \cdot I$	−.0055	−.0068	−.0034	−.0031
	(−0.98)	(−1.79)	(−1.13)	(−1.07)
SE	.0422	.0352	.0310	.0296
R^2	NA	NA	.887	.890
No. obs.	16	17	18	19

t-statistics are in parentheses.

See the text and the Appendix for the definitions of the variables: g is gYR for the 1976 equation and $g2$ for the others; p is $p2YR$ for the 1976 and 1980 equations and $p8$ for the others.

in Fair (1990). The general form of the equation remained unchanged over this time, although there were some modest changes in the definition of the variables. For example, from the 1980 equation on, g was changed from being GDP growth rate in the year of the election to the growth rate in the second and third quarters in the year of the election. From the 1984 equation on, p was taken to be the absolute value of the inflation rate in the eight quarters prior to the election, with the last quarter being the third quarter of the election year. Earlier, the last quarter had been taken to be the fourth quarter of the election year. Finally, for the 1988 equation the time trend was stopped in 1976 and its value after 1976 was taken to be the 1976 value.[4]

The estimates in Table 1 are based on a smaller number of observations, and a number of the coefficients are not precisely estimated. The growth rate is always significant, but the inflation rate is not. However, the coefficients on the inflation rate do have the expected sign. The time trend is meant to pick up possible trend effects on the Democratic share of the vote since 1916, and it was a t-statistic close to 2 by the fourth version. The variable reflecting whether the president himself is actually running for reelection (*DPER*) has a t-statistic greater than or equal to 2 after the first version. The standard errors of the 1984 and 1988 equations are about 3 percentage points.[5]

Data mining is a potentially serious problem in the present context, given the small number of observations. Much searching was done in arriving at the final specification, and it may be that an equation was found that fits the historical data well, but that is, in fact, a poor approximation of the way that voters actually behave. Put another way, the equation may be overparameterized: since there are a relatively high number of parameters for the number of observations, small changes in the data or the specification can lead to substantial changes in the estimates. How can one test for this?[6] The most straightforward test is to see how the equation predicts outside the estimation period. If the equation is badly misspecified, it should not predict the future well even if the actual values of the economic variables are used.

Prior to 1992, the equation looked good. Using the actual economic values, the 1980 equation makes a prediction error of only .028 for the 1984 election and the 1984 equation makes a prediction error of only .017 for the 1988 election. Also, the coefficient estimates do not change much as new observations are added. But the 1992 election was a bad one for the equation. The 1992 error for the 1988 equation, for example, is .098 (using actual economic values), which is over three times the estimated standard error of the equation. In 1992 President Bush had the incumbency advantage, the inflation rate was modest and the growth rate was not too far below average; and so the 1988 equation predicted that he should have had an easy victory, which he did not.

The 1992 Update

The main concern of the most recent revision was trying to account for the large error in predicting the 1992 election. Several possibilities deserve consideration: how the presence of the Perot vote disrupted the equation, whether recent revisions to economic data might offer a more precise fit and whether to add one or two new variables to the basic equation. Certain adjustments do improve the fit of the equation for the 1992 election, but the need for such adjustments provides less confidence in future predictions.

Treatment of Third-Party Votes

Except for the 1924 election, where the votes for Davis and LaFollette have been added together and counted as Democratic,[7] no adjustments have been made in my work for third-party votes: V is the Democratic share of the *two*-party vote. By not making an adjustment, it is implicitly assumed that the percentage of the third-party votes taken from the Democrats is the same as the Democratic share of the two-party vote. For example, President Clinton got 53.5 percent of the two-party vote in 1992, and there were 20.4 million third-party votes, mostly for Perot. If it is assumed that Clinton would have received 53.5 percent of the third-party votes had there been no third-party candidates, his share of the *total* vote would also have been 53.5 percent. Haynes and Stone (1994, p. 125) cite exit polls suggesting that Perot took about equal amounts from both Clinton and Bush, which is close to the implicit assumption made here of 53.5 percent being taken from Clinton. However, Ladd (1993) argues that Perot may have taken most of his votes from Bush. If this is true and one were to allocate most of Perot's votes to Bush, then the equation no longer would show a large prediction error for 1992. This would be an easy way of rescuing the equation, but I have chosen to stay with the assumption that Perot took roughly equal amounts of votes from Clinton and Bush.

New Economic Data

In calculating rates of past GDP growth, it is necessary to use a price index. Earlier work had relied on fixed-weight price indexes, but these have well-known problems associated with using fixed weights over long periods of time: the weights become less representative of actual spending patterns over time, until they are abruptly updated, at which point their quality again begins decaying. However, chain-link price indexes dating back to 1959 have now become available, which avoid many of the problems of fixed-weight indexes. The update after the 1992 election was able to use the GDP chain-link price index to deflate nominal GDP for the 1959:1–1992:4 period.[8] The other major data change was to use quarterly GDP data prior to 1946, as constructed by Balke and Gordon (1986). In the earlier work, only annual data were used.

A key question when dealing with revised data is whether one should use the latest revised data or the data as it was known at the time. I have always used the latest revised data in this context, based on the view that voters look at the economic conditions around them—how their friends and neighbors and employers are doing—and not at the numbers themselves.

The use of the updated data made a noticeable difference to the equation. When the 1988 equation was estimated over the original period, 1916–1988, using the new data, the time trend became insignificant and the coefficient on the growth rate fell by more than half, while the coefficient on the inflation rate more than doubled.[9] The other three coefficient estimates had noticeable changes as well. The fit of the equation using the updated data was not as good, with a standard error of .0325, and it had a larger outside-sample prediction error for 1992—.120 versus .098. This degree of sensitivity to the use of revised data is, of course, of some concern. As noted earlier, it may be a sign that the equation is, in fact, overparameterized, so that even small changes in the data can lead to large changes in the coefficient estimates.

Given the updated data and the new observation for 1992, searching was done to see which set of economic variables led to the best fit, and several changes were made. The growth rate in the three quarters before the election did better than the growth rate in only the last two. The inflation rate over the whole 15-quarter period before the election did better than the inflation rate only over the last eight. The time trend was dropped from the equation because it was clearly not significant. However, even with these changes, the basic equation still led to a large error in predicting the 1992 election.

A New Variable: The Number of Quarters of Good News

At the time of the election in 1992, the inflation rate was modest and the growth rate was not too bad. One might have thought that people would have been at least neutral about the economy, but surveys of consumer sentiment and voter attitudes in 1991 and 1992 revealed that people were quite pessimistic. Many possible reasons have been suggested: Bush wasn't interested enough in the economy; foreign competition seemed threatening; white collar workers were hit harder than usual in the 1990–1991 recession; the press was overly negative; or people were worried about growing income inequality and a lack of "good jobs at good wages."

Answers like the above are all plausible, but for a testable explanation, one needs a variable for which observations can be collected back to the election of 1916. With hindsight, what struck me about the 1989–1992 period was there was no quarter within the overall 15-quarter period before the 1992 election in which the growth rate was especially strong. The news was either bad (as during the 1990–1991 recession) or just OK. Maybe the lack of good news began to wear on people and led to their gloom.

To test this idea, a "good news" variable, denoted n, was constructed. This variable is the number of quarters of the first 15 quarters of each period of a presidential administration in which the growth rate is greater than 2.9 percent (which is the value that gave the best fit). By this measure, the Bush administration experienced zero quarters of good news. It is the only administration since 1916 for which this is true (as shown in the Appendix in Table A), and this obviously helps explain the 1992 result.[10]

An Additional Incumbency Variable

It has been argued that voters eventually get tired of a party if it has been in power a long time. A number of authors have used some measure of how long a party has been in the White House without a break to help explain votes for president (Abramowitz, 1988; Campbell and Wink, 1990; Haynes and Stone, 1994; Fackler and Lin, 1994). For the work here, five versions of a duration variable, denoted DUR, were tried. The general version of DUR was taken to be 0 if the incumbent party has been in power for only one or two consecutive terms, 1 $[-1]$ if the Democratic [Republican] party has been in power for three consecutive terms, $1 + k$ $[-(1 + k)]$ if the Democratic [Republican] party has been in power for four consecutive terms, $1 + 2k$ $[-(1 + 2k)]$ if the Democratic [Republican] party has been in power for five consecutive terms, and so on. Values of k of 0, .25, .5, .75 and 1.0 were tried, and DUR is defined here for $k = .25$, where the best results were obtained.

The Final Version

The final variables in the equation are listed in the first column of Table 2. The equation differs from the 1988 equation in ways that have already been mentioned. The time trend is dropped. The growth rate in the three quarters before the election replaces the growth rate in just the two quarters before. The inflation rate over the entire 15-quarter period replaces the inflation rate over only the last eight quarters. The good news variable n is added. The coefficients of the inflation rate and n are assumed to be 0 for the 1920, 1944 and 1948 elections (the "war" elections, as discussed in note 10). Finally, the duration variable DUR is added. One interesting implication of lengthening the time period for the inflation variable and adding the good news variable is that voters are being assumed to look back further than they did in previous versions of this model.

Ordinary least squares estimates for the three sample periods, 1916–1992, 1916–1988 and 1916–1960, are presented in Table 2. The coefficient estimates for the growth rate, the inflation rate and n are all significant and of the expected sign. Based on the coefficients for the first sample period (through

TABLE 2. Estimates of the 1992 Update

Sample:	1916–1992	1916–1988	1916–1960
cnst	.468	.466	.463
	(90.62)	(124.05)	(88.08)
I	−.034	−.015	−.028
	(−1.26)	(−0.75)	(−1.31)
$I \cdot d$	.047	.016	.031
	(2.09)	(0.88)	(1.50)
$g3 \cdot I$	.0065	.0070	.0076
	(8.03)	(11.60)	(8.95)
$p15 \cdot I \cdot (1 - d)$	−.0083	−.0093	−.0066
	(−3.40)	(−5.21)	(−1.98)
$n \cdot I \cdot (1 - d)$	.0099	.0064	.0068
	(4.46)	(3.40)	(3.10)
DPER	.052	.061	.063
	(4.58)	(7.10)	(5.80)
DUR	−.024	−.017	−.016
	(−2.23)	(−2.14)	(−1.98)
SE	.0190	.0138	.0133
R^2	.960	.981	.990
No. obs.	20	19	12
$\hat{V}_{1992}$	.501	.467	.463

t-statistics are in parentheses.
See the text and the Appendix for the definitions of the variables.

1992), one sees: an increase of 1 percentage point in the growth rate in the three quarters before the election increases the vote share by .65 percentage points; an increase of 1 percentage point in the inflation rate over the 15-quarter period decreases the vote share by .83 percentage points; and each quarter in which the growth rate is greater than 2.9 percent adds .99 percentage points to the vote share. The coefficient estimates of DPER and DUR are of the expected signs, positive and negative respectively. The estimated standard error of the equation is less than two percentage points at .0190, and the (within-sample) prediction for 1992 actually has Clinton winning with 50.1 percent of the two-party vote!

The second sample period in Table 2 drops the 1992 observation, which has a noticeable effect on some of the coefficient estimates. The coefficient estimate for the good news variable falls, which makes sense because it was important in helping to explain Bush's low share of the vote. The coefficient estimate for DPER rises, which makes sense because Bush was an incumbent running again. The (outside-sample) prediction for 1992 is .467, which, given that Clinton actually received 53.5 percent of the two-party vote, is a prediction error of .068. The estimated standard error of the equation is only .0138 (which then rises to .0190 when the 1992 observation is added).

The third sample period in Table 2 ends in 1960. The main result here is that the coefficient estimates for this sample period are very similar to the coefficient estimates for the 1916–1988 period, except perhaps for the coefficient estimate for inflation. The equation is quite stable in this respect.

The predictions and prediction errors for the equations estimated for the first and third sample periods in Table 2 are presented in Table 3. The errors for the 1916–1992 equation are all within-sample, but the errors for the 1916–1960 equation are outside-sample from 1964 on. All the predictions used the actual values of the economic variables. As expected, given the small estimated standard errors, the prediction errors are generally small in Table 3. The largest error for each equation occurs in 1992.

Perhaps the most remarkable feature of the errors in Table 3 is the string of very small errors between 1964 and 1988 for the equation estimated only through 1960. These are all outside-sample errors, and, for example, the error for the 1988 election is outside sample by 28 years. The mean absolute error for these seven errors is only .014. If the 1992 error of .072 is added, the mean absolute error rises to .021. This seems to me to be the strongest evidence in the paper in favor of the new voting equation.

A voting equation like the present one should be judged according to the size of its errors and not according to how many winners it correctly predicted.

From a least squares point of view, a close election predicted incorrectly as to winner but with a small error is better than a landslide predicted correctly as to winner but with a large error.[11]

Of course, most people can't resist pointing out the elections in which the winner was not predicted correctly. For the 1916–1992 equation, the elections that were predicted incorrectly as to the winner are the elections of 1916 (error of .022), 1960 (error of .007) and 1968 (error of −.008). For the 1916–1960 equation, the elections are 1960 (error of .012), 1976 (error of .020) and 1992 (error of .072). The errors for these elections are all small— except the error for the 1992 election.

Evaluation

What judgment should one make of the equation? If one just looks at the final equation estimated for the 1916–1992 period, it does a remarkable job in explaining votes for president. The estimated standard error is less than 2 percentage points, and the largest within-sample error is only 3.4 percentage points. Also, when the equation is estimated only with data through 1960, it

TABLE 3.   Prediction Errors for Table 2 Equations

Winner		V	1916–1992 eq.		1916–1960 eq.	
			$\hat{V}$	$V - \hat{V}$	$\hat{V}$	$V - \hat{V}$
Wilson	1916	.517	.495	.022	.507	.010
Harding	1920	.361	.382	−.021	.363	−.002
Coolidge	1924	.418	.419	−.001	.424	−.006
Hoover	1928	.412	.427	−.015	.426	−.014
Roosevelt	1932	.592	.607	−.015	.591	.001
Roosevelt	1936	.625	.629	−.004	.633	−.008
Roosevelt	1940	.550	.553	−.003	.551	−.001
Roosevelt	1944	.538	.522	.016	.531	.007
Truman	1948	.524	.518	.006	.528	−.004
Eisenhower	1952	.446	.449	−.003	.446	−.000
Eisenhower	1956	.422	.417	.005	.413	.009
Kennedy	1960	.501	.494	.007	.489	.012
Johnson	1964	.613	.617	−.004	.603	.010
Nixon	1968	.496	.504	−.008	.495	.001
Nixon	1972	.382	.392	−.010	.376	.006
Carter	1976	.511	.507	.004	.491	.020
Reagan	1980	.447	.446	.001	.453	−.006
Reagan	1984	.408	.387	.021	.373	.035
Bush	1988	.461	.489	−.028	.480	−.019
Clinton	1992	.535	.501	.034	.463	.072

does a good job of predicting the elections outside the sample from 1964 through 1988. In this sense the equation is very stable. The fact that the good news variable, n, is significant even when the equation is estimated only through 1960 suggests that it is not merely a dummy variable for the 1992 election.

On the other hand, there is plenty of reason to be cautious. The estimates are based on only 20 observations, and much searching was done in arriving at the "final" equation. This included searching for the best variables, for the best threshold values for the good news n and duration DUR variables, and restricting the sample period to elections from 1916 on. Strategic decisions that helped the statistical fit were made about how to treat the inflation and good news variables in war years (see note 10) and about not categorizing Ford as incumbent running again because he had not been elected vice president (see note 4). Finally, the outside-sample prediction errors for 1992 are large, and adding the 1992 observation to the estimation period results in fairly large changes in some coefficient estimates.

It may be that the equation is better at explaining the past than the future. Time will tell. If the equation predicts the next two or three elections within two or three percentage points, there may be something to it. Otherwise, I will have to keep searching or do something else in my updating week every four years.

Conditional Predictions of the 1996 Election

Any of the equations discussed in this paper can be used to make a prediction of the 1996 election conditional on the economy. Since Clinton is running for reelection, all the incumbency variables are known. For example, given the incumbency information, the equation in Table 2 estimated for the 1916–1992 period is: $V = .4859 + .0065g3 - .0083p15 + .0099n$. The first term is calculated by plugging in the coefficients for the known variables, multiplied by their coefficients, and adding the intercept term. In applying this equation, remember that the growth rate $g3$ and quarters of good news n pertain to growth rates of *per capita* real GDP. Since the U.S. population is currently growing at an annual rate of about 1 percent, the growth rates to use for the present calculations are 1 less than the growth rates for the aggregate economy normally quoted in the press.

Table 4 presents predictions of the 1996 election using the four equations in Table 1 and the three equations in Table 2. The economic forecasts used for these predictions are my own, and they are presented in the Appendix in the last row of Table A. These forecasts differ little from the "consensus" view.

TABLE 4. Forecasts of the 1996 Election
Democratic Share of the Two-Party Vote

Equation	$\hat{V}$
Table 2, 1916–1992	.495
Table 2, 1916–1988	.512
Table 2, 1916–1960	.508
Table 1, 1916–1988	.549
Table 1, 1916–1984	.564
Table 1, 1916–1980	.578
Table 1, 1916–1976	.588

The four equations from Table 1 predict a substantial Democratic victory. Since these equations do not take into account the defeat of incumbent Bush, it makes sense that they offer a larger incumbency advantage for Clinton. However, all three equations from Table 2 are predicting a close election. The equation estimated through 1992 has a predicted Democratic share of the two-party vote of .495 (which is a narrow Republican victory), and the other two equations have the predicted value slightly above .5. If the economic forecasts are accurate and if the election is close, then the Table 2 equations will have done well, regardless of which party wins. On the other hand, if the economic forecasts are accurate but the election is not close, then the equations will not have done well, again regardless of which party wins.

So as not to be accused of presenting so many predictions that one of them is bound to be right, let me say that I take the equation from Table 2 estimated through 1992 to be my "final" choice. However, if one felt that Perot contaminated the 1992 election so much that the observation should not be used, then the second equation in Table 2 is a possible choice. It also predicts a close election. One would only use the previous version of the equation (like the fourth equation in Table 1) if it was felt that none of the changes for the 1992 update were any good.

Appendix:
Data for Econometrics and Presidential Elections

Let Y be real GDP divided by population and let P be nominal GDP divided by real GDP. The construction of Y and P is explained in Fair (1996). Let subscript k denote the kth quarter within the 16-quarter period of an administration and let (-1) denote the variable lagged one 16-quarter period. Finally, let q_k be the growth rate of Y in quarter k (at an annual rate), which is $((Y_k/Y_{k-1})^4 - 1) \times 100$ for quarters 2 through 16 and $((Y_1/Y_{16}(-1))^4 - 1) \times 100$ for quarter 1. Then:

$$g2 = ((Y_{15}/Y_{13})^{(4/2)} - 1) \times 100$$
$$g3 = ((Y_{15}/Y_{12})^{(4/3)} - 1) \times 100$$

$$gYR = ((Y_{16} + Y_{15} + Y_{14} + Y_{13})/(Y_{12} + Y_{11} + Y_{10} + Y_9) - 1) \times 100$$

$$p8 = |((P_{15}/P_7)^{(4/8)} - 1) \times 100|$$

$$p15 = |((P_{15}/P_{16}(-1))^{(4/15)} - 1) \times 100|$$

$$p2YR = |(((P_{16} + P_{15} + P_{14} + P_{13})/(P_8 + P_7 + P_6 + P_5))^{.5} - 1) \times 100|$$

n $\quad$ = Number of quarters in the first 15 in which q_k is greater than 2.9.

NOTES

1. Alas, four years later Ashenfelter's equations predicted that Ford would be elected in 1976, which was not to be. This is the first of a number of warnings in this paper not to become too confident with any of the equations.

2. Although Kramer (1971) used both data on congressional and presidential elections, he did not find that the presidential vote was very responsive to economic conditions. This may be because he constrained the coefficient estimates in the equation explaining the presidential vote to be the same as the coefficient estimates in the equation explaining the congressional vote. The results in Fair (1978) are only for presidential elections, and one of the maintained assumptions is that voters hold the party in the White House responsible for the state of the economy.

3. I have collected the data back to 1880, and some experimentation was done using

TABLE A.   The Data

	V	I	DPER	DUR	g3	p15	n	g2	gYR	p8	p2Y
1916	0.5168	1	1	0.00	2.229	4.252	3	−1.213	6.035	6.752	8.1
1920	0.3612	1	0	1.00	−11.463	16.535	5	−14.496	−8.147	17.240	16.8
1924	0.4176	−1	−1	0.00	−3.872	5.161	10	−9.777	−1.009	0.737	1.2
1928	0.4118	−1	0	−1.00	4.623	0.183	7	6.043	−0.225	0.242	0.7
1932	0.5916	−1	−1	−1.25	−15.574	6.657	3	−16.249	−14.369	10.127	10.1
1936	0.6246	1	1	0.00	12.625	3.387	9	18.765	12.933	0.928	1.3
1940	0.5500	1	1	1.00	2.420	0.553	8	10.350	6.708	0.542	0.7
1944	0.5377	1	1	1.25	2.910	6.432	13	3.317	5.768	3.737	3.9
1948	0.5237	1	1	1.50	3.105	10.369	3	3.976	2.289	8.852	9.5
1952	0.4460	1	0	1.75	0.910	2.256	7	0.632	1.935	3.542	4.
1956	0.4224	−1	−1	0.00	−1.479	2.132	6	−0.576	0.338	2.958	2.
1960	0.5009	−1	0	−1.00	0.020	2.299	5	−2.940	−0.038	2.314	2.
1964	0.6134	1	1	0.00	4.950	1.201	11	3.334	4.374	1.375	1.
1968	0.4960	1	0	1.00	4.712	3.160	9	4.125	3.599	3.775	3.
1972	0.3821	−1	−1	0.00	5.716	4.762	6	5.216	4.247	4.611	4.
1976	0.5105	−1	0	−1.00	3.411	7.604	6	0.923	4.406	7.288	7.
1980	0.4470	1	1	0.00	−3.512	7.947	5	−5.494	−1.330	8.718	8.
1984	0.4083	−1	−1	0.00	5.722	5.296	7	3.965	6.114	3.692	3.
1988	0.4610	−1	0	−1.00	2.174	3.392	5	2.285	2.943	3.737	3.
1992	0.5345	−1	−1	−1.25	1.478	3.834	0	1.102	0.979	3.325	3.
1996[a]		1	1	0.00	2.100	3.000	2	2.200	1.500	2.200	2

[a]Economic values are forecasts made May 3, 1996.

observations prior to 1916. As was the case for the original work in Fair (1978), however, the results using the elections before 1916 were not as good, and so the sample period was chosen to begin in 1916. The data prior to 1916 are presented in Fair (1996).

4. For the estimation of the 1976 and 1980 equations, Ford was counted as an incumbent running again in the construction of *DPER*. From the 1984 equation on he was not so counted, which improves the fit of the equation. Excluding Ford in *DPER* is justified (?) on the grounds that, unlike other vice presidents who became president, he was appointed rather than elected.

5. An attempt was made in Fair (1978) to account for the independent vote-getting ability of someone who ran more than once. This was done by postulating certain restrictions on the covariance matrix of the error term when a person had run before. In the econometric work, a parameter of the covariance matrix was estimated along with the structural coefficients by a nonlinear procedure. The 1976 and 1980 equations in Table 1 are estimated using this procedure, but from the 1984 equation on the restrictions were not imposed and the equations were just estimated by ordinary least squares. I have always liked this treatment of the covariance matrix, and I hope that some students may look it up; but it is probably too clever by half given the limited number of observations. The estimates of the parameter in the covariance matrix were never very precise.

6. With so few observations, structural stability tests are not really practical.

7. A slightly different procedure, based on the analysis in Burner (1971), was used for the 1992 update. LaFollette was assumed to have taken only 76.5 percent, rather than 100 percent, from Davis.

8. Some of the early data are data on GNP, gross national product, rather than GDP, gross domestic product. The differences between GDP and GNP are trivial for the early years, and for ease of reference GDP will always be used in referring to the national output data.

9. Specifically, the coefficient on the time trend fell from .0036 with a t-statistic of 1.97 to $-.0007$ with a t-statistic of -0.35. The coefficient estimate for the growth rate went from .0104 with a t-statistic of 5.30 to .0042 with a t-statistic of 2.49, and the coefficient estimate for the inflation rate went from $-.0031$ with a t-statistic of -1.07 to $-.0070$ with a t-statistic of -2.12.

10. The use of n, which pertains to the entire 15-quarter period before the election, and the use of the inflation rate over this same period brings up the question of how to treat the war years. The 15-quarter period before the 1920 election is dominated by World War I, and the 15-quarter periods before the 1944 and 1948 elections are dominated by World War II. These periods may differ in kind from the other periods. To try to account for this problem, the assumption was made that the coefficients for n and for inflation are zero for these three elections. Voters are assumed to consider the other variables in the equation, including the growth rate in the year of the election, but not n and the inflation rate. This assumption leads to one extra coefficient being estimated. The new variable introduced is denoted d, which is 1 for the 1920, 1944 and 1948 elections and 0 otherwise.

11. If, on the other hand, the aim is not to explain vote share, but to predict the winner correctly, a different procedure from least squares may be desirable. There are some interesting econometric issues here, but these are beyond the scope of the present paper.

REFERENCES

Abramowitz, Alan I., "An Improved Model for Predicting Presidential Election Outcomes," *Political Science & Politics*, 1988, *21*, 843–47.

Balke, Nathan S., and Robert J. Gordon, "Appendix B Historical Data." In Gordon, Robert J., ed., *The American Business Cycle: Continuity and Change*. Chicago: University of Chicago Press, 1986, pp. 781–810.

Burner, David, "Election of 1924." In Schlesinger, Arthur M., Jr., ed., *History of American Presidential Elections 1789–1968, Volume III*. New York: McGraw-Hill Book Co., 1971, pp. 2459–2553.

Campbell, James E., and Kenneth A. Wink, "Trial-Heat Forecasts of the Presidential Vote," *American Politics Quarterly*, 1990, *18*, 251–69.

Downs, Anthony, *An Economic Theory of Democracy*. New York: Harper and Row, 1957.

Fackler, Tim, and Tse-min Lin, "Political Corruption and Presidential Elections." Paper presented at the 1994 meetings of the Midwest Political Science Association, Chicago, Illinois, April 14–16, 1994.

Fair, Ray C., "The Effect of Economic Events on Votes for President," *Review of Economics and Statistics*, 1978, *60*, 159–73.

Fair, Ray C., The Effect of Economic Events on Votes for President: 1980 Results." *Review of Economics and Statistics*, 1982, *64*, 322–25.

Fair, Ray C., "The Effect of Economic Events on Votes for President: 1984 Update," *Political Behavior*, 1988, *10* 168–77.

Fair, Ray C., "The Effect of Economic Events on Votes for President: 1988 Update." Yale University, New Haven, Conn., 1990. Mimeographed.

Fair, Ray C., "The Effect of Economic Events on Votes for President: 1992 Update," *Political Behavior*, 1996, *18*, 119–39.

Haynes, Stephen E., and Joe A. Stone, "Why Did Economic Models Falsely Predict a Bush Landslide in 1992?" *Contemporary Economic Policy*, 1994, *12*, 123–30.

Ladd, Everett Carll, "The 1992 Vote for President Clinton: Another Brittle Mandate?" *Political Science Quarterly*, 1993, *108*, 1–28.

Kramer, Gerald H., "Short-Term Fluctuations in U.S. Voting Behavior, 1896–1964," *American Political Science Review*, 1971, *65*, 131–43.

Stigler, George J., "General Economic Conditions and National Elections," *American Economic Review*, 1973, *63*, 160–67.

Taxes and the Electoral Cycle: How Sensitive Are Governors to Coming Elections?

Anne Case

Review Questions

1. What factors affect the ability for governors to get reelected? How do these factors affect gubernatorial policy?
2. How do term limits affect tax policy?
3. How do neighboring states' policies affect a state's tax policy and gubernatorial reelection prospects?

Recent tax increases in several eastern states have received attention from both voters and the press. In 1991, New Jersey Republicans gained veto-proof majorities in both houses of the legislature for the first time in 20 years. Shortly after the election, the *New York Times* of November 13, 1991, attributed the outcome to "[Governor Florio's] unpopularity and the $2.8 billion tax package he pushed through the legislature." In the wake of Governor Weicker's income tax legislation, 40,000 Connecticut residents "carried signs

---

Case, Anne. "Taxes and the Electoral Cycle: How Sensitive Are Governors to Coming Elections?" *Federal Reserve Bank of Philadelphia Business Review*, March/April 1994, 17–26.

that called for everything from impeachment to lynching for the Governor and his budget officers," according to the *New York Times* of October 7, 1991. History suggests these tax changes may have cost the governors their jobs. In New Jersey, Governor Florio was unsuccessful in his re-election bid in November 1993. In Connecticut, Governor Weicker has announced he will not stand for reelection. Thad Beyle documents that "tax loss" governors have been a common sight on the political landscape since the 1960s.

Political economists, pollsters, and the popular press have long understood the tension that taxes create between elected officials and their constituents. Such tension is to be expected: governors are at times called upon to introduce or increase taxes in order to carry out the wishes of the electorate. Voters understand that tax increases are sometimes unavoidable, but they have limited information with which to assess each call for higher taxes. The electorate also has few tools available with which to punish or reward officials for their performance, and this may add to the tension. Citizens may protest tax increases, as was seen in both Trenton and Hartford, or reduce their political donations in the face of unwelcome tax changes. The electorate may also vote with its feet, leaving the state for one more frugal. These strategies, however, are limited in the size of the punishment they can bring to bear on incumbents. Exit may impose a larger cost on those who choose to move than on the errant official.

A more effective strategy for disciplining elected officials is, often, the ballot box. Threatening to unseat an incumbent may provide the most powerful lever under the electorate's control. However, fiscal decisions are made by elected officials who understand that their re-election odds depend upon their tax policies. For this reason, tax decisions may be based not only on their economic merits but on their political merits as well. This gives way to two potentially important phenomena. Voters, with limited access to information on the need for new taxes, may evaluate and vote on their governor's performance by comparing his fiscal policies with those of governors in neighboring states. Governors who would like to be re-elected may, for this reason, time state tax changes to coincide with those in states nearby. This would lead to a correlation between tax changes in states in close geographic proximity. In addition, tax increases may be postponed until a governor no longer fears the ballot box: tax changes may be timed to correspond with term limits.

Conventional wisdom suggests that voters react to recent changes in taxes. This article quantifies that reaction and shows how it depends upon what neighboring states have done. It also examines the impact of voters' comparisons between tax changes at home and in nearby states on a governor's tax setting behavior. Overall, the results tend to support Ferejohn, who suggests "the key to the voting decision is found not in the earnest pledges of the contenders but, rather, in the infamous remark of a Kansas farmer: 'But what have you done for me lately?'"

Effects of Tax Changes and Economic Performance On Re-election

Data on state tax changes and economic performance indicate some clear differences in states in which the governor was re-elected from those in which he or she was not. We present data on state economies for the two years leading up to each election from 1979 to 1988 (Table 1). We use two-year changes in state economic and fiscal performance because it sometimes takes governors a full fiscal year to implement their fiscal policies.[1] States in which the governor was re-elected and those in which he or she was not differ dramatically in their taxing behavior. Increases in state income tax liabilities, measured in constant dollars, were significantly lower in those states in which governors were re-elected compared with states in which governors were not. On average, the tax liability of joint filers earning $25,000 increased by $10 in the two years leading up to the elections in which the incumbent was returned to office. This contrasts with the $74 increase on average in states in which the incumbent was not re-elected. This difference, of $64, amounts to roughly 10 percent of the income tax liability of filers earning $25,000.[2] Voters appear to

TABLE 1. A History of Gubernatorial Re-elections 1979–1988

	All States Holding Elections	Governor Re-elected	Governor Not Re-elected	Significance Level of Difference[c]
Number of observations	74	47	27	
Change in income tax liability[a]	34.03	10.81	74.44	0.033
Change in state unemployment rate[b]	0.49	0.24	0.92	0.178
Change in state income per capita[b]	353.46	464.14	160.81	0.075

All changes are two-year differences: that is, the change between the fiscal year ending just prior to the election and two years before the election.

[a]Change in income tax liability for joint filers with no dependents who earn $25,000 annually, calculated for filers taking average deductions for this income category. Sample here restricted to states with income taxes.
[b]Source: Statistical Abstract of the United States.
[c]Significance level of difference between the average among governors re-elected and those unseated.
Source: National Bureau of Economic Research, TAXSIM data.

take tax increases during an incumbent's term into account when standing in the voting booth.

The overall economic health of the state also seems to influence whether a governor is re-elected. Changes in state income per capita during a governor's watch significantly affects the probability of his or her re-election. States in which governors were re-elected had lower increases in state unemployment rates (a 0.24-percentage-point increase versus a 0.92-percentage-point increase, on average) and significantly larger increases in income per capita ($464 versus $160, on average) than did states in which governors were not re-elected.

Thus, tax changes and economic performance seem to influence election outcomes. Can we quantify the effects? We can estimate the impact of changes in taxes on a governor's re-election odds and also the effects of state unemployment and income by using a statistical technique known as probit analysis. From 1979 to 1988, incumbents were eligible to stand for re-election in 74 races under study and were returned to office roughly 60 percent of the time. Governors ineligible to stand for re-election due to a binding term limitation are not included in this part of the analysis. In addition, we do not study races in which the governor was eligible to run again but chose instead to run for the United States Congress. Governors eligible for re-election who chose not to run again and who did not run for Congress are included as governors "not re-elected." Voluntary retirement from public office is often a masked defeat: some governors would rather retire than go down to defeat at the polls.[3]

The results of our probit analysis suggest that an increase in tax liability significantly increases the probability that a governor will not be re-elected. (See *Increasing Taxes Lowers the Probability of Re-election,* in which the effect of an increase in tax liability on the probability of re-election is estimated to be .146.) If a governor were to increase taxes by $34.03, which is the average tax change observed during this period, this would reduce the probability of re-election by 5.0 percent (.3403 × .146), holding all else equal.

Voters appear to hold the governor more accountable for the impact of tax policy on their disposable income than for the impact of overall economic conditions within the state. In the period from 1979 to 1988, increases in state unemployment also appear to reduce the odds of re-election, but its effect is not as clear as that of tax changes.[4] The probability of re-election does not depend significantly upon changes in state income per capita. Gubernatorial sensitivity toward tax changes may, for this reason alone, be well placed.[5]

Tax Changes in Neighboring States

Do tax increases always reduce re-election odds? Good governors must raise taxes or cut services, or both, when costs rise more quickly than revenues. How does the electorate decide whether a tax increase is "appropriate"? Evidence from a study by Besley and Case (1992) suggests voters may look to neighboring states when determining whether a given tax increase is out of line. For example, a recession-driven revenue shortfall may require that taxes be raised if the government is expected to provide a minimum level of services. Voters without access to perfect information about the magnitude of such a recession may find it difficult to assess the need for a tax increase. However, if the recession has a regional component, voters may be able to add to their information base by noting how neighboring states have responded. Voters in New Jersey, for example, may look to the tax changes occurring in Pennsylvania and New York to determine whether a tax increase is appropriate. Neighboring states may provide a benchmark against which a given state's performance may be measured. Information on tax levels and changes within a region is available in local newspapers. For example, at the time income taxes were introduced in Connecticut, the *New York Times* ran a front page article under the headline "Neighbors Challenge New York's Tax Reputation." The article compared effective tax rates for filers in different income categories living in a variety of cities in New Jersey, New York, and Connecticut. Such articles appear at regular intervals and may provide information adequate to allow voters to evaluate their governor's relative performance.

Our data suggest that voters gather and use such information. (See ... *But Neighbors' Tax Policy Matters, Too.*) Tax increases in neighboring states appear to offset the effect of home-state tax increases. Governors are not penalized for tax increases if neighbors are raising taxes simultaneously. If neighboring states increase their tax liability by $34, holding all other things equal, this will increase the probability of re-election for the home-state governor by 6.6 percent (.34 × .194), almost exactly offsetting the reduction in the likelihood of re-election that (as we showed earlier) results from the same-size tax increase in his own state. This may have implications for gubernatorial behavior. Governors, recognizing that voters are making comparisons between tax changes at home and in neighboring states, may wait until neighbors are raising taxes before calling for a tax increase at home. Therefore, governors may become responsive to what neighboring states are doing.

We find tax changes are positively and significantly correlated between neighboring states during the 10-year period 1979–88.[6] There are several possible explanations for this correlation. Neighboring states may face shocks to their economies that are regional in nature, as argued above. Furthermore, changes in the national economy may cause neighboring states' tax changes in a given year to appear significantly correlated. We do not want to attribute to re-election concerns a correlation that is actually due to regional or national economic conditions. One natural way around this is to look separately at governors who are eligible to stand for re-election and those who are not. If correlation between neighboring states' taxes is due primarily to political concerns, we should find a positive and significant relationship between changes in home-state taxes and changes in neighbors' taxes only in those states in which the governor can stand for re-election. This is indeed what we find: in states in which the governor is ineligible to stand for re-election, there is no correlation between tax changes in home and neighboring states; in states in which the governor is eligible to run again, there is positive and significant correlation between tax changes.[7]

These relationships are presented graphically (Figures 1 and 2) for two-year tax changes observed in 1983 for joint filers earning $25,000 in each state. Similar patterns are present in every year. In Figure 1, the tax change in a given state is marked on the vertical axis, and the average tax change in that state's neighbors is marked on the horizontal axis. For example, Michigan had a very high change in taxes from 1981 to 1983, and so did Michigan's neighbors. Fiscal year 1983 ends before the elections of 1983. Comparing states whose governors were eligible to stand in their states' next election, held sometime between 1983 and 1986, we see that states with large tax increases have neighbors with large tax increases, and states with small tax increases have neighbors with similarly small tax increases. In contrast, among states run by governors who are ineligible to stand for re-election, there is no observable pattern between neighbors' tax changes.

Regional shocks could cause state tax changes to be correlated between states in a region, regardless of whether the state is run by a governor eligible to stand for re-election. The data suggest, however, that only states in which the governors can run again show a positive and significant correlation with neighboring states' tax changes. We take this behavioral difference as evidence that the sensitivity to neighbors' taxes is due to electoral effects.

Contrary to textbook public finance models in which state taxation decisions are based solely on economic criteria, our evidence suggests that the governors' political timetable and the behavior of neighboring states may influence state taxation decisions.

Increasing Taxes Lowers the Probability of Re-election

To estimate the effect of tax increases net of changes in income and the unemployment rate, we include all three variables in a probit equation. The dependent variable equals 1 if the governor was defeated in the primary or election or was eligible to run but "retired" and did not run for Congress; it equals 0 if the governor was re-elected. Changes in tax liability is the change in the effective state income tax liability of joint filers earning $25,000, expressed in hundreds of 1982 dollars. Change in state income per capita is also expressed in hundreds of 1982 dollars. The coefficients reported here are changes in the probability of incumbent defeat, evaluated at sample means.

Governor Defeat = 0.146 × change in − 0.005 × change in + 0.026 × change
(t=1.94)   tax   (t=0.47)   state   (t=0.73)   in state
    liability   inc./cap   unemp.

Governor Defeat = 0.126   × change in + 0.007 × change in + 0.082 × change
(t=1.77)   tax   (t=0.54)   state   (t=1.70)   in state
    liability   inc./cap   unemp.

    + 0.022 × gov.'s + 0.245 × pres. − 0.139 × pres.
    (t=2.75)   age   (t=1.42)   election   (t=0.82)   coattails
                        yr.

Number of observations = 74.

If state income tax liability for joint filers were to increase by $100, this would act to reduce the probability of an incumbent's re-election by almost 15 percent. When changes in taxes, income and unemployment are entered simultaneously, it appears that the change in taxes is the dominating force behind incumbent defeat.

In addition to changes in state economic variables, many political variables may influence election results. For example, incumbents who must run in presidential election years may find it relatively more difficult to win re-election, given the larger voter turnout from both parties that occurs in presidential election years. In addition, there may be presidential "coattails." That is, if an incumbent is of the same party as the winning contender in the presidential race, he may receive votes that reflect the popularity of a president-elect. While this is possible, we find no evidence for either effect in the period studied here.

Term Limits, Electoral Cycles, and Taxation

The timing of tax changes may be affected not only by changes in neighboring states but also by the presence of term limits. The political economy literature discusses the potentially offsetting effects of such limits. James Adams and Lawrence Kenny suggest that, in the absence of term limits, it may be rel-

... But Neighbors' Tax Policy Matters, Too

We define geographic neighbors as states that share a common boundary. "Neighbors' tax change" is the average tax change experienced in a given state's geographic neighbors. In results presented here, all neighbors are given equal weight. Changes in taxes and state income are in hundreds of 1982 dollars.

Governor Defeat =

0.110	×	tax	−	0.194	× neighbors' +	0.004	× change +	0.090
(t=1.66)		change	(t=1.74)		tax change	(t=0.29)	in	(t=1.97)
		$25,000			$25,000		state	
		filers			filers		inc./cap	

× change	+	0.025 ×	gov.'s	+	0.269	× pres.	− 0.112 ×	pres.
state		(t=3.03)	age		(t=1.66)	election	(t=0.72)	coattails
unemp.						yr		

Governor Defeat =

0.017	×	tax	−	0.059	× neighbors' −	0.010	× change +	0.053
(t=1.68)		change	(t=2.69)		tax change	(t=0.79)	in state	(t=1.29)
		$100,000			$100,000		inc./cap	
		filers			filers			

× change	+	0.029 ×	gov.'s	+	0.165	× pres.	− 0.138 ×	pres.
state		(t=3.42)	age		(t=1.21)	election	(t=0.91)	coattails
unemp.						yr.		

Number of observations = 74.

Increases in neighboring states' taxes offset the effect of tax changes at home on an incumbent's re-election odds; the absolute value of the coefficients on own tax changes and neighbors' tax changes are not statistically different from one another.

The effect of changes in income taxes on the probability of re-election is present in different parts of the income distribution. The increase in the probability of gubernatorial defeat when taxes are raised at home, and the offsetting effect of increases in neighbors' taxes, are seen here for both $25,000 joint filers and $100,000 joint filers.

atively easy for one party to put a lock on the governor's office, especially in small states. Political capital may accrue to the party in office, acting to increase the odds of gubernatorial re-election. States may perceive term limits as a way to block the accrual of political capital and, thus, as a means to broader representation.

While term limitations provide a guarantee that a state will not be stuck with a bad incumbent indefinitely, this guarantee may come at a price. In addition to the costs associated with learning about candidates and voting, there is also the possibility that incumbents, as lame ducks, may change their be-

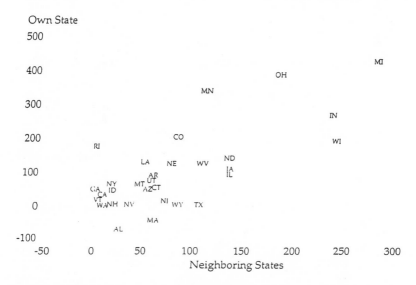

Figure 1. The Relationship Between Own and Neighbors' Tax Changes (1981–83) When the Governor Is Eligible for Re-election[a]
[a]Increased tax liability in dollars for joint filers with incomes of $25,000.

havior to better suit their own long-term goals. Some analysts do not believe such a change in behavior is likely. Given that parties live forever even when incumbents do not, Alberto Alesina and Stephen Spear suggest that the incumbent's political party could compensate the official to keep him in line and, in this way, protect others within the party from being punished in response to the lame duck's behavior. Lott (1990) provides some evidence of this among congressmen.

We find differences in many aspects of the taxing behavior of governors eligible to stand for re-election and those facing term limitations, in addition to the difference in sensitivity toward neighbors' tax changes discussed above. Our data suggest that governors who are hitting term limits increase taxes more than those who can stand for re-election. For example, controlling for state income per capita, state unemployment, and state-specific effects, we find that in each year of the term of an incumbent ineligible to stand for re-election, state income tax liability for $25,000 joint filers increases by $26 more per year than it does when that state is governed by an incumbent who can run for re-election.[8] Over a four-year term, this amounts to a tax increase of $106 (26.49 × 4), or roughly 15 percent of the tax liability of $25,000 filers. This is true even though, on average, states with term limits have lower income tax liability for $25,000 joint filers: $650 versus $783 on average from

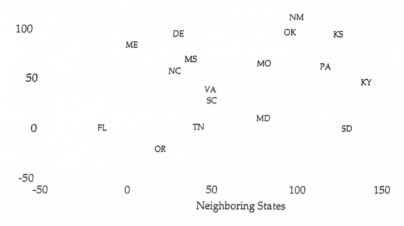

Figure 2. The Relationship Between Own and Neighbors' Tax Changes (1981–83) When the Governor Is Ineligible for Re-election[a]
[a]Increased tax liability in dollars for joint filers with incomes of $25,000.

1977 to 1988. This lower tax is maintained through gubernatorial behavior in the years in which the governor is eligible to run for re-election. In many states with term limits, a governor can serve for two consecutive terms. In the first term, the governor holds tax changes below the state's average. If re-elected, the governor raises taxes more than the average for that state. In this way, term limits lead to electoral tax cycles.

Conclusion

Models of fiscal decision-making must take political variables into account if they are to adequately capture reality at the state level. The analysis of gubernatorial behavior suggests re-election looms large in choices made by incumbents. The common perception is that governors who raise taxes do not get re-elected, and therefore, governors are reluctant to propose tax increases (at least in the two years prior to an election). In fact, the situation is more complicated. The experience of neighboring states in raising taxes has a great deal of influence. Moreover, governors who are not eligible for re-election may raise taxes more than other governors, producing an electoral cycle in tax policy.

NOTES

1. The results presented in this article are similar when three-year changes are used.

2. Throughout this article we use joint filers with $25,000 in income as the basis for our analysis, but the basic results hold for other income levels as well.

3. Inclusion of governors who voluntarily retire improves the precision of (reduces the standard errors on) our estimates but does not otherwise affect the analysis. We could also model transitions in the governor's chair from one party to another and, in this way, include in the analysis decisions made by governors who cannot stand for re-election because of term limits. Party loyalty may force elected officials to behave prudently even though they personally will not benefit at the ballot box. However, Besley and Case (1993) find that party loyalty does not appear to play a role in the decisions made by governors facing term limits, and for this reason, governors facing term limits are excluded from the current analysis.

4. The statistical significance level of the unemployment rate effect varies greatly depending on what other variables are entered into the equation. (See *Increasing Taxes Lowers the Probability of Re-election.*)

5. For a detailed analysis of the relationship between tax changes and gubernatorial re-election, see Besley and Case (1992). It is possible that when states face fiscal crises they simultaneously raise taxes and reduce expenditures. The effect of tax changes on re-election odds may be in part proxying for the impact of reduced expenditures on re-election odds. To test for this, changes in state expenditures per capita were added to the re-election equation. We found that the probability of gubernatorial re-election in this period is insensitive to changes in total state expenditures per capita, whether or not change in taxes is used as an explanatory variable.

6. The correlation coefficient is 0.17.

7. The correlation coefficient for these states is 0.19. We continue to find a positive and significant relationship between neighbors' tax changes in states where governors can run again, even when we control for state income and unemployment, state demographic variables (proportion elderly and young in the state population), year effects, and state-specific fixed effects. We continue to find no relationship between neighbors' tax changes in states governed by lame ducks. See Besley and Case (1992) for tests based on alternative econometric specifications.

8. This result comes from the regression: Tax liability $= 26.49 \times$ an indicator that the incumbent is ineligible to run again ($t = 2.33$), controlling for state income per capita, state unemployment, and state-specific fixed effects. (Number of observations $=$ 480: 48 states for the period 1977–86. Regression run with heteroskedasticity consistent standard errors.) The sample is larger than that for gubernatorial re-elections because we have tax data for every year of an incumbent's term, not just election year data. In addition, the sample covers both governors who can and cannot run for re-election. Indicator variables were used to see if taxes varied within the four years of a term. We found no evidence that they did. Taxes were higher by about the same amount in every year of a lame duck's term.

REFERENCES

Adams, James D., and Lawrence W. Kenny. "Optimal Tenure of Elected Public Officials," *Journal of Law and Economics*, 29 (October 1986), pp. 303–28.

Alesina, Alberto, and Stephen E. Spear. "An Overlapping Generations Model of Electoral Competition," *Journal of Public Economics*, 37 (December 1988), pp. 359–79.

Bartlett, Sarah. "Neighbors Challenge New York's Tax Reputation," *New York Times* (September 22, 1991), p. 1.

Besley, Timothy, and Anne Case. "Incumbent Behavior: Vote Seeking, Tax Setting and Yardstick Competition," National Bureau of Economic Research Working Paper 4041, March 1992.

Besley, Timothy, and Anne Case. "Does Electoral Accountability Affect Economic Policy Choices? Evidence from Gubernatorial Term Limits," National Bureau of Economic Research Working Paper 4575, December 1993.

Beyle, Thad L. "Governors," in V. Gray, H. Jacob, and K. Vines, eds., *Politics in the American States.* Little, Brown and Company, 1983.

Ferejohn, J. "Incumbent Performance and Electoral Control," *Public Choice*, 50(1), (1986) pp. 5–25.

Gray, Jerry. "Embattled Florio Says He'll Seek Guidance From the Voters," *New York Times* (November 13, 1991), p. B1.

Johnson, Kirk. "Lawmakers Tell 40,000 at Rally Connecticut Income Tax Will Die," *New York Times* (October 6, 1991), p. I34.

Lott, John R., Jr. "Attendance Rates, Political Shirking, and the Effect of Post-Elective Office Employment," *Economic Inquiry*, 28 (January 1990), pp. 133–50.

Suggested Additional Readings

Alesina, Alberto. "Politics and Business Cycles in Industrial Democracies." *Economic Policy* 10 (1989): 55–98.

———. "Elections, Party Structure, and the Economy." In *Modern Political Economy: Old Topics, New Directions*, ed. Jeffrey S. Banks and Eric A. Hanushek. Cambridge: Cambridge University Press: 1995.

Blais, André, and Richard Nadeau. "The Electoral Budget Cycle." *Public Choice* 74 (1992): 389–403.

Chowdhury, Abdur R. "Political Surfing over Economic Waves: Parliamentary Election Timing in India." *American Journal of Political Science* 37 (1993): 1100–1118.

Chubb, John E. "Institutions, the Economy, and the Dynamics of State Elections." *American Political Science Review* 82 (1988): 133–54.

Erikson, Robert S. "Economic Conditions and the Presidential Vote." *American Political Science Review* 83 (1989): 567–73.

Hansen, Susan B. "Life Is Not Fair: Governors' Job Performance Ratings and State Economies." *Political Research Quarterly* 52 (1999): 167–88.

Heckelman, Jac C. "Historical Political Business Cycles." In Eh.net Encyclopedia, ed. Robert Whaples. *http://www.eh.net/encyclopedia/heckelman.political.business.cycles .php*, 2001.

Hibbs, Douglas A. "Partisan Theory after Fifteen Years." *European Journal of Political Economy* 8 (1992): 361–73.

Keech, William. *Economic Politics: The Costs of Democracy.* Cambridge: Cambridge University Press, 1998.

Peltzman, Sam. "Economic Conditions and Gubernatorial Elections." *American Economic Review Papers and Proceedings* 77 (1987): 293–97.

Sheffrin, Steven M. "Evaluating Rational Partisan Business Cycle Theory." *Economics and Politics* 1 (1989): 239–60.

Soh, Byung Hee. "Political Business Cycles in Industrialized Democratic Countries." *Kyklos* 39 (1986): 61–76.

Tufte, Edward R. *Political Control of the Economy.* Princeton: Princeton University Press, 1978.

Advanced Readings

Alesina, Alberto, Uriel Roubini, and Gerald D. Cohen. *Political Cycles and the Macroeconomy.* Cambridge: MIT Press, 1999.

Drazen, Allan. *Political Macroeconomics.* Princeton: Princeton University Press, 2000.

Ito, Takatoshi, and Jin Hyuk Park. "Political Business Cycles in the Parliamentary System." *Economics Letters* 27 (1988): 233–38.

Lupia, Arthur, and Kaare Strom. "Coalition Termination and the Strategic Determination of Election Timing." *American Political Science Review* 89 (1995): 648–65.

PART III
Social Choice Theory

Choosing Decision Rules

When individuals form groups, conflicts naturally occur, and decisions must be reached as to how these conflicts will be resolved. In a democratic environment, voting is the main avenue for deciding how to proceed. The issues may involve selecting representatives or specific proposals. If everyone in the group agrees on the best choice, there is no reason not to choose that. The larger the group, however, the less likely unanimous consent will be reached. In the typical case of differing opinions, a mechanism must be invoked to select the winning alternative.

The advantage to requiring unanimous consent is that everyone must agree on the outcome. Every person has the ability to veto a proposal. Assuming individuals favor the candidate or proposal that generates the largest net benefit for them (purely selfish individuals may consider only their own personal benefits and costs, whereas altruistic individuals may also consider how others are affected as part of the cost and benefits), agreeing to a new proposal must mean those individuals in favor receive at least some positive net benefit. Unanimous consent ensures everyone in the group receives positive net benefit, and thus any new policy is socially enhancing. If policy is socially efficient, that is, the total social benefits outweigh the total social costs, then by definition there must be at least one way to distribute the costs (for example, the taxes required to pay for the proposal's agenda) such that no one individual would have negative net benefits.

While unanimous consent ensures that any proposals passed would not be objected to by anyone, one problem with this requirement is that unanimous consent may never be reached, or possibly only after a long period of time amending the policy to everyone's satisfaction. In the interim, nothing happens. The group remains stuck at its original position and loses out on potentially socially efficient improvements that may contain some degree of redistributive element as well. In the case of selecting candidates, the office remains unfilled until a new candidate emerges that every person agrees is the best. By protecting the interests of a small subgroup, which may be even a single individual, unanimous consent may create larger problems than it prevents. In fact, since every person's agreement is required for any proposal to pass, such a requirement gives individuals the incentive to hold out for alterations more in their favor even if they consider the current proposal to be beneficial.

This suggests that unanimous consent is not practical for most cases. Furthermore, if one of the alternatives is to keep current policies the same (for instance by voting no on a new referendum), the unanimity rule builds in a bias to those who favor current policy since anything other than unanimous consent retains the status quo. If unanimous consent is rejected as a way to make decisions, there are many potential alternative rules that could be invoked. For example, perhaps only a majority, but less than 100 percent, could be required. Even here, with more than two alternatives from which to choose, no single alternative may obtain an absolute majority, again protecting the status quo although to a lesser degree than the unanimity rule.

It is unclear what is the best criteria to consider when deciding how to select a decision rule. One way is to estimate the costs of using various rules and choose the rule with the lowest cost. Another way is to consider various normative properties of each rule and select the rule satisfying the most attractive properties. Unfortunately, in probably the most famous proof in all of social choice theory, Nobel Laureate Kenneth Arrow has proven that no voting rule satisfies a specific set of fairly minimal normative requirements. What is shocking is not so much that the common rules often utilized, such as majority or plurality rule, fail to satisfy these requirements but that it is mathematically impossible to design any voting rule that would suffice. Thus, any voting rule will be subject to problems, and it is unlikely to get the group to agree on even which rule to use. No rule will emerge to be purely superior to all others.

According to Arrow's proof, any voting rule will possibly generate incoherent outcomes in the sense that it is possible that the group decision could lose out to another alternative already dismissed. For example, consider the

case of majority rule on three alternatives A, B, and C. For certain sets of individual preferences, it could be that a majority favors A over B, and a (different) majority favors B over C. We might then expect that A must generate
a majority preference over C, but actually it is possible for the opposite to be
true. Thus, the group decisions may not be transitive. This paradox is especially troubling since it means that even if we reduce our requirements to
only force majority satisfaction, rather than unanimous agreement, majority
rule does not ensure that a majority will in fact prefer the chosen outcome.
It is not clear which particular majority group should prevail in this case.
Arrow's proof shows the only way to ensure transitive outcomes on any potential set of alternatives without imposing any restrictions on the preferences each person has is to ignore everyone's preferences except for one single individual. This person would be appointed dictator over all decisions.
Obviously, this is not a very satisfactory mechanism since it is the antithesis
of democratic outcomes and is not, in the broad sense, truly a group decision
rule since no one in the group has any input except for the lone individual.

When decisions affect only the individual doing the choosing, such as in
private free markets without externalities, this system of dictatorship makes
sense. Any choice made (which may include no purchase at all) is the best for
that individual involved (among existing available alternatives). Here there is
no conflict between limited dictatorship (on these specific choices) and
unanimous consent since only one person is involved in the decision and the
outcome. When externalities are present, however, choices even in private
markets do affect others who may be harmed by the chooser's actions. Dictatorial decisions can then be inefficient. This is certain to be the case for group
decisions.

Buchanan's "Individual Choice in Voting and the Market" is an introductory piece to social choice theory at the start of the public choice movement.
Buchanan explains the differences in incentives for economic agents making
public-joint decisions through voting versus private-individual decisions in
the market. In large group settings, collective decisions rarely can rely on
unanimous consent, and therefore functional democracy needs to accept
rules with lesser criteria. Spindler's "Constitutional Design for a Rent-Seeking Society" explains how rent seeking affects the optimal size decision rule.
In "Social Choice and Arrow's Paradox," MacKay presents a nontechnical
treatment of Arrow's result and discusses the meaning of each included normative criteria.

Individual Choice in Voting and the Market[1]

James M. Buchanan

Review Questions

1. How are voter decisions in elections similar to consumer choices in markets? In what important ways do they differ? What issues does the simple one-dollar/one-vote analogy obscure?
2. In what sense are individuals "less corruptible" in market activity compared with voting? Why might voters not choose the alternatives they personally favor? Why are choices made in markets a clearer representation of desires than choices made with voting ballots?
3. What "indirect" coercion occurs prior to voting? What direct coercion occurs after voting?
4. When is the market the preferred choice process? When is voting the preferred choice process? Why?

This paper will compare individual choice in the political voting process and in the market process, with both considered as ideal types. A substantial portion of the analysis will be intuitively familiar to all social scientists, since it serves as a basis for a large part of political theory, on the one hand, and

---

Buchanan, James M. "Individual Choice in Voting and the Market." *Journal of Political Economy* 62 (1954): 334–43.

economic theory, on the other. Perhaps as a result of disciplinary specialization, however, the similarities and the differences between these two methods of individual decision-making in liberal society are often overlooked. The state of things is illustrated in the prosaic "one-dollar-one-vote" analogy, which is, at best, only partially appropriate and which tends to conceal extremely important differences.

It is necessary to emphasize the limitations of this analysis. No attempt will be made to compare market choice and voting choice in terms of the relative efficiency in achieving specified social goals or, in other words, as means of *social* decision-making. Many comparisons of this sort have been made. In the great debate over the possibility of rational socialist calculation, the discussion has been concerned primarily with the workability of political decision-making processes when confronted with the social criterion of economic efficiency. The issue has been framed, appropriately, in terms of the relative efficiency of centralized and decentralized decision-making. Collective choice implies centralized choice, whatever the process of choosing; hence the market has been compared with the whole subset of political choice processes ranging from pure democracy to authoritarian dictatorship.

This paper will compare the *individual* choices involved in the price system and in a single form of centralized decision-making—pure democracy. The individual act of participation in the choice process will be the point of reference. The comparison does not, of course, imply that these two processes will be presented as genuine alternatives to the individual, even in their somewhat less pure forms. A more complete understanding of individual behavior in each process should, however, provide some basis for deciding between the two, if and when they do exist as alternatives.

The following distinctions between individual choice in voting and the market will be discussed: (1) the degree of certainty, (2) the degree of social participation, (3) the degree of responsibility, (4) the nature of the alternatives presented, (5) the degree of coercion, and, finally, (6) the power relations among individuals. Quite obviously, these distinctions are somewhat arbitrarily isolated from one another, and in a broad sense, each implies others. After these are discussed, some attention will be given to their influence on the selection of voting or the market as a decision-making process for the social group.

I

It will be assumed that the individual chooser possesses the same degree of knowledge concerning the results of alternative decisions in the polling place that he does in the market place.[2] It is essential that this assumption be made at this stage, in order that the first important distinction, that of the degree of certainty, between individual choice in voting and individual choice in the market may be made clear.

In market choice the individual is the acting or choosing entity, as well as the entity for which choices are made. In voting, the individual is an acting or choosing entity, but the collectivity is the entity for which decisions are made. The individual in the market can predict with absolute certainty the direct or immediate result of his action. The act of choosing and the consequences of choosing stand in a one-to-one correspondence.[3] On the other hand, the voter, even if he is fully omniscient in his foresight of the consequences of each possible collective decision, can never predict with certainty which of the alternatives presented will be chosen. He can never predict the behavior of other voters in the polling place. Reciprocal behavior prediction of this sort becomes a logical impossibility if individual choice is accepted as meaningful.[4] This inherent uncertainty confronting the voter can perhaps be classified as genuine uncertainty in the Knightian sense; it is not subject to the application of the probability calculus.

This uncertainty must influence to some degree the behavior of the individual in choosing among the possible social alternatives offered to him. Whereas the chooser in the market,[5] assumed to know what he wants, will always take the attainable combination of goods and services standing highest on his preference scale, the voter will not necessarily, or perhaps even probably, choose the alternative most desirable to him. The actual behavior of the voter must be examined within the framework of a theory of choice under uncertainty. As is well known, there is no fully acceptable theory of behavior here, and there are some students of the problem who deny the possibility of rational behavior in uncertain conditions.[6]

II

The second fundamental difference in the two choice processes is found in the sense or degree of participation in social decision-making. In the market the individual is confronted with a range of commodities and services, each of which is offered at a given price. Individually, the buyer or seller considers both the range of alternatives and the set of prices to be beyond his power to alter.[7] He is able, therefore, to assume himself apart from, or external to, the social organization which does influence the alternatives made available. He is unconscious of the secondary repercussions of his act of choice which serve to alter the allocation of economic resources.[8] The individual tends to act *as if* all the social variables are determined outside his own behavior, which, in this subjective sense, is nonparticipating and therefore nonsocial.[9] The influence of the individual's actual behavior on the ultimate social decision made has no impact upon such behavior.[10]

The individual in the polling place, by contrast, recognizes that his vote is influential in determining the final collective choice; he is fully conscious of his participation in social decision-making. The individual act of choosing is, therefore, social, even in a purely subjective sense.

The sense of participation in social choice may exert important effects on the behavior of the individual. It seems probable that the representative individual will act in accordance with a different preference scale when he realizes that he is choosing for the group rather than merely for himself. There are two reasons for this. First, his identification will tend to be broadened,[11] and his "values" will be more likely to influence his ordering of alternatives, whereas in market choice his "tastes" may determine his decision.[12] As an example, the individual may cast a ballot-box vote for the enforcement of prohibition at the same time that he visits his bootlegger, without feeling that he is acting inconsistently. Even if the individual's welfare horizon is not modified in a shift from market to voting choice, or vice versa, there is a second, and perhaps equally important, reason for a rearrangement of his preference scale and hence for some difference in behavior. The individual's ranking of alternatives in market choice assumes no action on the part of other individuals in specific correspondence to his own. In voting, the choice is determined from a ranking of alternative situations in each of which the position of the individual is collectively determined for him and for *all* other individuals in the group.[13] As an example of this difference, businessmen in a perfectly competitive industry marketing a product with an inelastic demand may vote to approve governmentally imposed production limitations, while, if left to operate independently, they would have no incentive to restrict production. A further example may be used to illustrate the case in which both these effects on individual choice may be operative. A man who in the unregulated market economy would construct a billboard advertising his produce might vote for the abolition of billboards because he considers such action preferable in terms of group welfare and/or because his own interests will be better served by such collectively imposed action.

III

The difference in the individual's sense of social participation has its obverse, however, which may be introduced as a third distinction between the voting and market processes. Since voting implies collective choice, the responsibility for making any particular social or collective decision is necessarily divided. This seems clearly to affect the individual's interest in the choosing process. Since a decision is to be made in any case, the single individual need not act at all; he may abstain from voting while other individuals act.

The responsibility for market decisions is uniquely concentrated on the chooser; there can be no abstention. There is a tangible benefit as well as a cost involved in each market chooser's decision, while there is neither an immediately realizable and certain benefit nor an imputable cost normally involved in the voter's choice.[14] This difference tends to guarantee that a more precise and objective consideration of alternative costs takes place in the minds of individuals choosing in the market. This does not suggest, however, that the greatest precision in the consideration of alternatives by individuals in the market implies that the costs and benefits taken into account are necessarily the proper ones from the social point of view.[15]

It seems quite possible that in many instances the apparent placing of "the public interest" above mere individual or group interest in political decisions represents nothing more than a failure of the voters to consider fully the real costs of the activity to be undertaken. It is extremely difficult to determine whether the affirmative vote of a nonbeneficiary individual for a public welfare project implies that he is either acting socially in accordance with a "nobler" ordering of alternatives or is estimating his own self-interest in accordance with a "collective-action" preference scale, or whether it suggests that he has failed to weigh adequately the opportunity costs of the project.

The difference in responsibility provides a basis for Professor Mises' argument that an individual is "less corruptible" in the market.[16] This might plausibly be advanced without necessarily contradicting the claim that ballot-box choice, if uncorrupted, is made in accordance with a more inclusive and modified value scale. A somewhat related point has been made by Professor Spengler when he says that there is, in voting as compared with the market, "the tendency of the individual (especially when he is a part of a large and disciplined organization) more easily to lose . . . political than economic autonomy."[17]

IV

A fourth distinction, and perhaps one of the most important, between individual choice in voting and the market lies in the nature of the alternatives offered to the individual in each case. Choice implies that alternatives are mutually conflicting; otherwise, all would be chosen, which is equivalent to saying that none would be chosen. It is in the precise way in which the alternatives mutually conflict that the voting process must be sharply distinguished from the market mechanism.

Alternatives of market choice normally conflict only in the sense that the law of diminishing returns is operative. This is true at the level both of the individual chooser and of the social group. If an individual desires *more* of a particular commodity or service, the market normally requires only that he take *less* of another commodity or service. If all individuals, through their market choices, indicate that *more* resources should be devoted to the production of a particular commodity, this requires only that *less* resources be devoted to the production of other commodities.

Alternatives of voting choice are more normally mutually exclusive, that is, the selection of one precludes the selection of another. This, too, is true at the level both of the individual chooser and of the whole system. The individual voter normally faces mutually exclusive choices because of the indivisibility of his vote. Group choices tend to be mutually exclusive by the very nature of the alternatives, which are regularly of the "all-or-none" variety.

For the individual, market choice amounts to the allocation of an unspecialized and highly divisible resource (income-yielding capacity) among a range of alternatives. On the other hand, few voting schemes include means which enable an individual to break his total voting strength down into fractional parts. The attribute of scarcity has never been applied to voting strength; an additional vote is granted to each individual when each new collective decision is made. In order for market choice to be made similar to voting in this respect, each individual would be required to devote his whole capacity in each market period to one commodity or service. If only the buying side is taken into account, this means that the consumer's whole expenditure should be on one commodity. It seems clear that this feature of the choice process can itself affect the nature of the alternatives presented. If the individual were required to spend the whole of his income on one commodity, market alternatives would tend to become mutually exclusive and to become severely limited in number and variety. Most of the normally available goods and services would disappear from the market places.

The major share of the difference in the nature of the alternatives presented in the two choice processes must, however, be attributed to fundamental differences in the objects of choice themselves. In a very real sense many voting choices can never be made in the market because they are inherently more difficult, involving, as they do, considerations which cannot be taken into account effectively by the individual choosing only for himself. The choice to be made is normally among two or more alternatives, only one of which may be chosen, with its very selection precluding the selection of the others. Even if the results of the voting were to be based upon the proportionate number of votes cast for each alternative, combinations or composite solutions of the market type would not be possible in most cases. Inherent in the market solution, by contrast, is choice among an almost infinite number of *combinations* of goods and services, in each of which some of almost every conceivable good and service will be included.[18] As a result of this difference, individual choice in the market can be more articulate than in the voting booth.

V

There follows directly from the difference in the nature of alternatives an extremely important fifth distinction between the voting process and the market process as faced by the individual choice-maker. If production indivisibilities may be disregarded (they would not be present in the ideally competitive world), each dollar vote in the market becomes positively effective[19] to the individual, not only in providing him with a unit of the chosen commodity or service, but also in generating changes in the economic environment. In either of these senses a dollar vote is never overruled; the individual is never placed in the position of being a member of a dissenting minority.[20] When a commodity or service is exchanged in the market, the individual chooses from among *existing* alternatives; at the secondary stage, of which he is unconscious, his behavior tends to direct economic resources in a specific manner.

In voting, the individual does not choose among *existing* but rather among *potential* alternatives, and, as mentioned earlier, he is never secure in his belief that his vote will count positively. He may lose his vote and be placed in the position of having cast his vote in opposition to the alternative finally chosen by the social group. He may be compelled to accept a result contrary to his expressed preference. A similar sort of coercion is never present in market choice. It has been argued that pressure toward social conformity "compels those outvoted to make an expenditure against their will."[21] While it is no doubt true that both the individual's earning and expenditure patterns are conditioned to a large degree by the average patterns of his social group, the distinction between this indirectly coercive effect involved in the social urge to conform and the direct and unavoidable coercion involved in collective decision seems an extremely important one.

If the assumption of production divisibility is relaxed, some modifications of this conclusion must be made. Given the presence of indivisibility, the individual's dollar vote may be overruled at the secondary stage of the market choice process. On the buying side, if the consumer's dollar vote is not accompanied by enough other votes to maintain the production of the particular good or service, it may be "lost," and, at this stage, the buyer may be in a position apparently equivalent to that of the ballot-box supporter of the losing side of an issue. On the selling side, if there are not enough final demand dollar votes to warrant production of those commodities or services embodying the individual's productive contribution, then the attempt to convert productive services into generalized purchasing power on former terms may be thwarted. But in each case, at the initial or primary stage of the market process, the individual's expressed choice is never overruled. The buyer would never have possessed the opportunity to choose, had not the commodity or service been existent in the market; and the seller of productive services would have never been able to develop particular skills, had not a derived demand for those skills been present. And since the one-to-one correspondence between the act of choice and its result is the only condition directly influencing the individual's behavior, there can never be present the sense of directly losing one's market vote. There may, of course, arise a sense of regret when the consumer returns to the market place and finds a desired commodity no longer available and when the individual no longer is able to market productive services previously adapted to particular uses. The consumer may also regret that certain desired goods have never been placed in the market in the first place, and the individual seller may be concerned that there has never existed a ready market for his peculiar talents. This sort of regret does not, however, apply uniquely to market choice. It applies equally to political voting, and it does not, therefore, constitute the market's equivalent of the "lost" ballot-box vote. It is true that there may be commodities and services not offered for sale which the individual would be willing to purchase, but there may also be many potential alternatives never presented for a vote which an individual might desire to support.

VI

Each of the five preceding distinctions in the individual participation in voting and market choice is present even when the relative power positions of individuals are made equivalent in the two processes, that is, when there is absolute equality in the distribution of income-earning capacity among market choosers. All these distinctions tend, therefore, to be neglected in the simple "one-dollar-one-vote" analogy, which concentrates attention only upon the

difference in the relative power of individuals. Market choice is normally conducted under conditions of inequality among individuals, while voting tends,
at least ideally, to be conducted under conditions of equality.

The essential point to be emphasized in this connection is that the inequalities present in market choice are inequalities in individual power and
not in individual freedom, if care is taken to define freedom and power in
such a way as to maximize the usefulness of these two concepts in discussion.
As Knight has suggested, it seems desirable for this reason to define freedom
somewhat narrowly as the absence of coercion and unfreedom as the state of
being prevented from utilizing the normally available capacities for action.[22]

VII

There remains the task of evaluating the foregoing differences in the position
of the individual chooser in voting and in the market, with a view toward determining the relative appropriateness of the two choice processes for the social group when they are, in fact, possible alternatives. If rationality in individual behavior is considered a desirable feature of a choice process,[23] there
would appear to be several reasons for claiming that market choice should be
preferred. The greater degree of certainty seems clearly to produce more rational behavior; the uniquely centered responsibility tends to work in the
same direction. Even if voting and the market are genuinely alternative means
of making choices in a particular situation (thereby eliminating the inherent
difficulties in voting choice when this is the only alternative), the difference
in the divisibility of voting tends to make market choices finer and more articulate. The fact that market choice tends to embody greater rationality in
individual behavior than does voting choice does not suggest that market
choice tends to produce greater *social* rationality.[24]

The market should also be preferred as a choice process when individual
freedom is considered in isolation. The absence of negative results of individual choices and, therefore, of the direct coercion which requires that the
individual accept unchosen alternatives makes for a greater degree of freedom in market choice.

On the other hand, voting should perhaps be preferred to the market when
individual motivation in choice is the attribute examined. Voting choice does
provide individuals with a greater sense of participation in social decision-
making, and, in this way, it may bring forth the "best" in man and tend to make
individuals take somewhat more account of the "public interest." This attribute of the voting process has probably been somewhat neglected by liberal

students and somewhat overemphasized in importance by socialists. It should be noted, however, that, even if this proves to be an important difference, voting will produce consistent or "rational" *social* choice only if men are able to agree on the ultimate social goals.[25] If men are not able to agree on what is genuine morality, the adoption of a choice process in which they act more morally cannot be justified on this ground.[26]

It is in the power structure among individuals antecedent to choice that the market may, and most often does, prove unacceptable. Political voting is characterized by an alternative power structure which may be deemed preferable to that of the market. And the selection of the one-for-one power relation among individuals appears to carry with it the selection of voting over market choice. If, however, the market power structure can be effectively modified independently of the choice process, this apparent advantage of political voting need not be present.

It should be noted that the fundamental decision to modify the power structure, as well as the extent of such modification, clearly must be made by the ballot box. And in this type of decision especially it is essential that individuals act in accordance with a value-ordering which is somewhat different from that motivating individual market choice. After a redistributive decision for the group is made, it must be further decided whether a particular choice shall be made by the market or by political voting. This decision on process must also be made by means of the ballot box. In this decision the market choices are considered by voters to produce a social state less desirable than that which is produced by individual voting choices.

The selection of the choice process, if the redistributive decision can be made separately, will depend to a large degree upon the relative positions of the various social goals in the value scales of individuals comprising the voting group. If consistency in individual behavior and individual freedom are highly regarded relative to other values, the market will tend to be favored. If, on the other hand, the somewhat vague, even though meaningful, concept of "social welfare" is the overriding consideration, voting choice may be preferred. But even here, if the individual's expressed interest is judged to be the best index of social welfare, the market may still be acceptable as a choice process (this was essentially the position of the utilitarians).

The selection of the choice process will also depend on whether or not the voters consider their own self-interest to be better served individualistically or collectively. If the "collective-action" preference scale allows the required majority of individuals to attain a more esteemed position than does the "individual-action" preference scale, voting choice will be selected regardless of the ranking of social goals. In this case it might be irrational for an individual to choose the market process, even though his behavior in the market, once this process was selected by the group, would be more rational than his behavior in the voting booth. The electorate should select the ballot box over the market place in those areas where individually determined market acts tend to produce results which are in conflict either with those which a large group of voters estimate to be their own or the "social welfare" and where the conflict is significant enough to warrant the sacrifice both of the individual freedom and the individual rationality involved.

In so far as market choice must be made under imperfectly competitive conditions[27] and voting choice under conditions of less than "pure" democracy, the analysis of individual behavior in each process must be appropriately modified and the conclusions reached earlier changed accordingly. No attempt will be made here to extend the analysis in this direction.

VIII

A major source of confusion in the discussion of economic policy stems from the failure to distinguish carefully between the selection of the power structure among individual choosers and the selection of the choice mechanism. This arises from the more fundamental failure to define freedom in such a way that market freedom and market power may be differentiated conceptually.[28] In many real world situations the market power structure cannot be effectively modified independently, that is, a redistributive decision cannot be made in isolation. It is nevertheless essential for analytical clarity that this ideational distinction be made.

The separation of the power structure and the decision-making process is less inclusive and less complex than the similar and more commonly encountered distinction between the "income" and the "resource" aspects of economic policy. The problem of selecting the desirable structure of power relations among individuals in the market is, of course, equivalent to the income problem broadly considered. The "resource" side of the "income-resource" dichotomy introduces an evaluation of policy in terms of the social criteria of economic efficiency, and these aspects of the market mechanism tend to be emphasized. The "choice" side of the "power-choice" dichotomy which has been developed here tends to concentrate attention upon individual behavior in making choices, and it tends to emphasize the greater range of freedom allowed the individual, as well as the greater degree of individual rationality in market choice.

NOTES

1. I am indebted to Marshall Colberg, Jerome Milliman, and Vincent Thursby for helpful comments and suggestions.

2. This is a simplifying assumption; there is reason for believing that the individual possesses a greater knowledge of alternatives in the market. This is due, first, to the greater continuity of market choice and, second, to the difference in the degree of knowledge required to compare alternatives in each case. The latter difference has been stressed by Professor Hayek (see F. A. Hayek, "Individualism: True and False," *Individualism and Economic Order* [Chicago: University of Chicago Press, 1948]; see also Robert A. Dahl and Charles E. Lindblom, *Politics, Economics, and Welfare* [New York: Harper & Bros., 1953], p. 63).

3. Cf. Kenneth J. Arrow, "Alternative Approaches to the Theory of Choice in Risk-taking Situations," *Econometrica*, XIX (1951), 405.

4. Cf. Frank H. Knight, "Economic Theory and Nationalism," in his *The Ethics of Competition* (London: Allen & Unwin, 1935), p. 340.

5. The device of considering productive services as negatively desired and hence carrying negative prices enables both the buying and the selling activity of the individual to be encompassed in "market choice."

6. See Arrow, *op. cit.,* for an excellent summary of the various theories of choice under uncertainty.

7. Cf. Ludwig von Mises, *Human Action: A Treatise on Economics* (New Haven: Yale University Press, 1949), p. 312.

8. The fact that individual behavior in the market sets off reactions which are not recognized or intended by the actor, but which do control society's utilization of resources, is stressed in a somewhat different context by Dahl and Lindblom (*op. cit.,* pp. 99–102). They are concerned with the "spontaneous field control" exerted over the individual in this manner. "Control" in this sense, however, is no different from that imposed by the natural environment or any other set of forces external to the individual (see Sec. V).

9. For a definition of social action see Max Weber, *The Theory of Social and Economic Organization,* trans. A. M. Henderson and Talcott Parsons (New York: Oxford University Press, 1947), p. 88.

10. It has been advanced as a merit of the price system that it does place the individual in a position of adapting his behavior to the anonymous forces of the market without at the same time feeling that he can participate in changing these forces. On this point see Hayek, *op. cit.,* p. 24.

Market behavior can, of course, become "social" if the individual is made to realize the secondary repercussions of his action. Exceptional cases of such realization may be present even in the perfectly competitive economy, e.g., "buyers' strikes."

11. Dahl and Lindblom, *op. cit.,* p. 422.

12. Cf. Kenneth J. Arrow, *Social Choice and Individual Values* (New York: John Wiley & Sons, 1951), p. 82.

13. Cf. William J. Baumol, *Welfare Economics and Theory of the State* (Cambridge: Harvard University Press, 1952), p. 15; Trygve Haavelmo, "The Notion of Involuntary Economic Decisions," *Econometrica*, XVIII (1950), 3, 8.

14. On this point see Alfred C. Neal, "The 'Planning Approach' in Public Economy," *Quarterly Journal of Economics,* LIV (1940), 251.

15. In cases where spill-over effects are significant, the costs taken into account by the individual in the market will clearly exclude some important elements of social costs (positive or negative) which should be considered in the making of a social decision (see Dahl and Lindblom, *op. cit.,* p. 419).

16. Ludwig von Mises, *Socialism* (new ed.; New Haven: Yale University Press, 1951), p. 21.

17. J. J. Spengler, "Generalists versus Specialists in Social Science: An Economist's View," *American Political Science Review,* XLIV (1950), 378.

18. The market is thus the only system of proportional representation which will likely work at all (cf. Clarence Philbrook, "Capitalism and the Rule of Love," *Southern Economic Journal,* XIX [1953], 466).

19. A decision to sell productive services may be considered as a vote for generalized purchasing power (i.e., dollars), and thus may be considered positively effective if the sale is consummated.

20. For an excellent summary discussion of this point see Von Mises, *Human Action: A Treatise on Economics,* p. 271.

21. Dahl and Lindblom, *op. cit.,* p. 424. A similar position is taken by Professor Howard Bowen (see his *Toward Social Economy* [New York: Rinehart & Co., 1948], p. 44).

22. See Frank H. Knight, "The Meaning of Freedom," in *The Philosophy of American Democracy,* ed. Charles M. Perry (Chicago: University of Chicago Press, 1943), p. 64; "Conflict of Values: Freedom and Justice," in *Goals of Economic Life,* ed. Dudley Ward (New York: Harper & Bros., 1953), pp. 207, 226. For supporting views see Michael Polanyi, *The Logic of Liberty* (Chicago: University of Chicago Press, 1951), p. 159; E. F. Carritt, *Morals and Politics* (London: Oxford University Press, 1953), pp. 195 f.

23. Rationality in individual behavior is defined in the normal manner, that is, the individual is able to rank alternatives, and such ranking is transitive.

24. It is on this basis that Dahl and Lindblom appear to reject the argument that market choice is more rational (*op. cit.,* chap. xv). They do so because they are concerned with rationality in the social sense, defined as that action which maximizes the achievement of certain postulated social goals. If rationality is defined purely in terms of individual behavior, their argument appears to support that of this paper, although they seem explicitly to deny this at one point (*ibid.,* p. 422).

25. Cf. Arrow, *Social Choice and Individual Values.*

26. If they cannot agree, the possible irrationality of collective choice may be a desirable rather than an undesirable feature, since a rationality could be imposed only at the cost of minority coercion (see my "Social Choice, Democracy, and Free Markets," *Journal of Political Economy,* LXII [1954], 114–23).

27. Imperfections include, of course, the presence of such monetary and structural factors as may lead to unemployment.

28. This constitutes one of the major weaknesses in Dahl and Lindblom's otherwise excellent comparison of voting and the market (*op. cit.,* pp. 414–27).

Constitutional Design for a
Rent-Seeking Society: Voting Rule Choice

Z. A. Spindler

Review Questions

1. What are the relationships between external and decision costs to the size of the group required to be in agreement for social decisions to be made? If a rule should be chosen in order to minimize the sum of these costs, what does this imply about the optimal required size?
2. Why might rent-seeking costs be greatest for simple majority rule? If these costs are added to the other interdependence costs, where do the new total minimum costs result?
3. Why might the decision cost curve have a discontinuity at the point of simple majority rule? If this is true, where is the point of minimum total cost?
4. How do the conclusions change if the rent-seeking cost function changed over time, depending on the decision rule in use?

Spindler, Z. A. "Constitutional Design for a Rent-Seeking Society: Voting Rule Choice." *Constitutional Political Economy* 1 (1990): 73–82.

Introduction

For Buchanan and Tullock (1965, Chapter 6), constitutional design was a matter of comparing the interdependence costs of public and private decisions over a range of activities to determine which activities would be assigned by the constitution to the state and to determine which voting rule or choice mechanism would be specified by the constitution for each state activity. The best public decision rule for each activity was the one that minimized interdependence costs. If the latter were less than the interdependence costs using the best private decision mechanism for that activity, then the activity would be assigned to the state by the constitution.

Further, Buchanan and Tullock specified that the representative individual perceived interdependence costs for an activity as the *sum* of the anticipated external costs levied on that individual if not part of the decision set and the anticipated decision cost experienced by the individual if part of the decision set. Since external costs were specified as a decreasing function of the number in (or the proportion of) the population whose agreement is required by the decision rule while decision costs were specified as an increasing function of the same number (or proportion), the sum of both external costs and decision costs necessarily had a unique minimum somewhere between the extremes of individual rule[1] and unanimity rule—the exact position depending on relative external and decision costs.

A few years after the publication of this classic analysis of constitutions, Tullock (1967) independently published his innovative ideas on what came to be called rent-seeking, which he argued entailed social costs. The latter were called "rent-seeking costs" or, by some, "Tullock Costs." These costs had not been totally ignored in Buchanan and Tullock's earlier constitutional analysis. Indeed their chapter on pressure groups is as relevant and as perspicacious now as when it was written. The historical increase in pressure groups activity was seen as increasing external costs, thus requiring more inclusive decision-making rules and more restrictive limits on collective activity.

However, what was missing from the original Buchanan and Tullock (1965) analysis, as well as from subsequent renditions of their work (Mueller 1989: 52–55), was an explicit specification of Tullock Costs as a function of the number in (or the proportion of) the population required for the decision rule. This may be an important oversight if the functional form for Tullock Costs is substantially different from those for external and decision costs—say, for example, a "trajectory" rather than rectangular-hyperbola functional form. Then, adding the Tullock Costs to the external and decision costs would not necessarily yield a total interdependence cost with a unique minimum. In fact, multiple local minima would tend to be closer to the individual rule and/or unanimity rule extremes. This, in turn, would have important implications for constitutional design. For example, direct-democracy majoritarianism would be expected to be the exception rather than the rule, as indeed appears to be the case for most decisions by most historical and modern governments.

The graphical illustration of the original analysis and this extension is discussed in the next two sections followed by the discussion of a rationale for abrupt regime or constitutional revision. A brief summary ends the paper.

I. External Costs, Decision Costs and Interdependence Costs

Mueller (1989) refers to the figure representing Buchanan and Tullock's analysis as "Choosing the optimal majority" although much more was actually intended by Buchanan and Tullock.[2] However, Mueller's figure is reproduced here as *Figure 1* where the vertical axis measures expected costs and the horizontal axis measures K, the "Number of Individuals Required to Take Collective Action", as well as N, the total population.[3] N could be considered as the entire population of a given polity or as the size of some decision-making body within the polity which itself is determined by Buchanan and Tullock's procedure. Consequently, K might represent simple-majority rule or even relative-unanimity rule on a (say) committee while at the same time representing minority rule for the population as a whole—as is the case for representative democracies.

The functions labeled C, D, and $C + D$ represent the present value of the external costs, decision costs, and total interdependence costs, respectively, that a representative individual expects to bear as a result of a collective decision made by any K individuals drawn from N.[4] Interdependence costs are minimized by a decision-making rule that requires K individuals (or K/N of the population or of a committee) to agree on a course of action in regard to a specific activity (say activity x). Buchanan and Tullock suggest that at the constitution-making stage—behind a veil of uncertainty over future position, tastes, etc.—a population of like-minded individuals might be able to agree unanimously on a constitutional decision rule of K (or K/N) for activity x.

A complete constitution would be composed of a set of decision rules over a set of collective activities which received unanimous approval at the constitution-making stage. All other activities, as the saying goes, "would be reserved for the people" to pursue by private competitive or cooperative means.[5]

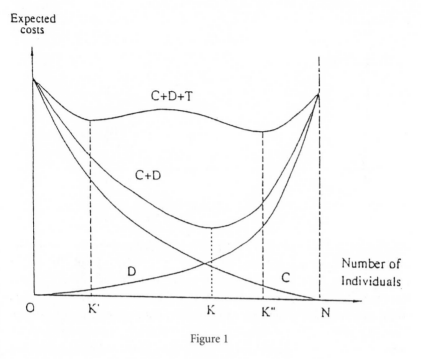

Figure 1

II. Tullock Costs and Interdependence Costs

Now suppose that Tullock Costs are considered a separate function of K (or K/N). There are, of course, many possibilities and the reader may choose to experiment with alternatives and, as a result, may reach different conclusions. Whatever the choice, both the position and form of the function will be determined by other institutional factors and constitutional rules. This is certainly implied by Buchanan and Tullock's discussion in Chapter 19. However, for purposes of argument, suppose Tullock Costs are given by some "trajectory" functional form, shown as T in *Figure 2*, which reaches a maximum at the point of simple majority rule. There may be a number of ways to justify this functional form, but only three will be given here.

The first rationale relies on the role of competition under various decision rules. An extensive literature on the dissipation of rents through rent-seeking activity suggests that complete dissipation, or even over-dissipation, is more likely the more competitive and unrestricted is the rent-seeking. The individual rule and unanimity rule extremes (*1* and *N*, respectively, in *Figures 1, 2*, or *3*) have been noted by Buchanan and Tullock and others as the extremes of monopoly in decision-making since in either case one individual can decide

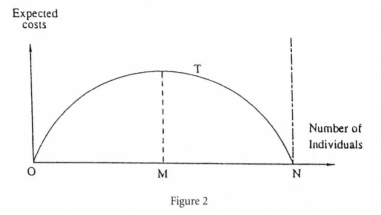

Figure 2

whether or not an action is taken. Simple majority, however, represents the point of maximum potential competition. Any fifty percent plus one of the population could be subject to "influence" while any fifty percent minus one could be producing "influence". Rent-seeking expenditures or transfers could well reach a maximum at that point unless constrained by natural forces, by rules of group formation (Olson 1965), by group norms or by other constitutional rules which, in turn, did not induce, or were not induced by, rent-seeking.[6]

The second rationale relies on the need to employ real resources for rent-seeking under various decision rules and can be given by way of example. Suppose the activity to be decided concerns the disposition of an entitlement to a natural monopoly. If there was "individual rule" where one and only one individual decides the matter, that individual could claim the title and the rents directly. With no rents to divvy up, there would be no need for rent-seeking by others.[7] If there was unanimity rule, any (and every) one individual can decide the matter in conjunction with all others. Each individual is like a dictator whose choice is limited to that with which all others would agree and whose agreement is required for a decision by all. Given such a "monopoly" position for everyone determined by the voting rule,[8] no specific real resources need to be devoted to rent-seeking from or by others; the costs of bargaining between potential dictators are already included in D.[9] However, with simple-majority rule, each individual must use real resources in order to enter the competition over the division of rents. With as much as half of the population competing with the other half, there could be considerable Tullock Costs. Thus, the representative individual may form an expectation of rent-seeking or Tullock Costs as rising from zero at individual rule to a

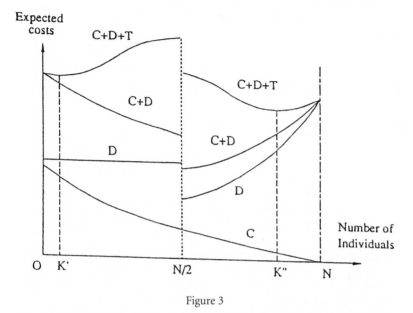

Figure 3

maximum at simple-majority rule and then falling back to zero at unanimity rule, as shown by curve *T* in *Figure 2*.

The third rationale is simply that a more interesting conclusion follows if Tullock Costs are assumed to have a trajectory functional form rather than, say, a flat, upward sloping, or downward sloping line. Specifically, the conclusion differs from Buchanan and Tullock.[10]

In order to observe what a difference a functional form makes, refer to curve *C* + *D* + *T* in *Figure 1* which adds Tullock Costs, or *T*, from *Figure 2* to *C* + *D* from *Figure 1* (Since this has been done freehand rather than by CAD, the result is approximate at best). This new curve has two local minima, one of which may be a global minimum if *C* is not reversely symmetrical with *D* or if *T* is not symmetrical around *M*.[11] This suggests that either "near-individual rule", at point *K'*, or "near-unanimity rule", at point *K''*, may be an appropriate antidote to rent-seeking. It also provides a possible explanation for the choice of either form over "simple-majority rule". For example, constitutional monarchy may have been an (implicitly) unanimous choice for some historical situations which were anticipated to entail both relatively high decision costs and Tullock Costs.

As also argued by Buchanan and Tullock (1965: 286–8), this analysis implies that the more rent-seeking activity anticipated, the smaller the scope of government chosen at the constitutional stage.[12] This can be seen by comparing the total interdependence costs at the minima on $C + D + T$ with the minimum point on $C + D$. Since the former are higher it is less likely that public provision will involve lower interdependence costs than private provision for this activity in the presence of rent-seeking.

III. Tullock Costs and Regime Stability

One other interesting variant can be developed on the basis of Buchanan and Tullock's suggestion that a discontinuity in decision costs might account for the popularity of simple majority rule. Mueller (1989: 56) presents a figure illustrating that case which is replicated here as Figure 3, where curve D, and hence curve $C + D$, have a distinct discontinuity at $N/2$. As Mueller explains:

> The committee could, when less than half of the voters suffice to carry an issue, become deadlocked in an endless series of offsetting proposals absorbing the time and patience of its members. The method of simple majority rule has the smallest possible required majority to pass an issue, which avoids the possibility of self-contradictory issues simultaneously passing.

However, if Tullock Costs are considered here, there are other possibilities since, with the "trajectory" functional forms, Tullock Costs peak precisely at the simple majority point. As can be seen from *Figure 3*, where T has been added to the two $C + D$ curves to form two $C + D + T$ curves, there are now three possible local minima, at K', K'', and, possibly, at $N/2$ (if the slope of C is steeper than the slope of D at that point, the lower $C + D + T$ curve will be upward sloping there—this is not shown precisely in *Figure 3*), of which any one may be the global minimum.

If Tullock Costs varied systematically over time in response to a particular voting rule regime, the optimum rule could jump precipitously between individual rule, minority rule, simple-majority rule, and qualified-majority rule. This would happen, for example, if the Tullock Cost function tended to rise under simple-majority rule and fall under either individual rule or qualified-majority rule. This might create a cyclical movement in $C + D + T$ in *Figure 3* such that the global minimum could change between K' and K'', between $N/2$ and K'' or between K' and $N/2$. If this systematically and simultaneously occurred for a wide range of collective activities within a given real world polity, the resulting adjustments might be seen as revolutions which replace less democratic (less inclusive decision-making) regimes with more democratic (more inclusive decision-making) regimes—and then *vice versa*.

While hardly a complete or testable theory, this explanation for abrupt constitutional shifts may be usefully applied to analyze selected cases of dramatic regime changes in Latin America (where rent-seeking cycles and, hence, revolutionary cycles may be relatively short), Eastern Europe (where long waves may apply for both rent-seeking and regime change), and elsewhere. Indeed, it could be used to give a constitutional perspective to Olson's (1982) tales of dynamic growth and decline.

Concluding Remarks

This paper was intended as a means for re-raising the issue of the effect of anticipated rent-seeking on constitutional choice. It has argued that rent-seeking costs—Tullock Costs—should be considered separately from external and decision costs since the static and dynamic functional forms for each may differ with respect to the decision set variable K. The particular functional form chosen here for Tullock Costs was meant to be suggestive rather than definitive. However, its use did lead to some interesting implications for constitutional choice which may have some correspondence to our current or historical world. In particular, non-majoritarian regimes, and revolution, may be viewed as compatible with unanimous "democratic" choice behind a veil of uncertainty at the stage of constitution formation.

NOTES

1. In this paper, "individual rule" refers to a single individual deciding about a collective activity on behalf of the polity. The terms "dictator", "dictatorial rule" or "dictatorship", which are sometimes used for this situation, are pejorative and seem inappropriate in a context where such a decision-making rule may be unanimously chosen at the constitutional level.

2. Mueller's *Figure 4.5* presents a standard treatment of Buchanan and Tullock's ideas even though this specific graph, which includes C, D, and $C + D$ together, was not included in their original book. Further, Buchanan and Tullock's (1965: 65–71) Figures 1–3 explicitly label the expected costs as present values.

3. Alternatively, K could represent a proportion in which case $N = 1$.

4. These costs functions will obviously be affected by how the specific individuals comprising K are determined when N represents the size of some decision-making group, such as a committee or a legislature, rather than the entire population of a polity. For example, self-selection or other (perhaps elite) selection may be anticipated to have higher external, and lower decision, costs than general election. Selection/election periodicity and maximum/minimum term of office may also be important issues in determining expected costs.

5. This is essentially a "positive" public choice view. From a "normative" public

choice perspective, an objection might be raised that some of the anticipated external costs for an individual may represent transfers to other individuals rather than pure deadweight costs, that this may create a difference between the optimum for the representative individual and the optimum for all individuals, that is, the so-called social optimum, and, as a result, that unanimous individual choice of constitutional form may not yield a constitution that is socially optimal. However, this will not be a concern in what follows.

6. Constitutional procedural constraints often rely on interest-group competition for their self-enforcing character. Even substantive constraints requiring judicial interpretation and administrative compliance are not free of rent-seeking possibilities (Gwartney and Wagner 1988: 35–49). Thus, such constraints may not ultimately limit Tullock Costs.

7. Of course, there could be a regress of unfettered competition to an earlier stage at which that decisive individual was chosen. That would rotate up the Tullock Cost curve in the OM range, giving it an elevated trajectory form. The limit might involve Tullock Costs as high at O as at M (not shown). However, in practice such competitions for select positions are naturally limited to those with special characteristics such as "noble birth" or "charisma", etc. On the other hand, others could still stake considerable resources on their favorite "contender". But then again, with few contenders, rules to conserve real resources and to restrict rent-seeking payments to transfers could more easily be enforced.

8. Each individual has essentially the same bilateral monopoly position with respect to everyone else, which will tend to result in an equal division of rents (Spindler 1974).

9. Bargaining or decision costs here might include the foregone opportunities to extract and share rents until a "deal" was struck. The shared incentive to minimize such costs provides the incentive to reach decisions under unanimity rule when positive net rents are expected.

10. Their analysis in Chapter 19 could be interpreted as suggesting a simple upward rotation of either C or D or an upward shift of $C + D$. The former two changes would simply increase or decrease, respectively, the crucial decision number (or proportion), while all three changes would imply that fewer activities should be undertaken by the state; that is, the size and scope of the public sector should decrease as Tullock Costs increase.

11. As A. Hamlin pointed out when this paper was presented, if all three separate cost functions, C, D, and T, have a quadratic form, the function obtained by their summation, $C + D + T$, will also have a quadratic form and, hence, only one minimum point. However, nothing in the above discussion suggests that all of these functional forms must be quadratic, so multiple minima are not precluded theoretically.

12. Alternatively, given the scope of government chosen at the constitutional stage, the size of the government will be larger the higher the level of rent-seeking activity.

REFERENCES

Buchanan, J. A. and G. Tullock (1965) *The Calculus of Consent: Logical Foundations of Constitutional Democracy.* Ann Arbor: University of Michigan Press.

Cebula, R. J. and M. Z. Kafoglis (1983) "In Search of Optimum 'Relative Unanimity.'" *Public Choice* 40: 195–201.

Gwartney, J. D. and R. E. Wagner (1988) *Public Choice and Constitutional Economics.* London: JAI Press Inc.

Mueller, D. C. (1989) *Public Choice II.* Cambridge: Cambridge University Press.

Olson, M. (1965) *The Logic of Collective Action.* Cambridge: Harvard University Press.

Olson, M. (1982) *The Rise and Decline of Nations: Economic Growth, Stagflation, and Social Rigidities.* New Haven: Yale University Press.

Spindler, Z. A. (1974) "Endogenous Bargaining Power in Bilateral Monopoly and Bilateral Exchange." *Canadian Journal of Economics* VII: 463–74.

Tullock, G. (1967) "The Welfare Costs of Tariffs, Monopolies, and Theft." *Western Economic Journal* 5: 224–232.

Tullock, G. (1980) "Efficient Rent seeking." In: J. M. Buchanan, R. D. Tollison and G. Tullock (eds) *Toward a Theory of the Rent-Seeking Society.* College Station: Texas A&M University Press. 97–112.

Tullock, G. (1989) *The Economics of Special Privilege and Rent Seeking.* Boston: Kluwer Academic Publishers.

Social Choice and Arrow's Paradox

Alfred F. MacKay

Review Questions

1. What is meant by a "rational" aggregation device?
2. What conditions does Arrow place on any reasonable voting mechanism? Why are each of these conditions individually so important?
3. Why has Arrow's proof attracted so much attention?

The *problem of social choice* is this: How can many individuals' preferences be combined to yield a collective choice? Various procedures have been, or might be, proposed to accomplish this feat, all of which differ from each other in many respects. We will call such procedures (mechanisms, combination rules) *aggregation devices*, or sometimes just *devices*. In democratic political theory, for example, the various possible voting schemes are all simply aggregation devices. The *theory of social choice* studies aggregation devices: what they are; how they work; how they differ; what they presuppose and imply; what can be said for and against the principal types; whether there is a perfect or ideal type, and if so, what features it has; and so on. Thus far, the main results of this the-

MacKay, Alfred F. "Social Choice and Arrow's Paradox." In *Arrow's Theorem: The Paradox of Social Choice,* chap. 1, 1–12. New Haven, CT: Yale University Press, 1980.

ory have been discouragingly negative. In the early 1950s the distinguished economist (now Nobel Laureate) Kenneth J. Arrow showed, in a demonstration that has come to be called Arrow's Impossibility Theorem, that given certain plausible assumptions, there can be no ideally rational aggregation device. We will attempt to come to terms with Arrow's justly famous result. We will try to explain what it is, understand why and how it works, examine its implications, and consider suggestions for evading it.

The present work contains little that is new concerning the technicalities of this area. It attempts no major contribution to the mathematics of the problem. Our approach is that Arrow's Theorem presents a fascinating problem in the philosophy of economics. It wears on its face that paradoxical aspect which is the hallmark of so many philosophical problems. It arises from a priori, conceptual sources, and provides scope for investigation by reflection and analysis rather than exclusively by experimentation. It has a good claim to be considered the outstanding problem in the philosophy of economics.

What, then, is Arrow's Theorem? Without now going into the details, Arrow proves, as we said, that it is impossible to construct a "rational" aggregation device. But there are many extant aggregation devices: for example, the voting systems in use every day. So everything depends on what is meant by "rational." The content of that notion is partially specified by four very general conditions which Arrow claims it is reasonable to require any aggregation device to meet. These seem almost innocuous, they are so weak. (Weakness is a virtue here. The weaker such constraints are, the less you have to take on faith when accepting them.) Listing them by name only, for future reference, they are:

(U) Unrestricted scope.
(P) Pareto principle.
(D) Nondictatorship.
(I) Independence of irrelevant alternatives.[1]

Arrow shows that no device can jointly satisfy four apparently reasonable requirements, and in that sense no reasonable or "rational" aggregation device is possible. Since his proof is nondefective (that is, formally valid), this naturally concentrates attention upon those four requirements. Indeed, one's evaluation of the "importance" of Arrow's result will depend in large measure upon one's assessment of the plausibility of his four conditions. If, as he sometimes suggests, they do embody canons of rationality—if, to use older language, they are clear dictates of reason—then his impossibility result takes on one aspect. If, on the other hand, one or more of them has some hidden flaw or can be forgone at small or no cost, then it takes on a different aspect.

Before turning to a detailed plausibility assessment, a process that will engage us throughout this work, it might be useful to locate Arrow's enterprise on the conceptual map, and to make various comparisons and contrasts, chiefly in the history of recent ethics. It has been said that anyone familiar with this somewhat depressing history will know that whenever you have even two independent, basic principles, they conflict. So why should it be surprising that Arrow shows how four taken together do? Arguments to the effect that certain very fundamental evaluative claims—each of which seems when independently considered to commend itself to right reason—in fact conflict and are logically incompatible, are staple fare in the history of ethics.[2] Why, then, should Arrow's very similar project cause such a stir?

Part of the answer may be that his work was not directed toward an audience of historians of philosophy, but toward economists and decision theorists. Such an audience is understandably ignorant of the disappointments, the "impossibility theorems," the generally negative results of classical modern ethics. So, like all reinventions of the wheel, Arrow's result astonishes the innocent. This, whether true or not, is not a sufficient explanation.

Another part of the answer might involve the ingenuity, the genius, displayed in devising a mathematically tractable formulation of a difficult and complex issue, rendering it susceptible of rigorous proof as opposed to persuasive argument. Again, no one familiar with standards of argument in moral philosophy, which, whether due to the intrinsic nature of the subject (only admitting of so much exactitude, as Aristotle claimed), or to the limitations of its practitioners, or to some other cause, contains a proportion of persuasion to proof that is perhaps higher than in any other area of philosophy, can fail to be impressed by the magnitude of this aspect of Arrow's achievement. It is an accomplishment not even approached in philosophical ethics, where the debate between utilitarians and intuitionists still continues, concerning in part whether there really is a conflict between the principle of utility and the precepts of justice. There can be no similar lingering doubts about the existence of a conflict among Arrow's four requirements. Settling that part of the question once and for all is a great leap forward. A similar advance in ethics would constitute that will-o'-the-wisp, Progress in Philosophy. Arrow's treatment of the conceptual problems of social choice stands, in this respect, as a model of the way some philosophical issues can be posed and occasionally brought to definitive resolution.

A related point is that Arrow's formal, axiomatic approach has the usual benefits regarding direction of further inquiry. In the first place, it forces exposure of operative assumptions and makes them relatively accessible to close examination. If the proof is valid—and it is—then the natural place to turn for further inquiry is to the premises. And there they all are, in plain view, clearly and exactly expressed. Furthermore, as we shall see, by exposing the formal structure of the argument, the axiomatic formulation aids in distinguishing form from content. This, in turn, enables reinterpretation of the normal content in nonstandard ways, often with illuminating results.

But important as these considerations are, they still do not adequately capture the boldness of Arrow's result. Its most striking feature is how unexpected and unobvious it is. To use an example from the history of ethics, everyone knew there was at least a prima facie conflict between duty and utility (or, expedience, as it is often termed), so it came as no great surprise when Sidgwick, and later Ross, argued its existence so forcefully. The naked, aggressive thrust for maximum utility plainly threatens the niceties of our stations and their duties. There, the challenging task is to construct a secular, ethical theodicy which harmonizes the apparent conflict—thus the attractions of rule-utilitarianism. With Arrow's Theorem, on the other hand, not only was the disclosed four-element conflict not widely suspected in advance, but even after thoroughly digesting the proof it can hardly be believed. His result is, in this broad sense, paradoxical. Although his four conditions demonstrably do conflict, one cannot (except for rehearsing the proof itself) see *why* they should. This, perhaps, finally accounts for the impact of Arrow's Theorem. It is a rigorous demonstration of an entirely unobvious, surprising, paradoxical result. Like all the great paradoxes, Arrow's result on collective rationality resists understanding and resolution equally as it demands the attempt.[3]

With these preliminaries behind us, let us turn to one of the problems discussed by Arrow. When we say that aggregation devices are rules or procedures for generating social choice based on individual preferences, we have not said very much. The notion of one thing's being "based on" something else is so open-ended that it cries out for further specification. One ultimate, overall aim of studies of social choice is to characterize good, desirable, or even acceptable aggregation devices. To do that, we have to say more than merely that the social output must be "based on" individual inputs. But what?

To see the problem, consider what Arrow dubs an "illfare" function, an aggregation procedure that completely reverses the individuals' preferences—that is, when everybody prefers X to Y, the device generates the social choice Y over X. Such a system would feature one, albeit perverse, way of basing social choice on individual preferences. So even if we are not prepared to legislate in advance the details of what any acceptable device will have to be like, we will surely want to say something about what, broadly speaking, we might call its directionality. Or again, consider a device that automatically repro-duces the preferences of some one person and designates them as the social choice. This would feature another perverse way of "basing" social choice on individual preference. And again, while not prescribing matters of detail, we might wish to require that the social choice be, in some sense, a genuinely col-lective affair.

It is at this very high level of generality that Arrow's four constraints op-erate. They represent normative judgments—requirements that embody a conception of the way aggregation devices ought and ought not to be. Yet they are, unlike many value judgments we can imagine in this area (for ex-ample, that a voting system ought to demand at least a three-fifths majority) relatively uncontroversial. Of course, they purchase their wide acceptability at the price of apparently innocuous minimality. They seem to be extremely weak requirements, leaving many important questions perfectly open, clos-ing off only what may seem ridiculously perverse options. No doubt a full characterization of desirability or acceptability for aggregation devices would need to include many more, and more specific, detailed constraints than these beginning four. But, as Arrow remarks, these are more than enough. He proves that no aggregation device can jointly satisfy even these:

1. (U) The first requirement is (U), *unrestricted scope.* This requires that an acceptable device be able to process any (logically) coherent set of individual preference rankings of any number of choice alternatives.[4]

Finitism is not particularly at issue here. All that Arrow's proof requires is at least three voters who can order three alternatives any way they please. On the face of it this requirement seems plausible enough. If you are going to consult the wishes of the multitude at all, you may as well let them express whatever preferences they really have, for whatever alternatives they happen to be faced with, under no artificially imposed restraints. One can imagine, of course, devices which only permit social choice between certain special, or special-sized, groups of alternatives, or which only accept certain preferred preference patterns as input. But it seems prima facie unreasonable to put up with such limitations if we can stipulate unrestricted scope, thus getting the preferred patterns and all the rest too.

2. (P) The second requirement is (P), the *Pareto principle.* This requires that when every individual without exception prefers X to Y, the device must rank X above Y in its social ordering. That is, whatever else it may do, an accept-able device must honor unanimity.

It is difficult to see how the social choice could be said to reflect individual preferences or be responsive to them in any significant sense if it failed to ratify unanimous consensus. Argument can arise over differences, but unanimity seems unquestionable. This requirement amounts to an exceedingly weak constraint on what we earlier called the *directionality* of the "based on" relation. Its innocuous weakness, and hence its relative uncontroversiality, springs from this: the only additional specification it applies to the vague notion of social choice's being based on individual preferences is that however "based on" gets embodied in detail, a device must implement unanimity.

3. (D) The third requirement is (D), *nondictatorship*. This prohibits an acceptable device from taking the preferences of any single individual and automatically making them the social ordering regardless of the preferences of all other individuals.

This enforces the judgment that an acceptable aggregation device should be a *collective* choice procedure, not merely rubber stamping one-person rule. Although clearly an evaluative postulate, the values it embodies seem uncontroversial.

4. (I) The final requirement is (I), the *independence of irrelevant alternatives*. This requires that the social ordering of a given set of alternatives depend only on the individuals' preference orderings of those alternatives.

The effect of this requirement is to place certain constraints on the information that an acceptable device can respond to. The social output of an aggregation device, we said, is to be "based on" individual preferences. But what aspects of individuals' preferences shall it respond to in thus "basing" its social ordering? Requirement (I) provides a twofold answer to this question. First, the social ordering of an acceptable device shall depend on, and only on, preference *orderings*. By this is meant that the device shall respond only to information concerning what is preferred, and what indifferent, to what. It shall not, for example, respond to how much one thing is preferred to another (that is, not to preference intensity information), nor to any other type of information. The first part of (I), then, requires that only the bare ordering of individuals' preferences is to be taken into account. The second part says that even among individuals' preference orderings, only a restricted class of them is to be responded to. In generating a social ranking of a given set of alternatives, only preference orderings of *those alternatives* (and no others) are to be taken into account.

In summary, (I) incorporates two prohibitions: (1) the social ranking of a set of alternatives shall not depend on anything other than preference orderings, and (2) it shall not depend on preference orderings for alternatives not in that set—so-called "irrelevant" alternatives. To these two negative prohibitions it adds the positive injunction that the social ordering of a set of alternatives *shall* depend on the individuals' preference orderings of alternatives in that set.

So much for what (I) requires. Why it should be thought a plausible requirement, let alone a dictate of reason, is another matter, to which we will return in due course. The first part of it, the ordinality injunction, has in its favor whatever is to be said for ordinality versus cardinality in the treatment of preference matters generally. This includes a mixed collection of considerations involving behaviorism, observability, and the proper scientific treatment of social phenomena, which we shall not pursue at this point. Theory aside, though, this much can be said on practical grounds alone: searching for reliable, direct, preference-intensity indicators seems to be chasing what cannot be caught. There is a certain plausibility in restricting oneself to what is possible. The plausibility of the second part of (I) will be examined extensively later. From one point of view its function is subservient to that of its mate. When joined to the first (ordinality) aspect, it serves to prevent any, even indirect, recourse to cardinality. The way this works is as follows. Some people have thought that even if preference-intensity information is not directly ascertainable—by introspection, say—there is nonetheless some hope of getting it in by the back door: that is, inferring it from (ordinal) information that is reliably available.

Such ways of imputing cardinality on the basis of ordinality often depend on noting how ordinally ranked alternatives are situated vis-à-vis some selected "irrelevant" alternative(s). For example, some would hold that we can infer that A prefers X to Y more intensely than does B, if A orders alternatives, X, α, β, γ, and Y, whereas B orders those same five alternatives, α, β, γ, X, and Y. The thought is that for A, the three alternatives, α, β, and γ intervene between X and Y, one of which he ranks first and the other last. Although B also prefers X and Y, he ranks them next to last and last, respectively, and places the other three alternatives ahead of them both. X and Y are immediately adjacent to each other in B's ordering, not widely separated (by three intervening ranks) as in A's. Hence, we infer that (relatively speaking) B barely prefers X to Y while A prefers X to Y more strongly. The second part of (I) frustrates this attempt to squeeze cardinal blood out of an ordinal turnip by forbidding the social ordering of any pair of alternatives to depend on information regarding any third. In socially ranking *X* and *Y,* a device can take account only of how individuals order *X* and *Y* themselves. It cannot consider how anybody ranks α, β, or γ, either vis-à-vis *X* or *Y* or anything else.

Arrow proves that it is impossible for an aggregation device with unrestricted scope, (U), to satisfy both the Pareto principle, (P), and independence of irrelevant alternatives, (I), and also be nondictatorial, (D). In other words, no device—no matter what its detailed, inner machinery—can have acceptable scope, (U), be minimally responsive to individual preferences, (P), be sensitive only to the actual ordinal rankings to which it is applied, (I), and not be dictatorial, (D). But why not? There appear to be no connections between the four conditions through which a conflict might arise. And in a sense this is so. What we are here faced with is an inconsistent quartet of requirements, no trio and no pair of which are themselves incompatible. Now it might be thought that such a four-element inconsistent set, no subset of which is itself inconsistent, simply overloads our logical attention span. That would explain why we cannot intuitively see the incompatibility that Arrow's proof establishes. However, although there must be some limits to our logical storage and processing capacity, they are not likely to occur so early in the number line. Generations of undergraduates have seen the point of the problem of evil—God is all good, all knowing, and all powerful, yet evil exists—an inconsistent quartet, no trio and no pair of which are inconsistent.

Be that as it may, a major factor contributing to the unobviousness of Arrow's result is surely this: the *content* of the four requirements is so diverse, they seem so mutually unrelated in substance, as not to provide opportunity for interaction of any kind. What can having acceptable scope have to do with not being dictatorial? What can implementing unanimous preferences have to do with responding only to preference orderings? No intuitive connections appear. The satisfaction of (U) is compatible with either (P) or non-(P), (I) or non-(I), (D) or non-(D). And similarly for the others. No one of them bears any logical relation to another, neither entailing it nor contradicting it. Yet taken together, they are incompatible.

NOTES

1. I follow Arrow's more economical presentation in "Values and Collective Decision-Making," in P. Laslett and W. G. Runciman, eds., *Philosophy, Politics, and Society,* 3d ser. (New York: Barnes & Noble, 1967), and in the 2d edition of *Social Choice and Individual Values* (New Haven, Conn.: Yale University Press, 1963), chap. 8, sec. 2. In his original monograph, *Social Choice and Individual Values* (New Haven, Conn.: Yale University Press, 1951), there were five conditions. The terminology (U), (P), (D), and (I)

is from A. K. Sen, *Collective Choice and Social Welfare* (San Francisco: Holden-Day, 1970), sec. 3.3. Sometimes I call Condition (U) "Unlimited scope."

2. See, for example, Henry Sidgwick's *Methods of Ethics*, 7th ed. (London: MacMillan and Company, 1907), and W. D. Ross's *The Right and the Good* (Oxford: Oxford University Press, 1930).

3. Omitted here, obviously, are more mundane considerations of "importance": that Arrow's Theorem allegedly sounds the death knell of democratic theory, welfare economics, and various other good things. As J. L. Austin once remarked, "Importance isn't important. Truth is." We have only attempted to account for the *intellectual* fascination of Arrow's result, not all the variously motivated attention it has drawn.

4. In *Social Choice and Individual Values*, Arrow calls his first requirement *collective rationality*. It includes, in addition to (U), a stipulation that preference and indifference be logically well behaved, that is, that they at least be transitive and connected. [What this means is that if alternative X is preferred (indifferent) to alternative Y, and Y in turn is preferred (indifferent) to Z, then X must be preferred (indifferent) to Z. That is what transitivity is. Connectedness means that for any two alternatives X and Y, either X is preferred to Y, or Y to X, or they are indifferent.] In the present work, logical well behavedness will be treated as a standing background assumption in order to concentrate attention on those aspects of Arrow's requirements that can intuitively be thought of as constraining the device itself. It is, however, true and worth keeping in mind that Arrow's result can be evaded by tinkering in various ways with the logical features of the preference relations; or, as some would say, by changing the subject.

Suggested Additional Readings

Arrow, Kenneth J. "Current Developments in the Theory of Social Choice." *Social Research* 44 (1977): 607–22.

Bernholz, Peter. "Instability of Voting Outcomes, Logrolling, Arrow, Coase, and All That: A Different Interpretation." In *Public Choice Essays in Honor of a Maverick Scholar: Gordon Tullock,* ed. Gary D. Fishback, Price V. Libecap, and Edward Zajac. Boston: Kluwer Academic Publishers, 2000.

Bonner, John. *Introduction to the Theory of Social Choice.* Chap. 4. Baltimore: Johns Hopkins University Press, 1986.

Brennan, Geoffrey, and Alan Hamlin. "Constitutional Choice." In *The Elgar Companion to Public Choice,* ed. William F. Shughart and Laura Razzolini. Cheltenham, UK: Edward Elgar, 2001.

Buchanan, James M. "A Hobbesian Interpretation of the Rawlsian Difference Principle." *Kyklos* 29 (1976): 5–25.

Buchanan, James M., and Gordon Tullock. *The Calculus of Consent.* Ann Arbor: University of Michigan Press, 1962.

Dahl, Robert A. *Democracy and Its Critics.* New Haven, CT: Yale University Press, 1989.

Dorn, James A. "Introduction: Government, the Economy and the Constitution." *Cato Journal* 7 (1987): 283–303.

Hardin, Russell. "Public Choice versus Democracy." In *Majorities and Minorities,* ed.

John W. Chapman and Alan Wertheimer. New York: New York University Press, 1990.

Holcombe, Randall G. "Non-optimal Unanimous Consent." *Public Choice* 48 (1986): 229–44.

Macey, Jonathan R. "Transaction Costs and the Normative Elements of the Public Choice Model: An Application to Constitutional Theory." *Virginia Law Review* 74 (1988): 471–518.

Mueller, Dennis C. "Constitutional Rights." *Journal of Law, Economics and Organization* 7 (1991): 313–33.

Riker, William H., and Barry R. Weingast. "Constitutional Regulation of Legislative Choice: The Political Consequences of Judicial Deference to Legislatures." *Virginia Law Review* 74 (1988): 471–518.

Saari, Donald G. *Decisions and Elections: Explaining the Unexpected.* Chaps. 2 and 3. Cambridge: Cambridge University Press, 2001.

Sen, Amartya K. "Social Choice and Justice: A Review Essay." *Journal of Economic Literature* 23 (1985): 1764–76.

Advanced Readings

Arrow, Kenneth J. "Values and Collective Decision Making." In *Philosophy, Politics, and Society,* ed. Peter Laslett and W. C. Runciman. Oxford: Blackwell Publishers, 1967.

Craven, John. "Liberalism and Individual Preferences." *Theory and Decision* 14 (1982): 351–60.

———. *Social Choice: A Framework for Collective Decisions and Individual Judgments.* Cambridge: Cambridge University Press, 1992.

Hanssen, Andrew F. "The Effect of Judicial Institutions on Uncertainty and the Rate of Litigation: The Election versus Appointment of State Judges." *Journal of Legal Studies* 28 (1999): 205–32.

Riker, William H. *Liberalism against Populism.* Chap. 5. Prospect Heights, IL: Waveland Press, 1982.

Sen, Amartya K. *Collective Choice and Social Welfare.* (Unstarred chapters.) San Francisco: Holden-Day, 1970.

Vickrey, William. "Utility, Strategy, and Social Decision Rules." *Quarterly Journal of Economics* 74 (1960): 507–35.

Majority Rule

The system of majority rule requires an alternative to receive at least one more than half the possible number of votes to be declared the winner. Suppose there is a single characteristic that defines the various alternatives, such as ideology for candidates or amount of bonds to be issued for a proposed public good. Further suppose that voters can be lined up based on their preferences for this particular characteristic. The person in the exact middle of the line, where there are an equal number of people on either side, is defined to be the median voter. If there are only two alternatives to consider, such as two candidates, two policies, or a simple yes-no vote on one policy, then whichever alternative is preferred by the median voter must also have at least all the voters on either side preferring the same alternative, and thus it will attract a majority of votes and be declared the winner. Therefore majority rule generates an incentive for candidates or policies to be moderated to coincide with the interests of the median voter. Since both candidates have the same incentive, the only equilibrium results in both candidates offering identical platforms.

Whether this is beneficial or not depends on interpretation. On the one hand, catering toward the middle implies compromise and benefits more people (in the case of a normal distribution) or at least harms fewer people compared with extremist candidates and policies. On the other hand, if both alternatives end up the same, no real choice is available despite a vote taking place.

In practice, exact convergence to the median position rarely occurs. It is unusual for the assumptions listed here to actually hold. Furthermore, institutional constraints, such as primary elections, may limit the incentive or ability for candidates to move toward the median position. Moderation in policy can still occur when voters balance the ideological positions of candidates against those of other politicians, such as president and members of Congress.

When there are more than two alternatives under consideration, the voting results may not be transitive, as presented in the previous section. These intransitivities, or cycles, suggest the order of pairwise voting, which can be purely arbitrary, can have as much of an impact on determining the winning outcome as the voters themselves. If these cycles can be predicted, then the person who decides the order of voting is in a position to put forward a specific order to ensure his or her preferred outcome is the winner. Likewise, voters have an incentive to vote strategically, that is, to vote for lesser alternatives that have a better chance of being the ultimate winner than their preferred choice. For example, primary voters may opt for more centrist candidates who have a better chance of winning the general election than the more extreme candidate they actually prefer.

Intransitive majority rule outcomes can leave a majority unhappy with the selected winner. In fact, the result can be even worse. Examples can be constructed where *everyone* would agree that another of the alternatives, already voted down, is preferable to the ultimate winner.

Although the notions of cycles and intransitivities do not apply when there are only two alternatives under consideration (such as yes/no on a specific proposal), majority rule vote outcomes may still be inefficient. The problem is that majority rule only considers the number of people in favor or opposition, and not the size of their gains or losses. Although it appears to be democratic, the notion of one person one vote under majority rule implies that the intensity of voter preferences is ignored. Small gains to the majority can be created at the expense of potentially large losses to the minority. Conversely, the majority can block efficient outcomes that impose even minimal losses on itself. As long as the majority coalition sticks together, it can impose its will on each and every issue, turning a seemingly democratic system into tyranny by the majority.

When the coalition members' individual preferences diverge across various issues, the coalition may fall apart, allowing other voters to become part of a new majority on particular votes. There are instances when two separate proposals, neither of which will generate a majority of votes in its favor individually, can both pass when combined, either through vote trading or more simply a single vote on the combined package. Such a process, known as logrolling, can allow two efficient proposals, where the gains to the minority in favor of each proposal outweigh the losses to the majority, to pass when they otherwise might not. On the other hand, logrolling can also entail passage of multiple inefficient proposals, each of which benefit a different narrow interest group, by creating a new majority in favor of the combined proposals. In both examples, each group would rather only have its own proposal pass but would prefer multiple passage to none. The incentive for any minority group is therefore to include only the minimum number of other interest groups into the coalition to just create an overall majority coalition.

In "Collective Decision Rules and Local Debt Choice: A Test of the Median-Voter Hypothesis," McEachern provides an early attempt to test the basic postulate of the median voter model with a simple yet compelling empirical framework. Dixit and Nalebuff's chapter, "The Strategy of Voting," considers voting strategies in multiple contexts but focuses primarily on majority rule decisions. Many surprising and potentially distressing outcomes are revealed. Mueller's "Probabilistic Majority Rule" offers a modification to the majority rule principle by using lotteries to threaten agents into fair bargaining, which would lead back to unanimity rule outcomes. He also considers how the normative implications of majority rule relate to the lottery system.

Collective Decision Rules and Local Debt Choice: A Test of the Median-Voter Hypothesis

William A. McEachern

Review Questions

1. What does the median voter theorem imply regarding the relationships between debt decisions made under majority rule referendum, under supermajority rule referendum, or by local officials? How are these relationships tested? Does the evidence support the relationships?
2. What affects an individual's preference for local debt? What other factors influence levels of local debt? Which factors are determined to be important in the actual level of local debt?
3. An early study implied referenda had no significant impact on local debt levels. Why do the results in this study differ?

Introduction

Nearly fifty years ago Harold Hotelling first discussed the logic underlying what has come to be known as the median-voter hypothesis [14]. Although

McEachern, William A. "Collective Decision Rules and Local Debt Choice: A Test of the Median-Voter Hypothesis." *National Tax Journal* 31 (1978): 129–35.

the theory has been greatly embellished over the years, the essential force of the argument has remained intact: if political opinion on a particular issue may be viewed as lying in a single dimension, then competition among political candidates will force them towards the position held by the median voter. A number of studies have employed the median voter hypothesis as an assumption in explaining public expenditure decisions [3;4;6;9;15], but direct tests of the hypothesis are almost nonexistent.[1]

One area that provides promise for testing implications of the median-voter hypothesis is the local debt decision. First, local debt is approved under a variety of collective decision rules, so contrasts can be made. In some states a simple majority on a referendum can pass a bond issue while in other states some fraction greater than majority is required, and in a third group of states no referendum is necessary. The debt decision is also appealing because, unlike the ordinary election in which candidates present a bundle of often competing issues, the bond referendum may be viewed by the voter as a one-dimensional decision. Moreover, as Buchanan and Tullock have noted, vote trading or logrolling are unlikely to occur with simple referenda.[2] As a result, individuals may be viewed as voting to reflect their true preferences.

Referenda outcomes have been examined in the past, but primarily to uncover those variables that contributed most to explaining the proportion of "yes" votes on particular referenda [e.g., 11;16;17;20]. None of this research is concerned with the median-voter hypothesis. In Section I a model is developed to examine the likely impact of alternative voting rules on a locality's debt preferences. These implications will be tested in Section II and the final section will present some concluding remarks.

I. Voting Rules and Debt Patterns

Local public outlay decisions may be divided into expenditure and revenue components. The first involves the choice concerning the kind and quantity of public goods to be provided, and the second involves the choice of financing schemes, including the "mix" of taxes and charges as well as the appropriate amount of debt financing. For several reasons local governments often choose to finance capital projects, such as school construction, through a bond issue rather than through current taxes or charges. Since local debt is usually used for capital goods, a local bond referendum may be viewed as a decision to change the quantity or quality of the existing capital stock, and the amount of debt in a community to some extent reflects the quantity and quality of this capital stock.[3]

Local debt preferences are likely to vary across individuals for a variety of reasons. Since local debt finances the stock of capital goods and since different voters are likely to have different perceptions of what might be an optimal stock of these capital goods, then views of what would be an appropriate debt level are apt to differ. Moreover, to the extent that certain functions could be financed by current taxes as opposed to debt, the timing of payments as reflected in the appropriate tax-debt mix may also differ across individuals. An individual's optimal tax-debt mix can be expected to depend on such factors as his expected income path, the existing tax structure, prevailing interest rates, his rate of time preference, plus his perception of the prospects of remaining in that community.[4]

A model will be developed to examine the impact of a simple-majority referendum, a greater-than-majority referendum, and no referendum on the level of debt in a community. Assume that debt level preferences in a community of a given population size are normally distributed[5] as in Figure 1, ranging between those with relatively low preferences for the use of debt to those with relatively high preferences for debt. In Figure 1, D_l and D_h represent low and high debt levels while D_m depicts the level preferred by the median voter.

A bond referendum presents the voter with two alternatives: one is to support the bond issue and the resulting higher debt level; the other is to vote against the bond issue and implicitly support the status quo. Assume individual voter debt preferences are single peaked, and that voters prefer the alternative that offers the highest utility. Over time the debt level in a community employing the simple majority referendum should approximate the level preferred by the median voter, depicted as D_m in Figure 1.

But what if some fraction exceeding a simple majority, for example, a two-thirds vote, is required to approve a referendum?[6] In Figure 1, D_g represents the debt level preferred by the voter at the 33.3 percentile. Assume a new community with a state-imposed two-thirds voting rule is in the process of funding the public capital goods required to operate the community. At the outset the status quo amounts to little or no debt. Debt issues will be preferred to the status quo by all those voters at or to the right of the proposed debt level. Additionally, some voters to the left of the proposed debt level will find the higher debt level preferable to the status quo. New issues will be approved until D_g is reached. Debt proposals to the right of D_g will not receive the necessary two-thirds support since all voters at or to the left of D_g will prefer the status quo (i.e., D_g) over the new proposal. Moreover, the further the new proposal is to the right of D_g the more voters to the right of D_g will

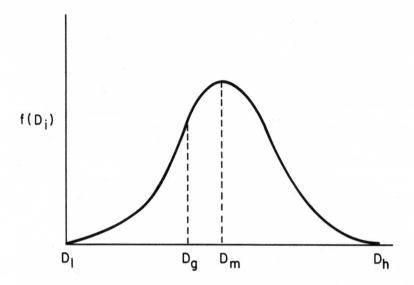

Figure 1. Debt Level Preferences

prefer the status quo to the new proposal, and therefore, the fewer votes for the new proposal. The equilibrium debt level under a greater-than-majority voting requirement will be lower, *ceteris paribus*, than under a simple majority voting rule.

Does this mean that once D_g is reached new referenda will never beat the status quo? No, because over time the real debt level falls below D_g both because existing debt is retired and because real income increases and/or general inflation reduce the debt level stated in real terms.[7]

The difference between the debt level preferred by a simple majority and the debt level preferred by two-thirds of the voters may provide some indirect measure of the external cost imposed by the simple majority on the voters between D_m and D_g in Figure 1. Specifically, the difference between the two debt levels represents debt unwillingly imposed by the simple majority on the voters at D_g, if the simple-majority rule is in effect.

Consider now the outcome if no local referendum is required and debt decisions are made by a locally-elected official. If there is competition in the political market then, according to the median-voter hypothesis, this competition will force the elected official to adopt a debt position that is, over time, consistent with the view of the median voter.[8] If the elected official prefers a different level of debt than that chosen by the median voter the official must revise his choice or he will be replaced.[9] As a result, there should be no difference in the debt level of a community whether it employs a simple-majority referendum or whether it has no referendum requirement.[10] However, if a greater-than-majority referendum is employed then debt levels will be lower than under either simple-majority voting or no referendum.

To examine the impact of alternative voting rules on actual debt levels one would ideally choose to view the outcome of the debt decision in a given community under each of the voting rules. But these voting rules are determined in each state by constitutional provisions and they seldom change for a given community. Consequently, the effect of various voting rules must be examined in a cross-section fashion; so we shall examine, *ceteris paribus,* differences in local debt levels across the fifty states based on the voting rules employed in each state.

The model discussed above focused on a single community; in comparing communities of varying size one must be sensitive to population differences. Clearly a voter would be less concerned with a one million dollar bond issue in a city of fifty thousand population than the same issue in a town of one thousand. The local per capita debt outstanding in each state will be the debt level measure. States will be divided into three groups based on their voting rules: (1) those states requiring a simple majority referendum, (2) those requiring some fraction greater than a majority (typically two-thirds), and (3) those states with no referendum requirement. We can obtain most efficient estimators to compare the debt levels of these three groups of states by including dummy variables to represent the voting rule. The dummy variables to be introduced are as follows: NR takes on the value of one if the state has no referendum requirement for local debt issues and zero otherwise; GM takes on the value of one if the state requires a fraction greater than a simple majority on a referendum to approve debt and zero otherwise. When both NR and GM are zero the state has a simple majority referendum requirement.

Local debt patterns in a particular state obviously are influenced by forces other than the voting rule. While these other factors are not of primary interest for this analysis, they must be carefully accounted for so as to minimize any specification error resulting from improperly omitting relevant information.

Local debt levels have been the focus of several previous studies employing data from the early 1960's [2;10;18;21], but the primary concern of that research has been to determine the effectiveness of state-imposed debt ceilings on the level of local debt. Accordingly, this study will include variables to account for the existence and stringency of state-imposed debt limits or ceilings. States may be divided into those with no debt limits, those with debt limits but with provisions (short of statutory reform) for exceeding the limit, and those with debt limits and no provisions for exceeding the limit. NDL and PEL will be dummy variables representing states with no debt limits and states with provisions to exceed the limit, respectively; when both variables are zero the state in question has a debt limit without provisions for exceeding that limit.[11] This latter case can be viewed as the most stringent of debt limits.

A local government's ability and desire to issue debt may also relate to the fiscal base in the community. The least ambiguous measure of a community's fiscal base is some measure of income.[12] Those localities with a greater need for schools and other capital projects funded may make more extensive use of debt to finance these expenditures. Several variables have been employed in the past in an attempt to account for those characteristics of the population that might indicate a greater need for capital expenditures, but the only variable that appeared to be at all of interest is some measure of population growth [21, p. 46], and such a measure will be used in this analysis as well.

In the absence of any theoretical justification for specifying the model otherwise, the linear form is adopted. The resulting equation amounts to a reduced-form expression to account for interstate differences in the ability (supply) and desire (demand) to issue local debt. Such an expression is presented in equation (1) as follows:

$$D_i = \alpha_0 + \alpha_1 NR + \alpha_2 GM + \alpha_3 NDL + \alpha_4 PEL + \alpha_5 PCI_i + \alpha_6 PG_i + \mu_i, \quad (1)$$

where D_i is the total outstanding local debt per capita (in dollars) for state i as of 1974;[13] NR and GM are no referendum and greater-than-majority referendum variables; NDL represents states with no debt limit, and PEL represents states with a debt limit but with provisions for exceeding that limit; PCI_i is per capita income in 1974; PG_i measures recent population growth and is the percentage growth in population between 1970 and 1974;[14] and μ_i is the random disturbance term.

Of primary interest here are the signs of the voting rule variables, NR and GM. If the median-voter hypothesis is correct, that is, if political competition forces elected officials over time to select the debt level preferred by the median voter, then there should be no difference, *ceteris paribus,* in the local per capita debt levels between states with no referendum requirement and those with a simple-majority referendum rule (i.e., $\alpha_1 = 0$). At the same time the discussion in the previous section suggests that states requiring a greater-than-majority referendum vote for approval will have lower debt levels per capita, *ceteris paribus,* than states requiring only a simple majority ($\alpha_2 < 0$).[15]

The effect of state-imposed debt limits remains an unsettled issue in the literature. One study concluded that local debt limits are largely ineffective [18], while two others found these limits have curbed the use of local debt [2;21]. The null hypothesis is that debt limits are not significant constraints on debt ($\alpha_3 = 0$), versus the one-sided alternative that states without debt limits have higher debt levels ($\alpha_3 > 0$). Those states with local debt limits, but with provisions for exceeding those limits (short of statutory reform) may have higher debt levels than those states with debt limits, but with no provisions for exceeding those limits ($\alpha_4 > 0$).

With respect to the remaining variables, the higher the per capita income the greater the ability to incur debt ($\alpha_5 > 0$). Also the more rapid the growth in population, the greater the demand for the sorts of capital projects financed by local debt (e.g., schools) and consequently the higher the debt levels ($\alpha_6 > 0$).

II. Estimated Effects of Voting Rules on Debt Levels

The results of least squares estimation of equation (1) employing the fifty states are as follows (with t-statistics in parentheses and asterisks denoting significance levels of 0.05 and above):

$$D = \begin{array}{l} -155.77 + 19.94 \, \text{NR} - 132.26^* \, \text{GM} + 426.22^* \, \text{NDL} + 51.08 \, \text{PEL} \\ (-0.63) \quad\;\; (0.22) \qquad\;\; (-1.68) \qquad\quad (3.74) \qquad\qquad (0.66) \end{array}$$

$$\begin{array}{l} + \; 0.13^* \, \text{PCI} + 2.08 \, \text{PG} \\ \quad (2.63) \qquad\;\; (0.74) \end{array}$$

$$\bar{R}^2 = 0.43 \qquad F(6,43) = 7.08^* \tag{2}$$

The results indicate that states without a referendum requirement do not have significantly different local per capita debt figures than states with a simple majority referendum.[16] In addition, as predicted, states requiring for approval a fraction exceeding simple majority have significantly lower debt levels than states with a simple-majority referendum requirement. The remaining variables all have the expected sign but only the no-debt-limit variable and the per-capita-income variable are significant. Debt limits appear to be an effective curb on the overall use of local debt, but provisions to exceed the debt limit do not result in significantly higher debt limits. The explanatory power of the model compares favorably with that found in previous research.

Since there is no significant difference in debt levels between states with a simple-majority referendum and those with no referendum, these two groups may be viewed as one and compared with those states requiring some fraction greater than a simple majority vote to approve bond issues.[17] The average per capita debt level for the fifty states is about $560 so the debt level in the greater-than-majority states is on average about 25 percent lower than in other states. And in simple-majority or no-referendum states, those in the minority are forced to bear more debt than they would prefer. The GM coefficient provides a crude measure of the external cost imposed by the simple majority on the marginal voter whose support would have been required had the greater-than-majority voting rule been in effect.[18]

Though his research did not consider the median-voter hypothesis, Pogue found that referenda had no significant impact on local debt levels [21, p. 45]. He drew no distinction, however, between simple-majority and greater-than-majority voting rules. Following Pogue's approach, if we simply contrast in our regression model all referendum states with those states without a referendum, we find no significant difference between the two groups. Thus the three-fold distinction of voting rules employed here uncovers effects that are masked by the two-fold approach employed by Pogue.

Although the issue has not been addressed here, one might ask whether the greater-than-majority voting rule simply changes the debt-tax mix or actually reduces the overall level of public expenditures. Pogue found after a rather detailed analysis that state ceilings on local debt actually depress both local spending and combined state-local spending [21, p. 47]. If the greater-than-majority restrictions operate in the same manner, then not only are per capita debt levels lower in states with that voting rule, but the overall level of spending is lower as well.

III. Summary

This paper tested the famous hypothesis of positive public choice that in an open, competitive political order constrained by majority voting rules, the tastes of the median preference holder dominate the margins of decision. Models that adopt the median voter hypothesis typically dismiss the real world fact that most public choices are made by representatives and not in referenda or by plebiscites. Such models assume that political markets function so efficiently as to make the question of representation or agency behaviorally uninteresting. This paper develops a model to test whether such liberties are empirically sound and finds that they are, at least with regard to the local debt choice. Specifically, there is no significant difference across states, *ceteris paribus*, in local debt levels between states employing a simple majority referendum and those with no referendum.

The model also predicts that when some fraction greater than a majority is required for referendum approval then observed debt levels in the community will be lower. This prediction is confirmed by the empirical evidence. Finally, state-imposed debt ceilings appear to be an effective curb on the level of debt issued by localities.

NOTES

1. When this study was undertaken there were no direct tests of the median-voter hypothesis. But a recent study by Holcombe [12] examines school spending levels, employing a methodology similar to that adopted here. His results will be discussed below.

2. They argue that with the standard referendum:

> ... the individual cannot easily trade his vote on the one issue for reciprocal favors on other issues because, first, he is uncertain as to when other issues would be voted on in this way, and, second, he and his immediate acquaintances represent such a small part of the total electoral that such trading efforts may not be worthwhile. Furthermore, the secret ballot, normally employed in such cases, makes it impossible for any external observer to determine whether voting commitments are honored or not [7, p. 132].

3. See the discussion by Mikesell and Blair [17] for a further development of this point.

4. See the analysis by Richard Wagner [27, p. 299] for a discussion of the tax-debt decision.

5. An equally weighted distribution or nearly any other distribution of preferences will yield the same general results.

6. One might ask why a greater-than-majority rule is adopted when a simple majority is optimal from a median-voter perspective. These rules were imposed by the state government decades ago, in part evidently to curb the local use of debt after widespread local defaults during the depression of 1873–78 [27, p. 297].

7. Population growth will also reduce each voter's perceived share of the debt. It is possible that in the initial stages of a town's capital formation, some bond issue to the right of D_g could capture the necessary two-thirds vote when paired against a status quo of little or no debt. But once this higher debt level is approved, subsequent bond issues over time will be defeated until the real debt level falls below D_g. Similarly, if the voting rule is changed from simple majority to a two-thirds requirement, the real level of debt will decline over time.

Of course, even if the prevailing debt level is below D_g (or below D_m with simple majority voting), new debt referenda may still be defeated if the capital good to be financed does not have the necessary support of the voters. But if the agent's ranking of projects is consistent with voters' ranking of projects, then bond issues will be approved as long as there is excess debt capacity.

8. To the extent that political competition is somehow lacking, then the elected official may not be forced to reflect the views of the median voter. See the research by Kasper on political competition and public expenditure levels [15]. For example, a political "machine" may run the city more in accord with the preferences of the politicians

and this could result in debt levels at odds with those preferred by the median voter. But where there is a margin for political discretion it is not clear whether elected officials would prefer higher or lower debt levels than those preferred by the median voter. If local officials derive utility from "empire building" through capital expenditures per se, then a greater amount of debt will result.

9. Two implicit assumptions must hold for referenda and elected officials to generate the same outcome. First, the same group of voters participate in bond referenda as participate in general elections. Second, where agents are making the debt decisions, logrolling among agents, to the extent that it exists, does not bias the outcome in a systematic way.

10. It is sometimes argued that voters experience a "debt illusion," and as a result prefer a higher level of debt than would be chosen if voters were aware of the full cost of debt. But even with this debt illusion, the vote-maximizing candidate will still choose the debt level preferred by the median voter.

11. All data concerning voting rules and debt ceilings are derived from the summaries of each state's constitution and statutes found in [1, pp. 153–58]. A total of 31 states have a simple-majority referendum, 11 have a greater-than-majority referendum, and 8 have no referendum requirement.

12. The value of property in a community may be another measure of the fiscal base, but the relationship between debt and property value is clouded by debt capitalization effects (see, e.g., [8; 27]). Specifically, to the extent that differential debt levels across communities become capitalized into the value of property, then the inclusion of property values to explain differences in debt levels across communities could give rise to simultaneous equation bias.

13. Previous research has argued that since debt limitations and referenda requirements often apply only to guaranteed debt, local officials are able to bypass these constraints by issuing nonguaranteed debt [18]. Similarly, it is argued that local officials can avoid state-imposed debt restrictions by creating new jurisdictions not subject to these debt restrictions [18]. To capture these possible effects debt is defined to include all long term "full-faith-and-credit" debt plus all nonguaranteed and short-term debt for all jurisdictions below the state level.

14. Debt figures are found in [25, Table 4] and [23, Table 22]. Personal income data are found in [24]; and population growth information is found in [22].

15. In fact one should expect the debt levels in greater-than-majority states to fall short of those both in simple majority referendum states and in no referendum states. This is tested below.

16. In recent, independent research Holcombe compared school spending levels, *ceteris paribus,* between states that required millage referenda on the school property tax and states with no referendum requirement. He found no significant difference between the two groups of states [12].

17. This is accomplished in equation (3) simply by omitting the NR variable. The results are as follows:

$$D = -171.26 - 135.77^* \text{ GM} + 426.60^* \text{ NDL} + 52.56 \text{ PEL} + 0.14^* \text{ PCI} + 1.97 \text{ PG}$$
$$(-0.73) \quad (-1.78) \quad (3.78) \quad (0.70) \quad (2.93) \quad (0.72)$$

$$\bar{R}^2 = 0.44 \qquad\qquad F(5,44) = 8.67^* \qquad\qquad (3)$$

Not surprisingly, the per capita debt level in the greater-than-majority states is significantly lower than the group of states consisting of both those with simple-majority referenda and those without referenda.

18. Of course, there always remains the possibility that some important variable was omitted, and to the extent that any omitted variable is correlated with the voting rule variables then the above results could be misleading. But care was taken to include all relevant factors. In addition, the voting-rule coefficients appear relatively insensitive to the inclusion or exclusion of additional variables. For example, although the no-debt-limit variable is large and significant, its exclusion has little effect on the size or significance of the voting-rule variables.

REFERENCES

1. Advisory Commission on Intergovernmental Relations, *Federal-State-Local Finances: Significant Features of Fiscal Federalism, 1973–74*, Washington: U.S. Government Printing Office, 1975.
2. Advisory Commission on Intergovernmental Relations, *State Constitutional Restrictions on State Borrowing and Property Taxing Powers*, New York: Government Affairs Foundation, Inc., 1965.
3. Barr, J. L. and Davis, O. A. "An Elementary Political and Economic Theory of the Expenditures of Local Governments," *Southern Economic Journal*, Vol. 33 (October 1966), pp. 149–65.
4. Bergstrom, T. C. and Goodman, R. P. "Private Demands for Public Goods," *American Economic Review*, Vol. 63 (June 1973), pp. 280–96.
5. Birdsall, W. C. "A Study of the Demand for Public Goods," in R. A. Musgrave (ed.) *Essays in Fiscal Federalism*, Washington: The Brookings Institution, 1965, pp. 235–94.
6. Borcherding, T. E. and Deacon, R. T. "The Demand for the Services of Non-Federal Governments," *American Economic Review*, Vol. 62 (December 1972), pp. 891–901.
7. Buchanan, J. M. and Tullock, G. *The Calculus of Consent*, Ann Arbor: University of Michigan Press, 1962.
8. Daly, G. C. "The Burden of the Debt and Future Generations in Local Finance," *Southern Economic Journal*, Vol. 36 (July 1969), pp. 44–51.
9. Davis, O. A. and Haines, G. H., Jr., "A Political Approach to a Theory of Public Expenditures: The Case of Municipalities," *National Tax Journal*, Vol. 19 (September 1966), pp. 259–75.
10. Heins, A. James, *Constitutional Restrictions Against State Debt*, Madison: The University of Wisconsin Press, 1963.
11. Hicks, R. E. "Influences on School Referenda in Ohio," *American Journal of Economics and Sociology*, Vol. 31 (January 1972), pp. 105–108.
12. Holcombe, Randall G. "An Empirical Test of the Median Voter Model," Paper Presented at the Public Choice Society Meetings, March 1977.
13. ———. "The Florida System: A Bowen Equilibrium Referendum Process," *National Tax Journal*, Vol. 30 (March 1977), pp. 77–84.
14. Hotelling, H. "Stability in Competition," *Economic Journal*, Vol. 39 (March 1929), pp. 41–57.

15. Kasper, H. "On Political Competition, Economic Policy, and Income Maintenance Programs," *Public Choice,* Vol. 10 (Spring 1971), pp. 1–19.
16. Lucier, R. G. "The Oregon Tax Substitution Referendum," *National Tax Journal,* Vol. 24 (March 1971), pp. 87–91.
17. Mikesell, L. and Blair, J. P. "An Economic Theory of Referendum Voting: School Construction and Stock Adjustment," *Public Finance Quarterly,* Vol. 2 (October 1974), pp. 395–410.
18. Mitchell, William E. "The Effect of Debt Limit on State and Local Government Borrowing," *The Bulletin,* New York University, Institute of Finance, 1967.
19. Piele, P. K., and Hall, J. S. *Budgets, Bonds, and Ballots,* Lexington, Mass.: Lexington Books, 1973.
20. Plotkin, N. "A Social Choice Model of the California Feather River Project," *Public Choice,* Vol. 12 (Spring 1972), pp. 69–87.
21. Pogue, T. F. "The Effect of Debt Limits: Some New Evidence," *National Tax Journal,* Vol. 23 (March 1970), pp. 36–49.
22. U.S. Bureau of the Census, *Statistical Abstract of the United States: 1975* (96th edition) Washington, D.C., 1975.

The Strategy of Voting

Avinash K. Dixit & Barry J. Nalebuff

Review Questions

1. The vice president only votes on pending legislation when the Senate vote is tied. Why did this situation occur more frequently earlier in U.S. history? If such a situation rarely occurs today, why is the power of the vice president still considered to be great?
2. What are the incentives for voters to be strategic in elections? How are these incentives affected if candidates adopt the median position?
3. If decisions are made by majority rule, why might a majority, or potentially even everyone, be unhappy with the outcome?
4. Why might the order of voting over paired alternatives affect the outcome? What does this imply about the power of the agenda setter?
5. When does strategic voting make the participants worse off than if everyone voted sincerely?

The foundation of a democratic government is that it respects the will of the people as expressed through the ballot box. Unfortunately, these lofty ideals are not so easily implemented. Strategic issues arise in voting, just as in any

Avinash K. Dixit and Barry J. Nalebuff. "The Strategy of Voting." In *Thinking Strategically*, chap. 10, 259–85. New York: W.W. Norton, 1991.

other multiperson game. Voters will often have an incentive to misrepresent their true preferences. Neither majority rule nor any other voting scheme can solve this problem, for there does not exist any one perfect system for aggregating up individuals' preferences into a will of the people.*

What this means is that the structure of the game matters. For example, when Congress has to choose between many competing bills, the order in which votes are taken can have a great influence on the final outcome. We begin by looking at the voting process more carefully, figuring out just when an individual's vote matters.

1. The Tie of Power

Recent presidential elections have emphasized the importance of the selection of the vice president. This person will be just a heartbeat away from the presidency. But most candidates for president spurn the suggestion of the second spot on the ticket, and most vice presidents do not seem to enjoy the experience. The prospect of twiddling one's thumbs for four or eight years, waiting for the boss to die, is hardly a fit occupation for anyone.† John Nance Garner, FDR's first VP, expressed this succinctly: "The vice-presidency ain't worth a pitcher of warm spit."

Only one clause of the Constitution specifies any actual activity for the vice president. Article I, Section 3.4 says: "The Vice-President of the United States shall be President of the Senate, but shall have no vote, unless they be equally divided." The presiding is "ceremony, idle ceremony," and most of the time the vice president delegates this responsibility to a rotation of junior senators chosen by the senate majority leader. Is the tiebreaking vote important, or is it just more ceremony?

At first glance, both logic and evidence seem to support the ceremonial viewpoint. The vice president's vote just does not seem important. The chance of a tie vote is small. The most favorable circumstances for a tie arise

---

*This deep result is due to Stanford University professor Kenneth Arrow. His famous "impossibility" theorem shows that any system for aggregating unrestricted preferences over three or more alternatives into a group decision cannot simultaneously satisfy the following minimally desirable properties: (i) transitivity, (ii) unanimity, (iii) independence of irrelevant alternatives, (iv) non-dictatorship. Transitivity requires that if A is chosen over B and B is chosen over C, then A must be chosen over C. Unanimity requires A to be chosen over B when A is unanimously preferred to B. Independence of irrelevant alternatives requires that the choice between A and B does not depend on whether some other alternative C is available. Non-dictatorship requires that there is no individual who always gets his way and thus has dictatorial powers.

†No doubt they console themselves by thinking of the even worse plight of Britain's Prince Charles.

when each senator is just as likely to vote one way as the other, and an even number of senators vote. The result will be roughly one tie vote in twelve.* Of course senators' votes are far from random. Only when the two parties are roughly equal or when there is an especially divisive issue that splits some of the party lines does the vice president's vote get counted.

The most active tiebreaking vice president was our first, John Adams. He cast 29 tiebreaking votes during his eight years. This is not surprising, since his Senate consisted of only 20 members, and a tie was almost three times more likely than it is today, with our 100-member Senate. In fact, over the first 200 years, there have been only 222 occasions for the vice president to vote. More recently, Richard Nixon, under Eisenhower, was the most active vice president, casting a total of 8 tiebreaking votes—out of 1,229 decisions reached by the Senate during the period 1953–61. This fall in tiebreaking votes also reflects the fact that the two-party system is much more entrenched, so that fewer issues are likely to cross party lines.

But this ceremonial picture of the vice president's vote is misleading. More important than how often the vice president votes is the impact of the vote. Measured correctly, the vice president's vote is roughly equal in importance to that of any senator.

One reason that the vice president's vote matters is that it tends to decide only the most important and divisive issues. For example, George Bush, as vice president, voted to save both the administration's chemical weapons program (twice) and the MX missile program. This suggests that we should look more closely at just when it is that a vote matters.

A vote can have one of two effects. It can be instrumental in determining the outcome, or it can be a "voice" that influences the margin of victory or defeat without altering the outcome. In a decision-making body like the Senate, the first aspect is the more important one.

To demonstrate the importance of the vice president's current position, *imagine that the vice president is given a regular vote as President of the Senate.* When does this have any additional impact? For important issues, all 100 senators will try to be present.† If the 100 senators are split 51–49 or more lopsidedly, then the outcome is the same no matter which way the vice president votes. *The only time the outcome hinges on the vice president's 101st vote*

---

*The biggest chance that a fixed group of 50 Senators votes Aye and the remaining 50 vote Nay is $(\frac{1}{2})^{50} \cdot (\frac{1}{2})^{50}$. Multiplying this by the number of ways of finding 50 supporters out of the total 100, we get approximately (1/12).

†Or senators on opposite sides of the issue will try to pair off their absences.

is when the Senate is split 50–50, just the same as now, when the vice president has only a tiebreaking vote.

We recognize that our account of a vice president's voting power leaves out aspects of reality. Some of these imply less power for the vice president; others, more. Much of a senator's power comes from the work in committees, in which the vice president does not partake. On the other hand, the vice president has the veto power of the president on his side.

Our illustration of the vice president's vote leads to an important moral of wider applicability: anyone's vote affects the outcome only when it creates or breaks a tie. Think how important your own vote is in different contexts. How influential can you be in a presidential election? Your town's mayoral election? Your club's secretarial election?

As with the Senate, the chance that the rest of the electorate reaches a tie, leaving you decisive, is at a maximum when each voter is just as likely to vote one way as the other. Mathematical calculation shows that the chances of a tie are proportional to the square root of the number of voters: increasing the electorate a millionfold reduces the chances of a tie by a factor of a thousand. In the Senate, with 100 voters, we saw that the chance of a tie in the most favorable circumstances was 1 in 12. In a presidential election with 100 million voters, it drops to 1 in 12,000. Because of the electoral college system, there is a greater chance that you will be decisive in affecting the electoral votes of your state. But the fact that the population is rarely split so evenly works the other way, and even a slight advantage for one candidate or the other reduces the chances of a tie drastically. So you might take 1 in 12,000 as an optimistic estimate of your influence in a presidential election. Considering these odds, is it worth your while to vote?

To explore this question, let us take a concrete example. Suppose one candidate, Mr. Soft Heart, has promised to raise the minimum wage from $3.50 to $5.00, and the other, Mr. Hard Head, is opposed to any increase. If you hold a minimum-wage job, work 2,000 hours a year, and expect to keep the job when the wage rises, Mr. Heart will mean $3,000 a year more in your pocket than Mr. Head. Over the four years, this will amount to $12,000. But the chance that your vote will bring this about is only 1 in 12,000. The expected advantage to you from your vote is only a dollar. It is not worth your while to vote if to do so you must sacrifice even 20 minutes of paid working time. Surveys find that most people value their leisure time at about half their wage rate. Therefore voting is not worth 40 minutes of your leisure time.

Even if you are unlikely to change the outcome, you can still add your voice to the crowd. But will it be heard? While it is clear that 100 million to 0 is a landslide, there is no apparent line where the change in one vote causes a landslide to become a simple victory. And yet if enough people change their vote, the landslide will become a tie and then a loss and finally a landslide in the other direction. This absence of a "bright line" dates back to the Greek philosopher Zeno, who tells the paradox in terms of creating a mound from grains of sand one at a time. It seems true that no one grain can turn a non-mound into a mound. And yet, enough grains will turn a molehill into a mountain. A vote is much like a grain of sand. It is hard to imagine how one additional vote will change anyone's perception of the outcome.*

What this tells us is that calculations of personal gains and costs cannot be decisive in motivating people to vote. For the proper functioning of democracy, however, it is very important that people do so. That is why we need social conditioning. From civics classes to elementary school to election-eve appeals to one's patriotic duty, societies work to get out the vote—even if individual voters don't have any major impact on the election.† Where patriotic duty is found insufficient, people are sometimes legally required to vote, as is the case in several countries, including Australia.

2. The Median Voter

So far our emphasis has been on pairwise elections. In such cases there is little strategy other than whether or not to vote. If you vote, you should always vote for the candidate whom you most prefer. Because your vote matters most when it breaks a tie, you want your vote to reflect your preferences honestly.‡ For elections with more than two alternatives, the decision is both whether or not to vote and what to vote for. It is no longer true that one should always vote for one's favorite candidate.

In the 1984 Democratic party primary, supporters of Jesse Jackson had the

---

*Even though any single individual's opinion of the outcome is ever so slightly changed, a small impact on a large number of people may still add up to something.

†A much cheaper and potentially more representative way of deciding elections would be to run a poll. The current practice is a glorified poll; anyone who wants to participate, does so. The theory of statistics tells us that if the vote from a random sample of 10,000 gives one candidate a 5% edge (5,250 or more votes), then there is less than a one-in-a-million chance the outcome will be reversed, *even if 100 million people vote*. If the vote is closer we have to continue expanding the survey size. While this process could greatly reduce the cost of voting, the potential for abuse is also great. The selection of a random voter is subject to a nightmare of problems.

‡Again, there is the qualification that you might care about the candidate's margin of victory. Specifically, you might want your candidate to win, but only with a small margin of victory (in order to temper his megalomania, for example). In that case, you might choose to vote against your preferred alternative, provided you were confident that he would win.

problem of trying to send a signal with their vote. They could predict that Jackson was unlikely to win. The polls told them that Gary Hart and Walter Mondale were the clear front-runners. There was a great incentive to vote for those at the head of the pack in order not to waste one's vote. This became an even bigger problem when there were seven candidates competing for the 1988 Democratic party presidential nomination. Supporters didn't want to waste their vote or campaign contributions on a nonviable candidate. Thus polls and media characterizations that pronounced front-runners had the real potential to become self-fulfilling prophecies.

There is another reason why votes may not reflect preferences. One way to help keep your vote from getting lost in the crowd is to make it stand out: take an extreme position away from the crowd. Someone who thinks that the country is too liberal could vote for a moderately conservative candidate. Or she could go all the way to the extreme right and support Lyndon LaRouche. To the extent that candidates compromise by taking central positions, it may be in some voters' interests to appear more extreme than they are. This tactic is effective only up to a point. If you go overboard, you are thought of as a crackpot, and the result is that your opinion is ignored. The trick is to take the most extreme stand consistent with appearing rational.

To make this a little more precise, imagine that we can align all the candidates on a 0 to 100 scale of liberal to conservative. The Young Spartacus League is way on the left, around 0, while Lyndon LaRouche takes the most conservative stance, somewhere near 100.

Voters express their preference by picking some point along the spectrum. Suppose the winner of the election is the candidate whose position is the average of all voters' positions. The way you might think of this happening is that through negotiations and compromises, the leading candidate's position is chosen to reflect the average position of the electorate. The parallel in bargaining is to settle disputes by offering to "split the difference."

Consider yourself a middle-of-the-roader: if it were in your hands, you would prefer a candidate who stands at the position 50 on our scale. But it may turn out that the country is a bit more conservative than that. Without you, the average is 60. For concreteness, you are one of a hundred voters polled to determine the average position.

If you state your actual preference, the candidate will move to $[99 \times 60 + 50]/100 = 59.9$. If, instead, you exaggerate and claim to want 0, the final outcome will be at 59.4 By exaggerating your claim, you are six times as effective in influencing the candidate's position. Here, extremism in the defense of liberalism is no vice.

Of course, you won't be the only one doing this. All those more liberal than 60 will be claiming to be at 0, while those more conservative will be arguing for 100. In the end, everyone will appear to be polarized, although the candidate will still take some central position. The extent of the compromise will depend on the relative numbers pushing in each direction.

The problem with this averaging approach is that it tries to take into account both intensity and direction of preferences. People have an incentive to tell the truth about direction but exaggerate when it comes to intensity. The same problem arises with "split the difference": if that is the rule for settling disputes, everyone will begin with an extreme position.

One solution to this problem dates back to the twenties and Columbia University economist Harold Hotelling. Instead of taking the mean or average position, the candidate chooses the *median* position, the platform where there are exactly as many voters who want the candidate to move left as to move right. Unlike the mean, the median position does not depend on the intensity of the voters' preferences, only their preferred direction. To find the median point, a candidate could start at 0 and keep moving to the right as long as a majority supports this change. At the median, the support for any further rightward move is exactly balanced by the equal number of voters who prefer a shift left.

When a candidate adopts the median position, no voter has an incentive to distort her preferences. Why? There are only three cases to consider: (i) a voter to the left of the median, (ii) a voter exactly at the median, and (iii) a voter to the right of the median. In the first case, exaggerating preferences leftward does not alter the median, and therefore the position adopted, at all. The only way that this voter can change the outcome is to support a move rightward. But this is exactly counter to his interest. In the second case, the voter's ideal position is being adopted anyway, and there is nothing to gain by a distortion of preferences. The third case parallels the first. Moving more to the right has no effect on the median, while voting for a move left is counter to the voter's interests.

The way the argument was phrased suggested that the voter knows the median point for the voting population, and whether she is to the right or the left of it. Yet the incentive to tell the truth had nothing to do with which of those outcomes occurred. You can think about all three of the above cases as possibilities and then realize that whichever outcome materializes, the voter will want to reveal her position honestly. The advantage of the rule that adopts the median position is that no voter has an incentive to distort her preferences; truthful voting is the dominant strategy for everyone.

The only problem with adopting the median voter's position is its limited applicability. This option is available only when everything can be reduced to a one-dimensional choice, as in liberal versus conservative. But not all issues are so easily classified. Once voters' preferences are more than one-dimensional, there will not be a median. At that point, the possibility of manipulating the system becomes real.

3. Naive Voting

The most commonly used election procedure is simple majority voting. And yet the results of the majority-rule system have paradoxical properties, as was first recognized over two hundred years ago by French Revolution hero the Marquis de Condorcet.

In his honor, we illustrate his fundamental paradox of majority rule using revolutionary France as the setting. After the fall of the Bastille, who would be the new populist leader of France? Suppose three candidates, Mr. Robespierre, Mr. Danton, and Madame Lafarge, are competing for the position. The population is divided into three equally sized groups, left, middle, and right, with the following preferences:

	Left's Ranking	Middle's Ranking	Rights' Ranking
1st	Danton	Lafarge	Robespierre
2nd	Lafarge	Robespierre	Danton
3rd	Robespierre	Danton	Lafarge

In a vote of Robespierre against Danton, Robespierre wins two to one. Then in a vote of Robespierre against Lafarge, Lafarge beats Robespierre two to one. But then in a vote of Lafarge against Danton, Danton wins two to one. Thus there is no overall winner. Who ends up on top depends on which vote was the last taken. More generally, this possibility of endless cycles makes it impossible to specify any of the alternatives as representing the will of the people.

Things become even more insidious when voting cycles are embedded in a larger problem. The will of the majority can leave everyone worse off. To show this problem, we update and expand the preferences above. Suppose the Seven Dwarfs are candidates in an election.* The voters are split into three

---

*Any similarity between this story and the early stages of the 1988 Democratic presidential primaries is purely coincidental.

equal factions—call them Left, Middle, and Right. The rankings of the groups are as follows:

	Left's Ranking	Middle's Ranking	Right's Ranking
1st	Happy	Grumpy	Dopey
2nd	Sneezy	Dopey	Happy
3rd	Grumpy	Happy	Sleepy
4th	Dopey	Bashful	Sneezy
5th	Doc	Sleepy	Grumpy
6th	Bashful	Sneezy	Doc
7th	Sleepy	Doc	Bashful

Note that the cyclic ordering over Happy, Dopey, and Grumpy is equivalent to the cyclic ordering of Robespierre, Danton, and Madame Lafarge above.

If we start with Happy versus Dopey, Dopey wins. Then Grumpy beats Dopey. And Sneezy beats Grumpy. Next Sleepy beats Sneezy. Then Bashful beats Sleepy, and Doc beats Bashful. This is remarkable. A sequence of majority votes has taken us from Happy, Dopey, and Grumpy all the way to Doc, when every voter agrees that any one of Happy, Dopey, and Grumpy is better than Doc.

How did this happen? The elections were all decided by two-thirds majorities. Those on the winning side gained a position, while those on the losing end went down four slots on average. All voters had four wins and two losses, which on net puts them four places worse than where they started.

At this point you would be justified in objecting that these voters were responsible for their own misfortunes; they voted in a shortsighted way. Each pairwise contest was decided as if it were the only one, instead of being a part of a chain of votes. If the voters had only looked ahead and reasoned backward they never would have allowed themselves to end up with Doc. That's true. But the presence of a voting cycle makes the outcome highly sensitive to the voting procedure. The next section shows how controlling the agenda can determine the outcome.

4. Order in the Court

The way the U.S. judicial system works, a defendant is first found to be innocent or guilty. The punishment sentence is determined only after a defendant has been found guilty. It might seem that this is a relatively minor procedural issue. Yet, the order of this decision-making can mean the difference between life and death, or even between conviction and acquittal. We use the case of a defendant charged with a capital offense to make our point.

There are three alternative procedures to determine the outcome of a criminal court case. Each has its merits, and you might want to choose among them based on some underlying principles.

1. Status Quo: First determine innocence or guilt, then if guilty consider the appropriate punishment.
2. Roman Tradition: After hearing the evidence, start with the most serious punishment and work down the list. First decide if the death penalty should be imposed for this case. If not, then decide whether a life sentence is justified. If, after proceeding down the list, no sentence is imposed, then the defendant is acquitted.
3. Mandatory Sentencing: First specify the sentence for the crime. Then determine whether the defendant should be convicted.

The difference between these systems is only one of agenda: what gets decided first. To illustrate how important this can be, we consider a case with only three possible outcomes: the death penalty, life imprisonment, and acquittal.* This story is based on a true case; it is a modern update of the dilemma faced by Pliny the Younger, a Roman lawyer working under Emperor Trajan around A.D. 100.[1]

The defendant's fate rests in the hands of three judges. Their decision is determined by a majority vote. This is particularly useful since the three judges are deeply divided.

One judge (Judge A) holds that the defendant is guilty and should be given the maximum possible sentence. This judge seeks to impose the death penalty. Life imprisonment is her second choice and acquittal is her worst outcome.

The second judge (Judge B) also believes that the defendant is guilty. However, this judge adamantly opposes the death penalty. Her most preferred outcome is life imprisonment. The precedent of imposing a death sentence is sufficiently troublesome that she would prefer to see the defendant acquitted rather than executed by the state.

The third judge, Judge C, is alone in holding that the defendant is innocent, and thus seeks acquittal. She is on the other side of the fence from the second judge, believing that life in prison is a fate worse than death. (On this the defendant concurs.) Consequently, if acquittal fails, her second-best out-

---

*Similar results hold even when there are many more outcomes.

come would be to see the defendant sentenced to death. Life in prison would be the worst outcome.

	Judge A's Ranking	Judge B's Ranking	Judge C's Ranking
Best	Death Sentence	Life in Prison	Acquittal
Middle	Life in Prison	Acquittal	Death Sentence
Worst	Acquittal	Death Sentence	Life in Prison

Under the status quo system, the first vote is to determine innocence versus guilt. But these judges are sophisticated decision-makers. They look ahead and reason backward. They correctly predict that, if the defendant is found guilty, the vote will be two to one in favor of the death penalty. This effectively means that the original vote is between acquittal and the death penalty. Acquittal wins two to one, as Judge B tips the vote.

It didn't have to turn out that way. The judges might decide to follow the Roman tradition and work their way down the list of charges, starting with the most serious ones. They first decide whether or not to impose a death penalty. If the death penalty is chosen, there are no more decisions to be made. If the death penalty is rejected, the remaining options are life imprisonment or acquittal. By looking forward, the judges recognize that life imprisonment will be the outcome of the second stage. Reasoning backward, the first question reduces to a choice between life and death sentences. The death sentence wins two to one, with only Judge B dissenting.

A third reasonable alternative is to first determine the appropriate punishment for the crime at hand. Here we are thinking along the lines of a mandatory sentencing code. Once the sentence has been determined, the judges must then decide whether the defendant in the case at hand is guilty of the crime. In this case, if the predetermined sentence is life imprisonment, then the defendant will be found guilty, as Judges A and B vote for conviction. But if the death penalty is to be required, then we see that the defendant will be acquitted, as Judges B and C are unwilling to convict. Thus the choice of sentencing penalty comes down to the choice of life imprisonment versus acquittal. The vote is for life imprisonment, with Judge C casting the lone dissent.

You may find it remarkable and perhaps troubling that any of the three outcomes is possible based solely on the order in which votes are taken. Your choice of a judicial system might then depend on the outcome rather than the underlying principles.

5. The Sophisticates

The problems with majority rule go beyond manipulating the outcome through control of the agenda. Even sophisticated voters who exercise foresight can collectively outsmart themselves. We tell a story that illustrates the point, freely adapting the saga of President Reagan's nominees for the Supreme Court.

Judge Bork was the first nominee. Judges Ginsberg and Kennedy were known to be high on the list, and likely to be nominated should Bork not be confirmed by the Senate. If the Senate turned down all three, the likelihood was that the seat would stay vacant for the next president to fill.

Imagine that the decision rests in the hands of three powerful senators. To avoid impugning the reputation of any actual persons, we will call the three A, B, and C. Their rankings of the four possible outcomes are as follows:

	A's Ranking	B's Ranking	C's Ranking
1st	Kennedy	Ginsberg	Vacant
2nd	Vacant	Kennedy	Bork
3rd	Bork	Vacant	Ginsberg
4th	Ginsberg	Bork	Kennedy

The first thing to observe is that leaving the seat vacant is *unanimously* preferred to nominating Judge Bork. Yet if these are the preferences and the senators correctly predict the order of nominations as Bork, Ginsberg, and Kennedy, the result will be that Bork is confirmed.

We figure out the voting patterns by working backward up the tree.

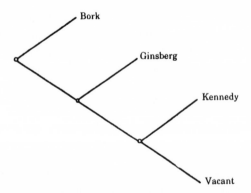

If the vote comes down to appointing Kennedy versus leaving the seat vacant, Kennedy will win. By looking ahead and reasoning backward the senators can predict a victory for Kennedy if Ginsberg is defeated. Therefore, if Bork is turned down the contest becomes Ginsberg or Kennedy. In the Ginsberg versus Kennedy contest, Ginsberg wins two to one.

Reasoning backward again, right at the start the senators should realize that their choice is Bork or Ginsberg. Here, Bork wins two to one. Everyone is looking ahead and correctly figures out the consequences of their action. Yet they collectively end up with a candidate whose nomination, everyone agrees, is worse than leaving the seat vacant.

Now in fact it didn't turn out that way, and there are several reasons. No one was quite certain who the next nominee would be. Preferences changed as more information was learned about the nominees. The senators' preferences may not have been as we represented them. Equally important, we have ignored any possibility for logrolling.

This was a perfect opportunity for logrolling to arise. There were three 2:1 votes. Each of the senators was on the winning side twice and on the losing side once. The gain from each win was worth one position in their ranking, but the loss pushed them down three. It doesn't help to win two small battles and lose the big war. The possibility for mutual gain opens the door for logrolling, and with these preferences we expect Bork would be defeated.

6. All-time Greats

After the White House, election to Cooperstown may be the next most coveted national honor. Membership in the Baseball Hall of Fame is determined by an election. There is a group of eligible candidates—for example, a player with ten years of experience becomes eligible five years after retirement.* The electors are the members of the Baseball Writers Association. Each voter may vote for up to ten candidates. All candidates capturing votes from more than 75 percent of the total number of ballots returned are elected.

One problem with this system is that the electors don't have the right incentives to vote for their true preferences. The rule that limits each voter to ten choices forces the voters to consider electability as well as merit. Some sportswriters may believe a candidate is deserving, but don't want to throw away the vote if the player is unlikely to make the cutoff. This same issue arose for vot-

---

*However, if the player has been on the ballot for fifteen years and failed to get elected, then eligibility is lost. For otherwise ineligible players, there is an alternative route to election. An Old Timers' committee considers special cases and sometimes elects one or two candidates a year.

ing in presidential primaries, and it appears in any election in which each voter is given a fixed number of votes to distribute among the candidates.

Two experts in game theory propose an alternative way to run elections. Steven Brams and Peter Fishburn, one a political scientist and the other an economist, argue that "approval voting" allows voters to express their true preferences without concern for electability.[2] Under approval voting, each voter may vote for as many candidates as he wishes. Voting for one person does not exclude voting for any number of others. Thus there is no harm in voting for a candidate who has no hope of winning. Of course if people can vote for as many candidates as they wish, who gets elected? Like the Cooperstown rule, the electoral rule could specify in advance a percentage of the vote needed to win. Or it could pre-specify the number of winning candidates, and then the positions are filled by those who gather the most votes.

Approval voting has begun to catch on, and is used by many professional societies. How would it work for the Baseball Hall of Fame? Would Congress do better if it used approval voting when deciding which expenditure projects should be included in the annual budget? We look at the strategic issues associated with approval voting when a cutoff percentage determines the winners.

Imagine that election to the different sports halls of fame was decided by approval voting, in which all candidates capturing above a fixed percentage of the votes are elected. At first glance, the voters have no incentive to misstate their preferences. The candidates are not in competition with one another, but only with an absolute standard of quality implicit in the rule that specifies the required percentage of approval. If I think Reggie Jackson should be in the Baseball Hall of Fame, I can only reduce his chances by withholding my approval, and if I think he doesn't belong there, I can only make his admission more likely by voting contrary to my view.

However, candidates may compete against one another in the voters' minds, even though nothing in the rules mandates it. This will usually happen because voters have preferences concerning the size or the structure of the membership. Suppose Dan Marino and John Elway come up for election to the Football Hall of Fame. I think Marino is the better quarterback, although I will admit that Elway also meets the standard for a Hall of Fame berth. However, I think it overridingly important that two quarterbacks not be elected in the same year. My guess is that the rest of the electorate regards Elway more highly and he would get in no matter how I vote, but that Marino's case will be a very close call, and my approval is likely to tip him over. Voting truthfully means naming Marino, which is likely to lead to the outcome in which both are admitted. Therefore I have the incentive to misstate my preference and vote for Elway.

Two players may complement each other, rather than compete, in the voters' minds. I think neither Geoff Boycott nor Sunil Gavaskar belongs in the Cricket Hall of Fame, but it would be a gross injustice to have one and not the other. If in my judgment the rest of the electorate would choose Boycott even if I don't vote for him, while my vote may be crucial in deciding Gavaskar's selection, then I have an incentive to misstate my preference and vote for Gavaskar.

In contrast, a quota rule explicitly places candidates in competition with one another. Suppose the Baseball Hall of Fame limits admission to only two new people each year. Let each voter be given two votes; he can divide them between two candidates or give both to the same candidate. The candidates' votes are totaled, and the top two are admitted. Now suppose there are three candidates—Joe DiMaggio, Marv Throneberry, and Bob Uecker.* Everyone rates DiMaggio at the top, but the electors are split equally between the other two. I know that DiMaggio is sure to get in, so as a Marv Throneberry fan I give my two votes to him to increase his chances over Bob Uecker. Of course everyone else is equally subtle. The result: Throneberry and Uecker are elected and DiMaggio gets no votes.

Government expenditure projects naturally compete with one another so long as the total budget is limited, or congressmen and senators have strong preferences over the size of the budget. We will leave you to think which, if any, is the DiMaggio project, and which ones are the Throneberrys and Ueckers of federal spending.

7. "Love a Loath'd Enemy"

Incentives to distort one's preferences appear in other situations, too. One instance occurs when you can move first and use this opportunity to influence others.[3] Take for example the case of charitable contributions by foundations. Suppose there are two foundations, each with a budget of $250,000. They are presented with three grant applications: one from an organization helping the homeless, one from the University of Michigan, and one from Yale. Both foundations agree that a grant of $200,000 to the homeless is the top priority. Of

---

*Marv Throneberry played first base for the '62 Mets, possibly the worst team in the history of baseball. His performance was instrumental to the team's reputation. Bob Uecker is much better known for his performance in Miller Lite commercials than for his play on the baseball field.

the two other applications, the first foundation would like to see more money go to Michigan, while the second would prefer to fund Yale. Suppose the second steals a march and sends a check for its total budget, $250,000, to Yale. The first is then left with no alternative but to provide $200,000 to the homeless, leaving only $50,000 for Michigan. If the two foundations had split the grant to the homeless, then Michigan would have received $150,000, as would Yale. Thus the second foundation has engineered a transfer of $100,000 from Michigan to Yale through the homeless. In a sense, the foundation has distorted its preferences—it has not given anything to its top charity priority. But the strategic commitment does serve its true interests. In fact, this type of funding game is quite common.* By acting first, small foundations exercise more influence over which secondary priorities get funded. Large foundations and especially the federal government are then left to fund the most pressing needs.

This strategic rearranging of priorities has a direct parallel with voting. Before the 1974 Budget Act, Congress employed many of the same tricks. Unimportant expenditures were voted on and approved first. Later on, when the crunch appeared, the remaining expenditures were too important to be denied. To solve this problem, Congress now votes first on budget totals and then works within them.

When you can rely on others to save you later, you have an incentive to distort your priorities by exaggerating your claim and taking advantage of the others' preferences. You might be willing to gain at the expense of putting something you want at risk, if you can count on someone else bearing the cost of the rescue.

The principle of forcing others to save you can turn the outcome all the way around, from your worst to your best alternative. Here we show how this is done using the votes of a corporate board of trustees facing a hostile takeover. Their immediate problem is how to respond. Four options have been proposed, each with its own champion.

The founding president is looking for a way to keep the company intact.

---

*One explicit example is the strategic game played between the Marshall and Rhodes Scholarships. The Marshall Fund's objective is to have the maximum influence over who is given a scholarship to study in England. If someone has the potential to win both a Marshall and a Rhodes, the Marshall Fund prefers to have the person study as a Rhodes Scholar; that brings the person to England at no cost to the Marshall Fund and thus allows the Marshall Scholarship to select one more person. Hence the Marshall Fund waits until the Rhodes Scholarships have been announced before making its final selections.

His first preference is to initiate a poison-pill provision into the company charter. The poison pill would be designed to prevent any outside party from attaining control without board approval.

The two young members of the board feel the situation is more desperate. They believe that a takeover is inevitable and are concentrating on finding a way to make the present transaction more acceptable. Their preferred action is to look for a white knight, a buyer who is acceptable to management and the board. The management representation on the board suggests a third possibility. The present managers would like the opportunity to buy the company through a management buyout, an MBO.

The fifth member of the board is an outside director. He is cautiously optimistic about the present raider and argues that there is time to see how the offer develops.

After these four options have been discussed, everyone ends up with a clear picture of where the others stand (or sit) on the four proposals. For example, the founder is a man of action; his worst outcome is the Wait & See position. The two young board members agree with the fifth that the MBO option is unattractive; whenever management competes with an outside bidder it opens the door to conflict of interest and insider trading, for managers are the ultimate insiders. The complete set of preferences is presented below.

	Founder's Ranking	Two Young Directors' Rankings	Management's Ranking	Outside Director's Ranking
1st	Poison Pill	White Knight	MBO	Wait & See
2nd	MBO	Poison Pill	Poison Pill	White Knight
3rd	White Knight	Wait & See	Wait & See	Poison Pill
4th	Wait & See	MBO	White Knight	MBO

Faced with these options, the board must make a decision. Everyone recognizes that the voting procedure may well influence the outcome. Even so, they decide there is a natural order to the decision-making process: begin by comparing the active courses of action and then decide whether the best one is worth doing. They first compare an MBO with a White Knight, and the more preferred alternative is then compared with the Poison Pill option. Having found the best active response, they decide whether this is worth doing by comparing it with Wait & See.

This voting problem is represented by the tree below.

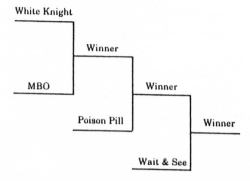

This tree should remind you of a tennis tournament in which some players are seeded. We are seeding "Wait & See" all the way into the finals, "Poison Pill" into the semifinals, and giving no seed to "MBO" and "White Knight."

Boxing and chess both work this way, too. There is a series of challenges that you must win in order to go against the presiding world champion. The U.S. presidential election process also works this way. When there is an incumbent president, that person is typically a shoo-in for his party's nomination. The opposing party runs a primary to decide who will go against the incumbent in the final elections. The primary process, the ensuing party nomination, and the presidential election can be thought of as a series of elimination elections. But back to the boardroom.

We suppose that the five board members have enough foresight to realize the consequences of their actions in successive rounds, and vote according to their true preferences. Backward reasoning makes this problem easy to solve. You can work out the solution and see that the White Knight option wins (or you can jump to the next paragraph), but that is not the point of this story. We are interested in showing how the founder can improve the outcome from his perspective by making a commitment to distorted preferences.

How is it that the White Knight option wins under foresighted voting? The last election must be Wait & See versus something. In this final election everyone has an incentive to vote honestly, since this will determine the actual outcome. The three possibilities are easy to calculate:

- Wait & See vs. Poison Pill, *Poison Pill* wins 4–1.
- Wait & See vs. MBO, *Wait & See* wins 3–2.
- Wait & See vs. White Knight, *White Knight* wins 3–2.

Now we go back one previous round. The contest will be either Poison Pill vs. White Knight or Poison Pill vs. MBO. In the first case, both Poison Pill and White Knight are preferred to Wait & See. So whatever wins the second round will be implemented. The board members prefer White Knight to Poison Pill, 3–2.

In the second case, a vote for MBO is in reality a vote for Wait & See. Board members can anticipate that if MBO beats Poison Pill for the active course, it will lose out in the next comparison with Wait & See. So when deciding between Poison Pill and MBO, board members will act as if deciding between Poisin Pill and Wait & See, with the result that Poison Pill wins 4–1. Thus the first-round comparison is truly between Poison Pill and White Knight. White Knight is chosen by a 3–2 margin and is then selected in each of the subsequent comparisons.

Once the founder recognizes what will happen, there is a strategy he can employ to get his most preferred option, the Poison Pill. Look what happens if the founder "adopts" the preferences of the outside board member. Of course it is essential that this change of preferences is credible and is made known to all the other voters. Suppose the founder simply gives his vote to the outside director and leaves the meeting.

At first glance this seems nothing short of crazy; the adopted preferences are almost the opposite of his true ones. But look at the effect. The votes will now go as follows:

- Wait & See vs. Poison Pill, *Poison Pill* wins 3–2.
- Wait & See vs. MBO, *Wait & See* wins 4–1.
- Wait & See vs. White Knight, *Wait & See* wins 3–2.

The only active option that can beat Wait & See is Poison Pill. Right from the start the board members should predict that if Poison Pill ever loses, the outcome will be Wait & See. Yet both MBO and White Knight supporters prefer Poison Pill to Wait & See. They are forced to vote for Poison Pill as it is their only viable alternative; thus Poison Pill wins.

By transferring his support to the opposition, the founder is able to make a credible threat that it is either Poison Pill or Wait & See. As a result, all but the die-hard Wait & See supporters dump the White Knight option (which can no longer beat Wait & See) in favor of the Poison Pill. Superficially, this transfer of a vote doubles the strength of the Wait & See supporters. Actually, it leads to an outcome that is worse from their viewpoint—Poison Pill rather than White Knight. In voting, strength can be weakness. Of course, if the outside director sees through the game, he should refuse to accept the founder's proxy.

If you regard this story as farfetched, something quite like it did occur in the 1988 Wisconsin presidential primary. The Republican governor of the state said that of the Democratic candidates, Jesse Jackson was the most interesting. Many commentators thought this was a Machiavellian attempt to get Republicans to cross over and vote for Jackson in the Democratic primary, thereby helping produce a more easily beatable opponent for Bush in the November election. Apparently, Michael Dukakis was sufficiently easy for George Bush to beat, even without this help.

8. Case Study #10: All or Nothing

Gin and vermouth: some prefer them straight, while others only drink them mixed, i.e., a martini. We've seen examples of both types of preferences. In election to the Football Hall of Fame, some would be happy with either Elway or Marino, but not both, while in cricket others find only the martini combination of Boycott and Gavaskar palatable.

Is the budget approval process all that different? How can it be improved? One suggestion is to give the president the power of a line-item veto.

> We ask the Congress, once again: Give us the same tool that 43 governors have, a line-item veto, so we can carve out the boondoggles and pork—those items that would never survive on their own.
> —Ronald Reagan, State of the Union Address, January 27, 1987.

Yet, it is possible that this may be a tool the president is better off without. How could that be?

Case Discussion

One reason is that without a line-item veto, the president is committed to taking what the Congress gives him; he cannot modify it piecemeal to better suit his preferences. Consequently, compromises made in Congress will be honored without fear that the president will pick and choose what segments to keep. Once Congress predicts they will lose all of the parts that would not survive on their own, the process of agreeing on a budget will become much more contentious, and a consensus compromise may not be found. Congress may be much less willing to serve the president a martini if he can remix it before presenting it to the nation.

Thus a president with a line-item veto might end up with less power, simply because the Congress is less willing (or able) to put proposals on his desk. A simple example helps illustrate the point. President Reagan wanted funds for Star Wars. Unfortunately for Reagan, the Republican party did not control the Congress. The Democrats' approval had to be bought. The budget offered the Democrats a package of social programs that made the defense spending tolerable. The willingness of the Democrats to approve the budget was contingent on the complete package. If they thought that Reagan could use a line-item veto to cut the social program (in the name of pork), they would be unwilling to give him the Star Wars funds.

The debate about the effectiveness of the line-item veto for reducing deficits is best settled by looking at the experience at the state level. Columbia University economist Douglas Holtz-Eakin has examined the historical evidence:

> Gubernatorial veto power is quite old. The President of the Confederacy had (but did not exercise) item veto power during the Civil War and 28 states (out of a total of 45) adopted a line item veto between 1860 and 1900. By 1930, 41 of the 48 states had a provision for line item veto power. The governors of Iowa and West Virginia acquired line item veto power in 1969.[4]

And yet, after looking at all these cases, Professor Holtz-Eakin was unable to see any reduction in the budget deficits of states whose governor had the line-item veto.

NOTES

1. The story of Pliny the Younger is first told from the strategic viewpoint in Robin Farquharson's 1957 Oxford University doctoral thesis, which was later published as *Theory of Voting* (New Haven, Conn.: Yale University Press, 1969). William Riker's *The Art of Political Manipulation* (New Haven, Conn.: Yale University Press, 1986) provides much more detail and forms the basis for this modern retelling. Riker's book is filled with compelling historical examples of sophisticated voting strategies ranging from the Constitutional Convention to the recent attempts to pass the Equal Rights Amendment.

2. The arguments are presented in their book *Approval Voting* (Boston, Mass.: Birkhauser, 1983).

3. This topic is addressed in recent economics working papers by Princeton professor Douglas Bernheim and University of Michigan professor Hal Varian.

4. This history of the line-item veto and the empirical results are reported in Douglas Holtz-Eakin's paper "The Line Item Veto and Public Sector Budgets," *Journal of Public Economics* (1988): 269–92.

Probabilistic Majority Rule

Dennis C. Mueller

Review Questions

1. Why is it important to distinguish between allocative efficiency and re-distribution? How does this limit the benefit of relying upon majority rule decisions?
2. What is the importance to the lottery system? How does the procedure work?
3. Interpret the expected utility equation (3). Why do risk averse voters prefer equal cost sharing rather than a lottery over all or nothing costs? What does this imply about any new proposals to be offered? Why does group size on each side affect this determination?
4. Why is the lottery a preferable mechanism to determine an outcome over a straight majority vote even if the majority favors one particular alternative over the other? What is meant by "tyranny of the majority"? How does the lottery serve to break this tyranny?
5. What normative properties does standard majority rule satisfy when there are only two alternatives under consideration? How does the lottery mechanism relate to these properties?
6. How is the rule affected when there are more than two alternatives under consideration? How does the presence or absence of a Condorcet winner affect the benefits of the lottery mechanism?

Mueller, Dennis C. "Probabilistic Majority Rule." *Kyklos* 42 (1989): 151–70.

One of the most useful pedagogical distinctions in economics is between allocative efficiency improvements and distributional changes, between movement to the contract curve and movement along it. It was one of Knut Wicksell's [1896] great insights to recognize the importance of this distinction to the choice of democratic procedures for making collective decisions. Wicksell focussed upon allocative efficiency improvements, and is perhaps most remembered for his advocacy of the unanimity rule to decide these questions. But in a footnote presaging modern arguments in favor of majority rule, Wicksell suggests that this rule be used to decide distributional questions [1896, p. 109, note *m*]. The work of May [1952], Barry [1965], and Rae [1969, 1975] can be interpreted as arguing that the majority rule, *under certain assumptions,* is an attractive procedure for resolving distributional issues. While the majority rule may have attractive properties for deciding distributional issues, the unanimity rule almost certainly does not. Indeed, under a narrow interpretation of the rational, self-interest postulate, there will be no redistribution under the unanimity rule.

When the majority rule is used to decide allocative efficiency improvements, on the other hand, the temptation to transform pure allocative efficiency changes into a combination allocative efficiency-redistribution issue will be too great for rational egoists to pass up. A majority coalition can transform a public good proposal that would make all better off into one that is even more beneficial to themselves, by reducing their share of its costs, and raising the minority's share. William Riker's [1982] evidence that 'grand' coalitions quickly change into minimal winning coalitions is consistent with this prediction. When the majority rule is used, all collective decisions are likely to have a redistributional component, and the redistributional tail may wag the allocative efficiency dog.[1]

The separation of allocative and redistributive decisions in the collective decision process is featured again in Buchanan and Tullock's *Calculus of Consent* [1962]. They argue not for different voting rules for the two types of decisions, favoring the unanimity rule for both, but rather that the different decisions should be taken up at different stages of the collective decision process: distributional questions at the constitutional stage, allocative efficiency questions at a legislative or parliamentary stage.

Constitutional conventions are seldom occurrences, however, and most distributional questions get resolved in the world's democracies by committees of representatives using the same voting rule to decide both these issues and those involving allocative efficiency. The strictures of Wicksell, Buchanan and Tullock and others from the public choice school have gone unheard.

This essay is also concerned with the questions of how best to resolve allocative efficiency and distributional questions using democratic institutions. It begins with the assumption that allocative efficiency and distributional questions are not easily separated, and constitutional conventions seldom convened. It presumes, therefore, that both kinds of issues are routinely decided by parliaments using a single voting rule. Given this constraint, a modification of majority rule is proposed with arguably superior properties to the simple majority rule.

We first describe the procedure and then discuss its properties.

I. How the Procedure Works[2]

Individuals are free to propose alternatives as in any committee under fair rules for recognizing motions. When two proposals are on the floor, P_i and P_j, the issues are decided using the following two step procedure. First, a vote is taken on the two proposals. If m_i voters support P_i and m_j support P_j, then the following probabilities are announced, $\pi_i = m_i/(m_i + m_j)$ and $\pi_j = m_j/(m_i + m_j)$. These probabilities are used to determine a winning proposal in a second step of the procedure using a random process (black and white balls in an urn), *unless* all members of the committee unanimously agree to a third proposal, P_u. If they do, then P_u is the committee's choice, unless some other proposal can achieve a unanimous majority against it. If no P_u is forthcoming, the winning proposal in the random process becomes the new status quo with members free to propose alternatives to it. The meeting proceeds with members free to propose new alternatives to any issue winning on a previous round by the random process until either a predetermined time limit is reached, with the last winning proposal via the random process being the committee's choice, or at some stage a P_u is proposed that all committee members prefer to the previously determined gamble.

Comment. Since it is possible in a groping toward the Pareto possibility frontier that several successive proposals are unanimously preferred to the previous winning proposal, an opportunity must be allowed for new proposals to be made once a P_u has been found.

II. Properties—Allocative Efficiency Issues

Consider a public good-externality decision in which a reallocation of resources could make everyone better off. To make the problem especially simple, assume that the decision is whether or not to provide a lumpy public good G, and if so how to share its costs. All members have identical, separable, concave utility functions defined over G and the private good, X,

$$U = u(G) + v(X) \tag{1}$$

$u' > 0$, $u'' < 0$, $v' > 0$, $v'' < 0$. All have identical incomes Y. Provision of the public good with equal cost sharing among the n citizens makes all better off.

$$u(G) + v\left(Y - \frac{G}{n}\right) > u(0) + v(Y) \tag{2}$$

But an equal sharing of the public good's costs is not necessarily the outcome of the collective decision process. As noted above, were majority rule employed the incentive would exist to shift the burden of the public good's costs on a bare minority.

To make the problem of coalition formation especially obvious, assume that a river divides the city in half, with m = n/2 citizens living in the east and *m* in the west. An obvious, at least to those living in the east, alternative to equal cost sharing is for all of the costs to be borne by those living in the west. Let this proposal from citizens in the east be P_e, with the west making the symmetric proposal P_w. If the choice were between these two proposals, and simple majority rule were used, the outcome would be decided in favor of whichever side of town turned out the largest number of voters.

Now consider the situation under probabilistic majority voting. The expected utility of a citizen from either side of town is

$$E(U) = \pi[u(G) + v(Y)] + (1 - \pi)\left[u(G) + v\left(Y - \frac{G}{n - m}\right)\right] \tag{3}$$

where $\pi = m/n = 1/2$ is the probability that the citizen's favored proposal wins. The public good is provided, whichever proposal wins, and the remaining terms in (3) correspond to a fair gamble between paying all and none of the public good's costs. All of the n risk averse voters prefer the provision of the public good with equal cost sharing to the fair gamble depicted in (3). To see this, we take Taylor expansions of (3) and (1) with X = Y − G/n. From (1)

$$U = \mu(G) + v\left(Y - \frac{G}{n}\right) = \mu(G) + v(Y) - v'(Y)\left(\frac{G}{n}\right)$$
$$+ \tfrac{1}{2}v''(Y)\left(\frac{G}{n}\right) + \text{higher order terms} \tag{4}$$

From (3)

$$E(U) = \frac{m}{n}\mu(G) + \frac{m}{n}v(Y) + \left(1 - \frac{m}{n}\right)\mu(G) + \left(1 - \frac{m}{n}\right)v(Y)$$
$$- \left(1 - \frac{m}{n}\right)v'(Y)\left(\frac{G}{n - m}\right) + \frac{1}{2}\left(1 - \frac{m}{n}\right)v''(Y)\left(\frac{G}{n - m}\right)^2 + \text{higher order terms} \tag{5}$$

Subtracting (5) from (4) while ignoring the higher order terms we see that all terms other than those including $v''(Y)$ cancel out.

$$U - E(U) = \frac{1}{2}v''(Y)\left(\frac{G}{n}\right)^2 - \frac{1}{2}\left(\frac{n-m}{n}\right)v''(Y)\left(\frac{G}{n-m}\right)^2$$

$$= \frac{1}{2}\frac{G^2}{n}v''(Y)\left(\frac{1}{n} - \frac{1}{n-m}\right) \tag{6}$$

The factor in parentheses on the right is negative and so too is v'' under the assumption that all voters are risk averse. The certain utility from an equal sharing of the public good's costs exceeds the utility of the risk averse voters under the fair gamble.

The dominance of the equal cost sharing proposal to fair gambles between paying none and all of the public good's costs is not restricted to situations in which two equal size coalitions oppose one another. If any coalition of size m $\leq$ n/2 proposes that its members pay none of the public good's costs, and the $(n - m)$ remaining members share all of the public good's costs equally, and this coalition is opposed by n/m coalitions of size m making symmetric proposals, then (3) describes the expected utility of a member of any of the n/m coalitions, and the fair gambles they propose are dominated by the equal cost sharing proposal. For example, if each individual would propose that she pay none of the public good's costs, and the other n − 1 citizens share the costs equally, and each proposal had a 1/n chance of winning, m would equal 1 in (3), and the superiority of equal cost sharing again holds.[3]

Under the probabilistic majority rule coalitions may choose to make initial proposals extremely favorable to themselves and unfavorable to other coalitions so as to force a 'compromise' highly favorable to themselves. Were this to occur, the outcomes might be better modeled as a bargaining game among the coalitions. Risk aversion would still drive the players toward solutions in which the gains from cooperative actions are shared.[4]

Of course, opposition coalitions need not be of equal size. In particular, when a coalition containing more than half of the community forms, its opposition must be of smaller size. When this happens, members of the larger coalition may prefer the gamble on their proposal's victory to acceptance of the equal cost sharing proposal. For example, if a coalition of size (n − 1) forms and proposes that the single citizen not in the coalition pay the full costs of G, and this citizen proposes that she pay nothing and the other n − 1 share the costs, then the coalition of size n − 1 may prefer gambling on their proposal's victory with probability (n − 1)/n to a full equal sharing of G's costs.

Three points need to be made with respect to this example. First, the coalition of n − 1 may not be stable. If the individual not in the coalition proposes that some second person pay all of G, and in addition that A dollars be taken from this second person and distributed equally among the remaining n − 1, this proposal will get n − 1 votes against the proposal to force the first person to pay all of G. The second person can pick a third, however, and propose that she pay for G and that 2A be distributed among the other members. At the beginning of a sequence of proposals of this type, each committee member will realize that there is a 1/n probability that she will be the person forced to pay all the costs of the public good and then some, when time runs out. Rather than engage in this taxpayer Russian roulette, all risk averse voters may again prefer a sure-bet-equal-cost-sharing proposal. All other coalitions of size m > n/2 are equally vulnerable.

Second, should a coalition of more than half of the committee prove stable, and the final choice be made by lot with the majority coalition's discriminatory proposal having a better than 50/50 chance of winning, the outcome would still be no worse under the probabilistic majority rule than under the simple majority rule. Under the simple majority rule, the proposals of a stable majority coalition win with probability one. Under the probabilistic majority rule, a minority of *m* retains at least an m/n chance of defeating a discriminatory majority.

Third, prior to the last exercise of the random process to determine a winning proposal, there will still exist a proposal P_u, in which the majority pays some of the costs of the public good, although less than an equal per capita share, and the minority pays a disproportionately large share, that all prefer to the gamble. The discriminated against minority is better off under this P_u, unanimously agreed to under the probabilistic majority rule, than it would be under the simple majority rule, where the majority coalition would force it to cover all of the public good's costs.

Returning to the case where a stable majority coalition cannot form, we note that the incentive properties of the simple and probabilistic majority rules are quite different. Under the former, the incentive is to move from a proposal all would unanimously support to one which is supported by only a bare majority, by increasing the benefits going to members of the majority coalition and reducing those of the minority. But under probabilistic majority rule, a proposal that achieves only a bare majority of the votes has only slightly more than a 50/50 chance of eventually winning. Risk averse voters will prefer to move the committee away from these gambles to outcomes under which all are sure to benefit.

Most public good-externality choices are not as simple as these examples. Nevertheless, if an allocation is possible that would make all citizens better off, there exists a sure thing proposal that risk averse voters prefer to a gamble between proposals promising them greater and lesser benefits.[5]

III. Decision Making Costs

Finding an allocation of costs that makes all better off is rather easy when the public good is lumpy and all citizens have identical preferences and incomes. With differing tastes and incomes, and alternative quantities and quality characteristics for the public good possible, the task of finding a quantity-quality-tax combination that makes all citizens better off may be formidable. It certainly will take some time.

In a now classic discussion of the effect of decision costs on the choice of voting rule, Buchanan and Tullock demonstrated two propositions [1962, pp. 63–91]: *1.* A single rule, like the simple majority rule, is not optimal for all committees and all types of issues. *2.* The higher decision making costs are for a given committee and class of decisions, the lower the majority required to pass an issue that this committee will find optimal to write into its constitution. Both propositions emerge naturally as characteristics of the probabilistic majority rule.

Consider the decision calculus of the representative voter deciding what time limit to set on the committee's deliberations prior to the application of the probabilistic majority rule. Decision making costs must be set against the expected gain in utility from a longer search for a proposal promising a higher, if not unanimous majority. Let C be the expected increment in utility of a representative voter if his preferred proposal wins from the final pair of issues voted upon. Let the units in which C is measured be the same as those in which decision costs, D, are measured. Define π as the probability that the representative voter's preferred issue from the final pair wins. Both π and D should be functions of t, $\pi' > 0$, $\pi'' < 0$, $D' > 0$, and $D'' > 0$. C might also depend on t, but this is less clear. If the status quo is, say, what was done last year, then this proposal contains a positive quantity of public good and set of tax shares. New proposals, as in the example of the previous section, may simply redistribute expected gains to raise π, without changing C at all. If we assume C independent of t, then the representative voter's task in setting a time limit on the committee's work is to maximize

$$E(U) = \pi(t)C - D(t) \tag{7}$$

Optimal t satisfies

$$\pi'C = D' \tag{8}$$

Committees which place a high marginal value on time set short time limits on their work. Final votes will generally exhibit lower majorities for the more preferred issue. Given whatever time limit is set, however, all issues will not be decided using the same majority-determined probabilities. When consensus can easily be obtained, high majorities, if not unanimous agreement, on one proposal will be observed. Thus, the effective majority used to pass an issue will vary under the probabilistic majority rule in the same manner as Buchanan and Tullock's analysis indicates is optimal.

IV. Properties—Distributional Issues

So far, we have described the procedure's properties with respect to the kinds of issues on which unanimous agreement is at least hypothetically possible, improvements in allocative efficiency. Critics of the unanimity rule and defenders of majority rule have generally argued that this is not what politics is all about, or at least not what it is exclusively about [Barry, 1965, pp. 312–4; Rae, 1969, 1975]. They focus upon distributional and property rights issues. The choice is between x and $\sim x$ with no compromise possible. Ownership of slaves is either allowed or prohibited, and no alternatives which all unanimously prefer exist.

It is instructive to compare probabilistic majority voting's properties when issues are of this binary character with those of majority rule. In a well-known paper, Kenneth May [1952] demonstrated that majority rule, when limited to binary choices, is equivalent to four axioms.[6]

Decisiveness. For a given set of voter preferences, the procedure either selects x, or $\sim x$, or declares them as socially indifferent.

Anonymity. A change in any voter i's ranking of x and $\sim x$ when coupled by the opposite change in ranking by any other voter j of the two issues, leaves the committee choice unchanged.

Neutrality. A relabeling of x and $\sim x$ with respect to all individual preference orderings produces the corresponding relabeling of the committee's choices.

Positive Responsiveness. If a committee vote declares x to be at least as good as $\sim x$ ($xR \sim x$), and one voter i's preferences switch from $\sim xP_ix$ to $xR_i \sim x$, or from $xI_i \sim x$ to $xP_i \sim x$, then the committee choice is $xP \sim x$.

It is easy to see that if we consider probabilistic majority voting's properties up through the first stage of the procedure, i.e. in the determination of the probabilities of x and $\sim x$ winning, that the procedure satisfies probabilistic restatements of the last three axioms.[7] Offsetting changes in any two voters' rankings of x and $\sim x$ leave the probabilities of the two proposals' winning unchanged. Relabel the proposals, and the probabilities switch accordingly. An increase in x's position in any voter's preference ordering increases the probability that x wins.

The normative heart of majority rule rests in the last three axioms. The fairness and egalitarian properties many see in majority rule are captured in the anonymity and neutrality axioms. Yet the rule retains an individualistic flavor by assigning any individual the power to break a tie. Probabilistic majority voting has all of these same normative properties in a probabilistic sense. Indeed, it has an even stronger form of positive responsiveness in that any change in one voter's preferences in the direction of favoring x increases the probability that x wins, regardless of the distribution of preferences for and against x prior to the change. Under simple majority rule, a change in one voter's preferences leaves the committee outcome unchanged, *unless* the votes of the committee were evenly split prior to the change.

The major axiomatic difference between the probabilistic and simple majority rules comes in their decisiveness properties. In a single application of the procedure, probabilistic majority rule does, of course, choose between x and $\sim x$. One of them must win, so that in this sense it is decisive. Indeed, it is more decisive than simple majority rule, for it will never declare x and $\sim x$ socially indifferent. A decision for or against slavery will be reached. But repetitions of the procedure with the same preference orderings could result in x winning one time, $\sim x$ the next. In this respect, the procedure is different and perhaps inferior to simple majority rule. Given the close similarities between the probabilistic and simple majority rules with respect to the other three axioms, normative arguments in favor of the single majority over the probabilistic majority rule must rest on their differences with respect to the decisiveness property. We discuss this issue further in the following and penultimate sections.

Before turning to that issue, however, let us briefly examine the assumption underlying May's theorem that distributional issues are inherently binary. This assumption is essential to the proof of the theorem, and thus for normative arguments in favor of the simple majority rule.

Perhaps slavery is such an issue, but many others would appear to allow for compromise. The right to buy alcoholic beverages is a property right-type issue if any is. But more choices are available than simply outright prohibition, and unrestricted market distribution. Some of the effects prohibitionists find objectionable can be avoided by restricting the sale to adults, restricting the hours of sale, and taxing its purchase. Probabilistic majority voting would encourage risk averse voters to propose and vote for such property right compromises rather than risk the victory of the polar alternatives.[8]

V. Properties—Over Time

A major difference between the probabilistic and simple majority rules is that the former can on successive applications produce different social choices from the same set of preferences, while simple majority voting always yields the same outcome if preferences do not change. This characteristic may be thought to be an advantage for the simple majority rule, particularly if we add an equal intensity assumption regarding the preferences of those favoring x and $\sim x$, as is commonly made [Buchanan and Tullock, 1962, pp. 128–30; Rae, 1969]. Simple majority rule then maximizes the net utility gain from the outcome.

The kinds of property rights issues that represent no-compromise binary choices, as envisaged in support of the use of simple majority rule, are often associated with differences in preferences based on the religious, ethnic or geographic characteristics of opposing groups. Slavery in the United States was such an issue. Differences in taste of this type change slowly. Over time numerous property rights issues are likely to arise, which divide the polity into the same majority-minority groups. Under simple majority rule, the larger religious, ethnic or geographic group always wins. This possibility is what critics of simple majority rule have in mind when they speak of a 'tyranny of the majority.'

Under probabilistic majority voting, the minority wins some of the time. Moreover, the bigger the minority group is, the more often it wins. This property makes the probabilistic rule a more equitable rule, in the long run, when differences in preferences on property rights issues reflect objective differences between groups, which change very slowly. If it is the existence of these differences, which gives rise to the appearance of no-compromise, either-or choices, then probabilistic majority rule's property of *not* selecting the same issue upon each application, when preferences do not change, is arguably an attractive property in that it destroys the majority's power to tyrannize.

VI. Three or More Mutually Exclusive Issues

Although normative arguments in favor of majority rule, such as May's theorem, assume that the committee faces only two choices, much of the public choice literature is concerned with the properties of voting procedures when there are three or more mutually exclusive alternatives. It is in these situations that the much discussed voting paradox or voting cycle occurs.

Consider first, however, the distribution of preference over the three mutually exclusive alternatives x, y and z in *Table 1*. The entries represent cardinal utilities scaled so that each voter's most preferred issue has a utility of 100, and her least preferred issue a utility of zero. The m_i are the potentially different

TABLE 1.   Voter Preferences in the Absence of
a Majority Rule Cycle

Voters	Issues		
	x	y	z
1	100	m_1	0
2	m_2	100	0
3	0	m_3	100

utilities for each voter for the middle ranked issues, $0 < m_i < 100$, i = 1, 2, 3.
Under the simple majority rule, y is the committee choice for it can defeat
both x and z in a pairwise vote. In this example, there is no cycle.

Now consider the outcome under the probabilistic majority rule. At the beginning of the application of the procedure, an unknown sequence of pairwise
votes is foreseen in which two issues first face one another. The winner of this
first pairwise vote faces the third issue, the winner of this vote faces the loser of
the first pairwise vote, and so on. At the beginning of the procedure, no voter
can predict which outcome will emerge the winner when time runs out. But
they can compute the probabilities of each issue's winning. The probability that
y will defeat x when they meet is 2/3. y wins with a probability of 2/3 when y
and z meet, and with a probability of 0 when x and z meet. Its expected probability of being the eventual winner is thus (2/3 + 2/3 + 0)/3 = 4/9. The expected probabilities of x and z eventually winning are 1/3 and 2/9, respectively.

Thus, the expected utilities for each voter from the application of the
probabilistic procedure are

$$EV_1 = 33\tfrac{1}{3} + \tfrac{4}{9}m_1$$
$$EV_2 = m_2/3 + 66\tfrac{2}{3}$$
$$EV_3 = 4m_3/9 + 200/9$$

Now y promises the three voters m_1, 100, and m_3 utility units, respectively. If
$m_1 = EV_1$, a risk neutral voter 1 is indifferent between the certain provision
of y, and the gambles over x, y and z inherent in probabilistic majority voting. If $m_1 \geq 60$ and $m_3 \geq 40$, all three risk neutral voters will unanimously
prefer a proposal to provide y with certainty, to the application of the probabilistic aspect of the procedure. If voters 1 and 3 are risk averse, then the more
risk averse they are, the smaller m_1 and m_3 can be, and still have the committee unanimously choose the certain provision of y.

Thus, when a Condorcet winner exists under the simple majority rule,
probabilistic majority voting *may* also lead to its selection with probability
one. When the utilities promised to those voters for whom this proposal is

TABLE 2. Voter Preferences in the Presence
of a Majority Rule Cycle

	Issues		
Voters	x	y	z
1	100	m_1	0
2	0	100	m_2
3	m_3	0	100

not their first choice are sufficiently high, they will vote for the certain provision of the Condorcet winner, and not allow the probabilistic part of the procedure to operate. This property of the procedure seems normatively reasonable. A glance at *Table 1* suggests that the normative case for choosing y is greater, the greater m_1 and m_3 are. If these values are low, near zero, for example, then allowing voters 1 and 3 a chance at having their most preferred proposal win can be defended as being at least as fair or even more so than giving the decision to y. Once again this point is strengthened if one envisages a sequence of votes over time with the same voters having roughly the same preferences over alternative issues.

Table 2 depicts the preferences of three voters over three issues, when no Condorcet winner exists. Since each proposal is ranked lowest by one voter, any proposal to provide one of the outcomes with certainty will not get unanimous support. The voter who ranks that issue lowest prefers a gamble with nonzero probabilities on the other issues.

Thus, when cycles exist under the simple majority rule, the probabilistic majority rule provides a fair mechanism for ending the cycle. When a Condorcet winner exists under the simple majority rule, probabilistic majority voting assigns this issue the highest probability of winning. When the Condorcet winner is sufficiently attractive to those voters who do not rank it first, a proposal to select this alternative will receive unanimous support under probabilistic majority voting. Probabilistic majority voting breaks the 'tyranny of the median voter,' however, by assigning positive probabilities to other issues, when the Condorcet winner provides relatively low utilities to those for whom it is not the first choice.[9]

VII. Are Probabilistic Voting Procedures Inherently Bad?

The above discussion illustrates several normatively attractive characteristics of the probabilistic majority rule. By implication it suggests that other procedures with probabilistic elements might warrant further research.

Voting procedures with chance elements have generally gotten short shrift in the public choice literature. William Riker, for example, dismisses all probabilistic voting procedures by noting that they violate Arrow's independence of irrelevant alternatives axiom, allowing x to win some of the time, y on other occasions with the same set of preferences [1982, pp. 118, 143]. Arrow does not discuss probabilistic voting mechanisms, but by implication eliminates them from consideration by rejecting information regarding voter preferences that would be affected by voter attitudes toward risk ('tastes . . . for gambling') [1951, p. 10].

But voter attitudes toward risk are a part of voter preferences, and are not obviously different from or inferior to their preferences for national defense or redistribution. Indeed, preferences for defense and redistribution may themselves depend upon 'tastes for gambling.' Moreover, Arrow's own theorem demonstrates that some otherwise attractive axiom has to be violated if we are to have a voting procedure that is not dictatorial. If one's only objection to probabilistic majority voting is that it violates the independence of irrelevant alternatives axiom by sometimes choosing x and sometimes y with the same set of preferences, then this disadvantage, if it is one, must be weighed against the disadvantages other nondictatorial procedures exhibit, since they too must violate one of the axioms.

A frequent reason for invoking the independence of irrelevant alternatives axiom is to avoid the strategic misrepresentation of preferences by voters. Under probabilistic majority voting, an individual's dominant strategy on the last round of voting is to vote sincerely. This property is ensured by the positive relationship between an individual's vote for an issue, and the issue's probability of winning [Gibbard, 1977].

Like all sequential voting procedures, however, situations may exist in which individuals have an incentive to vote strategically, i.e. to vote against their preferred issue, in an early round of voting so as to increase the likelihood of a more preferred issue's eventual victory.[10] While strategic behavior of this type cannot be excluded in principle, in practice it would involve rather complicated, high risk calculations on the part of an individual voter acting alone, for the success of the strategy depends on both the identity of the proposals that subsequently come up for a vote, and their relative probabilities of victory. Neither of these pieces of information are likely to be in an individual's hands at the time when a strategic vote might be optimal. Nor is it obvious that strategic behavior of this type would necessarily worsen the final outcomes of the procedure, since these depend only on the final pair of issues to be voted upon, where sincere voting is the dominant strategy, and the possibility that a sure bet proposal all prefer to a gamble on the final pair exists.

Probabilistic majority rule would be strategy proof if there were only one initial vote on a set of issues. Such a variant on the procedure might be used by a parliamentary system. Each party could put up one proposed resolution of a given issue, and the probabilities of each proposal's victory made proportional to the number of votes cast for the party in the previous election. Risk aversion would again drive all parties towards unanimous acceptance of a compromise proposal rather than chancing the victory of some other party's proposal through the random process.

VIII. Summary and Conclusions

In a polity ideally protective of individual rights, all collective decisions would be made using the rule of consensus. To achieve consensus on both allocative efficiency decisions and property rights issues, the latter would need to be decided separately in a constitutional setting where differences in individual preferences and positions were hidden from view by a self-imposed veil of ignorance [Buchanan and Tullock, 1962, ch. 13; Rawls, 1971]. Allocative efficiency improvements could be decided with full knowledge of preferences, by parliaments patient enough to seek out expenditure-tax combinations benefitting all.

In the real world, the costs of decision making preclude the achievement of full consensus on allocative efficiency issues, and no constitutional convention has been convened under rules which have instilled sufficient impartiality into its participants to yield consensual agreement on outstanding property rights issues. Moreover, the task of separating distributional and allocative efficiency decisions is difficult, so that most parliaments are routinely engaged in resolving both without drawing distinctions. In practice, both kinds of decisions are made in parliaments using a single set of parliamentary rules. Final votes are inevitably by the simple majority rule.

It is in this real-world setting that the probabilistic majority rule may be attractive. Given the constraint that both allocative efficiency and property rights issues are decided by the same committee using a single voting rule, probabilistic majority rule seems to have several attractive normative properties. Where compromise is possible, as when a collective decision benefitting all individuals can be made, the procedure encourages risk-averse voters to accept the compromise. Where compromise is impossible, the procedure produces a fair resolution of an issue, and avoids the possibility of one group's perpetual tyrannization of another.

In contrast to other new voting procedures, it is also a rather straightforward extension of the simple majority rule, and thus should appear less alien to those who tend to equate democratic procedure with the use of majority rule. Thus, it ranks relatively high both with respect to its normative properties and the feasibility of its application as a voting rule for tackling the knotty problems of collective choice.

NOTES

1. This theme is developed in Mueller [1989, ch. 6].

2. The properties of differing probabilistic voting procedures have been discussed by Coleman [1973, pp. 61–153] and Fishburn and Gehrlein [1977].

3. This is true for all $n \geq 3$. Ignoring higher order terms in the Taylor expansion we have

$$U - E(U) = \mu + v - v'\left(\frac{G}{n}\right) + \frac{1}{2}v''\left(\frac{G}{n}\right)^2 - \frac{n-1}{n}u$$

$$-\frac{n-1}{n}v - \frac{1}{n}u - \frac{1}{n}v + \frac{1}{n}v'\left(\frac{G}{n-1}\right) - \frac{1}{2n}v''\left(\frac{G}{n-1}\right)^2 =$$

$$-\frac{G}{n}\left(1 - \frac{1}{n-1}\right)v' + \frac{1}{2}\frac{G^2}{n}\left(\frac{1}{n} - \frac{1}{(n-1)^2}\right)$$

Both terms are negative for all $v' > 0$, $v'' < 0$, and $n \geq 3$.

4. Luce and Raiffa [1957, pp. 136–137] discuss two solutions originally proposed by Raiffa to an analogous, two-person bargaining game. A central point on the Pareto frontier emerges as the 'reasonable' arbitrated solution to this bargaining game. See also Moulin [1982, pp. 254–255] and Sutton [1986].

5. For a general discussion and proofs of theorems regarding the dominance for risk averse individuals of sure thing proposals over gambles with greater and lesser payoffs, see Rothschild and Stiglitz [1970].

6. We present simplified statements of these axioms with their commonly used names.

7. For a rigorous analysis, see Fishburn and Gehrlein [1977].

8. It is also true, of course, that we often observe the compromise choices being made even under majority rule. The reason for this may be that the cycling characteristic of majority rule also makes forming a minimum-winning-coalition risky. One might be a member of a minimum coalition today and not tomorrow. Risk averse citizens may then choose to distribute benefits and costs equally and reach distributional compromises. That most bills do not attain unanimous approval suggests that uncertainty over positions in coalitions does not go as far toward achieving consensuses as one might hope. This point is related to Gordon Tullock's [1981] explanation of the stability of outcomes from congressional logrolling.

9. Note from *Table 1* that when the issues are viewed in a single x-y-z dimensionality, the Condorcet winner *y* is the median of the three ideal points.

The examples and results of this section resemble those used by Zeckhauser [1969].

10. Experimental work with other iterative voting procedures indicates that indi-

viduals do not succumb to the temptation to engage in sophisticated strategic behavior at intervening steps in the procedure [Smith, 1977].

REFERENCES

Arrow, Kenneth J.: *Social Choice and Individual Values,* Second Edition, New York: John Wiley, 1951, 1963.

Barry, B.: *Political Argument,* London: Routledge and Kegan P., 1965.

Buchanan, J.M. and Tullock, G.: *The Calculus of Consent,* Ann Arbor: University of Michigan Press, 1962.

Coleman, James S.: *Mathematics of Collective Action,* Chicago: Aldine, 1973.

Fishburn, Peter C. and Gehrlein, William V.: 'Towards a Theory of Elections with Probabilistic Voting,' *Econometrica,* Vol. 45 (1977), pp. 1907–1923.

Gibbard, Allan: 'Manipulation of Voting Schemes: A General Result,' *Econometrica,* Vol. 41 (1973), pp. 587–601.

Gibbard, Alan: "Manipulation of Schemes That Mix Voting With Chance,' *Econometrica,* April, Vol. 45 (1977), pp. 665–681.

Luce, R. Duncan and Raiffa, Howard: *Games and Decisions,* New York: John Wiley, 1957.

May, K. O.: 'A Set of Independent, Necessary and Sufficient Conditions for Simple Majority Decision," *Econometrica,* Vol. 20 (1952), pp. 680–684.

Moulin, Herve: 'Non-Cooperative Implementation: A Survey of Recent Results,' *Mathematical Social Sciences,* Vol. 3 (1982), pp. 243–257.

Mueller, Dennis C.: *Public Choice II,* Cambridge: Cambridge University Press, 1989.

Rae, D. W.: 'Decision-Rules and Individual Values in Constitutional Choice,' *American Political Science Review,* Vol. 63 (1969), pp. 40–56.

Rae, D. W.: 'The Limits of Consensual Decision,' *American Political Science Review,* Vol. 69 (1975), pp. 1270–1294.

Rawls, J. A.: *A Theory of Justice,* Cambridge: The Belknap Press of Harvard University Press, 1971.

Riker, William H.: *Liberalism Against Populism,* San Francisco: W.H. Freeman, 1982.

Rothschild, Michael and Stiglitz, Joseph E.: 'Increasing Risk I: A Definition,' *Journal of Economic Theory,* Vol. 2 (1970), pp. 225–243.

Satterthwaite, Mark A.: 'Strategy-Proofness and Arrow's Conditions: Existence and Correspondence Theorems for Voting Procedures and Social Welfare Functions,' *Journal of Economic Theory,* Vol. 10 (1975), pp. 187–217.

Smith, Vernon: 'The Principle of Unanimity and Voluntary Consent in Social Choice,' *Journal of Political Economy,* Vol. 85 (1977), pp. 1125–1139.

Sutton, John: 'Non-Cooperative Bargaining Theory: An Introduction,' *Review of Economic Studies,* Vol. 53 (1986), pp. 709–724.

Tullock, Gordon: 'Why So Much Stability?' *Public Choice,* Vol. 37 (1981), pp. 189–204.

Wicksell, K.: 'A New Principle of Just Taxation,' *Finanztheoretische Untersuchungen,* Jena, 1896, reprinted in: Musgrave, Richard A., and Peacock, Alan T., *Classics in the Theory of Public Finance,* New York: St. Martin's Press, 1958, pp. 27–118.

Zeckhauser, Richard: 'Majority Rule with Lotteries on Alternatives,' *Quarterly Journal of Economics,* Vol. 83 (1969), pp. 696–703.

Suggested Additional Readings

Bell, Colin E. "What Happens When Majority Rule Breaks Down?" *Public Choice* 33 (1978): 121–26.

Black, Duncan. *The Theory of Committees and Elections.* Cambridge: Cambridge University Press, 1958.

Blais, André, and Richard Nadeau. "Measuring Strategic Voting: A Two-Step Procedure." *Electoral Studies* 15 (1996): 39–52.

Born, Richard. "Policy-Balancing Models and the Split-Ticket Voter, 1972–1996." *American Politics Quarterly* 28 (2000): 131–62.

Coleman, John J. "United Government, Divided Government, and Party Responsiveness." *American Political Science Review* 93 (1999): 821–35.

Downs, Anthony. *An Economic Theory of Democracy.* Chap. 8. New York: Harper & Row, 1957.

Enelow, James M., and Melvin J. Hinich. *The Spatial Theory of Voting: An Introduction.* Chap. 2. New York: Cambridge University Press, 1984.

Fiorina, Morris P. *Divided Government.* New York: Macmillan, 1992.

Grofman, Bernard, and Thomas L. Brunnell. "Explaining the Ideological Differences between the Two U.S. Senators Elected from the Same State: An Institutional Effects Model." In *Congressional Primaries and the Politics of Representation,* ed. Peter F. Galderisi, Marni Ezra, and Michael Lyons. Lanham, MD: Rowman & Littlefield, 2001.

Rae, Douglas W. "Decision Rules and Individual Values in Constitutional Choice." *American Political Science Review* 63 (1969): 40–56.

Rae, Douglas W., and Eric Schickler. "Majority Rule." In *Perspectives on Public Choice: A Handbook,* ed. Dennis C. Mueller. New York: Cambridge University Press, 1997.

Southwell, Priscilla. "Open versus Closed Primaries: The Effect of Strategic Voting and Candidate Fortunes." *Social Science Quarterly* 72 (1991): 789–96.

Advanced Readings

Coughlin, Peter J. "Majority Rule and Election Models." *Journal of Economic Surveys* 3 (1990): 157–88.

Holcombe, Randall G. "An Empirical Test of the Median Voter Model." *Economic Inquiry* 18 (1980): 260–74.

Riker, William H. *Liberalism against Populism.* Chaps. 3, 6, and 7. Prospect Heights, IL: Waveland Press, 1982.

Stratmann, Thomas. "Logrolling." In *Perspectives on Public Choice: A Handbook,* ed. Dennis C. Mueller. Cambridge: Cambridge University Press, 1997.

SECTION III

Alternative Voting Procedures

Although the most popular (in use, not among theorists), majority rule is certainly not the only possible way in which society can reach collective decisions. The problems inherent in majority rule decision making have led to the development of alternative voting schemes. Although most represent some degree of improvement over simple majority rule, as we have seen from Arrow's theorem, no rule can satisfy even certain minimal normative properties. Thus the dismal science strikes again. We are left to choose only among various flawed procedures.

In order to determine what is the best (or perhaps more honestly the least problematic) voting rule, we need to understand how each rule works, what incentives voters face under each system, how manipulable the outcomes are, and which properties each rule does or does not satisfy. It is likely no consensus may emerge (it certainly has not among the theorists), and thus a vote may be necessary to decide what voting procedure the group will utilize. Of course, what rule is used to decide the voting procedure may be a point of contention as well. Alas, an endless backward induction of voting over voting rules will result.

One glaring problem with majority rule is the requirement that a winner actually needs a majority of votes in its favor. When there are more than two alternatives from which to choose, no alternative may generate enough votes. For this reason, in practice, strict majority rule is rarely used. The term *majority rule* is often inappropriately applied to either of two other similar rules. Plurality rule requires that whichever alternative captures the most votes, regardless of whether or not it represents a majority of voters, is deemed the winner. Majority rule run-off requires a majority of voters to be selected. If no alternative nets a majority, a run-off is then held between the alternatives that receive the most and second-most votes. In the run-off, limited now to only two alternatives, whichever alternative receives the most votes must by definition have a majority. While the two rules are very similar, the winning outcome can differ under the two schemes due to the presence of majority rule cycles. Thus, the choice of voting rule can affect group decisions as much as the preferences of the people themselves.

Consider the following simple example. Candidate A is most preferred by 40 percent of the group and least preferred by the rest. Candidate B is most preferred by 35 percent and is ranked second by the other 65 percent. Finally, Candidate C is ranked first by 25 percent, second by 35 percent, and last by 40 percent. No alternative achieves a pure majority of votes. Under plurality, Candidate A is selected even though a strong majority rank this candidate last. Under majority rule run-off, a second vote would take place between Candidates A and B, which B would win 60–40. The difference occurs in this example because the majority that likes A least splits its preferences between B and C, enabling A to emerge victorious with a plurality, but not majority, of votes. In the run-off, C is no longer available, and the majority unite in favor of B. Put another way, altering the set of available candidates affects the outcome, even when the only change is the presence or elimination of an alternative that gets the fewest votes. In Arrow's terminology, this outcome was described as violating the independence of irrelevant alternatives.

Another way to avoid a minority-favored candidate winning simply because the majority split over its top two choices is to use a rule that takes account of voters' preferences over all the candidate choices. One example is a Borda rule that gives more points to each alternative the higher it is ranked by the voter. In this example, Borda's rule would give two points to each voter's top choice, one point to the voter's next choice, and zero points to his or her bottom choice. Under a Borda rule vote, Candidate B would get the most points, followed by Candidate C, and finally Candidate A.

Each rule discussed so far is identical to majority rule when there are only two alternatives. When there are more than two, however, majority rule cycles can occur, and the outcomes from the various procedures can differ. The more alternatives, the more likely no one alternative will achieve a pure majority, and the more likely the voting rules will lead to differing outcomes. Borda's rule is sufficiently different from the other rules in that even an alternative receiving a majority of first-place votes may not win under the Borda rule if there are several alternatives and the majority differs on the rest of its rankings. Borda's rule, while not necessarily selecting the alternative ranked highest by the greatest number of people, will tend to select the alternative ranked higher more often in the voters' preferences.

An alternative that does not generate a pure majority of votes when all alternatives are simultaneously considered may still generate majority support in every potential paired matchup. Condorcet's rule is that when such an alternative exists, it is selected as the winner. In the previous example, B beat A when paired against it and would also beat C in a vote of B versus C. Thus, B is the Condorcet winner. Majority rule cycles imply the absence of a Condorcet winner.

All of these rules can be manipulated to varying degrees by voting against one's true preferences in order to alter the winning alternative. A proof similar to Arrow's informs us that no rule which does not contain a random element can be devised that is completely immune to strategic voting behavior. Lottery rules are dismissed out of hand by many but do contain some beneficial properties, including, depending on the type of system, the elimination of strategic voting.

There are many other voting systems that have been devised, some more complicated than others. Various professional associations, such as the American Mathematical Association, seem the most willing to experiment with complicated voting rules, perhaps in part because they are better able to understand the alternative systems and their importance in avoiding particular problems to which the simpler rules will succumb. From these elections, other scholars are able to observe the rules in practice and glean additional insights.

In "An Introduction to Vote-Counting Schemes," Levin and Nalebuff outline various alternatives to majority rule and how they work in principle and practice. Martin, Shields, Tolwinski, and Kent offer a rare case-study application of social choice theory in "An Application of Social Choice Theory to U.S.D.A. Forest Service Decision Making" by contrasting potential outcomes under the Borda and Condorcet rules.

An Introduction to Vote-Counting Schemes

Jonathan Levin & Barry Nalebuff

Review Questions

1. What is the difference between rank-scoring and paired-comparisons rules? How do they relate to the "paired-comparisons matrix" and the "win-loss" matrix? The Borda rule is listed as a paired-comparisons rule. Can it also be considered a rank-scoring rule?
2. When there are only two candidates under consideration, plurality rule is the same as majority rule—why? Which other rules are also the same as majority rule in this limiting case of two candidates?
3. The authors have several considerations for the voting rules, such as minority support, simplicity, and others. For each rule, which criteria are met and which are not? What other considerations do you think are important?
4. What does it mean to be the Condorcet winner? Is the guaranteed selection of a Condorcet winner more or less important than other criteria?
5. Why might voter and candidate behavior depend upon the voting rule employed?
6. Which rule(s) do you feel is (are) the best? Does your choice depend upon the context, such as election or referendum, or the size of the group making the decision? Why or why not?

Levin, Jonathan and Nalebuff, Barry. "An Introduction to Vote-Counting Schemes." *Journal of Economic Perspectives* 9 (1995): 3–26.

The design of an electoral system is fundamental to any democracy. Motivation for understanding how electoral system design matters comes from many directions: the creation of new constitutions in eastern Europe; the recent trauma of a three-way presidential election in the United States; the ongoing debate over U.S. redistricting and gerrymandering; the furor caused by Lani Guinier's call for a more representative voting system. The status quo adds another incentive. Plurality rule is pervasive even though it is a flawed system. Fortunately, there is no lack of suitable alternatives. One of the purposes of this symposium—and this paper in particular—is to help illustrate and motivate the remarkable variety of alternative mechanisms that aggregate individual preferences to decide an election. This overview offers a summary of sixteen distinct methods and demonstrates by example how some of the more complex systems work.

One can speculate on why alternatives to plurality rule have had such a difficult time being adopted. Part of the cause may be Arrow's general possibility theorem. Arrow (1951) demonstrates that any voting system applied to an unrestricted collection of voter preferences must have some serious defect; we must always choose between flawed alternatives. With conflicting theoretical guidance to help select the least-flawed option, people evaluate a system by its likely effect on the status quo outcome. Since those in power tend to want to preserve the status quo—the status quo electoral system is what brought them into power—we should not be surprised by the difficulty of implementing electoral reform.

An electoral system has to balance multiple objectives: establishing legitimacy, encouraging participation, discouraging factionalization. We focus on the goal of representativeness. How do we go about choosing a representative outcome? What is meant by representation?[1] Should we examine the position of the elected representatives or the position of the policies that they pass? How do we trade off these objectives? We do not believe that there is any one right answer (although there are certainly many wrong ones).

The point of this paper is to move away from theoretical discussions of various properties; our aim is to provide the motivation behind different counting schemes. Are they better suited for choosing a single winner or for ranking the candidates? Do they tend to favor candidates with loyal minorities or candidates who are acceptable to all and the favorite of none? Are they simple enough to be used for a general political election where voters may only be familiar with one or two candidates, or are they more applicable in a board of directors situation where each voter possesses more detailed information? We try to give some examples of how and why they work and where they fail. We have also taken several of the methods and applied them to voting data gathered from British Union elections (data collected separately by N. Tideman and I. D. Hill). An interesting feature of these British elections is that voters are required to rank the candidates. As a result, knowing the voter ranking, we can simulate elections under a variety of electoral systems. It is perhaps remarkable that among the 30 elections we examined, with the exception of plurality rule and single transferable vote, none of the other seven alternatives considered gave a different top choice (see later section). The systems differed in the rankings of the lower candidates. This empirical regularity suggests a connection to some recent theoretical work (Caplin and Nalebuff, 1988, 1991): when voter preferences are sufficiently similar, a variety of voting systems lead to similar choices, and these choices have desirable properties. The difficulties in aggregating preferences arise in the case of a population with a lack of a consensus; this is the situation where the choice of electoral system can make the greatest difference and where apparently minor differences can directly influence the outcome.

The next section of our paper describes the basic information on which most vote-counting schemes rely: voter rankings and paired comparisons. We then describe five voting rules directly from the voter rankings, six paired-comparisons rules, and two additional rules derived from sports rankings. An Appendix then offers a few additional rules. We then attempt to point out how differences between rules might affect candidates' strategies and the outcome of a real election. In the final section, we address different factors that distinguish the methods and attempt to provide a basis to choose between methods. In our description of the various vote-counting rules, we have benefited greatly from the excellent surveys done by Lowell Anderson (1990, 1994) and Nicolaus Tideman (1993).

Voter Rankings and Paired Comparisons

Before describing the various counting rules, we need to consider their general structure and the information they rely on. Even if we actually had knowledge of all the voters' utility functions, there is the quandary of trying to make interpersonal comparisons of utility. This leads us to take as data a voter's ordinal ranking of the various candidates. However, there is a fundamental problem of getting people to reveal their true preferences accurately, since all voting systems encourage strategizing. Even if we had truthful rankings, there remains the issue of how to take averages over these rankings. Our focus is on this last step. Most of the variety in electoral schemes comes from the choice of different metrics for measuring the distance between one ranking and another.

From the start we should note that in a multi-candidate election, simple plurality rule throws away too much data. The voter's first choice is a poor summary statistic of preferences. Information regarding second and later choices is valuable in helping aggregate preferences. At the other extreme, we cannot reasonably ask people to vote in all possible pairwise elections. Even if there were only seven dwarfs running in a primary, this would require a voter to make 21 choices. Fortunately, we can easily infer pairwise preferences from ordinal voter rankings. For example, if a voter ranks the candidates $a >$ $b > c$, we infer that a is preferable to b and c and that b is preferable to c. (Of course, making these inferred rankings imposes a consistency condition that voters might not obey.) With one exception (approval voting), all the methods we discuss use as their base data the voter's ranking of the individual candidates. In general, these rankings provide more information than we need to tally the election. For our purposes, we assume that voters rank all the candidates on their ballots, and do not score candidates as tied.[2]

Voting theorists from the Marquis de Condorcet to Kenneth Arrow have shared the conviction that we should judge candidates on the basis of their pairwise performance. A candidate who wins every head-to-head matchup is called a Condorcet winner, in honor of Condorcet's *Essay on the Application of Mathematics to the Theory of Decision-Making* (1785). A Condorcet winner will win an election under most of the rules we describe below (although in some instances a good argument exists for not choosing the Condorcet winner. Most of the difficult issues in vote counting arise when no Condorcet winner exists; instead there is a voting cycle, i.e., three candidates a, b, c such that a beats b, b beats c, and c beats a.[3] Each method treats cycles differently, leading to discrepancies in how they rank the candidates.

Once we translate the voter rankings into paired comparisons, we often organize the information into a "paired-comparisons matrix." In this matrix, the ijth entry is the number of votes for i over j. The entries on the diagonal are all 0. Writing down this matrix actually loses information contained on individual ballots. That is, the matrix might show that candidate i received 45 votes over j, but it does not reveal whether those voters placed i first on their ballots and j last, or i sixth and j seventh. We may make an informed guess, but we cannot recover individual rankings from the paired-comparisons matrix.

Some voting rules further distill this information by only distinguishing the winner of each head-to-head comparison. They utilize a "win-loss matrix," where the ijth entry is 1 if more voters prefer candidate i to j and -1 if more voters prefer j to i. If there is a tie between candidates i and j, we enter a 0. Once again, all entries on the diagonal are 0 by definition.

The first five voting rules discussed are categorized as "rank-scoring" rules because they score directly from the rankings. The following six rules are "paired-comparisons" rules because they rely on that matrix. The final set of rules use a variety of different approaches.

1–5. Rank-Scoring Rules

1. Plurality Voting

Plurality voting is the most common method of ranking candidates in an election and is used in almost every political election in the United States. Under plurality election rules, each voter picks a single most preferred candidate. The candidate with the most votes wins. In an election with more than two candidates, a candidate does not necessarily need a majority vote to win. Bill Clinton won the 1992 presidential election with less than 50 percent of the vote.

When there are only two candidates in an election, plurality voting is the natural choice as an election rule: it is simply the rule of the majority. With three or more candidates, however, plurality voting can lead to disturbing results. Suppose there is an election with three candidates, two of whom have closely related views, while the third candidate has a radically different platform. Even if a large majority would choose either of the two related candidates over the third candidate, the third candidate might win if the majority split its votes between the two similar candidates.

In an indirect way, this coordination failure may have even changed the presidency of the United States. As told by Lowell Anderson (1990), the story starts with the 1966 Democratic primary for the governor of Maryland:

> George P. Mahoney received about 40 percent of the vote while his two opponents, Thomas Finan and Carlton Sickles, each received about 30 percent. Both Finan and Sickles are relatively liberal, and Maryland is a relatively liberal state. Mahoney is an unabashed ultraconservative, and it is extremely unlikely that he could have beaten either Finan or Sickles in a one-on-one contest. Maryland is a heavily Democrat state. However, in the main election, many Democrats could not support the ultraconservative Mahoney, and sufficiently many crossed over to vote Republican that the Republican candidate won. It is widely believed that had either Finan or Sickles won the

Democrat primary, then he would have beaten the (at that time) relatively obscure Spiro T. Agnew, in the main race. Agnew won, was later elected vice-president, and then resigned under pressure. Richard Nixon nominated Gerald Ford in Agnew's place and, when Nixon resigned, Ford became president.

The rest, as they say, is history.

While most presidential elections involve only two serious candidates, re-distributing the votes that went to serious third-party candidates (Wallace, Anderson, Perot) would have had the potential to swing an election. The co-ordination failures of plurality rule tend to be most glaring in a primary, where one often finds more than two serious candidates.

However, we should emphasize that the number of candidates in an election is not exogenous. It is partly determined by the type of electoral system in use. One of the consequences of using plurality rule is that it leads the outcome towards a two-party system. This empirical result is known as Duverger's law. When there are more than two parties, people tend to abandon the third party so as not to waste their votes.[4] This may not be a bad thing; an electoral voting rule that did a better job of representing preferences over more than two candidates might result in a proliferation of candidates, and the resulting factionalization could be worse for the democracy in the long run. Since the job of winnowing a large number of candidates in a primary is quite different from the job of choosing between a smaller number in the general election, society might consider using a different voting rule for primaries and for the general election.

1a. Multiple-Winner Extensions

If an election is to produce multiple winners, there are several extensions of plurality rule. One option, used to elect the legislature in Japan, is the "single nontransferable vote." Everyone gets one vote, and we simply pick the top several candidates based on the plurality voting. Under cumulative voting, voters are given a number of votes equal to the number of winners desired.[5] Depending on the rules, voters may or may not assign more than one of their votes to a single candidate. The candidates with the highest vote totals win the election.

In theory, cumulative voting is designed to foster minority representation. In an election with ten positions to fill, any group that controls 10 percent of the vote has the opportunity to elect one candidate. How these coalitions might form is less clear, and failure to coordinate could result in a loss of electoral power. In this regard, the single transferable vote electoral system (discussed below) is a more satisfactory method, although it is more complicated.

2. Approval Voting

Approval voting was invented in the 1970s. It is the only method we consider that does not require voters to rank the candidates. Instead, voters approve or disapprove each candidate on the ballot—that is, they select some subset of candidates. Candidates are ranked by the number of voters who approve them, and the highest ranked candidate (or candidates if more than one winner is required) wins. Thus with three candidates A, B and C, a voter has the opportunity either to vote for A or against A (by approving both B and C). Approving all three candidates is equivalent to not voting since it has no differential impact. Approval voting is the most frequently adopted alternative to plurality rule and is now used by several professional associations to elect their officers (Brams and Nagel, 1991).

A variant of approval voting can be used if we do not require a fixed number of winners, but rather a level of acceptance. We can set a quota and declare as winners any candidates reaching that quota. The election of baseball players to the Hall of Fame employs this form of approval voting. Sportswriters vote up or down on each candidate, and candidates who receive a certain (previously specified) number of votes head for Cooperstown.[6]

3. Runoff Voting

In runoff voting, or a "double election," voters rank the candidates, and votes are tabulated just as in a plurality election. If one candidate commands a majority vote, that candidate wins the election. If no candidate receives more than half the votes, we have a runoff election between the two candidates. The winner of the head-to-head runoff wins the election. Again, variations exist to runoff voting. In New York City primaries, the top two candidates engage in a runoff if the top candidate receives less than 40 percent of the vote in the primary. In France, candidates must also garner a certain minimum vote in order to participate in the runoff election. This has sometimes led to the peculiar result of a runoff election with only one candidate on the ballot, which then leads to imaginative and colorful voter responses (Rosenthal and Sen, 1973)!

In a multi-candidate election, runoff voting can prevent some of the potentially skewed results generated by a plurality count. Suppose we have four candidates, three similar candidates who evenly divide 70 percent of the vote, and a radically different candidate who commands a 30 percent minority. The 30 percent candidate would win outright under plurality, but would suffer a sound defeat in a runoff against any one of the other three candidates.

4. Single Transferable Vote

The single transferable vote, also known as "Cincinnati Rules" or "Hare voting," extends the logic of runoff voting by eliminating no more than one candidate at a time. A single transferable vote election with only one winner is sometimes called the "alternative vote." We consider this case first. Voters begin by ranking the candidates. If any candidate is ranked first by a majority, that candidate wins immediately. If no winner exists, we eliminate the candidate with the fewest first place votes and tabulate the ballots again as if that candidate never existed. This means votes for the losing candidate get redistributed to one of the remaining candidates. If still no candidate controls a majority, we again delete the candidate with the fewest votes and repeat the process. Eventually, barring a tie, a winner must emerge.

When there are many candidates and multiple winners, the algorithm for a single transferable vote becomes considerably more complex. However, it still works quite well in theory and in practice, finding use in New York City school board and Cambridge city council elections. With multiple winners, each one cannot control a majority, but rather should control some dominant share. Following the logic of the majority winner, we want this share (or quota) to be as small as possible, yet big enough to allow no more than the desired number of winners. For example, with two winners, we would require a winning candidate to control at least 34 percent of the vote. This is the smallest percentage that could be gained by no more than two candidates.[7]

Now suppose there are w winners and a corresponding quota q. The election runs as above until we find the first winner. When a candidate exceeds the vote quota, single transferable vote rules specify that the winner's surplus—that is, the number of votes the candidate receives over the quota—be redistributed to the voters' second-place choices. We call the surplus s, where $s = \text{total votes received} - q$, and divide it up using the following method: the winner receives a score of q and is then deleted from the ballots. Next, we tabulate who receives the transferred votes, but count them not as one full point, but as $s/(s + q)$. This weighting ensures that the sum of all candidate's scores remains equal to the number of votes originally cast, which in turn guarantees that we do not exceed w winners (recall that we chose the quota big enough so that not more than w candidates could control a share

q). If the transferred votes result in another winner, we repeat the surplus distribution process for the new winner. The election ends when w candidates reach the quota.[8]

One attractive feature of single transferable vote in a multi-winner election stems from the fact that it theoretically leads to proportional representation. A united minority can elect candidates in proportion to the size of the minority, ensuring diverse representation and avoiding tyranny of the majority. Suppose a region can elect six representatives. Any candidate who can control 17 percent of the vote will win, so that of course a dominant majority candidate will win, but beyond that, a candidate ranked second or third by a majority may or may not defeat a candidate with a small but loyal minority base. Also, unlike cumulative voting, there is no need to coordinate. If two candidates appeal to the same group, some voters can rank them 1 and 2 and the others 2 and 1, and the group will not lose its voice. In particular, single transferable vote avoids gerrymandering district lines to ensure minority representation (as discussed in Pildes and Niemi, 1993). If congressional elections were done on a statewide basis using single transferable vote, there would be no need to engage in the time-consuming and controversial act of redistricting following each census.

5. Coombs Voting

Clyde Coombs (1964) suggests a variant of the alternative vote. In successive rounds, instead of deleting the candidate with the fewest first-place votes, we eliminate the candidate with the most last-place votes. The election ends when only the desired number of winners remains. Unlike Hare voting, where candidates may qualify as winners in early rounds, Coombs voting always requires the full number of rounds. Duncan Black (1958, p. 69) describes an identical scheme called "exhaustive voting," which requires voters to approve all but one of the remaining candidates in each round. After each round of voting, the candidate with the fewest votes is eliminated. Again, the election ends when we reach the desired number of winners.[9]

Coombs voting loses some of its appeal in the light of analysis by Myerson (1993) and Cox (1990). Under Coombs voting, a candidate who takes a stance favored by a majority of voters may lose if all the other candidates take the opposite position. For example, suppose 75 percent of the electorate favors a certain proposition, but only one of five candidates supports it. The views of the candidates are identical on all other issues. Then 25 percent of the voters will rank the differing candidate last, while the majority, the 75 percent, if they split their last place votes equally, give each of the other four candidates less than 20 percent of the last place votes. Even though 75 percent of the electorate agreed with the proposition, the candidate in favor will be the first eliminated.

6–11. Paired-Comparisons Rules

6. Borda Voting

Jean-Charles de Borda, in a paper that marks the beginning of serious study in voting theory, proposed this elementary rule to the French Academy of Sciences in 1770. Suppose there are k candidates. Voters submit their rankings, and candidates receive $k - 1$ points for every first place vote, $k - 2$ points for every second place vote, and so on. We rank the candidates by their total points. Borda voting is a familiar scheme and is widely used to rank candidates or teams—the AP football poll is one example. Since every point a candidate receives may be considered a head-to-head vote against some other candidate, Borda scores are equal to the total number of head-to-head votes a candidate receives. This means we can count Borda scores by writing a paired-comparisons matrix and summing the rows to generate the candidates' scores.[10]

Interestingly, a Condorcet winner will not necessarily win a Borda election. We show a very simple example of this phenomenon with the pairwise-comparisons matrix and three candidates:

	a	b	c	Borda	a	b	c
a	0	51	51	Scores	102	114	84
b	49	0	65	a is a Condorcet winner but
c	49	35	0	b wins under Borda rules.

Here, the Condorcet winner a defeats b and c by a minimal margin, 51–49, while b beats c, 65–35. This election raises the question of whether one winner is intrinsically better than the other. As b beats c so decisively, we can be fairly sure that b is preferable to c, but less sure about the contests involving a. On a different day, with slightly different voter turnout, b or c might well beat a, but it is unlikely that c would beat b. In such cases, the Borda winner may have a better claim on the election.

We should note that there are an infinite number of possible variations to the basic Borda scheme.[11] For example, the choice of a linear point system is somewhat arbitrary; there is no reason to suppose that ordinal rankings should translate neatly into linear preferences. By manipulating the point values, we could arrive at dozens of alternative schemes.

Additional variations to Borda can be created by coupling it with other systems such as Coombs voting. E. J. Nanson, an Australian mathematician, worked on voting theory between 1875 and 1922. He proposed a variation of Borda voting that applies the Borda score in successive rounds. Under the Nanson rule, any candidate with a below-average Borda score is eliminated.[12] We then recompute Borda scores and repeat the elimination procedure. The last remaining candidate wins the election. This resembles Coombs voting as described earlier, except that low Borda scores substitute for last-place votes.

7. Copeland Voting

A. H. Copeland (1951) proposed the obvious paired-comparisons scheme where candidates are scored by their win-loss record across all head-to-head competitions. Employing the win-loss matrix, we sum the rows to determine each candidate's Copeland score. The sum of row i is equal to the number of pairwise wins candidate i has minus the number of losses. Equivalently, we might rank candidates by their winning percentages.

An example of Copeland scoring in sports occurs when competitors play a round-robin, and the teams or individuals are ranked by their number of victories. The first rounds of the Olympic hockey competition and the World Cup finals use this method.[13] When we use a Copeland system, we must also adopt a contingency plan for ties, since they may occur in the case of a cycle. Both the Olympics and the World Cup use total goals as a tiebreaker.

We might say intuitively that since professional sports leagues rank teams by winning percentages, they are using Copeland rules; but, if we consider each game between two teams as equivalent to the decision of a single voter, they are actually using Borda scoring. That is, teams are ranked by their total number of victories (or votes) over all head-to-head contests. In baseball, for example, teams in the same league play each other either 12 or 13 times each season, and 12 or 13 decisions are scored—under Copeland scoring, the winner of the season series would get one point. Of course in sports, rather than having ballots with rankings, we are truly interested in observing the $n(n-1)/2$ pairwise contests separately.

A Copeland winner must defeat all other candidates if a Condorcet winner exists. Even when there is no Condorcet winner, the Copeland winner dominates every other candidate in the sense that he either defeats him directly or defeats a third candidate who defeats him (Maurer, 1978; Miller,

1980). We say he can defeat any other candidate through a chain of length one or two.[14] However, just as several candidates might tie for first in a Copeland election, more than one candidate could dominate each of the others through a chain of length one or two.

8. Minimum Violations

Minimum violations is the first computationally difficult method we cover. After voters rank the candidates, we tabulate the head-to-head votes to determine the winner of each matchup. We then consider each permutation of the candidates *a, b, c,* and so on, as a potential ranking. The best ranking, according to the minimum violations criteria, is the permutation that has the fewest "contradictions," where by contradiction we mean that a candidate with lower rank defeats a candidate with higher rank.

One method to compute a minimum violations ranking is to use the win-loss matrix and maximize the sum of the entries above the diagonal by permuting the rows and columns. From this algorithm, we can see that the winning list of candidates will never display the feature that a candidate is ranked *immediately* above another who defeated her head-to-head. If this were the case, the list that switches only these two candidates would result in one less violation and no other changes.

If there are no cycles, the minimum violations will be identical to the Copeland ranking, and this order will be a zero violations ranking. Problems can arise if there are voting cycles, because in this instance a zero violations ranking does not exist, the best ranking is not necessarily unique, and the minimum violations criterion provides no particular way of resolving these ambiguities.

9. Ranked Pairs

Condorcet's (1785) seminal paper expresses the idea that a candidate who would defeat each of the others head-to-head should win the election. If no such candidate exists, then large majorities should take precedence over small majorities in breaking cycles. In his own words, the general rule was "to take successively all the propositions that have a majority, beginning with those possessing the largest. As soon as these first decisions produce a result, it should be taken as a decision, without regard for the less probable decisions that follow." How is this idea implemented? Consider all the possible lists that order the candidates from top to bottom. Find the largest margin of victory in any pairwise match—and then eliminate all potential rankings that contradict this preference. For example, if the largest victory is for candidate *a* over candidate *b*, eliminate all potential rankings which place *b* above *a*. Next, consider the second largest margin of victory, and eliminate all potential rankings that disagree. Continue this process until only one ranking remains.

With only three candidates, this method is well defined and is equivalent to ignoring the election with the smallest margin of victory. The problem is that in elections with four or more candidates, considering the largest unconsidered margin of victory may, at some point, force us to eliminate all remaining potential rankings (by locking in a cycle). Condorcet does not discuss this possibility, an omission which has led to criticism and some confusion.

T. N. Tideman suggests one solution to the dilemma of cycles: simply skip over a head-to-head result that will lock in a cycle. Tideman further notes that if ties exist, there may be more than one potential ranking left even after we have considered all victories. In this case, we declare a tie among the candidates who have first-place ranks in the remaining potential rankings. Tideman calls this scheme "ranked pairs."

In the pairwise-comparisons matrix below, we first lock in $a > b$, then $b > c$. This implies that $a > c$. The next largest victory is $c > a$, but this locks in a cycle, so we ignore that head-to-head result. We then lock in $a > d$, $b > d$, $c > d$, which leaves us with a final ranking $a > b > c > d$.

	a	*b*	*c*	*d*
a	0	61	41	51
b	39	0	60	51
c	59	40	0	51
d	49	49	49	0

We further discuss this example in the Kemeny-Young section.

10. Simpson-Kramer Min-Max Rule

The Simpson-Kramer min-max rule adheres to the principles offered by Condorcet in that it emphasizes large majorities over small majorities. A candidate's "max" score is the largest number of votes against that candidate across all head-to-head matchups. The rule selects the candidates with the minimum max score. A Condorcet winner will always be a min-max winner. When there is a cycle, we can think of the min-max winner as being the "least-objectionable" candidate. It is the person whose biggest defeat is the closest to 50 : 50. Large majorities take precedence over small majorities in that we are willing to ignore defeats if they are close enough to 50 : 50.

While the min-max rule works well for choosing the winner of an election, it may be less effective as a ranking technique, especially when a dominant Condorcet winner exists. In the election below, candidate *a* defeats all others by a large margin. As a result, the other candidates are ranked solely by their performances against *a*, while their head-to-head matchups are disregarded. Despite beating *b* and *c* head-to-head, candidate *d* places last in the election by virtue of having the poorest score against *a*.

	a	*b*	*c*	*d*							
a	0	61	63	64		Min-Max	*a*	*b*	*c*	*d*
b	39	0	49	45		Scores	39	61	63	64
c	37	51	0	44							
d	36	55	56	0							

11. Kemeny-Young Method

H. Peyton Young (1988) concluded that Condorcet intended to rank candidates in the order with which the most voters agree. In other words, we should maximize the number of head-to-head votes that agree with the ranking (or minimize the number of votes that disagree). As it turns out, Kemeny (1959) had suggested a method identical to the Young interpretation.

Kemeny-Young voting is very similar to the minimum violations method, except that it emphasizes decisive wins over smaller majority margins. Again, begin by considering all possible rankings of the candidates. However, instead of maximizing the sum of the entries in the upper diagonal of the win-loss matrix, Kemeny-Young voting uses the paired-comparisons matrix. The example nearby demonstrates this process. The left-hand pairwise-comparisons matrix shows the original rankings. The sum of entries in the upper right half is 51 + 45 + 58 + 53 + 44 + 49 = 300. Note that a cycle exists in these rankings: *c* > *a*, *d* > *c*, and *a* > *d*. Kemeny-Young resolves this cycle by placing *c* > *a*, *a* > *d* and *c* > *d*. In the right-hand matrix, the sum of the upper diagonal is 55 + 49 + 47 + 58 + 51 + 56 = 316.

	a	*b*	*c*	*d*			*c*	*a*	*d*	*b*
a	0	51	45	58	⇒	*c*	0	55	49	47
b	49	0	53	44		*a*	45	0	58	51
c	55	47	0	49		*d*	51	42	0	56
d	42	56	51	0		*b*	53	49	44	0

How do these rankings make *c* end up first? After all, although *c* beats *a* decisively, it loses to both *b* and *d*. Well, *c* must beat *a*, because the largest majorities must be respected. However, *c* cannot be *immediately* ahead of either *b* or *d*. Just as in the minimum violations ranking, a candidate cannot be ranked directly above another candidate who defeated her head-to-head. If *c* must be ahead of *a*, but cannot be one place ahead of either *b* or *d*, then the one possible position for *c* is first. Because *a* defeats *d* decisively, we place *a* ahead of *d*, and the rest follows. If *b* or *d* complain that they "should" have won the election, based on pairwise results with *c*, the Kemeny-Young answer is that both *b* and *d* clearly deserve to be defeated by *a*, and thus have a weak claim to victory.

When there is a Condorcet winner, Kemeny-Young and minimum violations both rank that winner first. Differences appear when there are cycles. The minimum violations winner in the above election is not *c*, but *a*. Minimum violations actually ranks *c* last.

It is also interesting to compare the min-max and Kemeny-Young methods. Again, both will rank a Condorcet winner first. But if there is a cycle, the Kemeny-Young and the min-max rule may not agree on the winner; and even if a Condorcet winner exists, they may not rank the lower candidates in the same order. In the example above, the min-max ranking is *cabd*; the Kemeny-Young rank is *cadb*. Examples can readily be created where the two methods pick dramatically different winners. In the example in the ranked-pairs section, candidate *d*, who receives 49 votes in each pairwise competition, is the min-max winner, and yet places last under Kemeny-Young rules. This disparity makes sense in that *a*, *b*, and *c* are locked in a cycle. It would be hard to make an argument that candidate *d* should be inserted into the middle of the cycle rather than placed above or below it. Interestingly, Caplin and Nalebuff (1988) prove that in a spatial voting model—where voters each have a most preferred point and each candidate occupies a position in Euclidean space— this outcome could not occur. In particular, the ranked-pairs winner will agree with the min-max winner because no cycle can occur if we restrict attention to majorities larger than the biggest margin involving the min-max winner.

12–13. Methods Derived from Sports Tournaments

12. Kendall-Wei/Power Rank Method

Kendall-Wei extends the Copeland method by attempting to account not only for a candidate's head-to-head wins but for the strength of the candidates beaten. To find the Kendall-Wei scores, we begin by giving each candidate a score equal to that candidate's number of pairwise wins. We then give each candidate a second score equal to the number of wins earned by candidates she defeated. In the third iteration, each candidate's score equals the sum of the second round scores of the candidates she defeated. The process continues; at each stage, the candidate's score is equal to the sum of the previous round scores of the candidates she defeated. This results in each candidate having an infinite sequence of scores. As it turns out, these sequences converge, and we call the convergent limits Kendall-Wei scores.

It would be impossible to carry these calculations ad infinitum. Fortunately, we can find the limits of these sequences through an elegant shortcut. Writing the win-loss matrix and counting 1 point for wins and 0 for losses (instead of -1), we find the eigenvector v associated with the largest positive eigenvalue of the matrix. If W is the win-loss matrix, and l is its largest positive eigenvector, we find a vector v, where $Wv = lv$. This vector is the candidates' Kendall-Wei scores.

This method only works if there is a cycle, otherwise the matrix W will have no nonzero eigenvalues. We present an example with a cycle below:

$$
W = \begin{array}{c|cccc}
 & a & b & c & d \\
\hline
a & 0 & 1 & 1 & 1 \\
b & 0 & 0 & 1 & 0 \\
c & 0 & 0 & 0 & 1 \\
d & 0 & 1 & 0 & 0
\end{array}
\qquad l = 1 \qquad
v = \begin{array}{c|c}
a & 3 \\
b & 1 \\
c & 1 \\
d & 1
\end{array}
$$

Because the Kendall-Wei method does not resolve cycles, we offer an extension called the power rank method. This compares to Kendall-Wei except that it uses the paired-comparisons matrix rather than the win-loss matrix, and does not require a voting cycle. Given the paired-comparisons matrix A, power rank scores are defined by the eigenvector belonging to the matrix's largest positive eigenvalue. We present an example below:

$$
W = \begin{array}{c|cccc}
 & a & b & c & d \\
\hline
a & 0 & 7 & 6 & 9 \\
b & 3 & 0 & 7 & 4 \\
c & 4 & 3 & 0 & 8 \\
d & 1 & 6 & 2 & 0
\end{array}
\qquad l \sim 13.9 \qquad
v \sim \begin{array}{c|c}
a & 34 \\
b & 24 \\
c & 25 \\
d & 17
\end{array}
$$

In this election, candidate a dominates the other candidates, and receives by far the highest power ranking. Although b beats c convincingly, 7–3, c earns the highest power score by virtue of stronger performances against a and d. As a comparison, the Borda method would agree with the power rank method, while the Kemeny-Young and ranked-pairs rules would rank b above c. The min-max rule, the Copeland rule, and the minimum violations method would place them in a tie.

13. Jech Method (Maximum Likelihood Estimation)

The Jech method, also proposed by Zermelo (1929), Bradley and Terry (1952), and Ford (1957), is a probabilistic ranking method. Jech's (1983) goal is to provide an ordering of the candidates that not only demonstrates whether i is superior to j, but also by how much. Each candidate i is given a strength T_i. Given these strengths, Jech defines a probability matrix p where the probability that i defeats j in a pairwise election (or game) is $pij = T_i/(T_i + T_j)$. Jech makes two assumptions: first, that odds multiply and second, that expected wins equal actual wins. Jech proves that only one matrix exists that satisfies this criteria. Candidates (or teams) receive a score equal to their expected winning percentage. In an election, this ranking is equivalent to the Copeland method. This can be viewed as an independent argument for using the Jech method. For sports teams, Jech's method works even if not all teams play one another. In this case, Jech's method predicts the number of wins a team might have in a full round-robin tournament (essentially an expected Copeland score).

Choosing an Appropriate Voting System

In the examples we looked at, there was surprisingly little difference between the winners under the various election methods. We tested nine of the methods—plurality, single transferable vote, Borda, Copeland, min-max, Kendall-Wei, power ranking, minimum violations, and Kemeny-Young—using voting data from British union elections. All elections were multi-candidate elections where voters ranked their preferences. With the exception of plurality rule, all the other methods obtained similar results. Plurality rule frequently resulted in a different winner than the other methods, and single transferable vote occasionally led to a different outcome. The other methods essentially differed only when there was a voting cycle, and even then, it did not affect the winner. While rankings were not identical, a Condorcet winner typically emerged, and this winner tended to be the Borda winner as well.

Given the variety of election formats, and that their results do not differ so dramatically, it is natural to ask how to choose among them. The answer may depend on which features of a voting rule are most important in a particular situation. We consider five aspects that distinguish the various methods.

Level of Complexity

A voting method should be relatively simple and transparent, both for voters and for those calculating the winner. The tolerable level of complexity depends on how many voters and candidates there are, who the voters are, and what purpose the election serves.

Simplicity helps explain why plurality voting is so widespread and why approval voting and Borda voting are the two most frequently used alternatives. The U.S. presidential election is something of an anomaly to this principle of simplicity—hence the periodic calls for a direct (plurality) election to replace the electoral college. In some cases, we accept greater complexity to gain accuracy. For example, the professional tennis rankings and *The New York Times* college football rankings (forms of power ranking) both require a computer for calculation. They can account for a great deal of information, much more than if we ranked tennis players simply by total matches won or tournaments won.

Voting in a single transferable vote election is straightforward; the main hurdle would be explaining the vote-counting procedure to voters and establishing the legitimacy of the system. Here, charts can be extremely useful. Edwin Newman and Miles Rogers (1952), in their analysis of the 1951 Cambridge city election, compare cumulative voting outcomes where the voters are given between 1 and 9 votes (there were nine city council seats). In their chart, presented as Table 1, we see how the candidates move up and down the rankings as voters are allowed more choices. The graph clearly demonstrates the importance of second, third and lower-place choices in capturing voter preferences. Note how candidate 20 rises from seventh to second place, candidate 06 rises from eighteenth to eighth position, and candidate 14 drops from fifth to twelfth.

The issue of how voters express preferences on a ballot is separate from how the preferences are combined. When a corporate board votes on a set of well-defined proposals, it would be reasonable to ask the board members to rank their preferences. A board member would presumably be well informed and interested, so we could use a more involved paired-comparisons technique to determine the winning choice. On the other hand, in an election for student government, with many candidates and mostly disinterested voters, ranking candidates could be capricious. Instead, we might ask voters to approve or disapprove each candidate, or approve a set number, or just pick their favorite. Simplicity is a relative term.

Voter Strategies

In an election, the possibility always exists for voters to cast their ballots strategically, rather than in accordance with their true preferences. All voting systems are susceptible to strategizing. For example, in a three-candidate plurality election, a voter might vote for her second choice if her preferred candidate lags far behind in preelection polls. An honest vote might be considered "wasted." Another person might vote for the lagging candidate as a

TABLE 1. Plurality Count with Each Number of Choices

Rank	P.R. Count	1	2	3	4	5	6	7	8	9
1	03	03	03	03	03	03	03	03	03	03
2	25	25	25	20	20	20	20	20	20	20
3	05	23	20	25	05	05	05	05	05	05
4	20	05	05	05	25	25	25	25	11	11
5	23	14	23	23	23	23	11	11	25	25
6	11	26	26	26	26	11	23	23	23	23
7	14	20	14	07	11	26	26	26	26	26
8	07	11	11	11	07	07	07	07	07	06
9	26	17	07	14	14	14	14	14	06	07
10	17	27	17	17	17	17	17	08	08	08
11	27	08	27	27	08	08	08	17	14	18
12	08	07	15	08	27	02	06	06	18	14
13	15	15	08	15	02	27	02	18	17	17
14	01	01	01	02	15	06	18	02	02	16
15	02	02	02	01	06	18	27	27	16	02
16	18	19	19	18	18	15	15	15	27	27
17	19	18	18	06	01	19	19	16	15	15
18	06	06	06	19	19	01	16	19	19	19
19	12	12	12	12	16	16	01	01	01	01
20	16	16	16	16	12	12	12	12	12	12
21	13	13	13	13	13	13	13	04	04	04
22	21	21	09	09	09	09	04	13	13	13
23	24	09	21	21	24	04	09	09	09	24
24	09	24	24	24	21	24	24	24	24	09
25	04	04	04	04	04	21	21	21	21	10
26	10	10	10	10	10	10	10	10	10	21
27	22	22	22	22	22	22	22	22	22	22

Note: Chart showing rank of candidates under assumption of vote by varying number of choices. Numbers in the table refer to candidates.

protest vote, even if she did not prefer that candidate over the others. Or suppose two of the three candidates—the ones with relatively similar views—are running neck and neck. Supporters of the first might rank their candidate first and the other last, even if in truth they would have chosen the other as their second choice. In recognition of this danger of strategizing, Borda wrote that his method was appropriate only for honest voters. For this reason, Borda counting works well when there is little incentive to strategize—for example, in the AP sports poll where writers, in general, have no vested interest in the outcome of the poll.

Voter strategizing provides a counterargument to the benefit of simplicity; the more complex schemes are harder to strategize and by their very complexity may help promote honest behavior.

Candidate Strategies

Electoral systems may influence candidate strategies as well. In plurality voting, a minority candidate could win if two similar candidates split the majority vote. Because of this, some candidates would do better to generate strong minority support instead of trying to attract a majority vote. Cox (1987, 1990) confirms this suspicion, finding that candidates do best by solidifying minority support rather than taking centrist positions. Myerson (1993) shows that in a two-candidate plurality election, candidates fare best when exactly half the electorate are promised benefits above the average. As the number of candidates increases, Myerson demonstrates that the optimum strategy shifts: candidates do better by promising the bulk of the resources to a smaller and smaller minority, seeking to cultivate a small bloc of strong support rather than widespread appeal.

When there are only two candidates, the approval voting and plurality rule lead to the same incentives. As the number of candidates increases, the incentives are different under approval voting. Here, to win broad approval, the optimum campaign strategy is to spread the bulk of the resources over a larger and larger segment of the electorate.

For single transferable vote elections, more than one possible equilibrium exists. Candidates might opt to seek majority support, but they might also choose to cultivate minority support at the expense of the majority. Suppose all but one candidate offer a distribution of benefits to voters that equals the distribution that each of these candidates would have gained in a plurality election with four candidates. The final candidate offers a uniform distribution of benefits, seeking majority support. She will be the very first candidate eliminated, even though head-to-head she would defeat any of the others. If the final candidate chooses the optimum strategy for a five-candidate plurality election, she will rank first in each stage until only four candidates remain, but will face elimination at this stage, as all the other candidates have taken the optimum four-candidate strategy.

All paired-comparisons methods, including the Borda rule, offer candidates precisely the same incentives. Rather than encouraging candidates to seek minority support, candidates in a paired-comparisons election do best to appeal to a majority.[15] We see this intuitively if we look at the head-to-head comparisons as simultaneous two-candidate plurality elections, all of which are symmetric. A candidate wants to do well in each of these individual head-to-head contests, hence the two-candidate plurality strategy.

Ranking vs. Picking a Winner

In an election to fill an office, we care solely about determining one winner. In other elections, we need to elect several candidates. In a weekly football poll, the number one team matters, but we also want to know the rankings of the other teams as well. These different goals suggest different voting rules. Methods that use a good deal of the information available on the ballots, such as Kendall-Wei, power rank, Jech, Borda, Copeland, and Kemeny-Young, work particularly well for ranking all the candidates. Each of these takes into account a candidate's or a team's head-to-head performance against each of the other teams. Kendall-Wei and Copeland count only wins and losses; the more complex of these ranking techniques, Jech, power rank, and Kemeny-Young, consider the margins of victory as well. Single transferable vote works well only when the quota is adjusted based on the number of candidates we seek to rank.

Plurality, approval voting, and min-max are better suited for choosing the winner of the election than ranking the candidates. Plurality works poorly for ranking mainly because it also takes into account only first-place rankings, and thus discards much of the available information. For example, a candidate who ranks second on every ballot, but first on none, probably deserves a relatively high rank, yet plurality gives that candidate zero votes. Min-max works poorly on the lower rankings when one candidate wins by an enormous margin. All the remaining candidates are then ranked solely by their performance against the strong candidate—because that will be their minimum vote—regardless of how they fare against each of the others. A candidate with only one head-to-head loss might wind up last with a bad enough defeat against the winner.

Minority Support and the Safe Choice

Suppose a business wants to introduce a new brand of cereal. They do not want to market a cereal that everyone picks as the second or third best but no one picks first. Consumers will buy the cereal they like best. It doesn't matter whether they like a cereal second best or fifth best; they won't buy it. The company should market a cereal that generates strong preferences, even if some tasters rank it very low. Counting systems such as plurality or weighted Condorcet, which emphasize strong preferences, work better for product testing than methods such as min-max or Borda, which reward consensus and wide approval.

Elections are different from product testing. The usual goal is a candidate who appeals to a large portion of the electorate, rather than one who draws forceful support from a strong minority. When the objective is to pick a "safe" choice, systems like approval voting or min-max will favor the least objectionable over more controversial candidates. Similarly, Borda rewards strong preferences to an extent, but a winning Borda candidate will probably not have alienated a large minority. A candidate who places second or third on each ballot stands a strong chance in a Borda, approval or min-max election, even though such a candidate has little hope of winning a weighted Condorcet or plurality election.

Conclusion

If the multitude of available vote-counting systems leaves you overwhelmed, you are not alone. Several of the relatively simple schemes—such as single transferable vote, Borda counting, min-max, Kemeny-Young, power ranking, and approval voting—possess qualities that are often desirable. Others, such as Copeland, minimum violations, or Jech may be useful for specific purposes. The diversity of questions we might ask about vote-counting procedures, their biases and their outcomes, is enormous. Many researchers, following Arrow's (1951) lead, have concerned themselves with stating various desirable or undesirable criteria and attempting to classify systems by these means. In contrast, there are far fewer papers written concerning the application of alternative systems in practice.

Despite the wealth of alternative voting mechanisms documented here, plurality rule remains the overwhelming favorite choice. Why do alternatives to plurality rule have such a difficult time being adopted?

Part of the answer is probably that when voter preferences are sufficiently similar, a variety of voting systems will lead to similar choices, and these choices will have desirable properties. In this case, the choice between voting systems will seem to make little difference. In many other cases, society does not have a consensus about what the goals of an electoral system should be. One is to establish legitimacy of the victor. A second is to encourage participation. A third may be to discourage the formation of a large number of political parties. A fourth is to assure a representative political system although the very definition of "representativeness" is part of the problem. For participants in the system, a fifth goal is often that "their side" improve its chances of winning.

No voting system will satisfy everyone on all of these dimensions; the choice is always between flawed alternatives. Between the entrenched power of the status quo, and with conflicting theoretical guidance to help select a second-best alternative, it is not surprising that electoral reform is difficult to implement. Most of the variety in electoral schemes comes from the choice of different metrics for measuring the distance between one ranking and another.

The Marquis de Condorcet (1785) believed that in an election, there exists some underlying truth to be discovered—that one candidate should be the "true" winner. We suggest a more modest conclusion, but one that might stop us from looking for some perfect Holy Grail of a voting method that meets all needs: a voting system can't find a consensus when none exists.

Appendix:
Additional Voting Rules

Young Method

Peyton Young, whose interpretation of Condorcet's work we have already described, proposed a separate method. Under the Young method, if there is no Condorcet winner, each candidate receives a score equal to the largest subset of voters for which that candidate is a Condorcet winner. The Young winner is the candidate with the highest score. In the example below, b is the Young as well as the min-max winner:

# Voters	Ballot							a	b	c
2	$a > b > c$	Young	a	b	c		a	0	6	4
3	$b > c > a$	Scores	3	9	7		b	5	0	7
2	$b > a > c$						c	7	4	0
4	$c > a > b$									

Here, a defeats the others if we count the two ballots that rank a first and any one other ballot. To compute b's score, we count the 5 first-place ballots and any 4 of the others, for a score of 9. Finally, for *c* we count the 4 first-place ballots and any three of the others, for final scores of 3, 9, and 7. The final ranking is *bca*. This method is similar to the min-max rule and will produce the same winner so long as the number of last-place votes each candidate receives is at least as large as that candidate's largest loss margin in a head-to-head match (Tideman, 1993, ch. 13).

Dodgson Rule

Charles Dodgson, mathematician and author of *Alice in Wonderland* (under the pen name Lewis Carroll) studied elections and lawn tennis tournaments at Oxford in the late 19th century. He agreed with Condorcet that a candidate who is undefeated head-to-head should win an election, but felt that if a Condorcet winner did not exist, the election should be called off. In discussing this opinion, he proposed this method of scoring candidates: if there is no Condorcet winner, the Dodgson rule holds that a candidate's score should be defined to be the total number of inversions on individual ballots necessary to make that candidate a Condorcet winner. More than one inversion may be needed on some ballots to make a candidate a Condorcet winner. This sounds difficult to compute, and it is.

A simplified Dodgson rule can be calculated directly from the paired-comparisons matrix. To compute the simplified Dodgson scores, we write the paired-comparisons matrix and for each candidate sum the vote difference in each of that candidate's head-to-head losses. The simplified Dodgson winner is the candidate who has the smallest total differential over all losses. The simplified Dodgson method bears a close similarity to the Borda rule, in that if we were to tabulate total differential over wins and losses, that is to sum the differential over all wins and subtract the simplified Dodgson scores, we would arrive at the Borda rankings.

Estimated Centrality

Discussed by T. N. Tideman and I. G. Good in 1976 (Tideman, 1993), estimated centrality assumes that each candidate occupies some spatial position, and that voters likewise have some ideal preferred point in space. Under estimated centrality, the candidate who occupies that point in space closest to the "median," or zero moment, of the voters' ideal points wins the election. (We might, in fact, take any moment of the voter's ideal points— here we take the zero moment.) Good and Tideman have proven that it is possible to use the fraction of voters who place the candidates in each of the possible orders to compute the estimated centrality winner, but the actual computation is still quite difficult.

NOTES

1. To give just the most simple example, if the population is uniformly distributed between positions 0 and 1, and we are to choose three representatives, should they be equally spaced [0.25, 0.5, and 0.75], or should they be selected so as to minimize the average distance traveled to the nearest legislator [0.16, 0.5, and 0.83]?

2. Many theorists have addressed the issue of how to deal with voters who either fail to rank some candidates, or rank two or more candidates as tied. Because of the immediate complications these issues generate, we try to avoid raising them in the general discussion. In a paired comparisons approach, there are basically two options when a voter ranks two or more candidates as tied. When we compare the candidates head-to-head, we can either ignore that voter, or give each candidate 1/2 point. If we do not count the voter, some head-to-head matches will have fewer total points than others. Since this leads to problems later, we could normalize all head-to-head scores so that a candidate's score is the percentage of the electorate won against the opponent. This method differs from giving each candidate 1/2 point in a tie. For example, if the score is 60 to 30 among 90 of the voters, with 10 ties, normalizing the scores results in a 66.6 to 33.3 election, while adding 1/2 point makes the score 65 to 35. What if a voter fails to rank some candidates? In our empirical work computing various schemes, we assume a ranked candidate is preferable to an unranked candidate. This means a single unranked candidate loses every head-to-head comparison and is effectively ranked last. If two or more candidates are unranked, we may place them in a tie for last place on the ballot and then treat the tie vote in one of the two ways described above.

3. If there is no Condorcet winner, there must be a voting cycle, but not vice versa. An example of an election with a Condorcet winner and a cycle is $a > b$, $a > c$, $a > d$, $b > c$, $c > d$, $d > b$. Here a beats the other three candidates, who are in a cycle.

4. This argument is a bit specious, since nearly all votes are wasted in the sense that they do not determine the outcome of an election. And votes are equally well wasted on a party with a large lead. Evidence from the '94 elections suggests that Duverger's law may be breaking down.

5. Endorsement of cumulative voting was one of the "radical" positions taken by Lani Guinier. For a popular discussion, see *The New York Times Magazine*, Feb. 27, 1994.

6. Actually, there is an upper bound on the number of players a sportswriter may list on his or her ballot. The limit is ten players, which is high enough that except in extraordinary years, the vote ceiling is rarely a factor.

7. In general, we define a quota $q = [n/(w + 1)] + 1$, where n is the number of voters, w is the desired number of winners, and the bracket notation $[x]$ means "greatest integer less than x." This choice achieves the goal of having the smallest possible quota such that no more than w candidates may exceed it.

8. In the Cambridge and New York elections, votes are hand counted, a practice fixed by law. Because of this, rather than assign transferred votes a weight of $s/(s + q)$,

$s/(s + q)$ ballots are randomly selected as transferred votes, and count as one full vote. Clearly, this is less preferable, because it adds an element of randomness to the election. Even with this time-saving procedure, Cambridge city council elections have taken as long as a week to be counted.

9. It is easy to imagine other reverse elimination schemes. For example, the Nanson rule eliminates candidates based on their Borda scores.

10. Obviously, from its original description, Borda voting could also be thought of as a rank-scoring rule.

11. Duncan Black (1958) proposed a compromise between Borda and Condorcet. Under the Black rule, we compare candidates based on their head-to-head performances. If a Condorcet winner exists, that candidate wins the election. Otherwise, the candidate with the highest Borda score wins.

12. If there are n voters and k candidates, the "average" score is $n(k/2)$.

13. In order to encourage aggressive offensive play, the World Cup now treats ties in a novel manner, awarding both teams one point. When one team wins a game, they receive three points to the loser's zero. Devaluing a tie is meant to provide both teams with incentives to play more exciting soccer.

14. However, Niemi and Riker (1976) note that under certain conditions, the Copeland method can choose as the winner a candidate who loses by near unanimity to the Borda winner.

15. Similarly, following Cox (1987), candidates have an incentive to adopt positions close to the political center. Cox uses a spatial model of voter preferences and shows that there is an equilibrium of candidate strategies when candidates adopt the position of the median voter.

REFERENCES

Ali, I., W. D. Cook, and M. Kress, "On the Minimum Violations Ranking of a Tournament," *Management Science,* June 1986, *32,* 660–72.

Anderson, Lowell, "Voting and Paired Comparisons." Extracted from Grotte, J., L. Anderson, and M. Robinson, "Selected Judgmental Methods in Defense Analyses." Institute for Defense Analyses paper P-2387, 1990.

Anderson, Lowell, "How to Take Votes: New Ideas on Better Ways to Determine Winners," research draft, Institute for Defense Analyses, 1994.

Arrow, Kenneth J., *Social Choice and Individual Values.* New Haven: Yale University Press, 1951.

Black, Duncan, *The Theory of Committees and Elections.* London: Cambridge University Press, 1958.

Board of Elections, Cincinnati, Ohio, "Proportional Representation Count: Rules and Instructions to Employees," 1955.

Bradley, R. A., and M. E. Terry, "The Rank Analysis of Incomplete Block Designs. I. The Method of Paired Comparisons," *Biometrika,* 1952, *39,* 324–35.

Brams, Steven, and Jack Nagel, "Approval Voting in Practice," *Public Choice,* August 1991, *71,* 1–17.

Caplin, Andrew, and Barry Nalebuff, "On 64%-Majority Rule," *Econometrica,* July 1988, *56,* 787–814.

Caplin, Andrew, and Barry Nalebuff, "Aggregation and Social Choice: A Mean Voter Theorem," *Econometrica*, January 1991, *59*, 1–24.

Condorcet, Marquis de, "Essay on the Application of Mathematics to the Theory of Decision Making," 1785. In Baker, K., ed., *Condorcet: Selected Writings*. Indianapolis: Bobbs-Merrill, 1976.

Coombs, Clyde, *A Theory of Data*. New York: Wiley, 1964.

Copeland, A. H., "A 'Reasonable' Social Welfare Function," mimeo, University of Michigan Seminar on Applications of Mathematics to the Social Sciences, 1951.

Cox, Gary W., "Electoral Equilibrium under Alternative Voting Institutions," *American Journal of Political Science*, February 1987, *31*, 82–108.

Cox, Gary W., "Centripetal and Centrifugal Incentives in Electoral Systems," *American Journal of Political Science*, November 1990, *34*, 903–35.

David, H. A., "Ranking the Players in a Round Robin Tournament," *Review of the International Statistical Institute*, 1971, *39*:2, 137–47.

Ford, L. R., "Solution of a Ranking Problem from Binary Comparisons," *American Mathematical Monthly*, 1957, *64*, 28–33.

Goddard, Steven T., "Rankings in Tournaments and Group Decision-Making," *Management Science*, December 1983, *29*, 1384–92.

Jech, Thomas, "The Ranking of Incomplete Tournaments: A Mathematician's Guide to Popular Sports," *American Mathematical Monthly*, 1983, *90*, 246–66.

Kemeny, John, "Mathematics Without Numbers," *Daedalus*, Fall 1959, *88*, 571–91.

Maurer, Stephen B., "The King Chicken Theorems," working paper, Princeton University Mathematics Department, 1978.

Miller, N., "A New Solution Set for Tournaments and Majority Voting," *American Journal of Political Science*, February 1980, *24*, 68–96.

Myerson, Roger, "Incentives to Cultivate Favored Minorities under Alternative Electoral Systems," *American Political Science Review*, December 1993, *87*, 856–69.

Newman, Edwin B., and Miles Rogers, "PR Voting: An Analysis of the 1951 Cambridge City Election," unpublished (available from Barry Nalebuff), 1952.

Niemi, Richard, and William Riker, "The Choice of Voting Systems," *Scientific American*, 1976, *234*:6, 21–7.

Pildes, Richard, and Richard Niemi, "Expressive Harms, 'Bizarre Districts,' and Voting Rights: Evaluating Election-District Appearances after Shaw," working paper, University of Michigan Law School, 1993.

Rosenthal, Howard, and Subrata Sen, "Electoral Participation in the French Fifth Republic," *American Political Science Review*, March 1973, *67*, 29–54.

Stob, Michael, "A Supplement to 'A Mathematician's Guide to Popular Sports,'" *American Mathematical Monthly*, May 1984, *91*, 277–82.

Tideman, Nicolaus, "Collective Decisions and Voting," draft, March 1993.

Young, H. Peyton, "Condorcet's Theory of Voting," *American Political Science Review*, December 1988, *82*, 1231–44.

Zermelo, E., "Die Berechnung der Turnier-Ergebnisse als ein Maximumproblem der Wahrscheinlichkeitsrechnung," *Math. Z.*, 1929, *29*, 436–60.

An Application of Social Choice Theory to U.S.D.A. Forest Service Decision Making

Wade E. Martin, Deborah J. Shields, Boleslaw Tolwinski, &
Brian Kent

Review Questions

1. When the USDA Forest Service began to incorporate more groups in its decision process, conflicts inevitably occurred. Why was it supposed these conflicts would be lessened when the Department of Interior adopted the ecosystem management paradigm? Does the analysis in the paper support this conjecture?
2. What difficulties arise in quantifying individual preferences if people do not solely pursue happiness, desire fulfillment, and choice? How can a social welfare function be determined?
3. Why is it argued the Condorcet and Borda rules will assist policymakers in determining preferences? Which normative properties does each satisfy or violate? Which rule is preferable in general or for the specific purpose of land-use planning?

Martin, Wade E., Deborah J. Shields, Boleslaw Tolwinski, and Brian Kent. "An Application of Social Choice Theory to U.S.D.A. Forest Service Decision Making." *Journal of Policy Modeling* 18 (1996): 603–21.

4. A specific ordered rule is suggested by Cases 1, 2, and 3. Do you agree with this proposed rule?
5. In the example generated, the authors note some voters may be given more than one vote. Which property would be violated if this were to occur? It is assumed in the example that each voter chooses the alternative in a pairwise comparison that if selected as the winner would yield the higher level of utility. Is this assumption necessary to the example? Why or why not?
6. What does it mean for preferences to be single-peaked? Verify that the preference rankings in Table 1 are single-peaked. Verify that A_4 is the Condorcet winner.

Introduction

The fundamental objective of social choice is to "combine individual preferences into collective choice" (MacKay, 1980, p. vii). Traditionally, the role of determining the collective choice for the management of public lands has been relegated to various administrative agencies within the government. For example, the U.S.D.I. Bureau of Land Management (BLM) had the authority to determine whether or not grazing was a socially desirable use of a particular parcel of land and, if so, the optimal level of that activity. Likewise, the U.S.D.A. Forest Service (Forest Service) could unilaterally decide whether a particular tract under its administration should be harvested for timber, based strictly upon the opinion of the agency's professionals as to the appropriate mix of land uses. The approach was essentially paternalistic; the agency knew best, and if there was disagreement, the public needed to be "educated" (Kennedy and Quigley, 1994).

Since the 1960s the centralized nature of land management within the federal government has been changing. The Multiple Use–Sustained Yield Act of 1960 was the last piece of legislation crafted by the Forest Service for the Forest Service (Bolle, 1987). Laws such as the Wilderness Act (1962) and Endangered Species Act (1973) enacted in the 1960s and 1970s reflected an emerging environmental ethic. The passage of the National Environmental Policy Act (NEPA) in 1969 and the implementation of guidelines developed by the Council of Environmental Quality provided specific means for the general public to be more actively involved in the management of public lands. Moreover, NEPA for the first time required federal agencies to justify actions with significant impacts. The Federal Land Planning and Management Act (FLPMA) (1976) and the National Forest Management Act (NFMA) (1976) combined these environmental laws with the statutory authority of the agencies, mandating interdisciplinary planning and broad public involvement (Bolle, 1987; Wilkinson, 1992).

As would be expected with the expansion of the parties involved in management decisions, the possibilities and areas for conflict also expanded. Land management agencies that continued to follow their traditional method of centralized land-use planning found their decisions challenged. Interested parties who felt their concerns had received inadequate attention sought redress in the courts. Unable to reach a consensus among the myriad of interested parties, the Forest Service retreated to following the letter of the law (NEPA, NFMA, etc.), while the Department of the Interior under Secretary Lujan attempted to limit the right to appeal agency decisions.

Attitudes of land managers in public agencies toward various (non-timber) uses of public lands have changed significantly over the last 15 to 20 years (see Kennedy, 1991; Brown and Harris, 1992). However, a change in the decision-making process will be necessary as well, if future conflicts are to be minimized. Partly in response to these concerns, federal agencies are replacing the previous commodity-oriented management paradigm with a new approach, ecosystem management (EM). EM emphasizes, among other concepts, maintaining ecosystem health and participatory decision making. It is hoped that the latter will reduce the frequency and intensity of the conflicts that have plagued agency planning efforts in recent years. Social choice theory can be used to provide insight into the direction that these changes in the decision-making process should proceed. This is particularly true in the area of conflict resolution where there is a need to focus on collective rather than individual choice.

This paper addresses one potential contribution of social choice theory to managing public lands. The search for consensus regarding alternative uses of publicly administered lands is framed as a group-decision problem, which can be solved through a voting mechanism. The Background section will review relevant literature from social choice theory and provide the necessary context for the subsequent voting models and application. This will be followed by a section presenting the voting models of Condorcet and Borda. These voting models will then be applied to an example from the Shoshone National Forest in Wyoming, where a resource company wants to explore for oil and gas in an area currently being managed to meet other goals. The Shoshone example will illustrate the difficulties involved in balancing the need or desire to produce commodity outputs with simultaneous maintenance of the health of the ecosystem providing them. This will be followed by a concluding section.

2. Background

The classic problem of economics concerns how to fulfill infinite desires with finite resources. To paraphrase Milton Friedman (1962), a resource management problem exists whenever scarce acreage is desired to satisfy two or more incompatible ends. If land is not scarce, there is no problem at all. If land is scarce, but there is only one end, the problem is a technological one. Unfortunately, the more typical case is one where land is scarce, the demands for it are numerous, and policymakers must find a balance among conflicting desires or preferences. One tool applicable to these kinds of problems is social choice theory.

The theory of social choice concerns the selection of some social alternative that has differing effects on individuals, each of whom have discrete preferences (Kreps, 1990). The preferences of individual i over social alternative x can be represented by an imputed value function V_i, such that

$V_i(x) = U_i(z)$ where $x = f(z)$ and $z = $ a consumption bundle.

The value of social alternative x to individual i is a function of the utility i receives from the consumption bundle z made possible by the decision to provide alternative x. The question facing the decision maker, which we will address below and in more detail in the section on voting models, is how to aggregate the V_is to arrive at a social choice.

When applied to public land management, social choice has a parallel definition: the selection of some planning alternative that affects the land and its suitability for various uses when those uses are diverse and frequently incompatible. Here V_i represents the value to some individual (spiritual, monetary, or otherwise) of planning alternative x, given that its choice would lead to the provision of resource bundle z. The objective of social choice in this context is to derive an ordering of management alternatives (the xs) based upon individual (or group) preference orderings of such alternatives (the V_is).

The social choice situation just described comprises four parts (MacKay, 1980, p. 13):

- voters or players (the is),
- choice alternatives (the xs),
- information on voter's preferences over the alternatives (the V_is), and
- an aggregation device (for this paper, voting models).

To apply social choice to ecosystem management, each of these four components needs to be integrated into the decision-making process.

This paper focuses on the fourth component, aggregation, with some consideration of its predecessor, individual or group preference functions. It addresses neither the identification of voters nor selection of management alternatives, although both of these are important and complex problems. It has been assumed that voters and choice alternatives have been identified in the NEPA scoping process.

2A. Preferences

Individual orderings of social states are presumed to be based on preferences, which are reflections of the individual's utility function. The assumption that individuals, or households, are the best judges of their own preferences is called individualism. By shifting to a more inclusive form of decision making, agencies are tacitly embracing the concept of individualism and rejecting, at least to some degree, paternalism. In the voting model, individual interests will be represented by group preference functions. While this represents a loss of autonomy for the individual, it is based upon a conscious decision on their part to let the group represent them. This differs significantly from the prior state where the agency simply assumed that the agency's preferences were both foremost and representative.

Three widely held perspectives on the quantification of individual preferences or well-being are happiness, desire fulfillment, and choice (Sen, 1987). Happiness as a measure of the utility generated by some object is linked to the utilitarian tradition; we value things for a reason, for example, the generation of pleasure. Through similar reasoning it can be argued that we desire things because their acquisition produces satisfaction, hence utility as fulfillment of desire. Finally, the choice perspective is the philosophical precursor to revealed preference theory, for example, A is revealed preferred to B, if A is chosen when B is available and affordable.

Happiness, desire fulfillment, and choice each have merit in quantifying utility; each can provide information on valuation and well-being. However, all these views are basically oriented toward consumption, income, wealth, and personal satisfaction. Were these factors the only ones of importance, a utility function derived from individual preferences could be represented by a money metric. This approach is commonly restricted to situations where individuals care only about their own consumption and not about that of others (Boadway and Bruce, 1984). While it is certainly true that self-interest plays a large role in motivation and preferences, humans are capable of acting contrary to their own best interest in the service of some higher goal. In analyzing problems where people evince concern for others and for future generations, a focus on wealth or money is inappropriate. As Sen states, "It is not clear that the relentless pursuit of self-interest is a good description of how people actually behave" (quoted in Klamer, 1989).

Clearly, a more complex conception of people's motivation is needed if we are to interpret estimates of utility in a way that is not misleading. A more inclusive view of utility might contain states of consciousness; that is, utility in the form of certain mental states is what would be available. This view is closer to that held by Sen (1985), who makes a case for abstracting from the things an individual owns or produces to the person's state of existence.

A conception of utility as the quality of the life one leads, rather than as a catalogue of one's physical and financial requirements, allows for a much more complex individual decision process. There is room for what might otherwise be thought of as irrational, for example, non-self-motivated behavior. The survival of species, or the needs of future generations, in addition to a desire for jobs, income, and commodities become legitimate concerns and influences on preferences.

It is impossible to know the degree to which altruism, sympathy, and concern for future generations, as opposed to pure self-interest, profit motive, or personal pleasure or convenience, affect preference rankings of forest plan alternatives. Nonetheless, it is reasonable to assume that individual preference rankings would be more consistent with this richer conception of utility than with one limited only to the instrumental valuation of wildlands. This view has been taken into consideration in estimating group preferences for this study.

For the voting models discussed in this paper, individuals are represented by interest groups. Aggregation of individual preferences to group preferences must be handled with care. The approach taken here has been to assign each interest group a single, representative preference function over forest plan alternatives. This form of aggregation is convenient, but is based on the assumption that intra-group individual utility functions are homothetic, or quasi-homothetic (Gorman, 1953). The "representative agent" approach has been severely criticized (Kirman, 1992). If the assumption of homotheticity is violated, the aggregation scheme proposed here may need to be replaced by an alternative approach such as one discussed by Stoker (1993) that utilizes individual and aggregate data.

2B. Aggregation

If the preferences described above are reflective, transitive, complete, and continuous, they can be represented by a utility function (Varian, 1984). Assuming the individual or, in our case, group orderings are represented by utility functions, successful aggregation generates a social choice rule, which can be thought of as a social welfare function (SWF) defined over utility space. Social welfare as a function of the utility of households is termed welfarism (Sen, 1977). However, in the voting model social welfare is a function of the utility of interest groups, some of which represent collections of individuals and others of which represent corporate entities or commodity producers.

It is not clear that this shift to group-preference functions automatically violates welfarism; however, the value sets upon which preferences are based could differ radically between groups. Consider business preferences, for example. Businesses have preferences centered on profit maximization and corporate survival; corporate welfare is not directly dependent upon altruistic factors such as intergenerational equity, or upon perceived quality of life. Including business interests as discrete groups in the social welfare function is essentially a value statement: Business preferences should have some say in public land management decisions.

We also make the assumption of independent utility functions across groups. Yet the actions that enhance well-being for one group could conceivably be detrimental to the well-being of some other group. This would violate the assumption of additive separability that is requisite to most aggregation schemes. All these difficulties surrounding group preferences warrant investigation.

Selection of the principles underlying selection of a SWF are important. For example, the axiomatic approach involves identification of a class of functions that satisfy some predetermined set of properties. Unfortunately, as Laffond, Laslier, and Le Breton (1994) point out, "Depending on the list [of properties], the class may be empty as illustrated by Arrow's Impossibility Theorem." In other words, Arrow demonstrated that it is impossible to move from individual choice to social choice while maintaining certain minimal rules. As will be noted in the following section, voting schemes are axiomatic in that the requisite properties are listed. They do not necessarily fulfill Arrow's original criteria for a social welfare function.

If the decision maker knows preference orderings and invokes individualism and the Pareto Principle, then a partial social ordering can be achieved. Usually a complete ordering is only possible with additional information about preferences or the inclusion of value judgments. Consider, for example, the additive form:

$SWF = \Sigma \alpha_j V_j(x) = \Sigma \alpha_j U_j(z)$ where a_j is the weighting coefficient for the jth voter.

Social welfare equals the weighted sum of the values each group j places on social alternative x, which equals the sum of the group utilities associated with choice x. Most voting models are related to this form, in which the weighting scheme represents a value judgment concerning the relative importance of groups' preferences.

The most important characteristic of a successful aggregation device is that it generate a social choice rule that can be used to determine the socially desirable outcome, if one (or more) exists. In the next section, the Condorcet model and Borda scoring model are discussed in detail. It will be argued that these voting models are useful aggregation devices that will assist managers in understanding conflicts among various interest groups.

3. Aggregation Devices or Voting Models

As noted in the previous section, there are four important components to a social choice decision problem. This section focuses on the aggregation device, or the fourth component. The voting models presented in this section will be applied to a social choice situation involving a land-use management issue facing the USFS concerning oil and gas leasing on the Shoshone National Forest in Wyoming.

3A. Main Types of Voting Rules

The two most popular families of voting rules are the Condorcet consistent methods, which elect the Condorcet winner whenever one exists, and Borda scoring methods that assign points to each candidate according to his ranking in the voter's opinion (Moulin, 1988).

> Definition 1 (Condorcet Rule).
> A *Condorcet winner* is a candidate a who defeats every other candidate in majority comparisons:
> *for all* b *(distinct from* a*) more voters prefer* a *to* b *than* b *to* a.
> A *Condorcet consistent voting rule* is one that elects a Condorcet winner when it exists.

However, a Condorcet winner does not always exist. A typical example of a preference profile without a Condorcet winner (i.e., where majority comparisons yield a cycle) is the following situation: There are nine voters and three candidates denoted by a, b, and c. Four voters have the ordering $a > b > c$ (a is preferred to b, and b is preferred to c), three have $b > c > a$, and two have $c > a > b$. Thus, in the majority comparisons, a is declared to be preferable to b by vote 6 to 3, b wins over c by vote 7 to 2, and c defeats a by vote 5 to 4.

Two alternative voting rules have been proposed as a way to resolve such situations.

(a) *The Copeland rule.* Compare candidate a with every other candidate x. Score $+1$ if a majority prefers a to x, -1 if a majority prefers x to a, and 0 if it is a tie. Summing up those scores over all x distinct from a yields the Copeland score of a. A candidate with the highest such score, called a *Copeland winner*, is elected.

(b) *The Simpson rule.* Consider candidate a, and for every other candidate x, compute the number $N(a,x)$ of voters preferring a to x. The Simpson score of a is the minimum of $N(a,x)$ over all x distinct from a. A candidate with the highest such score, called a *Simpson winner*, is elected.

Both these rules are Condorcet consistent. A Condorcet winner uniquely achieves the highest Copeland score $p - 1$, where p denotes the number of candidates and a Simpson score above $n/2$, where n is the number of voters. The Copeland and Simpson rules always produce subsets of winners (each may contain several tied candidates), even for preference profiles without Condorcet winners. For the particular preference profile of the above example, all candidates are Copeland winners with scores 0. On the other hand, the Simpson scores of a, b, and c are 4, 3, and 2, respectively; hence a is the winning candidate.

The Condorcet voting rule is simple and intuitively appealing whenever a Condorcet winner exists. When it does not, additional and less straightforward conditions must be imposed in order to define a winner. Thus, to win with a Copeland rule a candidate must defeat, even by a tiny margin, as many other candidates in pairwise majority voting as possible; while with the Simpson rule, he wins if no other candidate rallies a large majority against him.

Definition 2 (Borda Rule).
Each voter reports his preferences by ranking the p candidates from top to bottom (ties are not allowed). A candidate receives no points for being ranked last, one point for being ranked next to last, and so on, up to $p - 1$ points for being ranked first. The candidate with the highest total score, called a *Borda winner*, wins.

Candidates a, b, and c in the example presented above have Borda scores 10, 10, and 7, respectively, therefore a and b are Borda winners.

The Borda rule is slightly more complicated than the Condorcet method, but it takes into account the additional factor of each candidate ranking in the voters' opinions. To consider which method is preferable for decision making in land-use planning we need to review their properties in more detail.

3B. Fundamental Properties of Voting Rules

Practical voting rules are generally expected to have the following three basic properties.

- *Pareto optimality.* If candidate *a* is unanimously preferred to candidate *b*, then *b* should not be elected.
- *Anonymity.* Voters' names do not matter: If two voters exchange their votes, the outcome of the election is not affected.
- *Neutrality.* Candidates' names do not matter: If candidates *a* and *b* are exchanged in the ordering of every voter, then in the results of the elections *a* is to be substituted for *b* and vice versa.

All voting rules discussed in the previous section are Pareto optimal, anonymous, and neutral. However, because any of these rules can produce more than one winner, anonymity or neutrality may have to be occasionally violated in order to break ties among candidates. In the land-use planning problem considered here, the Forest Service may be the agent whose name does matter (violation of anonymity) and who, in situations when voting produces more than one winner, uses their special position to select from among them the one that it prefers.

Other criteria frequently used to evaluate voting rules include:

- *Monotonicity.* If *a* wins the elections under a given preference profile, then he or she will remain a winner under any other profile obtained from the original one by improving *a*'s ranking in voters' opinion without affecting relative rankings of all other candidates.
- *Reinforcement.* Suppose that two disjoint groups of voters face the same list of candidates and both elect *a*. Then, if these two groups vote together, they should still elect *a*.
- *Participation.* Suppose that a group of voters elect *a*. If this group is augmented by one additional voter, then the new electorate should elect *a* or a candidate that the new voter strictly prefers to *a*.

All voting rules of the previous section are monotonic while the Borda scoring method satisfies reinforcement and participation as well. The case of Condorcet consistent rules is more complicated. There is no Condorcet consistent voting rule that satisfies reinforcement or, when the number of candidates exceeds four, participation across all possible voters' preference profiles. This difficulty disappears, however, if the voting is restricted to profiles that produce Condorcet winners.

There are two other voting-related issues that need to be considered, namely a possibility that voters can benefit by misrepresenting their preferences (instead of voting for his favorite candidate a, a voter supports his second choice b whom he prefers to c, recognizing that a has no chance of winning) and that the election outcome can be manipulated by coalitions of voters.

- *Strategy-proofness.* A voting rule is *strategy-proof* if each individual voter maximizes his utility by truthfully reporting his opinion.
- *Core Stability.* A voting rule is *core-stable* if no winning coalition can find a voting strategy that would increase the utility of each coalition member. A *winning coalition* is a set of voters that can force election of any candidate a no matter how the remaining part of the electorate votes.

The Gibbard-Satterthwaite theorem states that for three or more candidates the only strategy-proof voting rules are dictatorial; that is, for every nondictatorial voting rule there exists a preference profile at which some agent may benefit by not reporting truthfully his preferences. On the other hand, non-dictatorial strategy-proof voting rules may exist for some restricted domains of preferences.

Theorem 1 (Moulin, 1988)
Consider an electorate with an odd number of voters and a restricted domain of preferences where each preference profile produces a Condorcet winner. Then the voting rule associating with each such profile its Condorcet winner is strategy-proof. Furthermore, it is coalitional strategy-proof, that is, no coalition of voters can jointly misrepresent its preferences and make every coalition member better off.

There is an interesting family of preference profiles that always produce Condorcet winners. These are the so-called *single-peaked preferences*.

Definition 3.
Suppose that A, the set of outcomes (candidates), can be ordered as $a_1 < a_2 < \ldots < a_p$. Then the preference u on A is *single-peaked* if there is an outcome a^*, called the peak of u, such that u is strictly increasing before a^* and strictly decreasing after it:

if $a < b < = a^*$, then $u(a) < u(b)$

if $a^* < = a < b$, then $u(a) > u(b)$.

Theorem 2 (Moulin, 1988)
If the number of voters is odd and the domain of preferences is restricted to single-peaked preferences, there is a unique Condorcet winner at any such profile (it is the median peak of the individual preferences).

Remark 1. In the land-use planning application, the outcomes can be ordered according to the degree of their negative environmental impact. The case of all agents having single-peaked preferences should be common in such situations.

Remark 2. The assumption about the number of agents being odd is not really restrictive because the Forest Service can always be given an additional (tie-breaking) vote.

Voting by pairwise majority comparisons is core-stable as long as the domain of preferences is restricted to those producing Condorcet winners, with single-peaked profiles as an important example of such a situation. A winning coalition for a Condorcet consistent rule consists of a strict majority of voters. If a strict Condorcet winner exists, it will be the unique outcome in the core of the voting game. In the absence of Condorcet winners, the core will be empty, making the voting rule core-unstable; that is, some coalitions consisting of at least half of the electorate plus one voter may be in a position to increase the utility of all its members by jointly coordinating to conceal their true preferences.

Winning coalitions for the Borda scoring method must include two thirds of the electorate or more. This can make manipulation of voting outcomes by coalitions more difficult but, in most cases, not impossible (in general, the Borda rule is not core-stable).

The above discussion suggests the following approach to conflict resolution by the Forest Service:

Case 1. If for a given preference profile, there is a unique Condorcet winner (possibly with an extra tie-breaking vote for the Forest Service), select it as the solution.

Case 2. If for a given preference profile, there is no Condorcet winner, but there is a unique Borda winner, select the latter as the solution.

Case 3. Otherwise (no Condorcet winners and several Borda winners), the Forest Service picks its preferred solution from among the tied Borda winners.

The case study presented in the next section will serve to illustrate these points.

4. An Application of Social Choice Theory

The Forest Service is attempting to use ecosystem management as the foundation for the forest plans that are required under NFMA. As part of the land-

se management approach, the Forest Service is developing a decision support
ʲstem of which participatory decision making is an important component
ʲhields et al., 1993). To assist in minimizing the potential for conflict in for-
ʲt planning when there are so many competing uses for the limited resources,
model is developed that defines the voters (players) involved and the choice
ʲternative scenarios for development and preservation.

The model is based upon the information that is provided in the Environ-
ʲental Impact Statement (EIS) required under NEPA. The NEPA process re-
uires that any major action (a forest plan) by a federal agency (the Forest
ʲrvice) be supported by an EIS that documents the environmental impact of
ʲe proposed action. An initial step in this process is "scoping." During the
ʲoping phase the federal agency identifies alternatives to the proposed action
ʲd then evaluates the impact of these alternatives. The identification of the
ʲternatives and individuals or groups that are affected provides the necessary
ʲformation for the first two parts of a group-decision model as defined by
ʲlacKay (1980) that can be used as a decision-making aid to reduce the pos-
ʲbility of conflict.

In accordance with the theory reviewed in the previous section, we need
ʲ define the set of "voters" (i.e., participants or players) in the decision pro-
ʲss, the set of "candidates" (i.e., choice alternatives), and the preference
ʲrofile defined by individual or group preferences of the participants. We
ʲote that some players (besides the Forest Service) may be given more than
ʲne vote to reflect their special position. An example of such a situation may
ʲe the preference given to hardrock mining in the United States by the Gen-
ʲal Mining Law of 1872 compared to other uses of public lands.

Define

$$\mathcal{P} = \{P_1, \ldots, P_n\}$$

ʲ represent the set of n players (voters) and let

$$\nabla = \{A_1, \ldots, A_m\}$$

ʲ the set of alternatives (candidates). Each player reports his or her prefer-
ʲnce by assigning a number from the set $\{1, \ldots, m\}$ to each alternative, with
ʲ corresponding to the favorite alternative, $m - 1$ corresponding to the next
ʲreferred alternative, and so on until the least liked alternative is assigned the
ʲalue 1. Notice that different alternatives have different numbers assigned to
ʲem. Let $\mu^i(A_j)$ denote the score assigned by player i to alternative A_u. We as-
ʲume that in pairwise comparisons between A_j and A_k player i votes for A_j if
ʲnd only if $\mu^i(A_j) > \mu^i(A_k)$. The set of n preference mappings of this type
ʲefines a *preference profile* for the problem.

Next, a case study of oil and gas leasing on Forest Service lands will be evaluated using this method. Dubois, Wyoming, is located near the Shoshone National Forest where a proposal for oil and gas leasing is currently being considered. The town of Dubois is particularly interested in the potential development of leases in the Brooks Lake/Lava Mountain area. This case study will focus on oil and gas leasing in this area, and identify the players and choice alternatives from the information available from the public documents.

Dubois is located in the Wind River Valley, in northwestern Wyoming, an area well known for its populations of game and watchable wildlife. The Shoshone National Forest surrounds the valley on three sides. The Dubois economy has historically been driven by recreation expenditures and commodity production. It has been the contention of many residents that local gains in terms of energy-based jobs and income, and increased tax collections, would not compensate for decreases in recreation-based income or amenity and life-style losses. The oil industry position has been that energy resource development is a legitimate use of public lands and that the area has high potential for an economic discovery. A complete discussion of the issues and economy of the area is available in Shields (1993).

Based upon the available documentation, seven players are identified. The players are:

- P_1: Oil Company that proposed leasing,
- P_2: Environmental Organizations,
- P_3: Local Tourist Industry,
- P_4: Local Timber Industry,
- P_5: Local Retail/Wholesale Merchants,
- P_6: Local Governmental Units, and
- P_7: Federal Government (Forest Service).

Based upon the diversity of the players and their respective preference functions, the opportunity for conflict exists. Using the group-decision model may provide insight into resolving the potential conflicts and achieving the goals of ecosystem management by the Forest Service.

An important component of conflict resolution is to identify the viable options that are available to the players. The institutional process that identifies the options is generally the NEPA framework for preparing an Environmental Assessment and/or Environmental Impact Statement. During the scoring phase of the NEPA process, seven alternatives were identified as applicable to this case study.[1] The seven alternatives are:

- A_1: Lease with standard lease terms only,
- A_2: Lease with standard lease terms plus minimal water quality and wildlife constraints,
- A_3: Lease with standard lease terms plus moderate water quality, wildlife, and recreation constraints,
- A_4: Lease with primary emphasis on wildlife protection and according to Forest Plan direction to protect soil, water, and recreation,
- A_5: Lease according to Forest Plan direction with additional emphasis on protecting wildlife and recreation,
- A_6: Minimize risk of impacts to all wildlife, soil and water, visual, and
- A_7: Do not lease administratively available land.

hese seven alternatives are listed from least environmentally restrictive (A_1)) most environmentally restrictive (A_7). An ordinal preference profile for the roblem is defined in Table 1. Clearly, the Oil Company (P_1) prefers the least nvironmentally restrictive alternative (A_1) to all others, the Environmental)rganizations (P_2) have a reverse preference ordering, and the preferences of ie remaining players lie somewhere between these two.

Applying Definition 3 to the preference ordering in Table 1, it is clear that ll preferences are single-peaked, and the ordered (according to environmen-al damage) list of peaks is A_1, A_2, A_3, A_4, A_6, A_6, A_7 (for P_1, P_4, P_7, P_5, P_3, P_6, nd P_2, respectively). Applying Theorem 2, the Condorcet winner is given by ie median of this list, which is Alternative A_4. Based upon Definition 2, Al-ernative A_4 is also the Borda winner with the score 26 (see Table 2). The re-ulting solution is strategy-proof and coalitional strategy-proof based upon heorem 1.

The finding that A_4 is both the Condorcet and Borda winner is not always ie case. This result is dependent on the voting weights and the complexity of ie preference function. This example used a straightforward ordinal prefer-nce function resulting in single-peaked preferences. More complex cardinal

ABLE 1.   Preference Orderings

	A_1	A_2	A_3	A_4	A_5	A_6	A_7
	7	6	5	4	3	2	1
2	1	2	3	4	5	6	7
3	1	2	3	5	6	7	4
4	6	7	5	4	3	2	1
5	1	2	6	7	5	4	3
6	1	2	3	4	6	7	5
7	3	6	7	5	4	2	1

preference functions could be used that would result in different and possible multiple solutions to the group-decision problem.

5. Conclusions

Ecosystem management attempts to acknowledge and incorporate individual (or group) responses to planning alternatives into the decision process. Although the land management agency is usually the ultimate decision maker regarding the specific land-use alternative, it is no longer able to make decisions in an autocratic manner. As previously noted, the NEPA process requires the involvement of other stakeholder groups (e.g., the voters). Their input may not be binding on the agency; however, it is important in the consensus-building process necessary for successful implementation of land-use decisions.

An application of social choice theory to group decisions was examined in this paper. The problem of choosing a forest plan alternative has been presented as a group-decision problem comprising four parts: voters, alternatives, preferences, and aggregation. Preferences of various interest groups or stakeholders over a set of forest plan alternatives for an oil and gas lease were aggregated using Condorcet and Borda voting models. It was demonstrated that if certain rules hold, consensus may be possible—in the case discussed here, "leasing with primary emphasis on wildlife." The solution is strategy and coalitional strategy-proof, implying that behaviors intended to influence the outcome, such as vote trading, would be unsuccessful.

One benefit of voting models to the decision-making process may be in helping participants understand the implications of and difficulties associated with attempting to aggregate their individual or group preferences to reach consensus. However, theoretical and applied problems remain. Further research focusing on whether the forest plan alternatives from which individuals are asked to choose actually reflect the values upon which their preferences are based. Differential levels of knowledge may also affect outcomes.

TABLE 2. Borda Scores

A_4: $3 + 3 + 4 + 3 + 6 + 3 + 4 = 26$
A_3: $4 + 2 + 2 + 4 + 5 + 2 + 6 = 25$
A_5: $2 + 4 + 5 + 2 + 4 + 5 + 3 = 25$
A_6: $1 + 5 + 6 + 1 + 3 + 6 + 1 = 23$
A_2: $5 + 1 + 1 + 6 + 1 + 1 + 5 = 20$
A_7: $0 + 6 + 3 + 0 + 2 + 4 + 0 = 15$
A_1: $6 + 0 + 0 + 5 + 0 + 0 + 2 = 13$

NOTE

1. Two of the alternatives considered in the EIS that were not considered in this model were the do-nothing option and the preferred alternative. These were omitted due to the belief that some action was going to occur and that the preferred option was a combination of other positions that was determined after scoping and the EIS were completed.

REFERENCES

Blackorby, C., and Donaldson, D. (1994) Information and Intergroup Transfers, *American Economic Review* 87(2):440–447.

Boadway, R.M., and Bruce, N. (1984) *Welfare Economics.* Oxford: Blackwell Publisher Ltd.

Bolle, A.W. (1987) Foreword. In *Land and Resource Planning in the National Forests.* (C. Wilkinson, H.M. Anderson, Eds.). Washington, DC: Island Press, pp 1–6.

Brown, G., and Harris, C.C. (1992) The United States Forest Service: Changing of the Guard, *Natural Resources Journal* 32:449–466.

Chichilnisky, G. (1994) Social Diversity, Arbitrage, and Gains from Trade: A Unified Perspective on Resource Allocation, *American Economic Review* 84(2):427–434.

Friedman, M. (1962) *Price Theory: A Provisional Text.* Chicago: Aldine.

Fudenberg, D., and Tirole, J. (1991) *Game Theory.* Cambridge, MA: The MIT Press.

Gorman, W.M. (1953) Community Preference Fields, *Econometrica* 21:63–80.

Keiter, R.B. (1990) NEPA and the Emerging Concept of Ecosystem Management on the Public Lands, *Land and Water Law Review* 25(1):43–60.

Kennedy, J.J. (1991) Integrating Gender Diverse and Interdisciplinary Professionals into the Traditional U.S. Department of Agriculture–Forest Service Culture, *Society and Natural Resources* 4(4):165–176.

Kennedy, J.J., and Quigley, T.M. (1994) Evolution of Forest Service Organizational Culture and Adaptation Issues in Embracing Ecosystem Management. In *Ecosystem Management: Principles and Applications.* Vol. II. (M.E. Jensen, P.S. Bourgeron, Eds.). U.S.D.A. Forest Service, Pacific Northwest Research Station. General Technical Report PNW-GTR-318, pp 16–26.

Kirman, A.P. (1992) Whom or What Does the Representative Individual Represent, *Journal of Economic Perspectives* 6(2):117–136.

Klamer, A. (1989) A Conversation With Amartya Sen, *Journal of Economic Perspectives* 3(1):135–150.

Kreps, D.M. (1990) *A Course in Microeconomic Theory.* Princeton, NJ: Princeton University Press.

Laffond, G., Laslier, J.F., and Le Breton, M. (1994) Social-Choice Mediators, *American Economic Review* 84(2):448–453.

Laitos, J.G. (1991) Paralysis by Analysis in the Forest Service Oil and Gas Leasing Program, *Land and Water Law Review* 26.

Lyden, F.J., Twight, B.W., and Tuchmann, E.T. (1990) Citizen Participation in Long-Range Planning: The RPA Experience, *Natural Resources Journal* 30:123–138.

MacKay, A.F. (1980) *Arrow's Theorem: The Paradox of Social Choice*. New Haven, CT: Yale University Press.

Martin, W.E., and Tolwinski, B. (1993) A Group Decision Analysis of U.S. Forest Service Ecosystem Planning, *Proceedings: International Symposium on the Application of Computers and Operations Research in the Mineral Industries* (Jorgen Elbrond and Xiaoli Tang, Eds.). Montreal, Canada.

Moulin, H. (1988) *Axioms of Cooperative Decision Making*. Cambridge, England: Cambridge University Press.

Sen, A. (1977) Social Choice Theory: A Re-examination, *Econometrica* 45:53–89.

Sen, A. (1985) *Commodities and Capabilities*. Amsterdam: North-Holland.

Sen, A. (1987) The Standard of Living: Lecture I, Concepts and Critiques. In *The Standard of Living*. (G. Hawthorne, Ed.). Cambridge: Cambridge University Press, pp. 1–19.

Shields, D.J. (1993) Allocation of Costs and Benefits from Crude Oil Production on National Forests: The Effects of Accounting Stance. Working paper. U.S.D.A., Forest Service, Rocky Mountain Forest and Range Experiment Station. Ft. Collins, Colorado.

Shields, D.J., Kent, B.M., Alward, G., and Gonzales-Vicente, C. (1993) Modelling Joint Rural Economy-Ecosystem Sustainability. In *Proceedings of the XXIV International Symposium on the Application of Computers and Operations Research in the Minerals Industry*. (J. Elbrond, and Xiaoli Tang, Eds.). Canadian Institute of Mining, Metallurgy and Petroleum, Montreal, pp. 54–63.

Stoker, T.M. (1993) Empirical Approaches to the Problem of Aggregation over Individuals, *Journal of Economic Literature* 31(4):1827–1874.

U.S.D.A. Forest Service (1992) Leasing for Oil and Gas Exploration and Development on the Shoshone National Forest. Final Environmental Impact Statement, December.

Varian, H. (1984) *Microeconomic Analysis*. New York: Norton.

Wilkinson, C.F. (1992) *The Eagle Bird: Mapping a New West*. New York: Vintage Books.

Suggested Additional Readings

Brams, Steven J., and Peter Fishburn. *Approval Voting*. Boston: Birkhauser, 1983.

Brams, Steven J., and Jack H. Nagel. "Approval Voting in Practice." *Public Choice* 71 (1991): 1–17.

Cox, Gary W. *Making Votes Count*. Cambridge: Cambridge University Press, 1997.

Dummett, Michael A. E. *Voting Procedures*. Oxford: Oxford University Press, 1984.

Heckelman, Jac C. "Probabilistic Borda Rule Voting." *Social Choice and Welfare* 21(2003): 455–68.

Joslyn, Richard A. "The Impact of Decision Rules in Multi-candidate Campaigns: The Case of the 1972 Democratic Presidential Election." *Public Choice* 25 (1976): 1–17.

Merrill, Samuel. "A Comparison of Efficiency of Multicandidate Electoral Systems." *American Journal of Political Science* 28 (1984): 23–48.

Tideman, T. Nicolaus. "The Single Transferable Vote." *Journal of Economic Perspectives* 9 (1995): 27–38.

Tideman, T. Nicolaus, and Gordon Tullock. "A New and Superior Process for Making Social Choices." *Journal of Political Economy* 84 (1976): 1145–59.

Volden, Craig. "Sophisticated Voting in Supermajoritarian Settings." *Journal of Politics* 60 (1998): 149–73.

Weber, Robert J. "Approval Voting." *Journal of Economic Perspectives* 9 (1995): 39–49.

Young, Peyton. "Optimal Voting Rules." *Journal of Economic Perspectives* 9 (1995): 51–64.

Zeckhauser, Richard. "Majority Rules with Lotteries on Alternatives." *Quarterly Journal of Economics* 83 (1969): 696–703.

Advanced Readings

Black, Duncan. "A Partial Justification of the Borda Rule." *Public Choice* 28 (1976): 1–15.

Dummett, Michael. "The Borda Count and Agenda Manipulation." *Social Choice and Welfare* 15 (1998): 289–96.

Mueller, Dennis C. "Voting by Veto." *Journal of Public Economics* 10 (1978): 57–75.

Riker, William H. *Liberalism against Populism.* Chap. 4. Prospect Heights, IL: Waveland Press, 1982.

The Calculus of Voting

As discussed in an earlier section, goods and services that are inexcludable create an incentive not to contribute to the costs of creating the good. Democracy is thought to possess such characteristics. Democracy cannot exist without fair elections (among others things), but the benefits of living in a democracy do not depend upon participating in the elections. Whichever candidate (or referendum) gains the most votes is selected, and the subsequently enacted policies affect the entire society, regardless of how, or even if, one voted. Furthermore, with a large enough base of voters, any individual vote added to or subtracted from the total will be inconsequential to the outcome. The costs of voting, however, such as time and travel, are only borne by those who decide to vote, and these costs do not depend upon the outcome. While the policy outcomes from voting are inexcludable to nonvoters, the costs of voting are privately borne by only those who do vote.

In small groups, such as committee decisions, it is more likely an individual vote can affect the final group decision. In a plurality election, this would occur if the group is otherwise deadlocked among its top two alternatives. Then adding one new person choosing among the top two alternatives will break the tie in that voter's favor. This is true no matter the group size, but in general the likelihood of such a tie occurring is inversely related to the size of the group. The efficacy of voting, then, is the probability of an exactly tied vote. In most mass elections, this probability is roughly equivalent to zero.

Thus, economic theory predicts free riding to be the dominant activity among potential voters.

Voting has received much attention because of this perceived paradox. Rational voters, considering the direct benefits and costs, would conclude the net benefits to participating in an election to be negative. Yet elections continue to occur, and a substantial proportion of eligible voters (although typically less than half) do turn out to vote. Theorists have posited several alternative ways to present the voting decision in order to explain why people do vote. Some are small tweaks on the benefit-cost analysis; others are unrelated. Unfortunately, none are without serious flaw.

For example, some have argued that voters care about the size of their candidate's victory. Although a particular candidate is elected in a plurality election as long as he or she generates more votes than anyone else, whether it is 50 votes more or 50,000 votes more, the degree of influence the particular politician has in affecting policy following the election may depend on the size of the plurality difference. For example, a governor elected by a landslide is thought to have more of a "mandate" from the people and find it easier to push his or her proposed budget through the state houses than one elected by a slim margin. While this is true in the aggregate, an individual voter only controls one of those votes, and a plurality difference of 51 as opposed to 50, or 50,001 compared with 50,000, will not alter the perceived voter support for the candidate. Thus, while it makes economic sense to try to influence a large number of voters, such as by holding a rally, which can alter the election outcome or increase the plurality by a sizable amount, when it comes time to actually vote this same person now directly controls only her single vote, which is not expected to affect the outcome. It is important to keep distinct the single vote an individual controls from the large number of votes a group controls. The group's contribution in total can be important, but individually no one person in the group is likely to be important, and free riding on election day should still be the norm.

Critics of public choice theory have focused on this issue to argue that economic analysis in the political arena is faulty since the prediction of complete free riding in elections does not hold true, even though abstention is prevalent. On the other hand, economic theory properly applied does not make predictions as to whether or not any specific individual will take a particular action, but rather it is concerned with how individuals respond to incentives. A better framework for analysis is to analyze activity at the margin. At the margin, does changing the benefits or costs to voting alter individual behavior? In this case, we would expect more voters to turn out when the costs to voting are lessened, and more to abstain when the costs are raised. By and large, the evidence is consistent with this notion which supports a rational benefit-cost approach to voting.

Unlike private market activities in which individuals are unable to benefit from a product without bearing the costs, voting is thought to be a public good in which the beneficial outcome of an election is not thought to be affected by any one individual. Aldrich's "Rational Choice and Turnout" is a survey article of rational choice voting models that attempt to explain the seeming paradox of why so many people do vote in general elections. Heckelman considers the role of legal institutions affecting the voting incentive and focuses on the transition to secret ballots in "The Effect of the Secret Ballot on Voter Turnout Rates."

Rational Choice and Turnout

John H. Aldrich

Review Questions

1. How does the calculus of voting differ from minimax regret? Why do they predict different actions for potential voters?
2. What change can be made to the calculus of voting to make voting rational? What are the critiques of this approach?
3. What type of evidence is supportive of the calculus framework?
4. Why is minimax regret not a rational way of making decisions?
5. Why might the absolute size of the benefits and costs affect the interpretation of the calculus and minimax regret models?
6. How does the recent decline in turnout for presidential elections relate to these models?

Turning out to vote is the most common and important act citizens take in a democracy and, therefore, is one of the most important behaviors for scholars of democratic politics to understand. And yet, it is not well understood. In rational choice theory, turnout holds a special place, as the most commonly used example of a major theoretical puzzle. So important is this puzzle that some

Aldrich, John H. "Rational Choice and Turnout." *American Journal of Political Science* 37 (1993): 246–78.

see turnout as the major example of the failure of rational choice theory. Here, I shall examine this problem and try to show that a richer choice theoretic accounting of turnout is possible. I hope to show that in solving the turnout problem in rational choice theory, that theory, itself, is enriched. Thus, I think of the problem in using rational choice theory to understand turnout not as a problem but as a challenge. Finally, I hope to show that in seeking to solve the theoretical challenge, we also learn more about electoral politics.

The problem of explaining turnout is not unique to rational choice theory. Earlier we argued (Aldrich and Simon 1986) that, while turnout is one of the most studied of political behaviors, all theoretical accountings of turnout are problematic. Extant theories are strong in finding variables that increase or decrease the likelihood of turning out. They do not, in a fundamental sense, however, tell us about the absolute level of turnout, that is, why some people vote and others do not.

While the empirical problem of understanding turnout is common to all known theories, turnout assumes a special place in rational choice theory. I begin by laying out the fundamentals of rational choice as applied to turnout. I then consider the two most important specific models that have been proposed and consider their problems. Finally, I turn to the challenge of proposing solutions to the theoretical problem.

The Basic Model

As Simon and I noted, virtually all scholars agree with what we called the "fundamental equation" of political behavior, which is that preferences (or attitudes, beliefs, values) determine behavior. Rational choice theory is about just how those preferences determine behavior. I begin with the basic choice model of turnout—"basic" because all rational choice accounts agree on it. This basic model cannot completely solve the decision problem facing the prospective voter. The theorist then faces a choice of how to complete the theory, and I examine alternatives in subsequent sections.

To begin, suppose that two candidates run for office, the only contest on the ballot. Citizens must choose among exactly three actions: vote for one candidate, vote for the other, or abstain from voting.[1] Citizens' preferences are defined over *outcomes*, from which preferences for actions are inferred and, in turn, from which choices of actions are determined.

While refined below, the basic set of possible outcomes is that one candidate or the other wins the election, or they tie. Citizens' *preferences* are transformed into *utilities* for outcomes when it matters how much the citizen prefers one outcome over another. Suppose the individual prefers the first candidate (A) to the second (B).[2] Let one (utile) represent the value of having the preferred candidate win, while that of the other candidate winning is zero.[3] The third outcome is a tie. Conventionally, it is assumed that both candidates are equally likely to win ties (e.g., by a coin toss).[4] If so, the individual receives an expected value of 1/2 utile. In general, *expected utility* is determined by multiplying the probability of an outcome happening by the utility obtained from that outcome and adding similar calculations for all other possible outcomes. Thus, there are three outcomes (A wins, tie, B wins) with their associated utilities for the individual (1, .5, 0).

Rational choice theories are theories about how the (expected) utility associated with outcomes generates or induces preferences for the particular actions at hand. Rational choice takes it as fundamental that the individual prefers outcomes with higher utility to those with lower utility and chooses actions to receive more highly valued outcomes. Actions are the means to obtain desired ends and have value only insofar as they affect outcomes. That is, actions are instruments to achieve outcomes, and this is known as an *instrument* or *"investment"* theory of turnout (Fiorina 1976). The vote is "invested" to achieve desired outcomes.

Clearly, there are *costs of voting*. Presumably, if voters decide to abstain, they do not have to pay these costs; if they vote, they do. These costs include the costs of obtaining information, processing it, and deciding what to do and the direct costs of registering and going to the polls. It is conventional, but false, to say that there are no costs for abstention. This is false, for rational abstainers must "pay" decision-making costs associated with deciding whether they do not, rationally, want to vote in this election. This situation will be considered later. For now, I follow convention and assign costs of voting, C, for choosing to vote, per se, whether that is for A or for B, and zero for abstaining, with $C > 0$. Now all the outcomes in which A wins (B wins, they tie) must be divided into two sets, those in which individuals voted and those in which they abstained. The value of A winning in the first case is $1 - C$, and in the second it is $1 - 0$.

The next step is to associate actions with outcomes systematically, from which it will be possible to assign values to the actions, and then to predict what the rational citizen should do. This is a key step, for elections are *collective actions* in which the outcome depends on actions taken by others as well as the decision maker. Thus, in figuring out what they should do, voters must give some regard to what others are going to do, insofar as possible to judge. Different characterizations of "what regard a voter gives to what others do" yield different rational choice models.

States of the World

Preferred Candidate is

Actions:	(1) Winning by More than One Vote	(2) Winning by Exactly One Vote	(3) Tied	(4) Losing by Exactly One Vote	(5) Losing by More than One Vote
(1) Vote for Preferred Candidate	$1 - C$[a]	$1 - C$	$1 - C$	$\frac{1}{2} - C$	$0 - C$
(2) Vote for Other Candidate	$1 - C$	$\frac{1}{2} - C$	$0 - C$	$0 - C$	$0 - C$
(3) Abstain from Voting	1	1	$\frac{1}{2}$	0	0

[a]Entry is payoff in utiles to decision maker. It is assumed that $0 < C < \frac{1}{2}$, where C is costs of voting. A tie is assumed to be broken by the flip of a fair coin. Utiles are normalized, so that the value of the preferred candidate winning is 1; the value of the opponent winning is 0.

Figure 1. Decision Table for Rational Choice Models of Turnout

Figure 1 presents a *decision table* that ties actions to outcomes. The rows represent the three possible actions open. The columns distinguish among the critical *"states of the world."* A voter should think of these as the outcomes before including his or her vote in the tabulations. There are five important states. The tied outcome is in the middle. The first two columns are cases in which A is winning by more than one vote and by exactly one vote. The last two columns make the same distinction for B. The first and last columns are cases in which the outcome does *not* depend upon what the voter does. The middle three columns represent *all* situations in which the voter's actions affect the outcome, by making or breaking a tie. In these three middle columns, voters are efficacious; in the others, they are not. The problem is that voters do not know the situation they face (i.e., which column is the true state of the world) before having to decide whether to vote or abstain.

The entries in the resulting 15 cells are the values of the outcome, given the state of the world and the action chosen. Thus, if a citizen votes for A (row 1) and the "state of the world" is column 1, the entry is the 1 utile for candidate A winning, less the costs, C, of having voted.

How do we analyze this table? The state of the world is unknown, so we must compare the value of voting for A, for B, or abstaining within each column. Consider column 1, for example. If that is the true state of the world, voters receive $1 - C$ if they vote for A or for B, and they receive 1 if they abstain. In this case, therefore, voters would rather abstain than vote for either candidate.

Notice that the entry in row 2 (vote for B) is either the same as the comparable column entry in row 1, or it is smaller. It is never better to choose row 2 than row 1, and sometimes doing so will make voters worse off. We can eliminate row 2, since row 1 *dominates* row 2. Therefore, we conclude the obvious; if citizens vote, they should vote for their preferred candidate. Never vote for the opponent.[5]

We are left with rows 1 and 3, voting for the preferred candidates or abstaining. In this case, it is sometimes better (columns 1, 2, and 5) to abstain than to vote. Columns 3 and 4 represent the cases in which a vote (for A) makes or breaks a tie. Whether the payoff for voting for A or for abstaining is greater depends on the costs of voting compared to the value of A and of B winning. Voting for A is better than abstaining in either column whenever costs are less than one-half, and abstaining is better when costs are one-half or greater.

If costs are one-half or greater, the voter should always abstain. There are two such situations. In one, costs of voting are high absolutely. Thus, as costs of voting increase, turnout should decline, ceteris paribus. In fact, of course, that is precisely what happens. When registration laws were passed, poll taxes were raised, or residency requirements were enacted, turnout fell. The second is when, holding costs constant, the difference in value between A and B winning declines. As citizens become more indifferent to who wins, even low costs become a larger and larger barrier to voting.[6] This circumstance connects citizens' choices to candidates' strategies. For example, in spatial models, candidate convergence makes all voters indifferent and therefore likely to abstain.[7]

To this point, all varieties of rational choice models yield the same conclusions. Rational choice models differ, then, over what to do if costs are less than one-half. Before turning to these differences, the conclusions of this basic (and thus all further) models are:

1. Never vote for the less preferred candidate;
2. If costs of voting are high (.5 or greater), always abstain;
3. If costs of voting are zero (or even negative—i.e., you get more value from voting, per se, than it costs to vote), then vote for A because voting for A dominates abstaining; and,
4. If $0 < C < .5$, the basic model is silent. Note that it is silent because of the middle columns. Thus, rational choice models of turnout differ over ways to handle these middle cases.

The Calculus of Voting Model

The "calculus of voting" was initially developed by Downs (1957) and extended and tested by Riker and Ordeshook (1968). The hallmark of this model is use of expected utility, assuming that citizens estimate the probability of the various states of the world. These probabilities are used to infer the expected utility associated with following each action. It is a decision-theoretic model.

They also made one other addition to the model that could, in principle, have been added to the basic model. I reserved it for here, however, because this addition is controversial, and some prefer to analyze turnout without it. Downs added a term, D, to represent the value of seeing democracy continue. If no one voted, he argued, the political system would fail. Therefore, he reasoned, some may vote to ensure the continued vitality of democracy. Riker and Ordeshook (1968, 1973) expanded his logic. Calling it "citizen duty," they argued that D represents the value of doing one's duty as a citizen, as well as an array of other values, such as expressing support for the country and the political system. These are called *"expressive"* components to the vote, for the voter receives that value from voting, per se, regardless of the outcome. In Fiorina's (1976) terms, voting on this basis is an act of *"consumption,"* a citizen "consumes" voting for its own sake, rather than voting being an act of investment (see also Crain and Deaton 1977; Hinich 1981). Fiorina added to D such concerns as expressing allegiance to a favored candidate or party.

Adding a D term is the same as subtracting a C term. Thus, C can be thought of as "net costs," that is, as costs of voting, less any positive values, such as doing one's duty. A positive C says that duty only partially outweighs costs of voting, but that net costs are increasingly likely to be less than one-half. Thus, the D term does not change the fundamental analysis, unless $D > C$, in which case it is better to vote for A than to abstain in all circumstances.

The key innovation of the calculus of voting is that each individual assigns a probability of each state of the world being true.[8] What is critical is the probability that one vote will make a difference, that is, that column 3 or 4 is true. Calling the probability that one vote (for A) will make or break a tie, P, and calling the difference in utility for A instead of B winning B (for the difference in "benefits"), Riker and Ordeshook determined the "rewards," or R, for voting as:

$$R = PB + D - C.$$

If R is positive, vote for A; if not, abstain.

An individual sees voting as a collective action, knowing that his or her decision is but one of many to be made in the election. In this model, the "regard given to what others are going to do," as I put it earlier, is captured in the *P* term. It represents an assessment of the probability of each state of the world being true and is often measured by how close the election was or is expected to be.

The probability or casting the deciding vote should be higher, the closer the election is, ceteris paribus. Of course, not all else is equal. For example, the size of the electorate matters, too. Two equally close contests, one for a town's mayor, the other for president, should be expected to have very different *P* terms. A large *P* term, therefore, reflects closeness of the expected vote and size of the electorate. Since this is a subjective estimate, it will vary from person to person.

In sum, the conclusion of the calculus of voting is that probability estimates are used to close the remaining gap in the basic model of turnout. Holding all else constant, the higher the *P* term, the more likely it is that an individual will vote. This model has been tested extensively, and all tests find that the *C, D,* and *B* terms are strong predictors of turnout. Many applications, especially those that use aggregate data, find that the *P* term is a significant predictor (e.g., Barzel and Silberberg 1973; Settle and Abrams 1976; Silberman and Durden 1975). Other tests using survey data (e.g., Ferejohn and Fiorina 1975; Foster 1984) have found it to be unrelated to the vote.[9] I will attempt to resolve this seeming paradox between aggregate and survey findings later. Ferejohn and Fiorina used their results as one reason to consider an alternative rational choice model of turnout.

The Minimax Regret Model

Ferejohn and Fiorina (1974, 1975) reject completing the basic model by assuming that people form probability assessments of the states of the world.[10] They argue that such assessments are difficult in many contexts. People may not form them and perhaps cannot form them in principle. If probabilities cannot be assessed, the calculus of voting cannot be used. Ferejohn and Fiorina propose a second decision-theoretic method of completion by transforming the problem. In place of expected utility maximization, they propose that people use the decision rule called "minimax regret."[11]

Citizens are uncertain about what to do. Suppose they decide to abstain, and their preferred candidate lost by exactly one vote. Presumably, they would greatly regret their decision to abstain. "Minimax regret" is a decision rule that makes this notion of regret precise.

The "regret" question is to ask, "If it turns out that a given state of the world is true, would you have any regret that you chose the action (voted or abstained) that you did, and if so, how much regret?" To measure regret, use the basic decision table (from Figure 1, repeated in Figure 2.A) to find the action within each column that yields the highest utility (see bottom, Figure 2.A). Thus, in column 1, the best action is to have abstained, yielding a return of 1 utile. Abstention also yields the highest payoff if column 2 is true (1 utile) and if column 5 is true (0 utiles). Columns 3 and 4 depend on the magnitude of the costs involved. If $C < 1/2$, the best action was to have voted for A (yielding $1 - C$ under column 3 and $1/2 - C$ under column 4). If $C > 1/2$, abstention would have been the best choice, yielding 1/2 and 0, respectively. Note that, before, $C > 1/2$ meant that abstention yielded the highest expected utility under every state of the world. So, too, does abstention yield the least regret in each column, so here, as before, abstain if $C > 1/2$.

Of course, we must choose without knowing the true state of the world, but we can compute a regret table to parallel the decision table. In Figure 2.B, the calculations are shown, while Figure 2.C contains the full regret table. Consider column 1. The regret from voting for A and finding out later that A was already winning by more than one vote would be 1 (the value if the best act, given that state of the world, had been chosen) minus $(1 - C)$, what you would actually get from voting for A and that being the true state. Thus, you would have C units of regret having voted for A. Obviously, if you choose the best action for that state of the world, you would have no regret. Thus, the larger the entry in the regret table, the worse it is—the greater the regret you would "suffer."

Now consider the act of voting for A. The worst thing that could happen, or the *maximum* regret, is needlessly paying the costs of voting, or C. If you voted for B (and $C < 1/2$), the maximum regret is to have turned the election from a tie to a one-vote win for B, yielding a regret of 1. The maximum regret for abstaining is to find out that your vote for A would have made A either tie with B or would have broken a tie, causing A to win. Finally, *minimax regret* refers to taking the action that yields the minimum of these maximum regrets. The maximum regret for voting for B is 1 (as listed at the end of Figure 2.C), which is larger than that for either other action. The maximum regret for voting for A is C (obtained if state of the world 1, 2, or 5 occurs). The maximum regret for abstaining is $1/2 - C$ (obtained if state of the world 3 or 4 occurs). The minimax regret decision rule says pick whichever of these two is smaller. That is, vote for A if C is smaller than $1/2 - C$. Thus, by the minimax regret rule, a person should vote (for A) if $C < 1/4$. Otherwise, it is better to abstain.

States of the World

Preferred Candidate is

Actions:	(1) Winning by More than One Vote	(2) Winning by Exactly One Vote	(3) Tied	(4) Losing by Exactly One Vote	(5) Losing by More than One Vote
(1) Vote for Preferred Candidate	$1-C$	$1-C$	$1-C$	$\frac{1}{2}-C$	$0-C$
(2) Vote for Other Candidate	$1-C$	$\frac{1}{2}-C$	$0-C$	$0-C$	$0-C$
(3) Abstain from Voting	1	1	$\frac{1}{2}$	0	0
Highest Payoff in Column	1	1	$1-C$ if $C<\frac{1}{2}$; $\frac{1}{2}$ if $C\geq\frac{1}{2}$	$\frac{1}{2}-C$ if $C<\frac{1}{2}$; 0 if $C\geq\frac{1}{2}$	0

B. Calculation of Table of Regrets, when $C < \frac{1}{2}$

	(1)	(2)	(3)	(4)	(5)
(1) Vote for Preferred Candidate	$1-(1-C)$	$1-(1-C)$	$(1-C)-(1-C)$	$(\frac{1}{2}-C)-(\frac{1}{2}-C)$	$0-(0-C)$
(2) Vote for Other Candidate	$1-(1-C)$	$1-(\frac{1}{2}-C)$	$(1-C)-(0-C)$	$(\frac{1}{2}-C)-(0-C)$	$0-(0-C)$
(3) Abstain from Voting	$1-1$	$1-1$	$(1-C)-(\frac{1}{2})$	$(\frac{1}{2}-C)-0$	$0-0$

C. Table of Regrets, when $C < \frac{1}{2}$, and Calculation of Maximum Regret for Each Action

	(1)	(2)	(3)	(4)	(5)	Maximum Regret
(1) Vote for Preferred Candidate	C	C	0	0	C	C
(2) Vote for Other Candidate	C	$\frac{1}{2}+C$	1	$\frac{1}{2}$	C	1
(3) Abstain from Voting	0	0	$\frac{1}{2}-C$	$\frac{1}{2}-C$	0	$\frac{1}{2}-C$

D. Calculation of Minimax Regret
(a) $1 > C$; $1 > \frac{1}{2} - C$; therefore row 2 is never the minimum of max regret
(b) $C > (\frac{1}{2} - C)$, if $C < \frac{1}{4}$, vote for preferred candidate
(c) if $C > \frac{1}{4}$, abstain

Figure 2. Construction of Minimax Regret Formulation of the Turnout Decision

This rule provides a complete specification of the decision-making problem, just as does the calculus of voting. Both yield the same results as the basic model; never vote for B, abstain if costs are prohibitively high ($C > 1/2$), and so forth. The two models differ over how to handle the middle columns.

Ferejohn and Fiorina (1974) argue that their model predicts turnout more often (i.e., for more people in more circumstances) than the calculus of voting. To see this, the minimax regret rule is to vote (for A) if $C < B/4$. By some rearrangements, they show that the calculus of voting rule is to turn out if $C < PB/2$. Minimax regret will yield voting more often when $B/4 > PB/2$, or, with a little algebra, when $[(B)(B/2)] > P$. Since $B = 1$, this reduces to $1/2 > P$. Thus, minimax regret leads to turnout more often whenever the probability of casting the tie-making or tie-breaking vote is less than one-half. Their argument, then, is that P, if it could be formed, is (almost) always smaller than that, so minimax regret predicts turnout for more people more often than does the calculus of voting. To see the full impact of this account, however, we must examine some of the problems found with these models. First, I briefly examine a third approach.

Game-Theoretic Accounts

The above are models based on decision theory, assuming the "regard given to others' decisions" is nonstrategic. That is, the decisions of others are, at most, highly aggregated (into estimates of P), and no one decision is assumed to affect the decisions of others. Game-theoretic models assume that decisions are based on taking others' decisions into explicit account. For instance, voters might reason that everyone will conclude that P is effectively zero, and no one will vote. Then, one vote will be decisive, breaking a 0–0 tie. But if that is true for one, it is true for all, so all will conclude it is rational to vote, leading to a large turnout. But then each concludes that his or her vote is indecisive, and on and on. Ledyard (1984) and Palfrey and Rosenthal (1985) examine such models, searching for game-theoretic equilibria to resolve strategic interaction. Often there are multiple equilibria, but the latter authors show that uncertainty about costs and others' preferences typically yield relatively low subjective estimates of P, and thus a low turnout rate, in equilibrium, in large electorates. These game-theoretic models clearly add more to our understanding of relatively small electorates. I argue elsewhere (1992) that the game-theoretic problem converges to a dominant choice similar to the calculus of voting results as the size of the electorate increases. Generally, true strategic interaction becomes attenuated as the size of the electorate increases, thus making game-theoretic solutions similar to the decision rule derived from the calculus of voting. As a result, it is reasonable to say that any problems associated with the calculus of voting are found as well, at least approximately, in game-theoretic models.

Problems with the Calculus of Voting

There are two important and commonly cited problems with the calculus of voting. The first problem is the D term. Whether or not the D term is considered relevant is not unique to the calculus of voting, although Ferejohn and Fiorina (1975) chose not to include it in their minimax regret model (to see it with a D term, see Aldrich 1976). Riker and Ordeshook's (1968) tests yielded support for all variables in the calculus. However, Barry (1970) pointed out that the strongest relationship appears to be due to the D term.[12] This, of course, is not a problem by itself.

Barry (1970) argues that the theoretical problem is that, if all the "action" is in the D term, turnout is not usefully understood by rational choice theory. To be sure, voting due to a high D term is perfectly rational. The answer to why someone voted, however, is simply that they valued voting on its own. If so, turnout is, effectively, noninstrumental. Moreover, if the answer to the question, "Why did you vote?" is that "I voted because I wanted to," then it moves the theoretically important question back one step to, "Why did you want to vote?" As Barry puts it, it makes turnout a "matter of taste," even though "taste" may mean "deeply held values." And rational choice models are not models of "where tastes come from," but how one acts, given tastes. Thus, theoretically, if turnout is due to the D term, rational choice models add nothing to the explanation of how preferences shape actions.

The more theoretically consequential problem concerns the P term. Simply put, in any large electorate, there is no reasonable basis for asserting that your vote will make or break a tie. Even in close elections, $PB/2$ will be very small and not outweigh even low costs of voting, unless $B/2$ is incredibly large. Those who take this position argue that the inevitable conclusion of the calculus of voting is that no one who has any plausible estimate of P should vote in a large electorate.

There is a sort of double whammy. The PB term should be *very* small, and P is the weakest, empirically, of all terms in the calculus. Empirically, the problematic D term is strong. Both BP and D point toward turnout as consumption. Therefore, an instrumental model of turnout yields, theoretically and empirically, a noninstrumental explanation of voting (but see Hinich 1981).

The empirical results of estimating the calculus of voting present something of a second paradox. Those who use aggregate data almost invariably find that electoral closeness is strongly related to the turnout rate (see sources cited above). Survey research finds it much less strongly related to the vote, if related at all. Of course, that may simply be because there is variation in the true closeness of elections over time or in different constituencies, thus showing up in aggregate measures, but no difference within a given election, thus showing up as random error in response to P-like questions on surveys.[13]

Problems with the Minimax Regret Model

There are also two theoretical problems with the minimax regret model. One concerns the P term. This may seem an odd assertion, since the whole purpose of turning to it was to develop a rational choice model in which there is no probability term at all. But refer to the regret table. If only the first and last columns are considered, abstention dominates voting. Thus, the only time there would be any regret from failing to vote is when it would make or break a tie. It may be that people do not, perhaps cannot, estimate probabilities, and they may reason by minimax regret logic. And it is theoretically consistent to say that individuals cannot say that these three columns have zero probabilities. If they do not estimate probabilities, there may be no way for such individuals to say column 1 (or 5) is more likely to be true than column 3. Such a statement is a probabilistic statement and is therefore inadmissible. Yet it seems clear that people may well have said, "Sure, it is more likely that Bush is ahead by at least one vote than it is that he is tied with Dukakis." They may say so without any coherent set of probabilities in mind, or using them in their decisions if formed. Perhaps there is a middle ground.

The question is not what specific probabilities people assign. The question is do people believe that there is *any* chance of an election being decided by exactly one vote, and can they do so without calculating (or using) probability terms systematically? Put alternatively, scholars have tried to make calculations of the probability of an exact tie in a very large electorate, but they do not need to know how small P is to believe that it is very, very small. You do not have to be able to say how close the election will be to believe that there is no chance that it will be decided by a single vote.

The second problem is also related to probabilities. The calculus of voting applied to multicandidate or multiparty elections predicts that some may well (rationally) choose to vote for a second-ranked party or candidate, rather than their first choice, to avoid "wasting" their vote on someone who has no chance of winning.[14] Ferejohn and Fiorinia (1974) show that the minimax regret model predicts that *all* voters will vote for their first choice. There is *no* wasted voting logic consistent with their model. Avoiding wasting a vote in the calculus of voting is dependent on P terms of the same form as a two-candidate case (i.e., on probabilities of ties or one-vote margins). One clear test between these two models is to examine multialternative contests to see whether voting occurs for candidates other than the first choice. It turns out that there is consistent evidence of the wasted-vote account in multiparty systems (Black 1978; Cain 1978), in voting in U.S. presidential primaries (Abramson et al. 1992), and perhaps in the three-candidate presidential contests (see below).

It would be an odd theory that applied to two-candidate contests only and failed in multicandidate races—especially if that means that it applies to some presidential races, but not others. We would need a theory about why the P term appears to be ignored in the first case and employed in the second, or why people *cannot* calculate probabilities in the first case, but magically can in the second. It is even more surprising because there is a lot of information about the expected closeness of two-candidate presidential elections, and it is relatively easy to process that information, while probability assessments are not as easy to assess in complicated multicandidate races, and when U.S. voters so rarely confront them. All this would point toward P terms being more likely to be employed in the first case and not in the second, just the opposite of the empirical findings.

It does not follow that the evidence that people do avoid wasting votes "saves" the calculus of voting. In fact, if the logic is compelling that the P term in a two-candidate contest should be considered effectively zero, then the logic is just as compelling that there is no chance that one vote will make or break a tie involving the voter's second-choice candidate. If a vote is "wasted" in the first case (i.e., a voter wastes the costs of voting by turning out), that vote will be just as wasted in multicandidate contests, no matter whom is supported. In 1980 Jimmy Carter argued that "a vote for John Anderson is a vote for Ronald Reagan" (i.e., that voting for the independent candidate instead of Carter was a wasted vote, since Anderson had no chance to win, while Carter [whom most Anderson supporters preferred to Reagan] could defeat the Republican nominee). In fact, a vote for Carter (or for Reagan) was just as wasted, since it had no chance of making or breaking a tie.[15]

The appearance of wasted voting, therefore, undermines the plausibility of the minimax regret formulation, since it is developed from expectational logic. The irony is that evidence for it does not strengthen the plausibility of the calculus of voting, if the arguments about the P term are credible, even if it undermines the universal applicability of minimax regret. The key question, therefore, is how to construct a model of turnout that is both theoretically tenable within a rational choice perspective and that conforms to basic empirical facts known about turnout.

The Rationality of Turnout

In this section, I suggest that turnout is not a particularly good example of the problem of collective action. The main reason is that turnout is, for many people most of the time, a low-cost, low-benefit action. Turnout is a decision almost always made "at the margin." Small changes in costs and benefits alter the turnout decision for many citizens. This argument applies to the basic model and thus all further formulations.

First, the models rest on the assumption that there is only one contest, whereas U.S. ballots are typically cluttered with numerous contests. It is not clear how to model turnout in such cases. One possibility is to assume that someone will turn out if R is positive (or $B > 1/4$) in any *one* contest. It does not follow that this person would therefore vote for all contests, but it does follow that this person will stand in the voting booth. Alternatively, the voter may be assumed to calculate a summary value for voting in all contests and will vote if the summary value is high enough, even if this is not true for any one contest considered in isolation. Whatever the case, the incidence of voting should be higher, and certainly no lower, in multiple, simultaneous elections than in separate ones. The result is that there will be "economies of scale" for voting in several contests at the same time, and the voter will need to associate lower (expected) benefits to find it worthwhile to vote in any one contest.[16]

Niemi (1976) argued that costs of voting are ordinarily low for most people, most of the time. With liberalization of registration laws, it is no longer as difficult or time-consuming to become registered. It does not take *that* long to vote, and for most people polling places are not *that* far away. To be sure, the United States differs from many democracies by requiring the individual to be responsible for becoming registered, and it does not go as far as other nations in making voting as convenient as possible. Still, the costs of registration and voting are relatively low and getting lower, which combines with the presence of multiple, simultaneous contests that reduce costs per contest.[17] Decision costs remain. As noted earlier, if one really believes in a rational choice model of turnout, some of these must be paid to decide that it is rational to abstain. Hence, the difference in decision costs between voting and abstaining is not as high as it appears in the various models.

Downs (1957) pointed out that many people come to the vote decision with "accidental" (or incidental) information. Simply in the course of ordinary life, most people pick up at least some information about at least some election campaigns, and as such these are not included in the C term. How much information a person acquires incidentally will vary from person to person and from election to election. Presidential contests are so heavily covered in the media that it is hard to avoid incidental information, perhaps in large quantities. At the other extreme are contests for which very little information is available even if purposefully sought (e.g., for nonpartisan contests to elect boards of trustees for state universities). Political scientists have studied turnout almost exclusively in high profile contests, in which case information acquisition (if not processing) costs can safely be considered small.[18] Of course, some people are exposed to more incidental information than others. Predictably, such people are, in fact, much more likely to vote, for decision-making costs are lower.

It is still necessary to process such information to decide which candidate is preferred and by how much. It is hard to say how costly such a process is. Virtually everyone will tell pollsters who they would like to see elected president (and forecast the outcome, see Lewis-Beck and Skalaban 1989), and this is true very early in the campaign, which suggests that, at least for important cases, decision-making costs are not particularly high.[19] Moreover, contests are partisan, and with the party affiliation of the candidates clearly labeled on the ballot, acquisition of this bit of information is very cheap. Even in an era of partisan dealignment, most citizens report at least some partisan leanings. V. O. Key, Jr. (1966), referred to party identification as a "standing decision." By this he meant that partisans would reason that they initially favor their parties' candidates, until and unless given good reason not to. Indeed, the very reason that they are partisans must be that, for most candidates, most of the time, they favor them over the opposition. Thus, an initial decision could be reached very easily and cheaply. While new information might give reasons to change that initial decision, preferences will exist before, as after, receiving that information. If anything, recent studies have analyzed new informational short cuts (such as voting retrospectively or for the incumbent in congressional elections) that also reduce decision-making costs.

If costs are, indeed, low, (expected) benefits are also low. Even in the minimax regret formulation, it is not at all clear that people perceive much difference about who wins most elections. This may be least true for president. But even there, it is not at all clear that having Dukakis as president would make my life, nor even the country's, all that different from having Bush as president. It is far less clear that it makes a great deal of difference who represents my district in Congress. After all, he or she is but one out of 435 to begin with, and it is not that obvious that having a Republican Senate from 1981 to 1987 made much difference from having it a Democratic Senate before or since then. There is some difference, to be sure, but not that much.

This is just as it should be. About half the electorate voted in 1988.[20] The decline in turnout from 1960 to 1988 has occasioned much concern, even alarm, but that massive decline is of about 13 percentage points. Low benefits to voting match well with low costs. For most people, I submit, turnout is a marginal decision. Change the costs of voting only slightly and turnout changes. As the level of partisanship has declined, so has the decline in turnout.[21] Modest changes in the costs or benefits of voting breed modest changes in aggregate levels of turnout.

Politicians know this. Registration and get-out-the-vote drives work. A national effort for registration or turnout is quite expensive, but the costs spent on any individual are low. A small expenditure per capita can increase turnout. Take registration forms door to door. Offer rides to the polls or an hour's worth of child care. These tactics work, and the cost of creating this new voter is quite low—$5 or $10 or less, which is sufficient to outweigh the costs of voting. The implications of "politicians knowing this" will be considered soon. First, however, there are some important consequences that flow directly from voting being a low-cost, low-benefit decision.

Some Initial Consequences of Low-Cost, Low-Benefit Choice

If turnout is a low-cost, low-benefit decision-making problem, small changes in costs and benefits can make a significant difference.[22] I believe that this explains four of the most important characteristics of the empirical literature on turnout.

1. Many variables are related to turnout; they are related to turnout consistently in study after study, election after election, but they are often moderately or weakly related to turnout.
2. Since turnout is, however, a close call for the typical citizen, we still do not know why the absolute level of turnout is what it is; we do not know, fundamentally, why some people vote and others do not. It may be a chimera to believe that we could assess all of the small bits of benefits and costs involved in the turnout decision. Therefore, it may be a chimera to expect to have a complete answer to "Who votes?" precisely because it is a low-cost, low-benefit decision.

3. Citizens may make many "errors" in these decisions, since it is not worth much effort to decide whether R really is positive (or B is greater than 1/4). In the aggregate, these "errors" might cancel out, but individual decisions will be consistent with these theoretical principles only probabilistically and not with the certainty implied by the theoretical equations.

4. Measurement error should also loom large in model estimation, attenuating estimates.

These all point to a major general conclusion. Low-cost, low-benefit actions are consistent with the empirical findings, in which there is weaker performance of turnout models than comparable models of other forms of participation or of candidate choice. There are more "errors" made by decision makers in low versus high cost-benefit contexts; measurement error will be more consequential; and a large range of variables that contribute small amounts of costs or of benefits and that are generally impossible to measure completely will have a greater impact on decisions.[23]

Like implication 4, implication 5 concerns social science rather than actual citizens' decisions. The fifth point, however, is an important theoretical issue.

5. Turnout is seen as a very central problem in rational choice theory because it is seen as the major and archetypical example of the problem of collective action. The turnout decision is an example of a collective action problem, but it is not a very good, nor even terribly problematic, example of it. The problem of collective action is, in large part, that people who share the same values for collective choices may find it difficult to attain and maintain the ability to act on those shared interests, precisely because there is little individual efficacy in action. While turnout is a collective action problem, it is not a good illustration because it differs from almost all other important collective action problems in a crucial regard. Collective action problems typically assume importance because they are high-cost, high (potential) benefit decisions, where small P terms mean that the high B terms are substantially discounted. Turnout is a low-cost, low-benefit decision and sheds little light on most important collective action problems.

6. I suspect that the low-cost, low-benefit nature of the turnout decision really means that most of the action is, in fact, in the intrinsic values of voting per se (i.e., in C and D terms). After all, these apply directly to the voter, regardless.

The problem at this point is to see whether there is an explanation of (nearly) expressive or consumptive voting that fits with the undeniably political and strategic nature of election campaigns. The problem is, if voting is primarily an expression of personal values, then there is little political or strategic content to the decision. Can it really be that voting is noninstrumental and nonstrategic, especially in this most strategic of political contexts? There is, I believe, a resolution to the conundrum.

Strategic Politicians and Rational Turnout

The actions of strategic politicians explain why turnout is higher in close elections, even if people ignore P terms in their own decisions. It is these actions that also explain why there is behavior consistent with the wasted-voting thesis, whether or not citizens weigh P term calculations.

Jacobson and Kernell (1983) proposed an answer to the following empirical puzzle about congressional elections. Economic conditions are often thought to affect voting choices. When times are bad, congressional candidates of the party of the president should be hurt, but those candidates should be helped by a strong economy. As Jacobson and Kernell show, aggregate analyses of this relationship find that economic conditions are, indeed, strongly related to the congressional vote. Survey research, however, typically finds that individual voters' perceptions of, experience with, and preferences over personal economic conditions are weakly related to vote choices (Jacobson and Kernell 1983; Kiewiet 1983; Lewis-Beck 1988). Jacobson and Kernell proposed a resolution of this puzzling disjuncture between aggregate- and individual-level data results, which they called the "strategic politicians" hypothesis.[24]

Congressional incumbents are very difficult to defeat, a fact known to the potentially strongest challengers (e.g., state legislators), who have much to lose if defeated. In bad economic circumstances, however, incumbents are relatively more vulnerable. Strong challengers, therefore, are more likely to run (and be able to raise resources) in such circumstances. Voters, of course, are much more likely to support a strong challenger than a weak one. Because there are more strong challengers, more citizens vote against incumbents in bad times than good. Even if voters paid no attention at all to economic circumstances in deciding how to vote, we would observe a relationship between voting for the incumbent and economic circumstances due to politicians' strategic decisions.

The strategic politician hypothesis provides an even more convincing explanation of an analogous empirical puzzle in turnout. As noted earlier, the relationship between the P term and turnout mirrors economic conditions and congressional voting. Empirical relationships are strong at the aggregate level, but are weak or nonexistent at the individual level.

While citizens may not care whether the election is close, politicians do.

Campaign resources are allocated by parties, PACs, and interest groups where those resources will do the most good, and they will do the most good where elections hang in the balance, rather than in elections that appear likely to be won or lost by large margins. Thus, analogous to strong challengers running in bad rather than good times, politicians (and politically active groups) allocate resources to close rather than to one-sided contests. This argument is not new. It was made, for example, by Key (1949). Moreover, Jacobson (1992) and others have clearly shown that in congressional elections, challengers to incumbents find it extremely difficult to raise enough money to make an effective race. They need to convince skeptical potential donors that they have a realistic chance of winning, and when they can do so, they can get money. This money, available primarily in close elections, can be "invested" by the candidate to turn-out-to-vote campaigns, thus stimulating turnout.

What of the people who must decide whether to vote? It may be that citizens are more likely to vote if the election is close. Even if not, they will be the recipients of greater campaign efforts if the election is expected to be close. Therefore, the costs of voting will, typically, be reduced, perhaps by more intensive registration and get-out-the-vote campaigns. A close, hard, expensively fought contest will, on average, increase interest in it, thereby increasing the likelihood that people will become informed about it out of general interest or incidentally due to more lavish advertising campaigns. Candidates, of course, seek to provide good reasons to vote for them and not their opponents, so higher amounts of incidental information may increase the perceptions of how different the candidates are, leading to higher B terms. It may even increase the feelings of duty or expression of allegiance to the favored candidate or party. Adding the strategic politicians hypothesis to the low-cost, low-benefits argument yields a seventh conclusion.

7. Strategic politicians will invest more heavily in the closest contests, and this investment will be reflected in increasing levels of turnout, even if voters do not consider the closeness of the contest. Hence, turnout should increase with the closeness of the contest at the aggregate level, even if perceived closeness is weakly related, or even entirely unrelated, to the turnout decision of any individual voter. Indeed, voters can be purely expressive voters or "consumers"—they could decide on the basis of C and D kinds of variables—and still a correlation would exist between closeness and turnout at the aggregate level.

While not put in these terms, several rational choice models have been developed based on this logic. Uhlaner (1989), for example, examines a model in which candidates adopt policy positions in part to receive support from interest groups. Group leaders use these policy benefits to acquire funds to invest in turning out their group members, thereby reducing costs. Morton (1987) has developed a closely related model. Aldrich and McGinnis (1989) have developed a model in which political parties allocate resources to candidates who invest these resources in get-out-the-vote campaigns. Recently, Cox and Munger (1989) have estimated a "strategic politicians" model using data from the 1982 congressional elections. They found that both the amount of money expended in the campaign and the closeness of the contest stimulated increased levels of turnout, controlling for a variety of other variables. Spending an extra dollar per capita increased turnout by 3.1%, and a race closer by one thousand votes increased turnout by 0.15%.[25]

More generally, empirical studies have consistently found that campaign efforts by parties and other groups stimulate turnout. Patterson and Caldiera (1983) provide a particularly good example, while Kramer (1970) demonstrates the impact of precinct-level campaigning on voting behavior. To illustrate, one of the most strategic politicians of all times was Martin Van Buren. He began constructing the first mass-based political party for the 1828 election. The Democrats in 1828 and 1832 effectively determined where there would be substantial attempts at mass mobilization.[26] I show (1995) that the national party organized state and local Democratic parties strategically, beginning with the closest expected contests of 1828 and then of 1832. In 1828, turnout increased 18.3% in the 13 states not organized. In the five states that the party succeeded in organizing, turnout increased 41.7%. In a more completely specified model, due to that organization, turnout in organized states was estimated to have increased 17.5% in 1828, 5.1% (on the already higher base) in 1832, and another 14.7% more in 1836, ceteris paribus.

I believe the strategic politicians hypothesis also can help explain why there is consistent evidence of the wasted-vote thesis. Under minimax regret, this kind of choice should never happen. Under the calculus of voting, we should observe very little such voting if the P term is small and weakly related to choice. Thus, it is a puzzle for each model.

In the 1968 and 1980 presidential elections, the third-party candidate stood much higher in public opinion polls in September than in November. According to National Election Studies (NES) survey data, over 95% of those who ranked a major-party candidate first voted for him, but only 85% of those who ranked George Wallace first voted for him, and only 57% of those who said John Anderson was their favorite candidate voted for him (Abramson, Aldrich, and Rohde 1983, 175). Wallace had strong regional appeal, actually carried several southern states and came close in others, while Anderson's support was not concentrated. This is consistent with the fact that Anderson's support fell more dramatically, since the wasted-vote logic was more compelling in his case. Moreover, Wallace supporters who "defected" (to their second choice, generally Nixon) were found in states where the Wallace vote was small. In strong Wallace states, he held much more of his support. In other words, the pattern of data is precisely what we would expect if voters made expected utility calculations. Why would this be true if the comparable probability calculations are all but ignored in deciding about turnout?

The strategic politicians hypothesis provides an answer. It is clearly in the interest of most politicians to support a major party because virtually all of them are successful politicians within one of those two parties. Indeed, both Wallace and Anderson had difficulty even finding a major politician to run with them. Interest groups benefit from maintenance of the current two-party system. Unions, for example, devoted great effort to convince their members to support Humphrey over Wallace, even though many members preferred Wallace. Unions also have a long-standing relationship with the Democratic party.

The two parties, their nominees, and interest groups, therefore, make the argument publicly that a vote for a third-party candidate will be wasted. Resources were systematically devoted to convincing people that "a vote for Anderson is a vote for Reagan," as Carter put it (i.e., that a vote for a third-party candidate is a wasted vote). Survey responses in 1980 suggest that the Democratic argument was heard by respondents, as 45% of those who had considered voting for Anderson said they decided not to because they felt he had no chance to win, while nearly 55% of them agreed with Carter's plea that a vote for Anderson would "help elect another candidate I dislike more." Of the 27% of the sample who had considered voting for Anderson, nearly half had changed to support a major-party nominee. Strategic politicians, whether the nominees themselves, other party figures, or even interest groups, clearly behave strategically. Voters appear to respond to this strategic prompting. Thus, an eighth conclusion is that

> 8. Strategic politicians inform voters of the wasted-vote argument and convince at least some voters that it is sensible to act as "strategic voters."

The Decline of Turnout and a Broader Theory of Preferences

Perhaps the single most studied and discussed fact about turnout in recent years is the decline in turnout in presidential and congressional general elections. Presidential elections hit a peak of turnout in 1960. Turnout has declined more or less continually since then, just as turnout in midterm elections peaked in 1962 and has declined since then. How are we to make sense of this in a rational choice context? Rational choice models are election-specific models, in which citizens choose based on the characteristics of the particular contest.

Suppose that people turn out, if at all, primarily to vote in the presidential election in relevant years.[27] It is very hard to imagine an election-specific explanation that would lead to the observed pattern of more or less monotonic decline in turnout from 1960 through 1988. In that period, we have had several very close elections (1960, 1968, and 1976) and several very one-sided contests (1964, 1972, and 1984). Turnout rose slightly in 1984, even though it was more one-sided than in 1980,[28] and it fell sharply between 1984 and 1988, even though 1988 was closer. Thus, P terms are not a very promising route.

Neither are B terms. Presidential nominees have been moderates, conservatives, and liberals. Sometimes (e.g., 1960 and 1976) the candidates have been fairly similar in policy stance; in most others, they have been very dissimilar. Sometimes a popular incumbent has run, sometimes an unpopular incumbent, and sometimes no incumbent at all (even once an unelected incumbent). We have had two candidates most of the time, but twice we have had three major candidates. There is no pattern to these that would yield an explanation for steadily decreasing turnout.

Changing costs are also an unlikely explanation. Material costs have, if anything, been reduced systematically due to liberalized registration laws, to the elimination of poll taxes, and so on. The civil rights movement, the Voting Rights Act, and Jesse Jackson's more recent efforts have made extensive gains among blacks, while conservative religious groups and others have made gains, especially among southern whites. It is true that candidates have tended to favor media and other "high tech" campaign strategies over the nuts and bolts of turnout drives, but Gibson et al. (e.g., 1983) show that state and local political parties are more professionalized and better financed now than in earlier decades. Levels of education and some other variables that might be expected to reduce decision costs have risen, not fallen.

Even the duty term is an unlikely explanation. The measures that Riker and Ordeshook (1968, 1973) examined have not been asked for some time. However, the so-called "internal efficacy" scale, which is about the closest surrogate measure that has been asked over this period, has not declined; indeed it has hardly changed at all in the aggregate. In sum, nothing about the specific elections seems able to account for even a portion of the decline in turnout. If anything, they predict an increase. More likely, they predict an erratic pattern.

Does this mean that election-specific models are the wrong way to think about turnout? I think not. There is no reason to imagine that people do not take election-specific characteristics, notably their preferences between candidates, into account in deciding whether to vote. It does suggest, however, the election-specific models are insufficient.

What variables do seem to account for the decline in turnout? Basically, these are long-term attitudinal and some demographic variables. Abramson and I (1982), among others, have pointed to the ability of party identification to predict turnout both cross-sectionally and over time, and this general conclusion holds even in models richer than ours (e.g., Teixeira 1987). In much the same fashion, "external efficacy," (i.e., the perception of the government's ability to respond to its citizens and to solve pressing problems) has declined over this period and seems to explain an even larger portion of the decline in turnout. Other variables have been proposed, such as increasing rates of residential mobility and others. Each of these shares the characteristic that they are not election-specific variables.

How can we reconcile the rational choice models with this argument that it is variables that are not election specific that shape the decline of turnout? The way to do this is simple: reexamine the D term. The D term is always understood to mean either maintenance of democracy or performing one's duty as a citizen, but Riker and Ordeshook had a more extensive interpretation of it, and Fiorina (1976) expanded it further to include expression of party affiliation (and he provided a rational choice model of partisanship, 1981; see also Achen 1989). If this is done, the portion of the decline that appears to be attributable to declining party attachments is included in the model. Moreover, the one "election-specific" variable used in tests of the calculus of voting that has declined along with turnout is the question that asks respondents how much they care which *party* wins the election. Therefore, its decline captures declining attachment to parties. Fewer strong partisans add up to fewer who care about party victories. The same could be done for other sorts of expressive values considered by Riker and Ordeshook.

If we agree with Fiorina's argument, then the B term appears in both the investment and the consumption portion of the model. That is, D is, in part, B. This concept not only allows us to understand how declining strength of party attachments has led to declining levels of turnout, but it also means that the "political" (perhaps even election-specific) nature of elections appears on the consumption side. In turn, this facilitates the strategic politicians hypothesis and "repoliticizes" the relatively politically inert appearance of voting as consumption.[29]

External political efficacy presents a slightly different, and perhaps theoretically more interesting, alternative. Low efficacy means that the respondent thinks that the government is unwilling or unable to solve current problems and to respond to the demands of its citizens. This fits nicely with choice-theoretic accounts. A citizen might see Bush and Dukakis as offering very distinct choices. Most did. A citizen might even have clear preferences between those policy options. This would suggest a big B term. But if the voter perceives that, no matter how much he or she prefers the options of one candidate over the other, neither can make any impact, that B term is reduced substantially. Declining efficacy implies that there are lesser benefits from electing any particular candidate to office. Problems are too complex, politicians are too corrupt or incompetent, and the political system is too unwieldy to expect that the election of any single individual will make any appreciable difference, no matter how desirable the program of the preferred candidate. Perhaps this is partially a consequence of lengthening experience with divided government.

Other long-term variables may also have an impact on the instrumental, as well as on the expressive, value of voting. Declining party affiliations, for instance, may be a measure of the declining perceptions of the ability or inclination of a party to impact on the fortunes of our nation, and hence on the B differential. Thus, long-term attitudes might not just expand the number of explanatory variables; they might even improve our understanding of election-specific forces. If consumption values can be expanded in these ways, we can reach some final conclusions.

9. The D term is not "politically inert" but may include highly political, even election-specific, values. The D term may also conflate investment with consumption factors (further suggesting why consumption terms appear so consequential).

10. If D includes, in part, B-like considerations, then the strategic politicians hypothesis provides even greater empirical leverage, as strategic politicians can both "manipulate" costs and, perhaps, sense of duty and stimulate turnout strategically, based on benefits.

11. An expanded view of the elements of D provides that ability to open the rational-choice account of voting to include long-term beliefs and values, as well as election-specific ones. As a result, the model can be seen to be consistent with many explanations of the decline in turnout.

Note that, in this account, turnout may be based in large part on consumption or expressive values, rather than on investment variables. However, that may be an overly narrow view. If D has genuine political content, it may better be thought of as *long-term* political considerations. These long-term considerations may be just as much "investments" as voting to make or break a tie (or avoid associated regrets), but just not as investing in this particular contest alone. This view of *D*-like variables as long-term investments is not new. It is, in fact, Downs's (1957) own position. Taking this view seriously would require a different model than the calculus of voting and, in particular, would require modeling *D* differently. The new model would not simply add some constant to the act of voting but would be modeled as any long-term investment. While beyond the scope of this paper, this account suggests a new modeling strategy with reasonably clear outlines, even if messy details remain.

Conclusion

The major purposes of this article have been to explain the nature of rational choice models of the turnout decision and to show how they can be used to explain broad patterns of behavior. A major lesson is that prior work using these models—and especially in criticizing these models—has been hampered by an overly narrow interpretation of the theoretical models. With the exception of wasted voting, all of the conclusions I have drawn apply to both the calculus of voting and minimax regret formulations.

The first major argument was that the turnout decision is a marginal decision with low costs and low (expected) benefits for many people, most of the time. Contrary to many interpretations, turnout is not a particularly good example of the problem of collective action because it is a relatively minor one. Further, many variables affect turnout because anything that affects benefits or costs even slightly can change individuals' choices. And yet, it is very difficult, perhaps practically impossible, to explain just who does and who does not vote in some absolute sense, precisely because marginal, small forces can be just enough to make the difference.

The marginality of the decision to turn out also provides an opportunity for political leaders and groups to affect turnout through their strategic actions. Thus, if we add the strategic politicians hypothesis to the low-cost, low-benefit assumption, we can explain why individuals are more likely to vote in close contests than in one-sided ones, even if they do not consider closeness of the contest in making their decisions. Theoretically, the strategic politician hypothesis has two important consequences. First, it permits the integration of the rational choice of voting or abstention into broader theories of political behavior by tying individuals' decisions with the actions of parties, groups, and candidates in campaigns. Second, the narrow interpretation of turnout makes that decision appear relatively apolitical, a "mere" matter of tastes. Turnout is "explained" by saying that people vote because they want to. The strategic politicians hypothesis, however, more broadly integrates even "mere matters of taste" into a richer, highly political, and strategic account of campaigns and elections.

The third major argument was that the D term has been overly narrowly interpreted in ways that remove it from politics of election campaigns. If there is a reward for expressing support for the preferred candidate or party, the D term assumes a genuine political and electorally relevant status. A response to Barry's criticism (1970) that the D term reduces turnout to a mere matter of tastes comes in three steps. First, if costs are low, these expressive values of voting need only be relatively small. Indeed, they must be so, if we are to explain why half of the electorate or less votes in most important U.S. elections. Second, the D term can be understood as a set of highly political and electorally relevant values. Third, use of these electoral values is part of the politicians' strategic repertoire; they are not merely a matter of tastes but play an integral and strategic role in campaigns and elections.

Finally, I have argued that the benefits part of the turnout equation has been interpreted too narrowly as election specific or as long-term forces that are "beyond politics." We should, instead, see nonelection-specific forces as reflecting longer-term political values and preferences. If so, we can begin to model turnout as a rational, long-term investment.

There is a genuine danger that interpreting cost and benefit terms broadly will make the rational choice explanation tautological. If everything is a cost or benefit, the theory predicts everything, which is the same as predicting nothing. One response is that the usual interpretation of the model is too narrow: it excludes too much, including long-established empirical regularities that any serious account must explain. But a stronger response is possible. If D term values are moved from the category of simple constants to a long-term investment category, there are well-developed models for such investments, models that can, in principle, be tested—and found wanting. Indeed, such a move would make even the narrower interpretations of the current models *less* tautological. Such investment decisions, to be rational, must fit certain patterns. Finally, if the strategic politicians hypothesis is examined rigorously, turnout models will be integrated into theories of campaigning and decision making by political elites. This integration will, in fact, provide more structure, more opportunities for testing, and more points at which the models could be found empirically insupportable. Thus, if theorized properly, this expanded view of the turnout decision may actually be less tautological than current, more isolated models.

The major argument is that the turnout decision can be fruitfully understood as an exercise in rational decision making. Current theories provide the basic framework for studying these decisions. Current interpretations of these theories, however, have been overly narrow. As a result, the conclusions drawn from them have been overly sterile, empirically narrow, or dubious. Narrow interpretations have led many to see, falsely I believe, rational choice in general as inappropriate for understanding politics, since narrow interpretations cannot make sense of one of the most common and important forms of political behavior. And overly narrow interpretations have missed genuine and important opportunities for developing more complete and insightful theoretical accounts of the politics of campaigns and elections and for providing a richer understanding of how and why people vote or abstain.

NOTES

1. Voting for minor, third-party candidates can be considered equivalent to abstaining.

2. Some, perhaps many, may not care which candidate wins (i.e., value A or B winning equally). While perfectly rational, such indifferent individuals will simply be predicted to abstain (or base their decision solely on the C and D terms introduced below).

3. Notice that the assignment of a metric utility to the individual is, like various temperature scales, interval but not cardinal. Utility is only comparable to the utility associated with other outcomes.

4. This may sound far-fetched, and its only theoretical role is convenience. I have, however, watched televised coverage of coin tosses to decide winners of tied contests for mayor in small cities!

5. Rational choice accounts conclude that one should never choose a dominated action. If one action dominates all others (e.g., as below if $C > 1/2$), then dominance alone solves the choice problem, and all rational choice models of turnout will conclude that the citizen should take that action. In interesting cases, however, one action rarely dominates all others. It is this fact that yields differing choice-theoretic models.

6. It is important to note that the costs of voting are actually compared to the *difference* to the voter for having A rather than B elected (not the one utile associated with A winning).

7. A good account is in Enelow and Hinich (1984). Another common form of abstention in spatial models (and also dependent upon candidates' strategies) is called "alienation," which arises when the preferred candidate offers too little in value (is too far away on policy) to be worth supporting. While indifference flows naturally from choice theory, alienation requires an additional, often ad hoc assumption about a threshold of minimal acceptability of the better choice, regardless of any comparison with the alternative.

8. If these are true probabilities, their sum across the five columns must be one.

9. They also examined the *PB* interaction, finding little evidence for it (see also Aldrich 1976).

10. More accurately, they argue that not all people use the calculus of voting's logic in deciding whether to vote. They suggest that some might do so, but some (presumably many) might not. Only the "pure" cases of everyone using the same decision rule are considered here, for ease of exposition.

11. Minimax regret is only one of several decision-making rules that have been proposed for decision making under uncertainty (see Luce and Raiffa 1957). There are good reasons for examining this particular decision rule (e.g., others always predict abstention).

12. Tests of turnout models that use survey data either have no measure of the costs of voting (e.g., Riker and Ordeshook 1968) or are forced to make problematic empirical decisions (e.g., that level of education is a measure of costs—and not of other theoretical terms). It might be supposed, however, that if good measures of costs were available in surveys, they would also show strong effects. If so, the arguments in the text would be largely unaffected, and in particular, the decision to vote would continue to be dominated by "consumption" terms and not investment terms.

13. I argued this position (1976) and provided some survey evidence to support it. Kramer (1983) made a much more elegant account, applied to a different problem (see below). Some psychologists argue that people are notoriously bad in estimating probabilities (e.g., Kahneman, Slovic, and Tversky 1982), which, of course, would also make the *P* term problematical.

14. Technically, it may be rational, by the calculus of voting, to vote for any candidate or party except the last-ranked alternative, depending upon the particular probabilities involved. It is easier to write this as voting for a second-choice alternative, so I shall do so here.

15. Tullock (1975) wrote a critique of the minimax regret formulation that he entitled "The Paradox of Not Voting for Oneself." Suppose that you write your name in on the presidential ballot and that you are your most preferred candidate. If so, it is not logically impossible that you could win (perhaps everyone else follows the calculus of voting logic, calculates small *P* terms and abstains, so you win one vote to zero). Minimax regret concludes that you always vote for your first-choice candidate, no matter what, if you vote at all. So minimax regret "predicts," according to Tullock's logic, that at least a great many should turn out and vote for themselves.

16. From the government's perspective, economies of scale in the costs of conducting elections are precisely why so many contests are on the same ballot.

17. This is not to say that the costs of registration and voting are low in some absolute sense or that they are equally low for all people. Obviously, even low costs may be an effective barrier to voting for the poor, and laws may still be manipulated to regulate who is more and who is less likely to vote. In this vein, see Piven and Cloward (1988). U.S. registration laws may have been generally liberalized, but not completely and not equally.

18. One exception that has received a great deal of attention (although not in terms of turnout, per se) is the often tremendous asymmetry between the information relatively easily available for the incumbent, but not the challenger, in U.S. House contests. This literature can be used to imply that, in general, voters do not seek information on challengers for the purpose of getting informed (just as Downs's "rational ignorance" ac-

count would imply), but many do have at least some limited information on incumbents. Moreover, they appear to construct decision rules about whom to support from this asymmetric informational base. All of this is consistent with the Downsian account of voting. Since the incumbent has an unusually high degree of control over this readily obtainable information in House elections, it should be no surprise that the rationally ill informed voter typically decides that the incumbent is doing at least an adequate job.

19. Such costs will be higher, the more similar the two candidates. For example, in 1976 Ford and Carter adopted relatively similar policy stances, requiring more information to decide whose platforms were preferred than in contests in which candidates' platforms were more distinct.

20. While our turnout is, of course, low, these figures overstate somewhat the incidence of (purposeful) abstention, since they include those not legally eligible to vote or even to register.

21. The decline in party affiliation is indicated by the increase in "pure" independents from a low of 6% in 1952 and an average preparty decline of about 8% to an all-time high of 15% in 1974 and 1976 and a postparty decline average of about 12%. On the relationship between the decline in strength of partisanship and turnout, see Abramson and Aldrich (1982).

22. Pomper and Sernekos (1989) argue along these lines. They entitle theirs a "bake sale theory" of voting because bake sales are held at the polls in their area. The attraction of a bake sale is another of those small benefits available to those who turn out. These are a part, of course, of the D term, and bake sales are consistent with Barry's (1970) argument that the D term is a matter of taste!

23. I put the "errors" in decisions in quotation marks because it is not a mistake in judgment or failure of rationality involved. It is an "error" only if the decision maker were fully informed. As Downs (1957) showed, however, it would be irrational to be fully informed, and thus the rational decision maker knowingly tolerates (and expects) "errors" at the margin, as here.

24. Kramer (1983) proposes another answer. He points out that surveys rely on respondents' assessments. Since these respondents are affected by the same national economic conditions, much of the variation in these assessments will be variations in perceptions of the same "reality" and simple measurement error. Overtime studies, such as the aggregate analyses, examine "true" variation in actual national economic circumstances. Hence, if economic conditions do matter, they should be revealed in over-time studies, but they will be greatly attenuated in cross-sectional studies. This parallels the P term. Survey data for a presidential election will have variation due not to differences in the "true" closeness of the election but to differences in perception, interpretation, and/or error in assessing the true closeness. Over-time studies, therefore, would find a stronger impact of the P term because there is true variation in expected closeness.

25. They report that these two variables had standardized betas of .33 and .45, respectively, in this aggregate data model. While betas are problematic, their magnitude suggests that these two variables are, indeed, strongly related to (aggregate) turnout.

26. This is not to say that they were the only groups that attempted to mobilize the electorate. Local groups opposed to Jackson may have countermobilized upon seeing the new Democratic party take to the field. In either case, the Democrats chose the locales of competition.

27. More specifically, assume that the decline is due primarily to the presidential contest (or forces independent of any particular contest). What needs to be avoided is declining turnout in presidential years due to changes in election-specific factors about contests on the ballot other than the presidency.

28. The 1980 election was "too close to call" in virtually all final preelection polls.

29. Citizen duty per se is often seen as not very political. I suspect that is one reason that Barry's (1970) arguments are persuasive. If, however, duty were derived from a well-formed theory of democratic citizenship, performing one's duty would appear both more political and more profound.

REFERENCES

Abramson, Paul R., and John H. Aldrich. 1982. "The Decline of Electoral Participation in America." *American Political Science Review* 76:502–21.

Abramson, Paul R., John H. Aldrich, Phil Paolino, and David W. Rohde. 1992. "'Sophisticated' Voting in the 1988 Presidential Primaries." *American Political Science Review* 86:55–69.

Abramson, Paul R., John H. Aldrich, and David W. Rohde. 1983. *Change and Continuity in the 1980 Elections.* Rev. ed. Washington, DC: Congressional Quarterly Press.

Achen, Christopher H. 1989. "Prospective Voting and the Theory of Party Identification." Unpublished paper, University of Chicago.

Aldrich, John H. 1976. "Some Problems in Testing Two Rational Models of Participation." *American Journal of Political Science* 20:713–34.

———. 1992. "Rational Choice Theory and the Study of American Politics." Paper prepared for delivery at the Conference on the Dynamics of American Politics, University of Colorado, Boulder, February 20–22, 1992.

———. 1995. *Why Parties?* Chicago: University of Chicago Press.

Aldrich, John H., and Michael M. McGinnis. 1989. "A Model of Party Constraints on Optimal Candidate Positions." *Mathematical and Computer Modeling* 12:437–50.

Aldrich, John H., and Dennis M. Simon. 1986. "Turnout in American National Elections." *Research in Micropolitics* 1:271–301. JAI Press.

Barry, Brian. 1970. *Sociologists, Economists, and Democracy.* London: Collier-Macmillan.

Barzel, Yoram, and Eugene Silberberg. 1973. "Is the Act of Voting Rational?" *Public Choice* 16:51–58.

Black, Jerome H. 1978. "The Multicandidate Calculus of Voting: Application to Canadian Federal Elections." *American Journal of Political Science* 22:609–38.

Cain, Bruce E. 1978. "Strategic Voting in Britain." *American Journal of Political Science* 22:639–55.

Cox, Gary W., and Michael C. Munger. 1989. "Closeness, Expenditures, and Turnout in the 1988 U.S. House Elections." *American Political Science Review* 83:217–31.

Crain, W. Mark, and Thomas H. Deaton. 1977. "A Note on Political Participation as Consumption Behavior." *Public Choice* 32:131–35.

Downs, Anthony. 1957. *An Economic Theory of Democracy.* New York: Harper and Row.

Enelow, James, and Melvin Hinich. 1984. *The Spatial Theory of Voting: An Introduction.* New York: Cambridge University Press.

Ferejohn, John A., and Morris P. Fiorina. 1974. "The Paradox of Not Voting: A Decision Theoretic Analysis." *American Political Science Review* 68:525–36.

———. 1975. "Closeness Counts Only in Horseshoes and Dancing." *American Political Science Review* 69:920–25.

Fiorina, Morris P. 1976. "The Voting Decision: Instrumental and Expressive Aspects." *Journal of Politics* 38:390–415.

———. 1981. *Retrospective Voting in American National Elections*. New Haven: Yale University Press.

Foster, Carroll B. 1984. "The Performance of Rational Voter Models in Recent Presidential Elections." *American Political Science Review* 78:678–90.

Gibson, James L., Cornelius P. Cotter, and John F. Bibby. 1983. "Assessing Party Organizational Strength." *American Journal of Political Science* 27:193–222.

Hinich, Melvin J. 1981. "Voting as an Act of Contribution." *Public Choice* 36:135–40.

Jacobson, Gary C. 1992. *The Politics of Congressional Elections*. 3d ed. New York: Harper Collins.

Jacobson, Gary C., and Samuel Kernell. 1983. *Strategy and Choice in Congressional Elections*. 2d ed. New Haven: Yale University Press.

Kahneman, Daniel, Paul Slovic, and Amos Tversky, eds. 1982. *Judgment under Uncertainty: Heuristics and Biases*. New York: Cambridge University Press.

Key, V.O., Jr. 1949. *Southern Politics in State and Nation*. New York: Knopf.

———. 1966. *The Responsible Electorate: Rationality in Presidential Voting*. Cambridge: Harvard University Press.

Kiewiet, D. Roderick. 1983. *Macroeconomics and Micropolitics: The Electoral Effects of Economic Issues*. Chicago: University of Chicago Press.

Kramer, Gerald H. 1970. "The Effects of Precinct-Level Canvassing on Voting Behavior." *Public Opinion Quarterly* 34:560–72.

———. 1983. "The Ecological Fallacy Revisited: Aggregate- versus Individual-level Findings on Economics and Elections and Sociotropic Voting." *American Political Science Review* 77:92–111.

Ledyard, John. 1984. "The Pure Theory of Two-Candidate Elections." *Public Choice* 44: 7–41.

Lewis-Beck, Michael S. 1988. *Economics and Elections: The Major Western Democracies*. Ann Arbor: University of Michigan Press.

Lewis-Beck, Michael S., and Andrew Skalaban. 1989. "Citizen Forecasting: Can Voters See into the Future?" *British Journal of Political Science* 19:146–53.

Luce, R. Duncan, and Howard W. Raiffa. 1957. *Games and Decisions*. New York: Wiley.

Morton, R. B. 1987. "A Group Majority Voting Model of Public Good Provision." *Social Choice and Welfare* 4:117–31.

Niemi, Richard G. 1976. "Costs of Voting and Nonvoting." *Public Choice* 27:115–19.

Palfrey, Thomas R., and Howard Rosenthal. 1985. "Voter Participation and Strategic Uncertainty." *American Political Science Review* 79:62–78.

Patterson, Samuel C., and Gregory A. Caldeira. 1983. "Getting Out the Vote: Participation in Gubernatorial Elections." *American Political Science Review* 77:675–89.

Piven, Frances Fox, and Richard Cloward. 1988. *Why Americans Don't Vote*. New York: Pantheon.

Pomper, Gerald M., and Loretta Sernekos. 1989. "The 'Bake Sale' Theory of Voting Participation." Presented at the annual meeting of the American Political Science Association, Atlanta.

Riker, William H., and Peter C. Ordeshook. 1968. "A Theory of the Calculus of Voting." *American Political Science Review* 62:25–43.

———. 1973. *An Introduction to Positive Political Theory.* Englewood Cliffs, NJ: Prentice-Hall.

Settle, Russell F., and Burton A. Abrams. 1976. "The Determinants of Voter Participation: A More General Model." *Publc Choice* 27:81–89.

Silberman, Jonathan, and Gary Durden. 1975. "The Rational Behavior Theory of Voter Participation: The Evidence from Congressional Elections." *Public Choice* 23:101–08.

Teixeira, Ruy A. 1987. *Why Americans Don't Vote: Turnout Decline in the United States, 1960–1984.* New York: Greenwood Press.

Tullock, Gordon. 1975. "The Paradox of Not Voting for Oneself." *American Political Science Review* 69:919.

Uhlaner, Carole. 1989. "Rational Turnout: The Neglected Role of Groups." *American Journal of Political Science* 33:390–422.

The Effect of the Secret Ballot on Voter Turnout Rates

Jac C. Heckelman

Review Questions

1. Why might a secret ballot reduce the incentive to vote? What other electoral laws might affect the incentive to vote?
2. Why is it not enough to simply compare a state's turnout rate after adoption of the secret ballot with its turnout rate before adoption?
3. Does the evidence support the notion that electoral laws affect turnout? What does this imply about the validity of the calculus of voting?
4. Why were doughnuts offered to voters in the Los Angeles mayoral election? How effective was this strategy?

1. Bribery and the Paradox of Voting

Rational economic agents evaluate their decisions in a benefit-cost analysis. According to Downs (1957), voters are rational economic agents. Thus, they

Heckelman, Jac C. "The Effect of the Secret Ballot on Voter Turnout Rates." *Public Choice* 82 (1995): 107–24.

engage in these same sort of calculations when deciding if and how to vote. Downs expressed his calculus of voting model as:

$$R = P * B - C \qquad (1)$$

where R is the net benefit from voting in utils, B is the net benefit from a particular candidate winning the election (usually referred to as the party differential), discounted by the probability, P, of the voter's action influencing the election, and C is the cost of voting. The net benefit of the party differential must be discounted because the voter will receive B regardless of his particular action as long as the candidate wins. This is the normal free-rider problem inherent in various collective-action situations.[1]

Tullock (1967) concluded that with the benefits from voting near zero, small costs leave net benefits less than zero. This can be seen formally by substituting P = 0 into equation (1).[2] We are left now with only R = − C and the net benefit from voting is negative regardless of the size of C. Even Downs (1957: 265) recognized that "since the returns from voting are often minuscule, even low voting costs may cause many partisan voters to abstain." Thus the paradox; voting appears to be an irrational act (Mueller, 1989: 350).

Downs (1957) was forced outside his model to find a rationale for voting. Voting is viewed as "one form of insurance" (p. 268) against the possibility that no one votes and democracy collapses. "Rational men are motivated to some extent by a sense of social responsibility" (p. 267). Downs recognized the free-rider problem in voting but conveniently ignored it for the preservation of democracy. If one man is unable to change an election, then he is not able to save democracy with his single vote, either.[3]

There have been numerous attempts to save the Downsian rational voter model from itself.[4] The calculus of voting models put forth all have one thing in common; they failed to incorporate monetary incentives. This can be remedied by introducing another simple variable into Downs' original equation:

$$R = P * B - C + \$ \qquad (2)$$

where $ represents the amount received through bribes.[5] As long as $ > C, which means the bribe covers all voting costs, R > 0. Since R is now positive, it is rational to vote.[6] The bribe value is not discounted because the voter receives the money only if he votes, and regardless of the outcome.

Secrecy in the voting act, ensured by the Australian (or secret) Ballot,[7] eliminated the monitoring mechanism, thereby ending the bribes. Candidates were not willing to risk their money on voters who were now able to cheat them without fear of retribution.[8] Having an Australian Ballot meant $ = 0 for all voters, whereas prior to this, $ was positive for those receiving bribes. Thus, for at least some voters, R was higher under the open balloting system. The secret ballot destroyed the vote market but in doing so eliminated a powerful voting incentive.[9]

Did the secret ballot reduce turnout? For this to have occurred, there must have been a strong vote market under the open ballot system. If the market was small, the secret ballot would not be expected to have had much effect in the aggregate.[10]

Anecdotal evidence that elections were routinely bought and sold is contained in most works concerning historical voting. This evidence suggests the vote market was, in fact, quite active. Harris (1929, 1934) provides detailed case studies and testimonials of rampant corruption. These include not only an active vote market, but strong-arm tactics as well. Voters were often threatened, kidnapped, and killed.[11] McCook (1892) chronicles venal voters in various small towns and city wards in Connecticut. Vote prices ranged from two to twenty dollars for an estimated 20,000 purchasable votes. In New York City, Speed (1905) found evidence that 170,000 vote sellers were "employed for the day" at a cost of five dollars. Argersinger (1985) details several other literary and legal sources for fraud evidence.

The importance of the secret ballot is not limited to its role in reducing turnout. Anderson and Tollison (1990) test for the impact of this law on government growth. They argue that the poor used the secrecy provided by the Australian Ballot to vote in their own interest. As rational wealth-maximizers, they voted for expansionary government policies in the form of redistribution. This reasoning would be supported by Converse (1974: 281) who notes the potential for a secret ballot to reduce corruption thus affecting *how* one voted, but decided "(t)here is, however, no obvious connection between the Australian Ballot reform and . . . any effect of the reform on turnout."[12]

The analysis here would not support such a conjecture. If voters accepting bribes were mainly the poor, they would certainly be more likely to vote in their own interest when bribery and coercion ended, but this applies only to those who remained active voters. Many of the voters who no longer were paid to vote responded by abstaining. It is therefore unlikely that the Australian Ballot was responsible for governmental growth. The focus of this paper remains on turnout changes, but the effect on turnout clearly has other implications as well that will not be pursued here.

In testing for the effect of various electoral laws, historical voter turnout studies have often relied solely upon simple correlations and bivariate regression analysis (Burnham, 1970, 1971, 1974; Rusk, 1970; Converse, 1972; Rusk and Stucker, 1978; Kleppner and Baker, 1980; Kleppner, 1982a).[13] Normally, hypothesis testing employs multivariate regression analysis which has two distinct advantages. First, economic theories usually involve more than one variable and the effect of each variable is easier to separate in this format. Second, other factors need to be controlled to account for possible spurious correlation. The contribution of equation (2), though, turns on only one key piece of legislation. Evidence that multivariate analysis is warranted can be shown by first testing for the influence of the Australian Ballot by itself. These tests support the notion that the secret ballot may have reduced turnout, thereby requiring further investigation.

2. Data Sources

The data needed to test this hypothesis can be divided into three categories: population, vote totals, and the year the law was first adopted. I define turnout as the total number of votes cast in a gubernatorial election divided by the age-eligible population. The census provides population figures in decade intervals. Non-census year populations are estimated using geometric interpolation.[14]

The Inter-University Consortium for Political and Social Research (ICPSR) has made state-level voting estimates for gubernatorial elections from 1824–1972 available on tape (Burnham, Clubb, and Flanigan, 1971). I began my sample in 1870 as this was the first census year after passage of the Fifteenth Amendment which made discrimination at the polls based on race illegal. Similarly, 1910 was the last census year before the so-called "Anthony Amendment" gave women full suffrage in 1919. A few Western states allowed women to vote prior to this, and have been accounted for by a simple adjustment of their population base.

The ICPSR tape also provides various census figures, including the total and age-eligible male populations in each state, but the off-decade estimates are based upon linear interpolations so they are not used in this paper.[15] Female population figures, when needed, were taken directly from the various censuses since the ICPSR numbers are labeled as estimates and do not match the census figures.

Ludington (1909), Evans (1917), and Albright (1948) have all included partial, and often conflicting, dates for adoption of the law in different states. They have been the principal sources used by others, including Rusk (1970) who studied the effect of the law on split ticket voting. Unfortunately, none of these sources have complete listings. Since he examined Presidential elections, Rusk's coding was not annual,[16] which is often needed for the gubernatorial election analysis.

Where the various sources all agreed, I have accepted their dating. For the remaining states, I supplemented these sources with various law code books.[17] The final dating used most closely resembles Rusk except for Mississippi and Vermont.

3. Before and after Tests

Table 1 shows the election turnout for each state adopting a secret ballot between the years 1870–1910.[18] A comparison is made between the gubernatorial elections immediately before (Ante) and after (Post) the law took effect.

The table shows that 2/3 of the states recorded a fall in turnout immediately after adopting a secret ballot. The mean fall-off is 5.22 percentage points, or an 8.2% drop compared to the previous election. The t-statistics at the bottom of the table are significant for both mean and percent changes.

The results in Table 1 give a strong indication that forces were at work to reduce turnout during this time. It could, however, be argued that the recorded drop in turnout is simply the continuation of a downward trend. This trend was first documented by Burnham (1965). Others have found fault in his reasoning for the trend but the trend itself is not in doubt (Rusk, 1971, 1974; Converse, 1974). Thus, Table 1 might be the result of mere timing.

Kleppner and Baker (1980) devised a detrending test for the passage of registration requirements. Regressing turnout against time, they are able to construct time trends to compute confidence intervals for turnout predictions.[19] If the actual turnout in the election after passage is lower than the lowest bound on the predicted value, turnout is concluded to be affected by the law in a way not accounted for by the time trend. This is done by comparing the difference between the predicted and the actual values, which should be positive and larger than the standard deviation. Kleppner (1982a) also used this procedure to test the impact of female suffrage.

A similar yet more straightforward test is to compute the law's effect directly in a regression format.[20] Accounting for the time trend, the law coefficient should be negative and significant. The time trend component is computed by regressing the election year interacted by a state code variable; the same is done for the first election after the law went into effect. In this way, each state is tested independently. A dummy variable is used to account for the higher turnout typically associated with presidential elections (Barzel and Silberberg, 1973); this is the only connection between the states.

$$\text{Turnout}_{it} = \alpha + \beta_{1i}\text{Secret}_{it} + \beta_2\text{Pres}_t + \beta_{3i}\text{Year}_t \qquad (3)$$

where variables are subscripted for state i at time t, Secret is a dummy variable coded 1 for the first election after the law and 0 otherwise, Pres is a dummy variable for presidential election years, and Year is the year in which a gubernatorial election was held. Both Secret and Year are interacted with

TABLE 1.   Before and After Test of Secret Ballot

ST	Law	Ante	Turnout	Post	Turnout	Change	% Change
AL	1893	1892	71.28	1894	54.26	−17.02	−23.88
AR	1891	1890	74.24	1892	58.23	−16.01	−21.56
CA	1891	1890	54.61	1894	57.67	3.06	5.60
CO	1891	1890	50.61	1892	54.98	4.37	8.64
CT	1909	1908	56.78	1910	47.80	−8.98	−15.82
DE	1891	1890	74.22	1894	78.19	3.97	5.35
FL	1895	1892	39.31	1896	33.94	−5.36	−13.65
IA	1892	1891	79.16	1893	75.27	−3.90	−4.92
ID	1892	1890	57.83	1892	57.25	−0.58	−1.00
IL	1891	1888	74.05	1892	77.16	3.10	4.19
IN	1889	1888	93.47	1892	88.81	−4.66	−4.98
KS	1893	1892	83.46	1894	75.98	−7.48	−8.96
LA	1896	1896	69.53	1900	23.58	−45.94	−66.08
MA	1888	1888	54.57	1889	40.69	−13.88	−25.43
ME	1891	1890	56.61	1892	63.72	7.12	12.57
MI	1891	1890	64.44	1892	73.60	9.17	14.23
MO	1891	1888	77.42	1892	73.76	−3.66	−4.73
MS	1890	1889	31.73	1895	21.14	−10.59	−33.38
ND	1891	1890	65.19	1892	58.08	−7.11	−10.90
NE	1891	1890	71.01	1892	65.52	−5.49	−7.74
NH	1891	1890	73.00	1892	72.19	−0.81	−1.11
NV	1891	1890	59.15	1894	53.46	−5.68	−9.61
NY	1895	1894	65.92	1896	69.73	3.81	5.78
OH	1891	1889	77.89	1891	76.91	−0.98	−1.26
OR	1891	1890	65.05	1894	70.34	5.29	8.14
PA	1891	1890	63.49	1894	59.76	−3.73	−5.87
RI	1889	1888	41.77	1889	44.25	2.48	5.93
SD	1891	1890	80.16	1892	70.58	−9.57	−11.95
VA	1894	1893	53.89	1897	40.08	−13.81	−25.62
VT	1890	1888	69.11	1890	53.02	−16.09	−23.28
WV	1891	1888	91.67	1892	88.72	−2.95	−3.22

	Mean	Std. error	T-statistic
Change	−5.22	1.87	2.80
% Change	−8.21	2.93	2.80

Note: Law refers to the year the secret ballot was adopted. Ante is the last election prior to adoption and Post is the first election after adoption.

the state code dummy variables. Following Kleppner and Baker (1980), each state vector consists of the five elections prior to adoption of the Australian Ballot, as well as the first election after. The hypothesis predicts $\beta_{1i} < 0$.

The results generated from this approach, reported in Table 2, are not much more hopeful than Kleppner and Baker's results in their study on registration. The coefficients imply that secrecy reduced turnout in 20 of the 28 states, but the t-statistics reveal that only 1/4 of these are significant. Forty percent of Kleppner and Baker's sample was found to be unsupportive of their hypothesis under this test.

TABLE 2.   State by State Effect of Secret Ballot[a]

State	Estimate	Std. err	T-stat
AL	−0.00805	0.08957	0.09
AR*	−0.21587	0.08949	2.41
CA	0.09312	0.09017	1.03
CO	−0.04837	0.08949	0.54
CT	−0.04086	0.08956	0.46
DE	0.16541	0.09031	1.83
FL*	−0.39493	0.09030	4.37
IA	0.02066	0.08871	0.23
IL	0.03699	0.09031	0.41
IN	−0.04575	0.09031	0.51
KS	−0.02633	0.08957	0.29
LA*	−0.43921	0.09146	4.80
MA	−0.01324	0.08868	0.15
ME	−0.09880	0.08949	1.10
MI	−0.02487	0.08949	0.28
MO	0.01857	0.09023	0.21
MS*	−0.24086	0.09106	2.65
NE	−0.09161	0.08949	1.02
NH	−0.06583	0.08949	0.74
NV	−0.02714	0.09031	0.30
NY	−0.04249	0.09050	0.47
OH	−0.01066	0.08871	0.12
OR	0.07106	0.09031	0.79
PA	−0.03722	0.09024	0.41
RI	0.15117	0.08868	1.70
VA*	−0.21006	0.09030	2.33
VT	−0.04843	0.08957	0.54
WV	0.03157	0.09031	0.35

Note: Dependent variable is state turnout rate. Regression controls for presidential election years and state time trends.

*Significant at 5%

[a]Idaho, North Dakota, and South Dakota are not included since they did not have enough Ante observations to develop a trend.

The problem with this approach can be found in the standard error column. The standard errors are large and nearly identical. By computing this statistic on a state-by-state basis, the sample size is effectively restricted to T = 5, resulting in large standard errors. Analogously, the large standard deviations for each state meant the prediction differences in Kleppner's tests had to be unrealistically large.

Pooling the data allows estimation of a national average, reducing the standard errors on the law coefficient while still accounting for the individual state trends:

$$\text{Turnout}_{it} = \alpha + \beta_1 \text{Secret}_{it} + \beta_2 \text{Pres}_t + \beta_{3i} \text{Year}_t \tag{3'}$$

The regression is the same as equation (3) except the interaction on Secret is replaced by a single Secret variable.

The results are more supportive of the existence of a national secret ballot effect. The state estimates in Table 3 lend support for the notion of a constant downward trend for each state during the five previous elections. The Secret variable implies that there was an immediate drop in turnout after passage of the law, on top of the downward trend.

Comparing Tables 2 and 3 reveals an important distinction made earlier. The Secret variable implies that turnout was reduced by an average of 4.9 percentage points after the time trend is accounted for. The estimates generated at the state level in Table 2 reveal larger drops in turnout for many states. Thus, the statistically non-significant t-statistics can be attributed to high standard errors, rather than low coefficient estimates. The pooled Secret variance is less than 1/13 that of the individual state Secret variances.

These tests imply the secret ballot is correlated with lower turnout. Other important legislation, including poll taxes and literacy tests, which has been shown elsewhere to hamper turnout (McGovney, 1949; Kelley, Ayers, and Bowen, 1967;[21] Silver, 1973; Kousser, 1974; Rusk, 1974; Rusk and Stucker, 1978; Filer, Kenny, and Morton, 1991), has thus far been ignored. A full legal-institutional model is needed to incorporate these and other factors. To my knowledge, this will be the first attempt at simultaneously assessing the true effect of various historical election laws. As noted above, these laws have only been tested independently of one another.

4. The Role of the Voter's Calculus

The role of the secret ballot in the voter's calculus has been shown above. No longer able to verify the voters' choices, political parties left the vote market altogether. Without anyone buying their votes, the monetary incentive for individuals to vote was dissipated. Less incentive implied less voting. For many voters, the benefits no longer outweighed the costs of voting. The secret ballot eliminated bribery, but in doing so removed an important voting catalyst.

The impact of other electoral laws can also be measured within this framework. Poll taxes and literacy tests[22] impose higher costs on voters (Kelley, Ayers, and Bowen, 1967; Silver, 1973). In contrast to the Australian Ballot System, the reduction in R in equation (2) from these laws comes through an increase in C. The predicted effect on turnout is the same.

TABLE 3. National Effect of Secret Ballot[a]

Variable	Estimate	Std. err	T-stat
Secret*	−0.04920	0.024026	2.05
Pres*	0.08140	0.020483	3.97
AL	−0.00111	0.001727	0.64
AR	−0.00105	0.001729	0.61
CA	−0.00114	0.001731	0.66
CO	−0.00114	0.001729	0.66
CT	−0.00112	0.001712	0.66
DE	−0.00107	0.001731	0.62
FL	−0.00110	0.001730	0.63
IA	−0.00102	0.001728	0.59
IL	−0.00106	0.001733	0.61
IN	−0.00096	0.001733	0.55
KS	−0.00099	0.001727	0.57
LA	−0.00114	0.001725	0.66
MA	−0.00119	0.001729	0.69
ME	−0.00107	0.001729	0.62
MI	−0.00105	0.001729	0.61
MO	−0.00107	0.001733	0.62
MS	−0.00119	0.001732	0.69
NE	−0.00107	0.001729	0.62
NH	−0.00104	0.001729	0.60
NV	−0.00111	0.001731	0.64
NY	−0.00106	0.001726	0.62
OH	−0.00100	0.001729	0.58
OR	−0.00107	0.001731	0.62
PA	−0.00108	0.001731	0.62
RI	−0.00124	0.001729	0.72
VA	−0.00110	0.001728	0.64
VT	−0.00110	0.001731	0.64
WV	−0.00100	0.001733	0.57

Note: Dependent variable is state turnout rate. The state estimates measure the time trend (β_{3i}) for each state.

*Significant at 5%

[a]The state estimates still rely on only 5 observations per state and consequently have uniformly small t-statistics. These coefficients were not reported in Table 2.

The final law included in the regression is female suffrage. The role of this particular law, though, is not unambiguous. Enfranchised women need not have different benefits and costs than male voters. Merriam and Gosnell (1924) surveyed residents of Chicago after the mayoral election of 1923. They found that 1/9 of the women did not believe in voting either out of ignorance or indifference to voting, or believing it to be men's work (p. 109). Kleppner (1982a) found gender-based differences in voting to be very weak in the presence of other short-term stimuli. When these short-run forces were absent, differences in voting between men and women became larger. Others have not been as ambivalent. "(A)s a result of female suffrage there is no question whatever but that over-all statements of turnout were drastically affected as a result"(Converse, 1972: 276).

The traditional female suffrage story is the same as the initial enfranchisement of any group. The older cohorts are not used to voting and the younger women only slowly become socialized to vote. Over time, a larger percentage of the younger group becomes socialized until they eventually reach the same level as men. This notion would be supported by Merriam and Gosnell (1924: 44), who found a disproportionate percentage of the older women were more likely to delegate voting as the man's responsibility.

This would almost certainly be true for most states after adoption of the 19th Amendment, a federal law encompassing all states at once. But for those states that allowed women to vote prior to this, there must have been strong forces within the state compelling their respective legislatures.[23] Thus it is not so obvious that women in these states were less interested in voting. This is consistent with Kleppner's (1982a) finding that women voted less after the 19th Amendment than their franchised cohorts did in prior years.

Furthermore, the novelty of a vote can act as a strong short-term stimulus. Once franchisement has been in place for a *long* time, this group might be less likely to vote since the right has been taken for granted. The initial franchisement of other groups did not always lead to a fall in the turnout rate (Kleppner, 1982a).

While it is usually *hypothesized* that women vote less than men,[24] sex variables are commonly found to not be significant in contemporary voting studies (Kelley, Ayers, and Bowen, 1967; Silver, 1973; Cassel and Hill, 1981). This result would be consistent with either the notion that gender was never important, or that it is simply no longer important because women by now have become socialized to vote. The percentage of women in a state was, however, found to be inversely correlated with turnout in Silberman and Durden (1975).

5. Data II

The sample used in the regressions represents an unbalanced panel covering all gubernatorial elections from 1870–1910. The number of observations differ across states for two reasons. Some states had not gained statehood by 1870 and the remaining states have unequal observations due to the frequency of their elections. For example, Rhode Island has twice as many observations as Arkansas, since Rhode Island held annual elections while Arkansas governors served two year terms.

"Split-states" (see note 18) have been removed from the sample. The only other states not included are Oklahoma, which had only one election prior to 1910, and South Carolina which had "true" turnout rates over 100% for 2 elections. This casts serious doubt on the validity of South Carolina's other election totals.[25]

The years each state had poll taxes and literacy tests in their elections were found in Porter (1918), McGovney (1949), and Kousser (1974). Again, these authors' findings were not entirely consistent, as each stressed different regions or time periods. Female suffrage states are listed in Beeton (1986) and Burnham (1986).

6. Econometric Estimation

Whenever the dependent variable of a regression is a percentage term, Ordinary Least Squares (OLS) yields biased estimates. The dependent variable must be constrained between zero and one but OLS can yield nonsensical predictions outside this range. To correct for biased and inefficient estimators, I have used the *Minimum Logit Chi-Square Method* (Maddala, 1983: 29–30).[26] The dependent variable is the logit of turnout. Turnout is assumed to represent the aggregation of the individual probabilities of voting. Heteroskedasticity is built into the model so the regression must be weighted.[27] The transformed model is:

$$\ln\left(\frac{P_{it}}{1 - P_{it}}\right) = \alpha + X_{it}\beta \tag{4}$$

where P is the percent of age-eligible persons that voted, and X is a regressor matrix of rank $N = K \times M$ of K observations on M state law dummies for a secret ballot, poll taxes, a literacy test requirement, a woman's suffrage law, and a presidential election year. The subscripts represent state i at time t.

For simplicity, I will refer to equation (4) as the Logistic regression and the weighted (corrected for heteroskedasticity) version as a Weighted Logistic.

The least-squares estimators (LSE) of equation (4) tell us the marginal effect from a given law on the logit of turnout. The LSE's are dY/dX, where $Y = \ln (P/1 - P)$. We are interested in finding dP/dX.

In the logit model, the derivative is equivalent to $dP/dX = P (1 - P) \beta$ (Greene, 1993: 639). Unfortunately, the X's in equation (4) are all dummy variables. Since X is not continuous, dP/dX does not exist mathematically. Instead, differences in predictions are calculated at each observation when the variable in question is assigned a zero or a one and the remaining explanatory variables are evaluated at their true values.[28] The average effect (which I label as Delta in Table 4) is then found by taking the mean of the differences:

$$\text{Delta} = \frac{1}{K} \sum_{k=1}^{K} [P_k(x_m = 1) - P_k(x_m = 0)].$$

The results are listed in Part 1 of Table 4. Derivates have also been calculated and are included for comparative purposes.

All the legal variables for equation (4) are negative and significant. The secret ballot law, the key variable under consideration here, appears to reduce

TABLE 4.   State Laws

	I. Base model			II. Fixed effect		
	LSE	dp/dx	Delta	LSE	dp/dx	Delta
Intercept	0.726*					
	(.0422)					
Secret	−0.219*	−0.048	−0.048	−0.317*	−0.069	−0.069
Ballot	(.0475)			(.0344)		
Poll	−0.771*	−0.170	−0.180	−0.551*	−0.120	−0.125
Tax	(.0600)			(.0654)		
Literacy	−0.694*	−0.153	−0.162	−0.579*	−0.126	−0.130
Test	(.0597)			(.0945)		
Female	−0.431*	−0.095	−0.098	0.353	0.077	0.074
Suffrage	(.1543)			(.2249)		
President	0.449*	0.098	0.098	0.446*	0.097	0.097
Election	(.0482)			(.0372)		
States[a]				25.53*		
R²	.619			.830		
Adj-R²	.615			.817		
F-value	157.53			62.149		

Note: Dependent variable is weighted logit of state turnout rate. Each regression contains 588 observations. Standard errors are in parenthesis.

*Significant at 5%

[a]States represents the joint test that all state coefficients are equal to zero in Model II. This is rejected at 5%. The individual state coefficients are not reported.

turnout 4.8 percentage points. This law, while not as strong a disincentive as the other restrictive laws, does impact upon the voter's calculus.

7. State Effects

Since the laws in question are all state laws, it could be argued that the independent variables are picking up various state effects. Each state has different characteristics which could be accounting for the turnout differences. Education and income, for example, have been found to be powerful determinants of voting (Kim, Petrocik, and Enokson, 1975; Wolfinger and Rosenstone, 1980; Cassel and Hill, 1981; Caldeira and Patterson, 1982; Durden and Gaynor, 1987; Filer, Kenny, and Morton, 1991).

An inexpensive mechanism to pick up the differences across states[29] is a fixed effects model.[30] State dummies are employed, allowing each state its own intercept term. It is still assumed that the laws would have the same effect (slope) in each state, but the state dummies can capture mean historical voting differences. The results are presented in Part II of Table 4.

Comparing these results to the previous regression, the marginal effects of all the laws are reduced, except for the secret ballot, which is enhanced. This result implies there was less variation across states in the effect of the secret ballot than from the other laws. The fixed effects model predicts turnout to be 6.9 percentage points lower in the secret ballot states. Literacy tests, which disfranchise the most directly, appear to have the largest effect on state turnout.[31]

A final note concerns the female suffrage variable. Female loses its significance in the fixed effects model. This is consistent with most of the current literature. Non-significance implies that the states which adopted female suffrage did not have a less than proportional female turnout when compared with the male turnout. This supports Kleppner's (1982a) analysis. Apparently these states had lower turnout to begin with, even before allowing women to vote. Women that were allowed to vote went to the polls in roughly the same proportions as the men. If voting under a closed ballot is indeed an act of irrationality as Mueller (1989) postulates, then women are no less irrational than men.

8. Conclusions

It has been shown that voting is directly tied to the institutions in place governing its behavior. Institutional arrangements affect the voter's incentives.

The secret ballot, by eliminating bribery, greatly reduced the benefit for many voters. Many of these voters responded by abstaining.

Previous research on the secret ballot limited its role to either specific regions (Kousser, 1974; Argersinger, 1980) or affecting only who one chooses to vote for (Rusk, 1970; Converse, 1972). The lack of effect of a regional dummy (see note 29) casts doubt upon the former and the strong results generated in Table 4 suggest the latter is not complete.

Lest anyone think the lessons of the secret ballot are not pertinent to contemporary elections, one need look no further than the June 1993 Los Angeles mayoral election for evidence to the contrary. The Democratic-backed (Michael Woo) and Republican-backed (Richard Riordan) candidates were running dead even on the eve of the election. To bolster its chances, the Democratic party offered bribes in the form of six free doughnuts to anyone providing proof of voting. These bribes cost the Democratic party $100,000 (Fiore, 1993). Although the Democrats were able to boost overall turnout, they still lost the election by a margin of eight percentage points.

There was a hole in the Democrats' doughnut plan. Since voters today are able to make their choices while cloaked under a shroud of secrecy, these enticements could not be limited to those voting for Woo. There is simply no mechanism to verify the voters' choice. Instead, the doughnuts were offered as payment to anyone who voted, relying upon goodwill to steer voters toward Woo's name once inside the booth. If the pre-election polls were accurate, the Democrats actually attracted a disproportionate percentage of Republican voters with the doughnut bribes. These bribes proved sufficient inducement to improve Los Angeles' previously abysmal turnout in municipal elections, but Woo was not the beneficiary of these extra votes.

The Democratic party could have saved themselves $100,000 if they had only remembered this historical adage: You can lead a voter to the polls, but you can't make him vote Democratic. At least not under a secret ballot.

NOTES

1. See for example Olson (1965).

2. A voter is decisive only if his vote causes or breaks a tie. Tullock assumed the probability of any single voter being decisive was equal to the reciprocal of the number of voters. More sophisticated attempts at calculating P include Barzel and Silberberg (1973), Good and Mayer (1975), Beck (1975), Margolis (1977), Owen and Grofman (1984), and Foster (1984). The conclusion from all of these formulae is that $P \approx 0$.

3. For a more elaborate probe into the shortcomings of Downs' analysis, see Barry (1970: 13–23).

4. See Riker and Ordeshook (1968), McKelvey and Ordeshook (1972), Strom (1975), Fiorina (1976), and Aldrich (1993) among others.

5. $ can also be viewed as the amount saved by voting under the intimidation of physical violence or the loss of one's job. In this case, $ represents the saving of a negative amount. The analysis is the same.

6. A psychic income term, alluded to by Downs and formalized as D by Riker and Ordeshook (1968), has been omitted from equation (2). The merit of this term has been debated (Barry, 1970: 15–19; Tollison and Willett, 1973; Ferejohn and Fiorina, 1974; Strom, 1975; Fiorina, 1976; Mueller, 1989; Aldrich, 1993) and its inclusion does not alter the analysis.

7. The Austrialian Ballot System replaced separate colored-coded party ballots with a single uniform ballot (Rusk, 1970).

8. Similarly, there is no longer an advantage in forcing voters into the booth through intimidation (Key, 1949: 597).

9. Alternatively, Kousser (1974) claimed the Australian Ballot effect was limited in the South to disfranchising Blacks and illiterate Whites. His argument is based on the inability of illiterates to vote without colored party ballots. However, most ballots contained party emblems to identify candidates (Ludington, 1909) and sample ballots were prominently advertised (and often distributed) prior to the election (Evans, 1917), so name recognition itself would not be problematic even for illiterates. Furthermore, most Southern states already had literacy test requirements for voting, a far more effective mechanism for disfranchisement.

10. Kleppner (1982b: 181, 10ff.) recognized that the elimination of corruption could lead to a decline in voting but doubted the existence of rampant corruption: "The case for the Australian Ballot's role in eliminating alleged vote fraud is dubious at best."

11. Harris (1934) also makes the point that it would be an inaccurate view to restrict the corrupt practices to urban areas.

12. Secret ballot advocates at the time often argued that eliminating corruption might actually spur turnout by restoring voters' faith in government (e.g., Evans, 1917).

13. Registration was the only electoral law Kleppner (1982b) included in his turnout regressions, although he controlled for various individual-level characteristics, such as age and wealth.

14. Geometric interpolations are calculated as:

$$\text{Population}_t = \text{Population}_0 * \left(\frac{\text{Population}_{10}}{\text{Population}_0}\right)^{\frac{t}{10}}$$

where subscript t refers to the tth year between the census endpoints labeled 0 for the starting year and 10 for the ending year.

15. Similarly, the turnout estimates available on the tape are also based on linear interpolations so they have not been used.

16. Correspondence from Rusk to the author.

17. These states include Maryland, Minnesota, Mississippi, Missouri, North Carolina, Oklahoma, Tennessee, Vermont, Wisconsin, and Wyoming.

18. Kentucky, Maryland, Minnesota, Tennessee, Texas, and Wisconsin are not included because they did not adopt the measure uniformly throughout the state. Missouri was also a "split-state" in 1889 but extended its law to apply to the entire state in

1890. Since there was no gubernatorial election in between these years, this state is included. Montana, Utah, and Wyoming have had the secret ballot since statehood, so a comparison is not possible for these states.

19. The time trends are based on the five previous elections in each state.

20. This is a state-specific model of Greene's proposed variation on Chow (1960) for prediction (Greene, 1993: 196–197).

21. Kelley, Ayers, and Bowen (1967) studied the registration decision. The economic incentives are the same.

22. These voting restrictions are often viewed as part of the "Southern system", limiting their application to the South (Burnham, 1970; Converse, 1974; Kousser, 1974; Rusk and Stucker, 1978) even though these laws were enacted by various states outside the South as well (Porter, 1918; Lewinson, 1932; McGovney, 1949; Filer, Kenny, and Morton, 1991).

23. These forces are described in Beeton (1986).

24. A notable exception is Durden and Gaynor (1987). They claim a positive relationship between women and voting to be the typical prediction without reason or references. Their results, however, are mixed.

25. Regressions were also run including the other South Carolina elections, but the results remained largely unaffected, so they are not reported.

26. See also Amemiya (1981) for a description of its properties, and Schroeder and Sjoquist (1978) for an application of the technique.

27. Filer, Kenny, and Morton (1991) used the unweighted logit for their dependent variable.

28. Since the prediction of $X\beta$ yields the logit of P, this value must be transformed via the expression $e^{X\beta}/(1 + e^{X\beta})$.

29. A south dummy was also employed prior to the fixed-effects modelling on the thought that all Southern states were equally different from the rest of the nation. None of the variables' signs or t-statistics were affected.

30. The fixed effects model can also capture possible problems caused by the unbalanced panel.

31. Each of the electoral laws considered here can possibly alter the benefits and costs of voting, which changes the likelihood of voting for any individual. Literacy laws act as an infinite cost to illiterates, removing them from the eligible voting population altogether.

REFERENCES

Acts of Tennessee. (1889). Nashville: Marshall & Bruce.

Albright, S.D. (1948). The American ballot. Washington, DC: American Council on Public Affairs.

Aldrich, J.H. (1993). Rational choice and turnout. American Journal of Political Science 37:246–278.

Amemiya, T. (1981). Qualitative response models: A survey. Journal of Economic Literature 19: 1483–1536.

Anderson, G.M. and Tollison, R.D. (1990). Democracy in the marketplace. In W.M.

Crain and R.D. Tollison (Eds.), *Predicting politics: Essays in empirical public choice*, 285–303. Ann Arbor: University of Michigan Press.

Argersinger, P.H. (1980) 'A place on the ballot': Fusion politics and antifusion laws. *The American Historical Review* 85: 287–306.

Argersinger, P.H. (1985). New perspectives on election fraud in the Gilded Age. *Political Science Quarterly* 100: 669–687.

Barry, B. (1970). *Sociologists, economists and democracy*. London: Butler & Tanner, Ltd.

Barzel, Y. and Silberberg, E. (1973). Is the act of voting rational? *Public Choice* 16: 51–58.

Beck, N. (1975). A note on the probability of a tied election. *Public Choice* 23: 75–79.

Beeton, B. (1986). *Women vote in the west: The woman suffrage movement 1869–1896*. New York: Garland Publishing, Inc.

Burnham, W.D. (1965). The changing shape of the American political universe. *American Political Science Review* 59: 7–28.

Burnham, W.D. (1970). *Critical elections and the mainsprings of American politics*. New York: Norton.

Burnham, W.D. (1971). Communications to the editor. *American Political Science Review* 65: 1149–1152.

Burnham, W.D. (1974). Theory and voting research: Some reflections on Converse's 'Change in the American electorate.' *American Political Science Review* 68: 1002–1023.

Burnham, W.D. (1986). Those high nineteenth-century American voting turnouts: Fact or fiction? *Journal of Interdisciplinary History* 16: 613–644.

Burnham, W.D., Clubb, J.M., and Flanigan, W. (1971). *State-level congressional, gubernatorial and senatorial election data for the United States, 1824–1972*. Ann Arbor: Inter-university Consortium for Political and Social Research. 1991 edition.

Caldeira, G.A. and Patterson, S.C. (1982). Contextual influences on participation in U.S. state legislative elections. *Legislative Studies Quarterly* 7: 359–381.

Cassel, C.A. and Hill, D.B. (1981). Explanations of turnout decline. *American Politics Quarterly* 9: 181–195.

Chow, G.C. (1960). Tests of equality between two sets of coefficients in two linear regressions. *Econometrica* 28: 591–605.

Constitution of the state of Mississippi. (1890).

Converse, P.E. (1972). Change in the American electorate. In A. Campbell and P.E. Converse (Eds.), *The human meaning of social change*, 263–337. New York: Russel Sage Foundation.

Converse, P.E. (1974). Comment on Burnham's 'Theory and voting research.' *American Political Science Review* 68: 1024–1027.

Downs, A. (1957). *An economic theory of democracy*. New York: Harper and Row Publishers.

Durden, G.C. and Gaynor, P. (1987). The rational behavior theory of voting participation: Evidence from the 1970 and 1982 elections. *Public Choice* 53: 231–242.

Evans, E.C. (1917). *A history of the Australian Ballot system in the United States*. Chicago: University of Chicago Press.

Ferejohn, J.A. and Fiorina, M.P. (1974). The paradox of not voting: A decision theoretic analysis. *American Political Science Review* 68: 525–536.

Filer, J.E., Kenny, L.W., and Morton, R.B. (1991). Voting laws, educational policies, and minority turnout. *Journal of Law and Economics* 34: 371–393.

Fiore, F. (1993). Gimmicks, glitches mark effort to get out the vote. *Los Angeles Times* 9 June.

Fiorina, M.P. (1976). The voting decision: Instrumental and expressive aspects. *Journal of Politics* 38: 390–413.

Foster, C.B. (1984). The performance of rational voter models in recent presidential elections. *American Political Science Review* 78: 678–690.

General laws of the state of Minnesota. (1889). Minneapolis: Harrison & Smith.

General laws of the state of Minnesota. (1891). St. Paul: The Pioneer Press Company.

Good, I.J. and Mayer, L.S. (1975). Estimating the efficacy of a vote. *Behavioral Science* 20: 25–33.

Greene, W.H. (1993). *Econometric analysis.* New York. Macmillan.

Harris, J.P. (1929). *Registration of voters in the United States.* Washington: The Brookings Institute.

Harris, J.P. (1934). *Election administration in the United States.* Washington: The Brookings Institute.

Inter-university Consortium for Political and Social Research. (1991). *Guide to resources and services, 1991–1992.* Ann Arbor, MI.

Kelley, S. Jr., Ayers, R.E., and Bowen, W.G. (1967). Registration and voting: Putting first things first. *American Political Science Review* 61: 359–377.

Key, V.O. (1949). *Southern politics in state and nation.* New York: Vintage Books.

Kim, J., Petrocik, J.R., and Enokson, S.N. (1975). Voter turnout among the American states: Systemic and individual components. *American Political Science Review* 69: 107–131.

Kleppner, P. (1982a). Were women to blame? Female suffrage and voter turnout. *Journal of Interdisciplinary History* 12: 621–643.

Kleppner, P. (1982b). *Who voted? The dynamics of electoral turnout, 1870–1980.* New York: Praeger.

Kleppner, P. and Baker, S.C. (1980). The impact of voter registration requirements on electoral turnout, 1900–1916. *Journal of Political and Military Sociology* 8: 205–226.

Kousser, J.M. (1974). *The shaping of southern politics: Suffrage restrictions and the establishment of the one-party south, 1880–1910.* New Haven: Yale University Press.

Laws of Maryland. (1890). Annapolis: State Printer.

Laws of Maryland. (1892). Annapolis: C.H. Baughman and Co.

Laws of Missouri. (1889). Jefferson City: Tribune Printing Company.

Laws of Missouri. (1891). Jefferson City: Tribune Printing Company.

Laws of Missouri. (1897). Jefferson City: Tribune Printing Company.

Lewinson, P. (1932). *Race, class & party.* New York: Oxford University Press.

Ludington, A. (1909). Present status of ballot laws in the United States. *American Political Science Review* 3: 252–261.

Maddala, G.S. (1983). *Limited-dependent and qualitative variables in econometrics.* Cambridge: Cambridge University Press.

Margolis, H. (1977). Probability of a tied election. *Public Choice* 31: 135–138.

McCook, J.J. (1892). The alarming proportion of venal voters. *The Forum* 14: 1–13.

Reprinted in A.J. Heidenheimer, (Ed.), *Political corruption readings in comparative analysis,* 411–421. New York: Holt, Rinehart and Winston, 1970.

McGovney, D.O. (1949). *The American suffrage medley.* Chicago: The University of Chicago Press.

McKelvey, R.D. and Ordeshook, P.C. (1972). A general theory of the calculus of voting. In J.F. Herndon and J.L. Bernd (Eds.), *Mathematical applications in political science,* 32–78. Volume 6. Charlottesville: University of Virginia Press.

Merriam, C.E. and Gosnell, H.F. (1924). *Non-voting.* Chicago: University of Chicago Press.

Mueller, D.C. (1989). *Public choice II.* Cambridge: Cambridge University Press.

Olson, M. (1965). *The logic of collective action.* Cambridge: Harvard University Press. 1971 edition.

Owen, G. and Grofman, B. (1984). To vote or not to vote: The paradox of not voting. *Public Choice* 42: 311–325.

Porter, K.H. (1918). *A history of suffrage in the United States.* Chicago: University of Chicago Press.

Public laws and resolutions of the state of North Carolina. (1909). Raleigh: E.M. Uzzell & Co., State Printers and Binders.

Public laws and resolutions of the state of North Carolina. (1929). Ft. Wayne, IN: Ft. Wayne Ptg. Co.

Revised statutes of the state of Missouri. (1889). Volumes One and Two. Jefferson City: Tribune Printing Company.

Riker, W.H. and Ordeshook, P.C. (1968). A theory of the calculus of voting. *American Political Science Review* 62: 25–42.

Rusk, J. (1970). The effect of the Australian Ballot on split ticket voting: 1876–1908. *American Political Science Review* 64: 1220–1238.

Rusk, J. (1971). Communications to the editor. *American Political Science Review* 65: 1153–1157.

Rusk, J. (1974). Comment: The American electoral universe: Speculation and evidence. *American Political Science Review* 68: 1028–1049.

Rusk, J. and Stucker, J.J. (1978). The effect of the southern system of election laws on voting participation: A reply to V.O. Key, Jr. In J.H. Silbey, A.G. Bogue and W.H. Flanigan (Eds.), *The history of American electoral behavior,* 198–250. Princeton: Princeton University Press.

Schroeder, L.D. and Sjoquist, D.L. (1978). The rational voter: An analysis of two Atlanta referenda on rapid transit. *Public Choice* 33: 27–44.

Session laws of Wyoming territory. (1890). Published by Authority.

Session laws of the state of Wyoming. (1890). Published by Authority.

Silberman, J. and Durden, J. (1975). The rational behavior theory of voter participation: The evidence from congressional elections. *Public Choice* 23: 101–108.

Silver, M. (1973). A demand analysis of voting costs and voting participation. *Social Science Research* 2: 111–124.

Speed, J.G. (1905). The purchases of votes. *Harper's Weekly* 49: 386–387. Reprinted in A.J. Heidenheimer, (Ed.), *Political corruption readings in comparative analysis,* 422–426. New York: Holt, Rinehart and Winston, 1970.

State of Oklahoma, (1908). *Session laws of 1907–1908.* Guthrie: Oklahoma Printing Co.

Strom, G.S. (1975). On the apparent paradox of participation: A new proposal. *American Political Science Review* 59: 908–913.

Tollison, R.D. and Willett, T.D. (1973). Some simple economics of voting and not voting. *Public Choice* 26: 59–71.

Tullock, G. (1967). *Toward a mathematics of politics.* Ann Arbor: University of Michigan Press.

U.S. Census of 1890. (1892). Volume II, Population Part II. Washington: U.S. Census Office.

U.S. Census of 1900. (1901). Volume II, Population Part II. Washington: U.S. Census Office.

U.S. Census of 1910. (1912). Volume I, Population Part I. Washington: U.S. Census Office.

Wisconsin laws. (1889). Madison: Democrat Printing Company.

Wolfinger, R.E. and Rosenstone, S.J. (1980). *Who votes?* New Haven: Yale University Press.

Suggested Additional Readings

Caldeira, Gregory A., Samuel C. Patterson, and Gregory A. Markko. "The Mobilization of Voters in Congressional Elections." *Journal of Politics* 47 (1985): 490–509.

Cebula, Richard J., and Dennis R. Murphy. "The Electoral College and Voter Participation Rates: An Exploratory Note." *Public Choice* 35 (1980): 185–90.

Darvish, Tikva, and Jacob Rosenberg. "The Economic Model of Voter Participation: A Further Test." *Public Choice* 56 (1988): 185–92.

Downs, Anthony. *An Economic Theory of Democracy.* Chap. 14. New York: Harper & Row, 1957.

Grofman, Bernard. "Is Turnout the Paradox That Ate Public Choice?" In *Information, Participation, and Choice,* ed. Bernard Grofman. Ann Arbor: University of Michigan Press, 1995.

Heckelman, Jac C. "Bribing Voters without Verification." *Social Science Journal* 35 (1998): 435–43.

Jackman, Robert W. "Political Institutions and Voter Turnout in Industrial Democracies." *American Political Science Review* 81 (1987): 405–24.

Kau, James B., and Paul H. Rubin. "The Electoral College and the Rational Vote." *Public Choice* 27 (1976): 101–7.

Knack, Stephen. "Does 'Motor Voter' Work? Evidence from State-Level Data." *Journal of Politics* 7 (1995): 796–811.

Mueller, Dennis C. "The Voting Paradox." In *Democracy and Public Choice,* ed. Charles K. Rowley. Oxford: Basil Blackwell, 1987.

Niemi, Richard G. "Costs of Voting and Nonvoting." *Public Choice* 27 (1976): 115–19.

Patterson, Samuel C., and Gregory A. Caldeira. "Getting out the Vote: Participation in Gubernatorial Elections." *American Political Science Review* 77 (1983): 675–89.

Tollison, Robert D., and Thomas D. Willett. "Some Simple Economics of Voting and Not Voting." *Public Choice* 26 (1973): 59–71.

Advanced Readings

Dhillon, Amrita, and Susana Peralta. "Economic Theories of Voter Turnout." *Economic Journal* 112 (2002): F332–F352.

Kanazawa, Satoshi. "A Possible Solution to the Paradox of Voter Turnout." *Journal of Politics* 60 (1998): 974–95.

Katosh, John P., and Michael W. Traugott. "Costs and Values in the Calculus of Voting." *American Journal of Political Science* 26 (1982): 361–76.

Knack, Stephen. "The Voter Participation Effects of Selecting Jurors from Registration Lists." *Journal of Law and Economics* 36 (1993): 99–114.

PART IV
Final Thoughts

Hopefully by now the reader has gained an appreciation for what public choice scholars do and the importance of the insights they have developed. As public choice analysis has evolved and developed, the field has grown from its relative infancy only a short period of time ago (relative to the history of economic analysis in general and to most other fields within economics) to a well-respected subdiscipline leading the interdisciplinary approach by combining the important tools of economics with topics previously analyzed almost exclusively by political scientists. This collection of papers is meant only as an introduction to the topic, and due to space and cost constraints, much has been left out. The suggested additional readings can help to clarify more of the details, reveal important related results, and uncover other issues not directly considered here.

As with economics in general, public choice analysis continues to branch out into new areas of inquiry, particularly the fields of law and sociology, as scholars become more conversant in formal theory modeling and advanced empirical techniques. The public choice framework has been increasingly applied to judicial behavior and the evolution of tort law, as well as models of group behavior and cognitive psychology.

Due to recent events, public choice scholars are likely to now turn their attention to the political-economic analysis of terrorism. Public choice methodology may very well be useful to help explain the existence of fanaticism and hatred, why individuals are so easily duped into engaging in these personal and socially destructive activities, and the collective action issues of martyrdom.

While in its infancy now, there will likely be greater adoption from the natural sciences in the future, especially evolutionary biology in survivor models that can be applied to the development of institutions. This has so far been slow to gain acceptance within the mainstream of public choice, but it continues to make limited progress.

Despite the advances made in the public choice field, the methodology is not without its critics. Traditional political scientists who reject the economic way of thinking resent public choice as a case of economic imperialism, forcing formal modeling techniques into a discipline that had formerly been purely descriptive in nature. This reaction is similar to what happened when the mathematics revolution swept through economics, leaving many of the older guard behind on the learning curve. Detailed case studies would help ground future research and prevent the growing complexity of public choice modeling from turning into an esoteric wasteland of notation understandable only to other scholars working in the same line of research.

A second concern has been the implications of the models rather than the models themselves. As we have seen, the actors in the public sector are no longer assumed to be without fault. Such a pessimistic view of public sector performance offends those with a predisposition toward governmental solutions. "Shoot the messenger" is their rallying cry. On the other hand, it is also likely that the early results showing cracks in the governmental armor specifically attracted economists and political scientists who had always been skeptical of government involvement in people's lives and business.

These views can be reconciled once it is noted that an important goal of public choice analysis is not simply to point out the fault in the policy process but, having now identified potential problems, to develop steps that can be taken to make improvements. Sometimes this may involve rolling back the state; other times, tweaking institutions to create the proper incentives for those in the public sector. It should be remembered that public choice scholars have identified, not created, the problems they study.

Brennan and Buchanan respond to the charge that public choice analysis is harmful to social cohesion by the nature of its cynicism toward public behavior in "Is Public Choice Immoral? The Case for the 'Nobel' Lie." They argue it is important to analyze the way things are, rather than just blindly believing everything actually is the way it should be.

Is Public Choice Immoral?
The Case for the "Nobel" Lie

Geoffrey Brennan & James M. Buchanan

Review Questions:

1. Why is public choice analysis attacked as being cynical? Is this justified?
2. What are the basic underlying assumptions public choice makes regarding political agents? How do these assumptions differ from those of conventional welfare economics and political science?
3. What are the consequences of public choice models for the behavior of political agents? Does public choice modelling simply describe or actually cause changes in behavior? How might this be harmful?
4. Is it immoral to describe problems inherent in our political institutions? Why or why not?
5. What distinctions are made between the normative and positive analysis of public choice? What are the moral values embodied in scientific inquiry?
6. It is argued that destroying illusions without offering any hope may be immoral. What hope does public choice offer through the "constitutional perspective"?

Brennan, Geoffrey, and James M. Buchanan, "Is Public Choice Immoral? The Case for the 'Nobel' Lie." *Virginia Law Review* 74 (1991): 179–89.

Cynical descriptive conclusions about behavior in government threaten
to undermine the norm prescribing public spirit. The cynicism of jour-
nalists—and even the writings of professors—can decrease public spirit
simply by describing what they claim to be its absence. Cynics are therefore in the business of making prophecies that threaten to become self-
fulfilling. If the norm of public spirit dies, our society would look bleaker
and our lives as individuals would be more impoverished. That is the
tragedy of "public choice."

> Steven Kelman, *"Public Choice" and Public Spirit*[1]

Public choice analysis—the application of the theoretical method and techniques of modern economics to the study of political processes—has come
increasingly to popular attention in recent years. The 1986 Nobel Prize in
economics is both a reflection of that increased attention and an occasion for
it. It is only to be expected that such attention would focus on the simpler
and/or more controversial aspects of public choice theory. In a sense, this is
what "good press" is all about. It is more surprising, and to some extent regrettable, that some of the allegedly "academic" evaluations have been similarly focused.

It has to be conceded that public choice theory *is* controversial, and not
just because some of its predictions are counterintuitive or its methods of
analysis unusual; the controversy goes well beyond the "scientific" level. There
is an apparent accompanying conviction on the part of many commentators
that the whole enterprise is *immoral* in a basic sense. Steven Kelman's discussion reveals this position nicely, as the initial quotation suggests. But Kelman's
position is by no means unique.[2] It merely takes up an anxiety that has been
aired on and off by orthodox welfare economists and mainstream political
scientists ever since the public choice revolution began.[3]

To some extent, this anxiety is based on a misconception. Public choice theory has been widely touted as being *defined* by the attribution of *homo economicus* motivations to actors in their political roles. *Homo economicus*—the
wealth-maximizing egoist—should be seen to play no more significant a
role in public choice analysis than in the whole program of economic theory
more generally. And it is simply wrong to conceive of economics as nothing
more than egoistic psychology. Also, as we have argued, there may be good reason to believe that *homo economicus* may be descriptively somewhat less relevant in the political setting than in economic markets.[4] The more appropriate
use of the *homo economicus* construction is to further the normative exercise

of investigating the incentive structures embodied in various institutional forms[5] rather than the descriptive exercise of providing predictions as to the likely outcomes of political interactions.

But definitions of public choice are, for the purposes of the argument here, somewhat beside the point. In fact, Kelman's anxiety is ultimately independent of whether political agents can be accurately described by egoistic motivations. Whatever the reality, the logic of Kelman's claim is that the responsible political analyst should err on the side of the heroic. If cynicism destroys politically useful illusions, then equally romanticism within limits *fosters* those illusions. This aspect of Kelman's argument is then not an argument for science but an argument for illusion. It is an argument designed to supply *additional* weight to, over and above any descriptive scientific critique of, the *homo economicus* postulate.

To this substantive charge we must, of course, plead guilty at least to this extent: although we do not believe that narrow self-interest is the *sole* motive of political agents, or that it is necessarily as relevant a motive in political as in market settings, we certainly believe it to be a significant motive. This differentiates our approach from the alternative model, implicit in conventional welfare economics and widespread in conventional political science, that political agents can be satisfactorily modeled as motivated solely to promote the "public interest," somehow conceived. *That* model we, along with all our public choice colleagues, categorically reject.

In doing so, however, whatever the scientific imperatives, we have to reckon with the moral implications. That is our object here—to investigate the substance of the morally based critique of public choice. To do this properly, it is useful to set the empirical/scientific issues on one side: We shall take our critics seriously on their own terms, and examine the purely *ethical* case against public choice scholarship.

Two related questions seem relevant to this ethical critique. The first deals with the consequences of public choice models for the actual or imputed behavior of persons as they act in political roles. To the extent that public choice analysis influences the behavior of political agents, is this behavioral response desirable? There are, in turn, two distinct dimensions to this first question. One involves the behavior of politicians/bureaucrats—those who exercise discretionary power within the given political order. The other involves the attribution of legitimacy by the citizen to that political order, and leads to the more general question of its stability and possibly to the feasibility of any long-term political order at all. Beyond this, there is the second question of whether public choice may not be "immoral" simply by virtue of its dispelling illusions about the nature of the political order, quite independent of any of its political consequences.

The final section of the paper will be devoted to what we may call a "moral defense" of public choice. As we shall argue, however, this defense depends on a prior specification of the purpose of public choice analysis—one that may not be endorsed, even if it is understood, by all our professional colleagues in public choice itself.

I. The Behavioral Consequences of Public Choice

A. Potential Effect on Political Actors

One of this century's scientific advances has been the recognition that what is being observed may be influenced by the fact of observation. Problems emerge from this source in *all* sciences; they appear in many guises and have many ramifications. In this respect, however, there is an important distinction between the human and nonhuman sciences.

In the nonhuman sciences, the interactions are restricted to those between the observer and observed. John Kagel and his colleagues must take into account how their own behavior might influence the behavior of the rats they study.[6] But they need not worry at all about the influence of their research on *the behavior of other rats*. Other rats do not read or understand economists' conversations about rats; the behavior of those other rats will remain totally unaffected by the reporting of the results of the experiments or by new analyses "explaining" such results to economists.

In the human sciences, no strict boundary between individuals who are observed and those who are not can be drawn for such purposes. Persons read research reports; they listen to social scientists talk about experiments; they understand and interpret models of behavior imputed to others of their species. And this fact matters scientifically to the extent that the reading of such reports and the consequent changes in people's understanding of themselves influence human behavior. It matters *normatively* to the extent that those changes in behavior have morally relevant consequences.

Second, and somewhat more subtly, ideas may change values themselves. Two examples may help here. Suppose that some Kinsey-like report has revealed that, in fact, over seventy percent of married couples in the United States indulge in some sexual practice commonly believed to be decidedly eccentric and perhaps morally somewhat dubious. It seems plausible to suggest that the release of this information may serve to change sexual standards in the direction of this practice: the "facts" somehow serve to legitimize the practice. The charge that "everyone does it" is normally regarded as at least a presumptive argument in favor of "doing it" oneself. As a second example within social science itself, one might hazard the conjecture that economists (at least those with a strong "price theory" orientation) are more likely to act like the *homo economicus* model they work with than are others not blessed with the "economist's way of thinking." This involves, in many cases, not only a greater attentiveness to the costs and benefits of alternative actions (particularly the financially measurable ones), but also a sort of cultivated hard-nosed crassness towards anything that smacks of the "higher things of life."

Suppose that we acknowledge this possibility—that analysis of social interactions in *homo economicus* terms influences individuals toward behaving more in the way persons are *modeled* to behave. In the context of well-functioning markets, this prospect may be of little normative concern. Within the market, self-interested behavior, given the appropriate legal constraints, does not necessarily inhibit "social interest" and may indeed further it. In this institutional setting, any legitimizing of self-interest that economic theory provides need have no moral consequences of any significance.

In extending the application of the *homo economicus* model to political contexts, however, any comparable response in the behavior of political actors may be of considerable normative account. Scientific enquiry—whether in the form of formal analysis or of the application of empirical tests to relevant hypotheses—may, in using the *homo economicus* construct to "explain" the workings of political processes, tend to further the notion that the behavior so modeled is the norm. To the critics, the very structure of enquiry here may serve to legitimize such behavior for those who exercise discretionary power in political roles. Voters, lobbyists, politicians and bureaucrats may face reduced public expectations of their behavior—standards of public life will be eroded, and persons in these roles may predictably lower their own standards in response. Such moral constraints as do apply to political behavior will be reduced by the spread of the conception that most persons, when in such roles, seek only private interest, and that such behavior is all that can reasonably be expected. However, because there is no invisible hand operative in majoritarian political institutions analogous to that operative in the market setting, any lapse in political morality is of normative significance.

Even if the explanatory power of public choice models of politics is acknowledged, therefore, the moral spillovers of such models on the behavior of political actors may be deemed to be so important as to negate any purely "scientific" advance made in our understanding of how politics actually works. The maintenance of the standards of public life, it could be argued, may require a heroic vision of the "statesman" or "public servant," because only by holding such a vision can the possibility of public-interested behavior on the part of political agents be increased. The empirical evidence may suggest that any such vision remains decidedly utopian, yet the effects on the morality of those who occupy positions of political power may still be held to override all such factual evidence. Hence, so the argument would go, those who engage in the ideas of politics must preserve a calculated hypocrisy about the conduct of political affairs, and they must talk only in terms of "ideal types." They must explicitly eschew the dull "scientific" talk of sordid realities; they must lift their gaze to the "good, beautiful, and true." The consequences for a tolerably acceptable political life in failing to keep this essential faith become potentially disastrous.

This argument deserves to be taken seriously, despite its apparent vulnerability to caricature when viewed from the "scientific" perspective. Moreover, we think that at some subliminal level, the force of argument is well recognized. Suppose, for example, that a public choice economist or political scientist is asked to talk to a group of young persons in training for employment in the bureaucracy. On what aspects of public choice would he or she focus? On explaining how to manipulate agendas? On showing how to maximize the size of an agency's budget? The public choice analyst would probably soft-pedal the cynical edges, and focus more on the prospects for institutional reform than on the maximization of career prospects.

More generally, consider the role of the public choice analyst in a setting where no change in the structure of political organization is considered to be possible. In this case, the only possible impact on policy outcomes lies in powers of persuasion over people who hold positions of political power. If all such persons are self-interested wealth-maximizers, the entire *raison d'être* of proffering policy advice collapses. Those who either actually or putatively offer advice to politicians must model their targets as something *other* than wealth-maximizers. We should hardly be surprised, therefore, when our political-establishment colleagues (indeed all those who do not understand, or have no taste for, the prospect of institutional reform) treat public choice as the heresy it is for their own church.

B. Illusion and the Citizen

To this point, we have focused on the possible feedback effects that public choice ideas may exercise on the behavior of "professionals" in the political process—effects that may well be judged undesirable by common normative standards.

The recognition of such consequences does not, of course, carry direct implications for the pursuit of scientific enquiry. But scientific enquiry embodies its own moral values—a belief in the value of knowledge for its own sake and predisposition towards the view that science is, on balance, "productive." In certain contexts, the importance of these values may be debatable.

We may agree that public choice analysis allows us to see politics without blinders. In that sense, we play the role of the boy who called attention to the emperor's nakedness. But the familiar story might be given quite a different twist if it went on to relate that the emperor fell into disgrace, that the nobles fought among themselves, that the previously stable political order crumbled into chaos, and that the kingdom was destroyed. The moral might then have been *not* that one should call a spade a spade, whatever the possible consequences, but rather that a sensitivity to consequences may require one to be judicious in exposing functionally useful myths.

In this argument, there are echoes of the Hobbesian concern about the precariousness of stable political order. Cynicism about the behavior of political agents, however empirically justified it may be, may wreak damage to the "civic religion." This is a danger that any enquiry into political arrangements must acknowledge. As scientists, we consider it our purpose to destroy myths. But we should recognize that the "myths of democracy" may be essential to maintenance of an underlying popular consent of the citizenry to be governed, in the absence of which no tolerable stable political order is possible.

The late-1981 action in which, by an amendment to a totally different piece of legislation, members of Congress substantially reduced their income tax liability[7] exemplifies the problem in a practical way. This action will surely induce ordinary taxpayers everywhere to become less moral in their own behavior vis-à-vis the Internal Revenue Service. In the United States, income tax arrangements continue to depend in large measure on taxpayer honesty—a dependence that makes effective income taxation infeasible in many countries. Public choice theory, in itself, does not induce politicians to behave as tax avoiders: it is not *responsible* for the recent tax change. But the theory does hold such cases up as being of the essential nature of political process, rather than an unfortunate and regrettable lapse. Public choice theory gives coherence and meaning to such events by providing an understanding of political process in the light of them. And this sort of understanding is not conducive to taxpayer honesty or to the good functioning of stable government, more generally.

As any good public choice theorist recognizes, *some* discretionary political power will remain in the hands of some political agents even under the best of feasible institutional arrangements: constraints are costly, and we must make the best of what we have. Economists are familiar with the proposition that not all "problems" are problems—that resources are limited, including "resources" of good will, altruism, honesty, and the like. In a world where political institutions were "optimal" in some sense, what useful purpose would it serve to destroy popular illusions about those institutions?

There is, of course, an aspect of the myth-destruction exercise that goes beyond the possible destruction of civic order. That is the more direct question of the ethics of destroying illusions—even when there is *no* behavioral response. As Eugene O'Neill's *The Iceman Cometh*[8] emphasizes, the destruction of illusion in and of itself without the offering of hope may be grossly immoral: it directly reduces individuals' perceived levels of welfare. The moral considerations involved in informing someone who has an incurable cancer of his condition, or in informing the recently bereaved and grieving widower that his wife had been having affairs for twenty years behind his back, do not obviously commend the virtues of "truth at all costs." Knowledge without hope, science without a conviction that it can lead to a better life—these are by no means unambiguously value-enhancing, and those who shatter illusions for the sheer pleasure of doing so are not so clearly to be applauded for their "work."

II. Public Choice in Constitutional Perspective

Public choice—the hardheaded, realistic, indeed cynical model of political behavior—can be properly defended on moral grounds if we adopt a "constitutional perspective"—that is, if the purpose of the exercise is conceived to be institutional reform, improvements in the *rules* under which political processes operate. This perspective requires that we shift attention away from the analysis of policy choice by existing agents within *existing* rules, and towards the examination of alternative sets of rules. Improvement, or hope for improvement, emerges not from any expectation that observed agents will behave differently from the way the existing set of incentives leads them to behave, but from a shift in the rules that define these incentives. The public choice theorist does not envisage his "science" as offering a base for "preaching to the players" on how to maximize welfare functions. His task is not the Machiavellian one of advising governors, directly or indirectly, on how they ought to behave. His task is that of advising all citizens on the working of alternative constitutional rules.

We suggest that this methodological stance is that which informed both the classical political economists and the political philosophers of the eighteenth century.[9] Within such a perspective, the delusion that political agents are saints becomes costly folly. Politics can be reformed without depending on moral suasion of kings and princes. The burdens of politics can be minimized independently of agent motivation.

What is the appropriate model of man to be incorporated in the comparative analysis of alternative constitutional rules? In our response to this question, we follow the classical economists explicitly, and for precisely the reasons they stated.[10] We model man as a wealth maximizer, not because this model is necessarily the most descriptive empirically, but because we seek a set of rules that will work well independently of the behavioral postulates introduced.

From our perspective, then, we agree that there is cause for some concern with public choice interpreted as a predictive model of behavior in political roles. Where public choice is used to develop a predictive theory of political processes in a manner typical of "positive economics"—that is, with the focus solely on developing an empirically supportable theory of choice *within* rules, and with the ultimate normative purpose of constitutional design swept away in footnotes or neglected altogether—then the danger is that it will indeed breed the moral consequences previously discussed.

The attainment of the "constitutional perspective" is by no means easy, surprising as that may be. It is somehow "unnatural" to many scholars, orthodox and otherwise. But what is intriguing in this connection is that the most intense resistance to public choice analysis arises from precisely those critics who cannot think in terms of constitutional alternatives. For such critics, it is apparently impossible to conceive of institutional arrangements within which political agents are constrained. They must then face a genuine dilemma: they must either model political man as he is and live with Schumpeterian despair, or model man as he "should be" and seek to make their dreams come true. Should we really be surprised that so many choose the second of these options?

NOTES

1. 87 Pub. Interest 80, 93–94 (1987).

2. For a more strident example, see John Foster's review note of our monograph, *Monopoly in Money and Inflation,* in which he accuses us of providing "another small step on the road to fascism." Foster, Book Note, 91 Econ. J. 1105 (1981).

3. See, e.g., Samuelson, The World Economy at Century's End, 34 Bull. Am. Acad. Arts & Sci. 44 (1981) (remarks about the tax revolt movement and those whom he sees as spawning it); Gordon, The New Contractarians (Book Review), 84 J. Pol. Econ. 573 (1976). In his review of J. Buchanan, The Limits of Liberty (1976), Gordon said that "Buchanan's reasoning eschews any moral considerations of duty or obligation." Gordon, supra, at 585.

4. See G. Brennan & J. Buchanan, The Reason of Rules 48–51, 145 (1985).

5. A point that we have reiterated consistently. See id. at 46–66; G. Brennan & J. Buchanan, Predictive Power and the Choice Among Regimes, 93 Econ. J. 89, 90, 97–104 (1983) [hereinafter Predictive Power]; G. Brennan & J. Buchanan, The Normative Purpose of Economic Science: Rediscovery of an Eighteenth Century Method, 1 Int'l Rev. L. & Econ. 155, 159–63 (1981) [hereinafter Normative Purpose].

6. See, as one example of their work, Kagel, Battalio, Rachlin & Green, Demand Curves for Animal Consumers, 91 Q.J. Econ. 1 (1981).

7. See Black Lung Benefits Revenue Act of 1981, Pub. L. No. 97–119, § 113, 95 Stat. 1635, 1641–43 (1981) (codified at I.R.C. § 280A (1982 & Supp. IV 1986)); see also N.Y. Times, Dec. 17, 1981, at B14, col. 3 (discussing passage of the provision that made it easier for members to deduct living expenses).

8. E. O'Neill, The Iceman Cometh (1940). Henrik Ibsen's play, *The Wild Duck* (1884), deals with the same problem with a more consequentialist orientation. Edward Albee's *Who's Afraid of Virginia Woolf?* (1962) deals with a similar issue, though ultimately with a more optimistic "triumph-of-truth-in-spite-of-everything" sort of flavor.

9. For discussion of this hypothesis, see Predictive Power, supra note 5, at 89; Normative Purpose, supra note 5, at 163–64.

10. See, e.g., D. Hume, On the Independency of Parliament, in 3 The Philosophical Works 117–18 (T. Greene & T. Grose eds. 1882 & photo. reprint 1964) (1742) ("[I]n contriving any system of government, and fixing the several checks and controuls of the constitution, every man ought to be supposed a *knave*, and to have no other end, in all his actions, than private interest."); J.S. Mill, Considerations on Representative Government, *in* 29 Collected Works of John Stuart Mill 505 (J. Robson ed. 1977) (1867) ("[T]he very principle of constitutional government requires it to be assumed, that political power will be abused to promote the particular purposes of the holder; not because it always is so, but because such is the natural tendency of things, to guard against which is the especial use of free institutions.")

Suggested Additional Readings

Buchanan, James M. *Explorations into Constitutional Economics.* Chap. 2. College Station: Texas A&M University Press, 1989.

Chrystal, K. Alec, and David A. Peel. What Can Economics Learn from Political Science and Vice Versa? *American Economic Review Papers and Proceedings* 76 (1986): 62–65.

Heckelman, Jac C., and Robert Whaples. "Are Public Choice Scholars Different?" *PS: Political Science and Politics* 36 (2003): 797–99.

McLean, Iain. "Economics and Politics." In *Companion to Contemporary Economic Thought,* ed. David Greenaway, Michael Bleaney, and Ian Stewart. London: Routledge, 1991.

Mikva, Abner J. "Foreword: Symposium on the Theory of Public Choice." *Virginia Law Review* 74 (1988): 167–77.

Mueller, Dennis C. "Public Choice in Perspective." In *Perspectives on Public Choice,* ed. Dennis C. Mueller. Cambridge: Cambridge University Press, 1997.

Rowley, Charles K., Friedrich Schneider, and Robert D. Tollison (eds.). *The Next 25 Years of Public Choice.* Dordrecht: Kluwer Academic Press, 1993.

Stretton, Hugh, and Lionel Orchard. *Public Goods, Public Enterprise, Public Choice.* New York: St. Martin's Press. 1994.

U 42 . U36 — Van Crelden